Central and East European Politics

Central and East European Politics

From Communism to Democracy

EDITED BY
SHARON L. WOLCHIK AND JANE L. CURRY

ROWMAN & LITTLEFIELD PUBLISHERS, INC.
Lanham • Boulder • New York • Toronto • Plymouth, UK

ROWMAN & LITTLEFIELD PUBLISHERS, INC.

Published in the United States of America
by Rowman & Littlefield Publishers, Inc.
A wholly owned subsidiary of The Rowman & Littlefield Publishing Group, Inc.
4501 Forbes Boulevard, Suite 200, Lanham, Maryland 20706
www.rowmanlittlefield.com

Estover Road, Plymouth PL6 7PY, United Kingdom

British Library Cataloguing in Publication Information Available

Library of Congress Cataloging-in-Publication Data

Central and East European politics : from communism to democracy / edited by Sharon L. Wolchik and Jane L. Curry.
    p. cm.
    Includes bibliographical references and index.
    ISBN-13: 978-0-7425-4067-5 (cloth : alk. paper)
    ISBN-10: 0-7425-4067-7 (cloth : alk. paper)
    ISBN-13: 978-0-7425-4068-2 (pbk. : alk. paper)
    ISBN-10: 0-7425-4068-5 (pbk. : alk. paper)
    1. Europe, Eastern—Politics and government—1989–   2. Post-communism—Europe, Eastern.   3. Democracy—Europe, Eastern.   4. North Atlantic Treaty Organization—Europe, Eastern.   5. European Union—Europe, Eastern. I. Wolchik, Sharon L.
II. Curry, Jane Leftwich, 1948–
DJK51.C437   2008
947.009'049—dc22   2007024391

Printed in the United States of America

The paper used in this publication meets the minimum requirements of American National Standard for Information Sciences—Permanence of Paper for Printed Library Materials, ANSI/ NISO Z39.48-1992.

This book is dedicated to the memory of Václav Beneš, who taught us to appreciate the complexities of Central and Eastern Europe and modeled for us the life of a caring teacher and scholar.

Contents

PART FOUR: CONCLUSION

Acknowledgments

We would like to acknowledge the support of the Institute for European, Russian, and Eurasian Studies at the George Washington University; the Centre for East European Studies at the University of Warsaw; and Santa Clara University.

We thank Melissa Aten, Nancy Meyers, Isabelle Chiardia, and Ashley Schweikert for their research assistance. Elwood Mills deserves special thanks for his seemingly unending work and patience in preparing maps and illustrations.

We thank all of our contributors for their patience, persistence, and diligence in preparing their contributions to this volume.

We also want to acknowledge the intellectual debts we owe not only to Václav Beneš, to whom this book is dedicated, but to others whose mentoring and teaching have shaped our views of Central and East European affairs and comparative politics. Our colleagues and friends in Central and Eastern Europe have challenged us and informed us, giving us valuable insights and untold hours of their time. For that, we owe them much. We are also grateful to the generations of students whose interactions with us helped us learn what students want and need to know about the politics of the region.

We are indebted as always to our families for their support in this endeavor, as in all others.

Finally, the idea for this book grew out of our common difficulty in finding up-to-date, accessible materials about the politics of Central and Eastern Europe after communism. But its origin actually dates to 1970 when we found ourselves beginning the study of what was then termed Eastern Europe with Václav Beneš at Indiana University. Our meeting at the reception for new graduate students led to a friendship that has seen us through graduate school, the births and growth of six children between us, and nearly forty years of professional and personal triumphs and tragedies. In addition to all those we have thanked for their role in this book, we are grateful for each other and for our friendship.

Illustrations

Maps

Photos

Tables

Part I

INTRODUCTION

CHAPTER 1

Democracy, the Market, and the Return to Europe

FROM COMMUNISM TO THE EUROPEAN UNION AND NATO

Sharon L. Wolchik and Jane L. Curry

In 1989, the unthinkable happened: communist rule collapsed, virtually like a house of cards, all over what had been the former Soviet bloc. As Timothy Garton Ash said, "In Poland it took ten years, in Hungary ten months, East Germany ten weeks: perhaps in Czechoslovakia it will take ten days!"[1] This statement, although not entirely accurate, captures several crucial aspects of the end of communist rule: it was fast, unexpected, and unplanned.

True, after almost fifty years of communist rule and of a Cold War that most assumed had irreversibly divided Europe between east and west, the countries of Central and Eastern Europe were once again free to chart their own course. But the return to Europe and transition from communism have not been easy for these states. Even when their institutions look like those in the established democracies of Western Europe, they often do not work the same ways.

Slightly more than a year later (October 3, 1990), not only had the Berlin Wall come down but Germany was no longer divided into the Soviet-occupied communist German Democratic Republic (GDR) and the richer democratic Federal Republic of Germany. As Germany came together, Czechoslovakia, Yugoslavia, and the Soviet Union came apart, creating from what had been eight states, twenty-nine states, nineteen of which are geographically in Europe. In the process, the collapse of Yugoslavia brought the first European war since the end of World War II.

A decade after the collapse of communist rule, the Czech Republic, Hungary, and Poland joined the North Atlantic Treaty Organization (NATO)—once the military bulwark of the Americans and what we then called the West Europeans against communism. Five years later, in 2004, NATO took in the Baltic states, Bulgaria, Romania, Slovakia, and Slovenia. That same year, fifteen years after the first roundtable negotiations between the Polish communists and their Solidarity opponents, the European Union (EU) expanded eastward to take in eight of the new democracies. Romania and Bulgaria became members in 2007. By 2005, Croatia, Macedonia, Albania, and Montenegro (as part of the Federal Union of Serbia and Montenegro) had begun accession talks. Since its Orange Revolution in 2004, Ukraine has also pushed to begin negotiations. Only Serbia and Bosnia remain far from even the discussion of their membership.

When communism collapsed, the new leaders and the citizens within the region hoped that democracy and capitalism would take root and flourish easily and quickly. The realities, though, proved more complicated. Almost all of these states had to catch up from centuries of being the backwaters of Europe, most often as a part of someone else's empire. State economies whose failures had helped bring down communist control had to be unraveled. Political systems in which elites shared power and citizens both had a voice and took responsibility had to be devised, established, and consolidated. Finally, both the leaders and the populations had to come to grips with their communist past.

These states are becoming part of European institutions, but they are not yet totally "European" in their politics or their economic developments. Politics and politicians in the region have ranged from the right to the left with little in between. Populism has begun to be the order of the day. Corruption is far more significant, and democracy less stable than elsewhere in Europe. Economic reform has brought private ownership and multinational corporations. At the same time, it has brought deep divisions between rich and poor; a decline in social welfare that has impacted the health and lives of much of the population; and, for many, real disappointment in capitalism.

Accession to the European Union was the logical outcome of the fall of the Berlin Wall, but it has complicated the EU's politics and economics. The postcommunist European countries are poorer than the original members. Many of their citizens face far higher unemployment rates. As a result, their citizens are easily tempted by the possibility of working in the West, provoking fears and hope in much of continental Europe that these job seekers might fill the least well-paid jobs in their societies. With the exception of those in Poland, Slovakia, and Hungary, citizens in this region proved to be far more skeptical of the EU than those in earlier member states. The result has been that some of these states, particularly Poland, have complicated EU debates and almost blocked key changes to the constitution and basic EU policies.

As the transition progressed, scholars debated whether these transitions would follow the models of democracy building in southern Europe (Spain, Portugal, and Greece) and in Latin America in the 1970s or whether their precommunist history and the impact of communism made the Central and East European countries different enough from each other and from the earlier transformations that they would follow different paths.[2] This book lays out the paths, the commonalities, and the differences that have marked the transitions from communism to democracy, from centrally planned economies to the market, and from the Soviet bloc and Iron Curtain to NATO and the European Union.

The countries dealt with explicitly in this volume are those from the old European communist world that have been the focus of attention for Europe and that have made substantial progress along the path to democracy. These include

Map 1.1.   Central and Eastern Europe Today

- Poland, Hungary, the Czech Republic, and the Baltic states, where there was an early and decisive break with the past and a clear turn toward building democratic institutions and politics in 1989 or, in the case of the Baltic states, with the fall of the Soviet Union in 1991
- Romania, Bulgaria, Croatia, Serbia-Montenegro, Ukraine, and Macedonia, where the initial collapse of communism led to semiauthoritarian rule, or Slo-

vakia, which experienced de-democratization[3] and where politics took a decisive turn toward democracy after critical elections or "electoral revolutions"
- parts of what was Yugoslavia (Bosnia-Herzegovina and Kosovo) where outside powers have occupied and ruled. Bosnia is formally independent even though its elected officials' decisions can be overruled by the OSCE supervisor. The independence of Kosovo has remained a highly conflictual issue: Kosovo is claimed by Serbia in its 2006 constitution as an integral but autonomous region, while Albanians in Kosovo and the United Nations commission hold that it should be made independent.

This volume deals only tangentially with Albania, which has begun the shift to democracy but remains less central to Europe as a whole than the other states. It also does not deal with East Germany, the former German Democratic Republic, which went through many of the same processes in its shift to democracy but in the context of reunification with West Germany rather than as a separate state.

The Rocky Roots of Central and Eastern Europe

History has not been kind to the peoples in the east of Europe. The landscape of the region is a mosaic of different nationalities which have their own languages, religions, and cultures. For most of their histories, the peoples of this region have not had their own states. They were underlings first of each other and then of the empires of Europe: the Ottoman Empire in the south, the Russian Empire to the east, and the Austro-Hungarian and Prussian empires to the west. In those empires, they were not the leaders. Instead, they served the empires' needs for food, cheap labor, or bureaucrats. Most often, they struggled to develop or preserve their national identities against attempts to assimilate or control them. Thus, when they became independent states, most after World War I, virtually all but what became Czechoslovakia were economically behind and politically troubled.[4]

The division into empires created a second layer of difference in this area. The lines drawn between the empires were more than geopolitical divisions. They resulted in clear differences in the trajectories of these states toward democracy and industrialization. Nearly a century after the empires collapsed, the differences between these states in the way their democracies work or do not work fall along the same lines as the empires' divisions of the nineteenth century. When new states were formed and old states re-created after World War I, the empires' boundaries reappeared in the differences in the economies and infrastructure of the new states. Each empire had made its capital its focus. The train lines went back and forth to Berlin, Vienna, and Moscow, not between Warsaw and Krakow or Prague and Bratislava.

The areas of southeastern Europe that became Serbia, Montenegro, Bulgaria, Bosnia, Albania, and parts of Romania and Croatia had been loosely ruled by the Ottoman Empire beginning in the thirteenth century. The Ottomans did little to develop this area. Corruption glued the empire together. It also brought it down after local

Map 1.2. *Empires in Central and Eastern Europe, 1800*

nationalism began to increase and the European empires, led by Austria-Hungary, moved in to take the pieces they could of most of these areas. Before World War I, Serbia, Bulgaria, and Romania were formally independent but internally torn apart. The battles that emerged over their borders and who belonged where have continued since. Their economies were based largely on subsistence agriculture.

The Russian Empire in Europe encapsulated the Baltic states (Latvia, Lithuania, and Estonia), the eastern part of Poland, and Ukraine. Unlike the Ottoman rulers, Russia's goal was to Russify and hold tight to these lands and their populations. In spite of Russia's stranglehold, though, these nations retained their memories of national glory and religions that were, at best, not Russian and, most often, anti-Russian. Many of their intellectuals escaped to Western Europe and the United States, creating strong ties with the West that defied Russia's attempts to seal the borders, keep out new democratic ideas, and make them "Russian." The Poles were the most determined. They fought against Russian control with uprisings and underground organizations that began in the 1700s when Russia, Austria, and Prussia partitioned Poland. Under Russian rule, Poland, Ukraine, and the Baltics remained largely agricultural economies with only a few pockets of industry and mining.

Until World War I, the German Empire extended into what is now western Poland. The Germans in western Poland and in the Czech Lands of Bohemia and Moravia had a long history of dominance and were also a large part of the population in much of this area. They dominated the economies of both western Poland and the border regions of what came to be Czechoslovakia. These areas were industrialized, and their agriculture the most modernized in Central and Eastern Europe.

The Austro-Hungarian Empire encompassed the Czech Lands, Slovakia, Hungary, Croatia, Slovenia, part of Poland, and what is now western Ukraine, as well as Bosnia after 1878. If foreign control can be good, Austrian control was. In the areas ruled from Vienna (the Czech Lands, part of Poland and Ukraine, and Slovenia), industrial development and local governance were allowed and encouraged. Citizens from these states participated in regional government and the Diet in Vienna. Schooling took place in German and also in the local languages. The Czechs flourished under Austrian rule; Bohemia and Moravia came to account for the majority of the industry in the empire. Citizens in the Hungarian part of the empire (Slovakia and Croatia) had fewer opportunities to develop national movements. In Slovakia, there was little education available beyond the elementary level in Slovak, and particularly after the 1870s, Slovaks came under heavy pressure to assimilate and adopt Hungarian as their language. Non-Hungarians had few political rights or opportunities to participate in politics even at the regional level. Opportunities for education and participation in local governance were somewhat greater in Croatia under Hungarian rule. However, given the domination of political life in Hungary by the landed aristocracy, there were few incentives for the development of industry. Apart from Budapest, much of the region remained dependent on agriculture.

World War I marked the birth of a new constellation of states in the east of Europe. It was triggered by the assassination of Austrian Archduke Ferdinand in Sarajevo by a Serbian who wanted Bosnia to be part of Serbia, not the Austro-Hungarian Empire. After the war, American president Woodrow Wilson's call for national self-determination for the peoples of Europe was reflected in the carving up of the old empires into nation-states. The boundary lines of the states established at this time were far from perfect. The results created serious problems within and between states in the interwar period and are evident in political conflicts between ethnic groups even today.

The Russian Revolution in 1917 and the attempts to spread the revolution beyond Russia created new ideological pressures and divisions that further complicated the political fortunes of these fragile new states. Ukraine had a brief period of independence that ended when it was conquered by Bolshevik armies in 1921. In Hungary, communist supporters, led by Bela Kun, established a short-lived experiment with communism, the Hungarian Soviet Republic. Ousted after only a few months, this experiment discredited the idea of communism in Hungary and contributed to Hungarian antagonism toward the Soviet Union. The communists also tried but failed to spread their revolution to Poland.

At the end of the war, the Treaty of Versailles drew the borders of the new Europe. But, although national self-determination was the call, ethnic groups were intermingled when the borders were drawn. The desire of the Allies to punish Germany, Austria, and Hungary; opposition to the new communist regime in Russia; and the constellation of military forces on the ground instead determined the borders of the new Europe. To punish Germany and Austria, the lands of the German and Austro-Hungarian empires were cut apart. Hungary was most affected. As the result of the Treaty of Trianon of 1920, it lost two-thirds of its territory and roughly 60 percent of its population to its neighbors.[5] Since many of the areas Hungary lost were populated largely by ethnic Hungarians, citizens and leaders in the shrunken Hungary saw this loss as unjust. The popular response to Trianon, "No, no never," was played out in the efforts of Hungarian leaders to reverse the treaty and regain Hungary's "historical lands," an effort that dominated Hungarian politics and poisoned its relations with its neighbors during the interwar period. With the breakup of Austria-Hungary, Germans lost their dominant positions in what became Czechoslovakia and the newly re-created Polish state. Bulgaria also was punished; it lost land to Greece, Romania, and Yugoslavia.

The boundaries of the new states of Czechoslovakia and Yugoslavia brought together ethnic groups that were very different in their religions, cultures, economies, and levels of development. These differences were most divisive in Yugoslavia. There the languages and religions, as well as the empires under which the different ethnic groups had developed, varied greatly. The political opportunities and experiences of the main groups in these countries also differed widely in the new states. Instead of being on equal footing, one group dominated the others in each state.

The Polish territories straddled German areas in the West and areas with mixed Lithuanian, Ukrainian, and Polish populations in the East. Like Poland, Romania emerged as a multiethnic state patched together from pieces of very different European empires. As in Czechoslovakia and Yugoslavia, the new leaders of these states had to create unified states from peoples who came with very different histories and resources. Very often, states were created from national groups whose historical memories included conflict with or resentment of each other.

The interwar period began with high hopes of building democracy in the new states. But, with the exception of Czechoslovakia, these new democracies disintegrated

Map 1.3.   Eastern Europe, 1914

rapidly into autocracies. Only Czechoslovakia, Hungary, and Poland had more than fleeting moments of democracy. In Hungary and Poland, these ended with authoritarian regimes under military rulers. In Bulgaria, Romania, and Yugoslavia, royal dictatorships quickly replaced parliamentary rule. In Albania, which had maintained its independence at the Paris peace conference despite the plans of many of its neighbors and the larger powers to partition it, parliamentary rule was disrupted by a coup and, in 1928, the proclamation of a monarchy by Ahmet Zogu.

Ruled by combinations of bureaucratic and military elites, supplemented in some cases by representatives of the rising industrial class, these governments paid little attention to the needs of citizens, who, after a brief period, had few avenues for effective political participation. As authoritarian governments usurped the powers of parliaments, most of the numerous small political parties that had begun to be active were outlawed. Citizens were channeled into movements or parties loyal to the government.[6] Communist parties were formed in 1921 in all of these states. They too were soon outlawed in most cases. Extremist parties and movements, particularly those on the far right such as the Iron Guard in Romania and the Arrow Cross in Hungary, flourished and were a real threat to political stability. In Bulgaria, the radical IMRO (Internal Macedonian Revolutionary Organization) ruled parts of the country briefly.

With the exception of Czechoslovakia, which was one of the most developed nations in the world during the interwar period because of the concentration of 70 to 90 percent of Austria-Hungary's industry in Bohemia and Moravia, these countries remained largely (Poland and Hungary) or overwhelmingly (the others) agrarian. The new leaders of all these states aggressively tried to industrialize. They achieved some success in the 1920s. Growth rates at this time were higher in Poland and Romania than in France or Germany. However, their economies continued to be heavily dependent on agriculture. In the less than twenty years between the wars, none of the largely agrarian states were strong enough to develop their infrastructures, build up their industry, or compete on the world market. Indeed, economic conflict over land distribution and ownership amplified ethnic conflict. The trauma of the Great Depression derailed early efforts to develop and increased the susceptibility of these economies to foreign penetration and economic and political domination. The degree of development these states did achieve also proved problematic from a political perspective. The bureaucracies and leaders of these new states proved incapable, in most cases, of meeting the increased demands for services and infrastructure that urbanization created. They also were generally unsuccessful in incorporating the growing working class into the national political community.

In the end it was the actions of outside powers and the advent of World War II that brought the end of the interwar system in Central and Eastern Europe. The inability of the interwar leaders to resolve old issues, such as ethnic conflict, or deal with the new demands resulting from the development that did occur, however, played a role; it also increased their vulnerability and made them easy prey for outside manipulation.

World War II was the watershed event for the fledgling democracies in Central and Eastern Europe. None of the new states had the time or resources to build real defenses against a German onslaught. The first steps to war began when the Germans took the Sudetenland from Czechoslovakia with the approval, in the now infamous

Munich Agreement, of Italy, France, and Britain in October 1938. After that, the move toward war continued with the Molotov-Ribbentrop Pact for the division of Poland between the Soviets and the Germans, and their simultaneous invasions of Poland in 1939. The German invasion triggered French and English declarations of war against Germany, starting World War II. Bulgaria, Hungary, and Romania fought alongside the Germans as part of the Axis Powers. Only at the end of the war did Romania manage to leave the Axis camp. Slovakia and Croatia emerged as "puppet states" of the Axis powers, although Croatia also was eventually occupied. Poland, the Czech Republic, the rest of former Yugoslavia, the Baltic states, and Ukraine were occupied by Germany. Two years later, in 1941 (the 149th anniversary of Napoleon's attack on Russia), the German-Soviet pact collapsed, and German troops swept across Poland into the Soviet Union.

World War II would prove devastating for Poland, Ukraine, Yugoslavia, and the Baltic states, all of which suffered great loss of life as well as physical destruction. For the others, although the physical damage was less, the destruction of their political and social leadership was dramatic. The sizable Jewish and Roma minorities, as well as many of the intellectuals and others who were perceived as threats or who fought

Map 1.4.   Axis and Allies, 1941–1944

against the Germans, were decimated by the Holocaust. The complicity of some domestic leaders in the deportation of the Jews to the death camps and the collaboration of some with the Nazis further diminished their moral claims to leadership once the war was over.

The Allied leaders of Britain, the Soviet Union, and the United States began to plan for Germany's defeat and the resurrection of Europe in 1943. At Yalta, the second of three conferences between British, U.S., and Soviet leaders, Britain and the United States essentially agreed to let the Soviet Union have a dominant role from Berlin east. By the end of the war, the slaughter of millions of Jews and Roma, boundary changes, the shift of Poland's borders to the west, the expulsion of Germans from Poland and Czechoslovakia, and population exchanges in border areas made most of these states more homogeneous ethnically than they had been before the war. The western Allies pushed provisions for free, competitive elections as soon as the war ended. With the partial exception of the 1946 elections in Czechoslovakia and the 1945 elections in Hungary, these did not happen. After the war, western Ukraine and the Baltic states were incorporated into the USSR. The other Central and East European states found themselves in the Soviet sphere of influence.

The Imposition of Communist Rule

In many of these states, communist rule came with the Soviet armies. Ukraine was retaken from the German armies in 1943 as the Soviets moved west. The Soviet army then conquered the Baltic states and much of Central and Eastern Europe as it fought the Germans and marched to meet the Allied forces in Berlin. As they pushed the German forces out, the Soviets installed a "baggage train government,"[7] led by communist leaders who had spent the war years in the Soviet Union and returned with the Red Army, that worked to take control of what remained in Poland and Czechoslovakia. In Czechoslovakia, a coalition government of communist and noncommunist leaders was allowed to rule the reunited country. Hungary and Bulgaria, as "Axis powers," were simply occupied by the Soviet Union. Soviet troops also brought handpicked Romanian communists with them when they marched into Romania, which had switched from the Axis to the Allies in 1944.

In Yugoslavia and Albania, the Soviets played a very limited role in establishing communism. Although the Soviet army helped liberate Belgrade, Josip Broz Tito and the Partisans liberated most of Yugoslavia through guerilla warfare against the German occupiers. Most of the aid they received came from the western Allies. The Partisans thus came to power largely through their own efforts; in the process, they also often fought nationalist Croatian Ustaše forces and Serbian Chetniks who, in turn, fought each other and the Axis occupiers. The Soviet role in establishing communism was also negligible in Albania, where resistance fighters with Yugoslav and Western support ousted the occupiers and established a provisional communist government in 1944.

In Czechoslovakia and Hungary, a period of modified pluralism followed the end of the war. Soviet forces withdrew from Czechoslovakia after the war but remained in Hungary. Although, initially, the Communist Party had a number of advantages in both countries, other political forces were able to play a role in political life for several years. In Hungary, the Communist Party was far less popular than its main political rival, the Smallholders Party. In the election of 1945, the Smallholders received 57 percent of the vote; the Hungarian Communist Party and the Social Democrats each received 17 percent. Over the next two years, the Communist Party's membership increased greatly, and party leaders succeeded in gradually restricting the freedom of action of other political parties and discrediting their leaders. The ultimate step in this process was the manipulated election held in 1947 in which the Communist Party emerged as the strongest political force. In Czechoslovakia, where the Communist Party won the largest number of votes in the generally free elections of 1946, decreasing support for the party and changes in the international environment led the Communists to orchestrate a government crisis in February 1948. After the democratic ministers in the coalition government resigned, a government dominated solely by the Communist Party took power.

When communist governments took over after the war, they installed their men and women at the local level and in the key ministries so that they controlled the economy, military, and police. Parties on the far right were tarred as collaborators and outlawed soon after the end of the war. The timing varied, but in all cases, noncommunist parties were either eliminated or allowed to exist under Communist Party control to mobilize sectors of the population unlikely to become members of the party. The socialist parties from before the war were forced to merge with the communist parties. Communists who had fought against the Germans in their countries were purged in favor of those who had come from the Soviet Union with the Red Army. This process generated purge trials and attacks on communist and noncommunist intellectuals and workers for their connections with the West, the prewar regime, or criticism of the new socialist state.

At the same time, the communist rulers had to start rebuilding from the destruction of the war. For the Polish communists, this process meant rebuilding most of the major cities and industries. In other countries, this task was less monumental. But, in all, there were population shifts and the need to create functioning economies. This process was begun by the collectivization of all agricultural land into farms owned by the state or cooperatives farmed by large groups of farmers. This was a bitter pill for those who, less than a generation before in many cases, had received their own plots. It also meant drawing young people from the farms to the cities to build and run new industries. In the 1950s, propaganda portrayed these developments as the great glory of these new socialist states. The dramatic growth in industry also resulted in a great deal of upward social mobility, as a generation went from being peasant children to being educated workers who went on to leadership positions. The old elites were pushed aside in the process.

Communist Rule and Its Realities

Communist rule was intended to put everything under the supervision and direction of the Communist Party and to insure that the various states in the Soviet bloc were themselves supervised and directed by the Soviet Union. No aspect of life or politics was to be excluded. Everything was owned and controlled by the governments. They, in turn, were led by the Communist Party. Ostensibly, this arrangement was to speed up the transformation Karl Marx predicted in which industrialization first brought capitalist exploitation of the working class and then increasing equality and power for the working class. But, since these were not the states or the economic conditions where Marx had said this transition would occur, Vladimir Lenin's turning of Marx on his head was used to justify establishing communist rule in places where the Industrial Revolution was delayed. The promise was that the state, rather than capitalists, could develop and own industry, and transform the working class into the ruling class.

In reality, the institutions and policies that were associated with communist rule in Central and Eastern Europe failed both economically and politically. As developments throughout the communist period in the region illustrate, in most cases, the Soviet model was not welcomed or implemented by the population, but imposed from above. It also came into conflict with underlying conditions and values in many of these societies.

The irony of communist rule in the east of Europe is that it never worked as it claimed and was never monolithic. As early as 1947, the Soviet bloc had its first breakaway. In the period immediately after he came to power, Tito in fact went faster in implementing the Soviet model (to be detailed below) than Stalin wanted, given his hopes that communist parties would come to power peacefully in Italy and France and his emphasis on "national roads to socialism." Tito refused to accept Soviet interference in Yugoslav affairs and also offended Stalin with his plans for a "Balkan Union" under Yugoslav leadership. Disagreement over the speed with which Yugoslavia was moving to establish a communist system and its own control of the secret police led to an open break between the two leaders. Soviet advisors withdrew and Tito became the icon of evil in communist rhetoric.

The break meant that the fragile multiethnic state of Yugoslavia was on its own, without access to Soviet bloc supplies or markets and, because it remained communist, without immediate aid from the West either. To explain away the split, Tito charged that Soviet-style communism was ideologically incorrect and proposed real decentralization of decision making in the party and government. In 1952, the party changed its name to the League of Communists of Yugoslavia, a step that symbolized its intention to lead by example rather than force. Over the next two decades, power devolved to the republics and away from the center. The Yugoslav leadership also instituted a system of "workers self-management" that involved workers in decision making in factories, even though management retained a good deal of power. Tito also became one of the founders of the nonaligned movement and positioned Yugoslavia between the Western and Eastern blocs.

Although Yugoslavia remained a one-party system in which no organized political dissent was allowed, Tito's innovations allowed a degree of openness in debate within the country and contact with the West that no other communist government in the region permitted. Many of the institutional innovations the Yugoslavs tried were directed at giving different ethnic groups a stake in maintaining a unified state. The system, in the end, gave each republic a veto over decision making at the federal level.

It worked for a decade after Tito's death. But it failed to overcome the divisions that played out in a series of brutal wars between the former republics in the 1990s.

After communist governments were established in the rest of the region, they implemented far-reaching institutional and policy changes. This process, which began in earnest after the Stalin-Tito rift and the February 1948 coup in Czechoslovakia, involved copying the Soviet experience in all areas. The early emphasis on the need to find national roads to socialism gave way to efforts to create a uniform system of political and economic organization throughout the region by 1948. The Soviet model that Central and East European leaders emulated was the model that existed in the Soviet Union at the time, which was the Stalinist pattern of political and economic organization, economic development, and social and value change. In 1989 and 1991 when communist rule collapsed, this model left the countries in the region with an elaborate set of institutions and huge bureaucracies all involved in coordinating and directing the economy as well as the state apparatus. The fused nature of political and economic power both contributed to the end of communism and complicated the transition away from it.[8]

The Communist Party was charged throughout this period with having the "leading role" in the system. Its goal as a party was not to win elections. Those victories were guaranteed because there was, in normal circumstances, only one candidate per seat and, whether or not he or she was a party member, that candidate was selected by the Communist Party. Its goal was to serve as the "vanguard of the proletariat" and to lead the state in the name of that proletariat. Membership in the party was selective rather than elective. To be one of the 10 to 20 percent of the population in the party required that people apply, serve a long candidacy, and be approved by the party as members.

The Communist Party was organized hierarchically from the primary party organizations found in every workplace up to the Politburo or Presidium led by the first secretary. Its basic rule was "democratic centralism." This organizational principle required all decisions made at the top to be supported and carried out by all party members without question. In reality, though, party membership had very little to do with any commitment to the ideology. It was, most often, simply a ticket to upward mobility. Decisions were not made by the membership and its elected bodies but by a huge party bureaucracy (*apparat*) that managed not only internal party issues such as organization, ideology, and propaganda but also directed and supervised the work of each state institution. It did this through a system of parallel hierarchies, whereby party leaders at every level supervised and directed the workings of state institutions at that level.

At the very top of the Communist Party, the Politburo—or Presidium, as it was sometimes called—members allocated to themselves the key party and state offices. From their perch, they served as the "interlocking directorate," coordinating the various branches of the party and state. Information came up to them from the various party organizations and bureaucracies, and their directives were translated downward. From the top down, the Communist Party structures were the skeleton of the state. The party selected or approved the managerial or politically significant personnel working at all levels of the state bureaucracy and economy (*nomenklatura*), channeled information between the top and bottom, took ultimate responsibility for all major policy, coordinated the work of different sectors of the state, and provided ideological guidance.

Although the Communist Party controlled and directed all political life, everyone was expected to participate in the system. In contrast to the interwar period, when a wide variety of charitable, professional, political, and interest organizations flourished in most of the region, the associational life of these countries was brought almost entirely under the control of the Communist Party. An elaborate system of mass organizations, ranging from trade unions to children's organizations, served as "transition belts" to carry the party's directives to the population and mobilize ordinary people to carry out the party's bidding.

Elections were also regularly held for national, regional, and local government bodies. The candidates for these positions (party and nonparty members), as in the Soviet case, were selected and assigned by the Communist Party, one for each open seat, even if they were not party members. Elections were to demonstrate support rather than to select. Opposition was shown by not voting or by crossing out the candidate. As the 99 percent turnout rates demonstrated, opposition, however meek, was virtually impossible in this system.

The Soviet model also included a system of economic institutions and policies as well as a strategy of economic transformation that subordinated economic life to the party's direction and control. These economies were centrally planned with large, party-directed planning apparatuses. Decisions about what would be produced, how much, where, and for whom, as well as what workers of different ranks were to be paid and what each product would cost, were made by the state Planning Commission. All parts of the economy from agriculture and industry to social welfare and the arts were owned and run by the state. The Planning Commission's decisions were based on general policy goals set by the Communist Party leadership rather than the market. Often, these policy goals were established for political reasons and were not based on economic rationality.

The establishment of state ownership of most, if not all, economic assets began almost as soon as the communists took power. Communist leaders expanded the process of nationalizing industry that started in most of these countries immediately after the end of the war. In line with Soviet practice, they adopted rapid industrialization as a goal. They also emphasized heavy industry, particularly metallurgy and mining, to the detriment of light industry, agriculture, and the service sector. Collectivization of agriculture was another component of the model. In many cases, peasants who had only recently received land confiscated from expelled Germans or collaborators resisted fiercely. Communist elites also reoriented foreign trade away from traditional patterns with the rest of Europe to the Soviet Union and other communist countries.

The impact of this model on economic performance varied at first by the initial level of development of each economy. Stalinist economic policies worked best, at first, in the least developed countries in the region. There they produced rapid growth rates and urbanization as well as high rates of social mobility. The inefficiencies of centralized economies and Stalinist strategies of development eventually plagued and doomed all the economies of the region. However, in the economies that began with a higher standard of living and industrialization, these failings became evident more quickly. Shortages of basic goods and the lack of adequate services resulted in poor worker morale and low rates of productivity. There was little incentive to innovate. As a result of these failings, these economies could not compete on the world market. These dismal economic conditions were facts of life everywhere in the region. What the population got from state control of the economy was cradle-to-grave welfare, very low-cost housing, guaranteed employment, little pressure to work hard, and prices that virtually never changed even as products disappeared from the shelves. To cope with the shortages and disappearances of goods, elaborate personal systems of barter and an entire second economy based on illicit trade emerged and became a prime part of the "marketplace" wherever it was possible.

Communism, though, involved far more than state ownership and Communist Party elite control of the state and the economy. The system demanded public conformity and loyalty. Direction and control of the media and public discussions blocked criticism of the system, its leaders, and their decisions. It also discouraged support for alternative institutions and beliefs. All the media were organized as the mouthpieces of the party, which ensured that views other than those the party sanctioned did not get reported. Lest the population see how others lived, travel and communications in and out of the country were controlled and restricted.

The Soviet model also involved social change and efforts to change the population's value systems. Elimination of most private property served to undermine the economic base of the old elites and minimize the resources they could use to resist the new system. In the process, it also helped to turn the social hierarchy virtually upside down. Restrictions on the ability of the children of the upper and middle classes to obtain higher education and admissions procedures that gave children of workers and peasants preference also promoted changes in the status of members of different social groups. Wage structures that rewarded manual labor in priority branches of the econ-

Photo 1.1.   Bread lines were infamous in Communist Europe due to frequent shortages in food and consumer goods.
(Source: Peter Turnley/CORBIS)

omy such as heavy industry, mining, and construction more than work in the "nonproductive" sectors of the economy, such as education, medicine, public trade and catering, and administration, served the same purpose. Even when these policies faded away in the 1970s and 1980s in some of these countries, the old national elite was disadvantaged in comparison to the men and women who had risen from peasants to working class in the 1950s and then moved up through the Communist Party. They had the power in the state and party to buy themselves into the new economy in ways many who had fought the system or had come out of the intelligentsia did not.

Political leaders also used education, art and culture, and leisure activities to try to change popular values. The humanities, social sciences, and even many of the hard sciences that did not contribute to national defense suffered from an infusion of ideology into their content. Certain disciplines, such as sociology, were branded bourgeois sciences and banned outright in the 1950s in Poland, Hungary, and Yugoslavia and far longer elsewhere. Antireligion campaigns were used to try to wean the population away from religion and toward a belief in Marxism-Leninism as a worldview everywhere but Poland. The goal was the creation of "new socialist men" (and women) who put "the collective" above individual interests and who worked tirelessly for the promotion of socialism. In the arts and culture in communism's early years, the doctrine of "socialist realism" required that all artistic expression be directed toward political ends.

Communism was also a system in which the leaders had little trust in those they worked with or in the population as a whole. The Soviet model was not chosen by the population, but was imposed from above. In most cases, the communist leaders who imposed it were in turn also perceived to have been chosen by outside actors (the Soviet Union). The changes the model required were far-reaching and affected all areas of life. As a result, these regimes relied heavily on coercion. The secret police were an important tool to control dissent and punish opponents and were also used to provide information to the party leadership on what the population did and thought. The military hierarchy was paralleled by a political force in the military to make sure soldiers and officers were politically trained. In the end, it was a society that was watched and directed from all sides.

This pattern was expanded into relations among communist parties and rulers. The central Soviet party in Moscow controlled what the party units and, through them, governments did in the Baltics, Ukraine, and elsewhere in the Soviet Union. Although formally independent, the other states in what came to be the Soviet bloc were not truly independent. Their party leaders had to be approved by the Soviet leadership, to consult with them and follow their lead on all aspects of domestic and foreign policy, and to work with their neighbors only under Soviet supervision. The result was that changes in the Soviet Union or elsewhere in the bloc impacted all its members.

Formally, all of the members of the Soviet bloc (which did not include Yugoslavia and, after 1961, Albania) were members of the Warsaw Pact and the Council for Mutual Economic Assistance (Comecon or CMEA). The Warsaw Pact, a response to the formation of the North Atlantic Treaty Organization, organized all the military units of the Soviet Union and the Central and East European states under the command of the Soviet military leadership. It had elaborate plans as to who would do what for both offensive and defensive battles in Europe. Perhaps more importantly, it allowed for a monitoring of the preparedness and attitude of the various nations' troops and also forced bloc states to coordinate their military hardware.

Comecon was the economic trade organization that coordinated the economies of these states. It too was led by the Soviet Union. Through Comecon, Soviet interests were played out in the distribution of economic specialties to individual Central and East European countries other than Yugoslavia and Albania (and, after 1961, Romania), the direction of trade within the bloc and with the West and Third World, and the management of all currency exchange, since the currencies of Soviet bloc states could not be exchanged outside the "ruble zone" as currency values were set as much for political reasons as for economic ones. In the process, tasks were divided up so no country could be economically independent.

In the early communist period, Soviet control played a critical role in determining the course of events in the region. After the death of Stalin in March 1953, Soviet control shifted from direction to guidance and from prescription to proscription. The leaders of Central and East European countries were urged to come to some sort of accommodation with their populations. The Soviet leadership served more as a watchdog lest orthodoxy be challenged too vigorously rather than the director of events. However, although the Soviet model could be reformed and adapted, there were limits. The Communist Party had to retain its "leading role." There could not be criticism of the Soviet Union or a turn from the Warsaw Pact to the West. Twice, popular demands on the street and disillusionment within the party went beyond these limits. Both times, in Hungary in 1956 and Czechoslovakia in 1968, Warsaw Pact troops invaded, put down the revolt, and installed "safe" leaders.[9] When the recognition of Solidarity as the only independent trade union in the communist world in Poland in 1980 led to challenges to the party's leading role, Poland's communist leaders under General Wojciech Jaruzelski imposed martial law in December 1981 to prevent a Soviet-led invasion.

On a day-to-day basis, though, the whole system worked to prevent things from spinning so far out of control. Individual leaders worked their way up through the ranks. They knew the Soviet leaders well enough to easily estimate what would be tolerated and what would not. What they did not know, they were told in meetings with the Soviet leaders. Soviet troops were stationed in every country (except Romania, Yugoslavia, and Albania—all of which were far enough away to be able to have separate foreign policies). Long-established economic ties and their dependence on cheap Soviet oil and natural gas further tied the bloc together. The Iron Curtain that divided Berlin snaked between East and West economically, politically, and militarily.

Yet, even with these controls and this grand divide, the Soviet model was modified over time in each country. The "Polish Road to Socialism" after Stalin's death and the Polish upheavals in 1956 brought in a nationalist leadership that was able to trade tolerance from its population for private agriculture, small-scale private industry, and legal rights for the Catholic Church, to which 98 percent of Poles belonged. As part of its mission in Comecon in the 1970s, Poland actively sought trade with the West. When excessive borrowing from the West to buy off workers brought the economy nearly to bankruptcy, Polish leaders in the summer of 1980 increased prices on foodstuffs. Polish workers went on strike and the free trade union Solidarity was established. In December 1981, the Polish government declared martial law, made Solidarity and the other movements that had emerged illegal, and interned Solidarity activists and others who had pushed for real changes in the system. But the communists were never able to recapture their power. In the late 1980s, Poland's communist leaders turned to Solidarity to share power and the responsibility for improving Poland's disastrous economic performance, only to lose the first partially free election in communist Europe in 1989.

In the 1960s, Romania took its own road. Its communist leaders imposed a form of communism that was both nationalist and highly repressive. Consumer needs were denied in order to support Romania's international position. Romania withdrew from Comecon because it was pressed to become a purely agricultural state and from direct participation in the Warsaw Pact's invasion of Czechoslovakia. It deviated from Soviet foreign policy by maintaining relations with Israel and China when the Soviet Union broke them. And it was courted by the West because of its foreign policy independence. All this was both tolerated and used by the bloc. It provided them with a channel to two critical international actors, the West and China. But Romania also served as the demonstration case of how repressive communist rule could become.

Hungarians also took advantage of the opening the death of Stalin and disunity among the Soviet leadership created to challenge the communist system in the mid-

Photo 1.2.   Deputy Prime Minister Mieczysław Rakowski (in photo) meets with the crew of the Gdańsk shipyard, where he criticized the activities of Solidarity. The emergence and tolerance of Solidarity for fifteen months in 1980–1981 and the martial law regime that followed were the final protest and repression before 1989, when the authorities gave in. Rakowski went on to become the last communist prime minister and, after the 1989 defeat of communist candidates, the last head of the Polish United Workers Party.

(Source: Stefan Kraszewski/PAP)

l950s. In what has now been recognized as the Revolution of 1956, Hungarians fought Soviet invaders in the streets of Budapest. When Hungarian leaders declared the country's neutrality and announced plans to adopt a multiparty system, the Soviets invaded again. After a period of harsh repression, Hungarian leader János Kádár presided over a process of gradual reform. Adopting the slogan "He who is not against us is with us," Kádár shifted to a more conciliatory posture toward the population that has been described as "goulash communism." In the late 1960s, the Hungarian leadership allowed progressively more elements of the market in an attempt to stimulate the economy. Private enterprises proliferated, and state-owned firms' earnings were determined more by what they produced than by what the plan ordered. To further improve the economy and regain the support of its alienated population, the "Kádár Compromise" also came to include the gradual withdrawal of the Communist Party from many areas of life and a corresponding increase in room for debate and independent activity. Hungary also followed Poland in shifting the balance of its trade with the bloc and the West. In the process, Hungary's economy moved further than any other toward the market.

In the late l960s, Czechoslovakia also experienced a period of reform. A delayed response to de-Stalinization and the failing of the economy, this process of renewal and reform at the elite level gained a mass following in early 1968. When Alexander Dubček and his colleagues proved unable or unwilling to rein in calls for even greater freedom, the Warsaw Pact once again intervened to "protect" socialism from its enemies. The so-called Brezhnev Doctrine enunciated at this time justified the invasion as the right of the Soviet Union and other socialist states to ensure that socialism was not threatened in any socialist country and reaffirmed the Soviet Union's role as the arbiter of the limits of reform.

As part of the Soviet Union, the Baltic states and Ukraine experienced shifts in policy and the degree of openness that occurred elsewhere in the USSR as leaders changed after Stalin's death. But, although de-Stalinization allowed somewhat more room for the republics to chart their own courses, the Soviet system remained highly centralized. Moscow often interfered in republic affairs to quell excessive nationalism or particularlism on the part of the republic's Communist Party leaders as well as their populations. National movements continued to develop in the 1970s and 1980s, however. These movements were particularly strong in the Baltic states, where the memory of independent statehood in the interwar period was still very much alive.

The Collapse of Communism

Much as Communist Party leaders and their minions tried to claim that communism was creating a better world, it did not. The plan failed to encourage or allow for the research and development needed for the economies to be effective or even to replace outdated and failing machinery. After the 1950s, workers no longer worked out of fear. They worked for a better life. But, in what was most often an economy of shortages with salaries paid whether or not workers and their factories produced, there was little incentive for productivity. And so as the machinery failed and workers did less and less, productivity dropped. With this, there was a vicious circle. Lacking the new equipment that Western firms had, communist economies sank further, and productivity decreased as did what was available on the market, so workers had even less reason to work. As less and less was available and the wait for apartments remained decades long, the population grew more alienated. At the same time, the continuing shortages meant that those with power claimed as much as they could for themselves. Corruption and connections were decisive in what people got and how they lived.

When Mikhail Gorbachev came to power in the Soviet Union, he tried to deal with the crumbling of the communist system. Soviet reforms moved from merely trying to "accelerate" production by making people work harder to revealing the faults in the system through glasnost and making an effort to restructure the economy through perestroika, to widespread changes in how the state and the party worked and the expansion of opportunities for people to organize independently and make their views known. The other countries in the bloc were pressed to follow the direction of the Soviet Union. For hard-liners in Czechoslovakia, East Germany, Bulgaria, and Romania, the reforms were far from welcome. For the Poles and the Hungarians, they were a justification to go even further in reforms they were already making. For all of the countries in Central and Eastern Europe, as well as the Soviet Union itself, the reforms were destabilizing. Not only did the once stable limits of reform suddenly seem flexible, but, as the Soviet leadership focused on solving its own serious problems, it in effect cut Central and East European communist leaders loose to please their populations while propping up their own economies and paying market prices for once cheap Soviet energy resources.

In the end, the softening of Soviet rule and the mounting pressures of young people and others who wanted more, systems that were increasingly unable to deal with their failings, and the disillusionment of the party faithful started the fall of the Soviet bloc dominoes, and it could not be stopped. Where there was an established opposition, the changes were smoother than where no opposition had been able to form or survive. But the system fell apart everywhere outside the Soviet Union in 1989, and in 1991, Gorbachev announced the end of the Soviet Union as a state.

Changes in the Soviet Union under Gorbachev and the Soviet leadership's decision to allow Central and East European countries to go their own ways (the so-called Sinatra Doctrine) clearly were important factors in bringing about the end of communism in the region. Similarly, Boris Yeltsin's decision to recognize the independence of the Baltic states in August 1991, after the abortive hard-line coup, and the dissolution of the Soviet Union in September of that year opened the way for the Baltic states and Ukraine to become independent states again. Developments in countries such as Poland and Hungary, which were at the forefront of the process of change, and the fall of the Berlin Wall also influenced developments elsewhere. But while outside factors facilitated the process and in some cases acted as the catalyst for the changes, the collapse of these systems also reflected the deep economic and political crises that communist systems had created in all of these states.

The end of communism in the region differed in the speed of the process, the extent of citizen involvement, and the level of violence involved. If we combine these dimensions, four main patterns emerge. The first occurred in Poland and Hungary, where the end of communist rule most closely resembled the pacted transitions in

Latin America and southern Europe. In both, reformist leaders in the Communist Party negotiated the end of communism with representatives of the opposition in roundtable discussions. In Poland, the regime and Solidarity leaders agreed to hold semifree elections in June 1989. Although the agreement guaranteed the party's candidates certain seats, Solidarity won an overwhelming victory and formed the first government not dominated by the communists since the end of World War II.

In Hungary, where the opposition was much smaller, its leaders used issues connected with the Revolution of 1956 to open roundtable negotiations with reformers in the Communist Party. In what was, in some ways, the most remarkable case, the Hungarian communists negotiated themselves out of power without any significant pressure from mass public action other than the peaceful crowds that came to the streets for the reburial of the leaders killed after the 1956 revolt, which gave the process of change a public face. In 1990, presidential and parliamentary elections formalized the change of regime agreed upon in 1989. In both the Polish and Hungarian cases, the end of communism reflected a longer-term process of opposition organization and change within the party as well as in the broader society.

In East Germany, Czechoslovakia, and Romania, the collapse of communism came about as the result of massive citizen protests. The process began in East Germany where peaceful demonstrations led by activists in several cities gained momentum and became explicitly political once the Hungarians opened their borders and allowed large numbers of East Germans trying to reach West Germany through Hungary to do so. In November 1989 the fall of the Berlin Wall, the most potent symbol of the division of Germany into two halves, had repercussions around the world and encouraged citizens in other communist states to press for change in their own countries.

In Czechoslovakia, the beating of peaceful protestors in Prague who had gathered on November 17 to commemorate a student killed by the Nazis in 1939 led to mass demonstrations in Prague and Bratislava that quickly spread to other towns and cities. Aware that the Soviet leadership would not come to their aid, Czech and Slovak leaders yielded power in negotiations with the opposition twenty-one days after the beginning of the demonstrations. The election of Václav Havel as president by a parliament still dominated by the Communist Party in December capped the victory of what came to be called the Velvet Revolution for its peaceful nature.

Mass demonstrations also brought down the extremely repressive, personalized dictatorship of Nicolae Ceauşescu in Romania. Protests in Transylvania spread to the capital and other cities. In contrast to the cases above in which Communist Party leaders yielded power peacefully, Ceauşescu's secret police force, the Securitate, fired upon the peaceful demonstrators. When this action failed to stop the protests, Ceauşescu's opponents within the Communist Party engineered a coup. Nicolae Ceauşescu and his wife Elena, who was also very deeply involved in the regime's politics, were tried in what can only be described as a show trial and executed on Christmas Day.

In Bulgaria and Albania, the transitions occurred in two stages. In the first, less repressive Communist Party leaders took over from the old guard. These leaders were, in turn, replaced by the opposition in later elections. In Bulgaria, the reformed Communist Party won in multiparty parliamentary elections in 1990, although the opposition gained a significant number of seats in parliament. The opposition won the 1991 elections only to lose to the reformed communists, now the Bulgarian Socialist Party, in 1993. It was only in the mid-1990s that a coalition of the democratic opposition returned to power. In Albania, the Communist Party won the 1990 elections. The newly formed opposition was able to form a noncommunist government only after the 1992 elections.

The transition from communist rule in Yugoslavia differed in many important ways from the end of communist rule elsewhere in the region. In Yugoslavia, the end of communism coincided with the breakup of the country. It also occurred in a series of wars that resulted in a large number of deaths as well as large waves of refugees as the result of "ethnic cleansing," widespread physical destruction, and economic devastation. With the exception of Slovenia, which succeeded in defending its independence in a three-week war in 1991, the transition to postcommunist rule in the states formed from Yugoslavia has followed a very different path, one complicated by the impact of the wars and the need to come to terms with their aftermath.

In the Baltic states, the transformation was torturously close and yet impossible until the whole Soviet Union collapsed. The Lithuanians in 1990 and the Latvians in 1991 tried to declare independence, only to have the Soviets move in. It was only during the crisis in Russia that developed after the attempted coup in the summer of 1991 that movements for independence were able to succeed in Latvia, Lithuania, and Estonia. In all three, groups that had originally supported cultural autonomy gained adherents within the respective communist parties who also supported self-determination and later independence.

In Ukraine, activists centered in the western part of the country gained supporters in the late 1980s and early 1990s. After Yeltsin recognized the independence of the Baltic states in August 1991, Ukraine's leaders declared Ukrainian independence. As in a number of postcommunist states, the first free elections in Ukraine resulted in the election of a former Communist Party functionary. Political life in Ukraine moved in a markedly democratic direction only after the Orange Revolution defeated President Leonid Kuchma's handpicked candidate and brought Viktor Yushchenko to power in 2004.

The Transition to Postcommunism

Despite the many ways in which they differed from each other and the different ways communism developed in each of their countries, the leaders of Central and Eastern Europe had to resolve a number of similar crises after the end of communist rule. The most visible of these were summarized by the election slogans of most political parties in the first free elections in these countries: "Democracy, the market, and a return to Europe." In the first area, the new elites had to create or re-create democratic political institutions, values, and practices. The process involved dealing with the economic and political power of the Communist Party and revising the legal system and constitutional structures to make them compatible with democracy, the establishment of a multiparty system, the repluralization of associational life, and the recruitment and training of new leaders. They also had to counteract the influence of the communist-era values on the political values and attitudes of the population and foster new values supportive of democracy.

The economic aspect of the transition was equally daunting. In addition to privatizing state assets and fostering development of new private enterprises, the new leaders in the region also had to devise redistribution policies to restore property confiscated by the state to its rightful owners or heirs. They needed to redirect trade patterns, particularly after the disbanding of the Council for Mutual Economic Assistance and the end of the Soviet Union, and begin to deal with the environmental devastation that communist patterns of development created. They also had to deal with the requirements of international financial institutions and the economic and social consequences of the dramatic drop in production that accompanied the shift to the market.

These policies had their counterparts in the arena of foreign policy. In addition to asserting their independence on the world stage and negotiating the withdrawal of Soviet troops when necessary, the new elites undertook a series of actions to reclaim what they perceived to be their rightful place in Europe. Many of these focused on efforts to join European and Euro-Atlantic institutions, with particular emphasis on the European Union and NATO. As of this writing, many of the postcommunist states have achieved these goals. In the remaining countries, political elites continue to push for inclusion.

The transition from communist rule has also had social and psychological dimensions. In the first area, there has been a major change in the social structures of these countries. New (or old, previously prohibited) groups, such as entrepreneurs, and numerous occupations associated with the rapid development of the previously neglected service and financial sectors have emerged. The status of different social groups has also changed. With the shift to the market, restitution of property, and the end of most state subsidies, visible income differentials, which were previously small, increased. Social inequality, poverty, and unemployment also increased substantially. While some people were able to take advantage of the new opportunities available in politics, the economy, and society, many others were not. For the latter group, the end of communist rule entailed largely new hardships, particularly in the early postcommunist period when production and the standard of living fell dramatically in most countries. The division of society into winners (those who were young, well educated, and urban) and losers (older, less skilled workers, those living in rural areas, and single parents, as well as many women) in turn had important political repercussions.

The end of tight political control and the opening of borders, coupled with the uncertainty and disruptions created by the transition itself, exacerbated old social pathologies and problems, such as alcoholism, juvenile delinquency, prostitution, violence in the home, drug use, and street crime, and allowed new problems to emerge. Organized crime, trafficking in persons, smuggling, and the sex trade are among the most visible of these. Certain social issues, such as tensions between various ethnic groups, the widespread discrimination against and marginalization of the Roma, and the xenophobia and anti-Semitism that often poison political discussions, all had existed in the communist era but were taboo. Now they are recognized as problems and discussed openly,[10] although they all too often continue to serve as sources of violence and repression. Support for extreme nationalist parties and the development of skinhead movements, particularly in economically depressed regions, are further reflections of these trends.

The experience of living in a time in which most aspects of life, from political choices to the organization of day care, were in flux also had predictable psychological consequences in the region. Although these effects were most widespread among those for whom the transition brought largely new hardships, it also affected those who could be seen as winners. As one Czech student put it soon after communism fell in that country, "Under communism, it was a question of whether I was allowed to do things; now it is a question of whether I will prove capable of doing them." Greater uncertainty as well as far greater choices, coupled with new pressure to perform well at work, increased competition, and the specter of unemployment, all contributed to the stress individuals and families experienced, even among those groups fortunate enough to be able to take advantage of new opportunities.

The Role of International Organizations and Outside Actors

In contrast to the interwar period in which outside actors either largely ignored the region (the United States, Great Britain, France) or had designs on it (Italy, Germany, at times the USSR), the international climate has been far more favorable to the success of efforts to create stable democracies and market economies and engineer a return to Europe in the postcommunist period. All of these countries have received substantial economic and democracy-building assistance from the United States, the EU, and many individual European countries. The postcommunist states have also been the recipients of economic assistance and loans as well as a great deal of advice from international financial institutions such as the IMF (International Monetary Fund) and World Bank. The latter, as well as the European Union, have exerted significant influence not only on the policies adopted by successive governments in the region, but also, in many cases, on the institutional design of these societies and polities.[11] In the case of the successors to former Yugoslavia, the international community intervened with negotiators, military force, and peacekeepers to resolve or prevent conflict. It has, in the form of the International Criminal Tribunal for the former Yugoslavia at The Hague, set standards of cooperation that have delayed or sidetracked the beginning of negotiations for EU accession and NATO membership for several of these countries.

At the same time that joining European and Euro-Atlantic institutions has brought many benefits to the countries involved, the asymmetrical nature of the relationship between these countries and these institutions, as well as powerful Western countries, has also led, predictably, to resentment and skepticism on the part of certain segments of the population in all of these countries, who ask whether they have traded rule by Moscow for rule by Brussels, the seat of the European Union and NATO headquarters.[12] The impact of this backlash on politics in the region should not be underestimated, as is clear from the victory of populist "Euroskeptics" in Poland and the demonstrations in Hungary in 2006 as well as the losses of the pro-Western

"Orange Coalition" in Ukraine less than two years after the Orange Revolution demonstrations brought millions to the street in 2004.

Membership in these organizations has also facilitated far greater contact with the rest of Europe and introduced new influences, both positive and negative, that go far beyond even the dense web of official contacts that link these states to older members and each other. Now that some of these states are part of the European Union and others are working to join, their leaders also face new challenges as European Union members. These include establishing themselves so that their interests are considered in debate and decision making and balancing the demands of their membership in both European and transatlantic organizations.

The leaders of these postcommunist states have tried different policies in dealing with issues they have faced since the end of communist rule. They have had varying degrees of success in meeting their common challenges and those specific to their societies. The chapters that follow examine these developments. The first section provides an overview of the main political, economic, foreign policy, and social issues postcommunist leaders have faced. The second part of the book focuses on these issues as they have been dealt with in individual countries. Chapters in this section also discuss questions of particular importance in the countries examined. As the pages to follow illustrate, the success of leaders in Central and Eastern Europe in dealing with these challenges has varied, as has the response of the international community to these states. In the process, many of these countries have gone forward and backward on their roads to democracy. What has seemed to be success has often been followed by failure. Just as underlying realities in the region led to diversity in the way communist institutions, policies, and ideology played themselves out in particular countries, so too the transition from communism, though it has involved the same tasks for all, has reflected the diverse social, economic, and ethnic composition of these countries as well as their individual histories and political traditions.

Notes

1. Timothy Garton Ash, *The Magic Lantern: The Revolution of '89 Witnessed in Warsaw, Budapest, Berlin, and Prague* (New York: Random House, 1990), 78.

2. See debate between Terry Lynn Karl, Philippe C. Schmitter, and Valerie Bunce in the following articles: Philippe C. Schmitter with Terry Lynn Karl, "The Conceptual Travels of Transitologists and Consolidologists: How Far to the East Should They Attempt to Go?" *Slavic Review* 53 (Spring 1994): 173–85; Valerie Bunce, "Should Transitologists Be Grounded?" *Slavic Review* 54 (Spring 1995): 111–27; Terry Lynn Karl and Philippe C. Schmitter, "From an Iron Curtain to a Paper Curtain: Grounding Transitologists or Students of Postcommunism?" *Slavic Review* 54 (Winter 1995): 965–78; and Valerie Bunce, "Paper Curtains and Paper Tigers," *Slavic Review* 54 (Winter 1995): 979–87.

3. Fareed Zakaria, *The Future of Freedom: Illiberal Democracy at Home and Abroad* (New York: W. W. Norton & Company, 2003).

4. Barbara Jelavich, *History of the Balkans, vol. 2, 20th Century* (Cambridge, UK: Cambridge University Press, 1983), 128–31.

5. Lonnie R. Johnson, *Central Europe: Enemies, Neighbors, Friends* (Oxford: Oxford University Press, 1996).

6. Andrew Janos, "The One-Party State and Social Mobilization: East Europe between the Wars," in *Authoritarian Politics in Modern Society*, ed. Samuel P. Huntington and Clement Henry Moore, 204–36 (New York: Basic Books, 1970).

7. Zbigniew Brzezinski, *The Soviet Bloc, Unity and Conflict* (Cambridge, MA: Harvard University Press, 1960).

8. See Bartlomiej Kaminski, *The Collapse of State Socialism: The Case of Poland* (Princeton, NJ: Princeton University Press, 1991) and Valerie Bunce, *Subversive Institutions: The Design and Destruction of Socialism and the State* (Cambridge, UK: Cambridge University Press, 1999).

9. Brzezinski, *The Soviet Bloc*.

10. See Zoltan D. Barany and Ivan Volgyes, eds., *Legacies of Communism in Eastern Europe* (Baltimore: Johns Hopkins University Press, 1995) and James R. Millar and Sharon L. Wolchik, eds., *The Social Legacy of Communism* (Cambridge, UK: Cambridge University Press, 1994).

11. See Wade Jacoby, *The Enlargement of the European Union and NATO: Ordering from the Menu in Central Europe* (Cambridge, UK: Cambridge University Press, 2004) and Jan Zielonka and Alex Pravda, eds., *Democratic Consolidation in Eastern Europe* (New York: Oxford University Press, 2001) for discussion of the influence of the EU in the region.

12. Ronald H. Linden and Lisa Pohlman, "Now You See It, Now You Don't: Anti-EU Politics in Central and Southeast Europe," *European Integration* 25 (December 2003): 311–34.

Part II

POLICIES AND ISSUES

CHAPTER 2

The Political Transition

Valerie Bunce

The collapse of the communist regimes and communist states from 1989 to 1992 has produced a number of remarkable changes in the political and economic landscape of Europe's eastern half. In particular, authoritarian regimes have given way to political orders that are, albeit to quite varying degrees, more competitive and more respectful of civil liberties. In addition, twenty-two new states have arisen from the rubble of the Soviet Union, Czechoslovakia, and Yugoslavia, while one communist state—the German Democratic Republic—has merged with its neighbor, the Federal Republic of Germany, to reconstitute a single Germany. As a result, a region that was once composed of nine states now features twenty-five—if we include all of the successor states of the former Soviet Union, together with Central and Eastern Europe and the Balkans. At the same time, open-market economies, again to varying degrees, have replaced state-owned, centrally planned, and highly protectionist economies. Finally, the post–World War II separation of Europe into two halves has ended, not just because of the economic and political liberalization of the Central and East European states, but also because of the eastward expansion of three international institutions: the Council of Europe, the North Atlantic Treaty Organization (NATO), and the European Union. What we have witnessed over the past fifteen years, in short, is a revolution in Central and Eastern Europe—in state boundaries, in the organization and practices of politics and economics at home and abroad, and, finally, in elite and mass identities and political preferences.

The purpose of this chapter is to assess the political side of this revolution. In particular, I will compare patterns of regime transition in Central and Eastern Europe since the dramatic events of 1989, draw some generalizations about what has transpired and why, and place these changes in the larger context of the global spread of democratic governance. My discussion will be divided into two parts. In the first section, I will focus on the short-term political consequences of the collapse of communism, or the forms of governance that came into being during the early years of the transition, or from 1989 to mid-1996. Of interest here are such questions as the following:

- Did the end of Communist Party hegemony lead, as many expected, to the immediate rise of democratic politics, or do we see in fact a more complicated political story?

33

- To what extent were the early political dynamics of postcommunist Europe typical or distinctive when compared with the collapse of dictatorships and regime change in other parts of the world?
- Finally, what factors seem to provide the most compelling account of the first stage of the political transition in postcommunist Europe?

In the second part of this chapter, I will shift my focus to developments beginning in the latter part of 1996 that continued through 2007. Here, the discussion will address one notable trend: the expansion of democratic polities since the mid-1990s. This expansion represented two convergent developments: the remarkable ability of the first democracies in the region to stay the political course coupled with the failure of the remaining and more authoritarian regimes in the area to maintain their political momentum. Put differently, there have been in fact several waves of democratization in postcommunist Europe, with the first occurring immediately after the fall of state socialism and the second occurring roughly a decade later. Indeed, it is precisely this pattern—democratization in stages—that explains the division of this chapter into two parts.

Postcommunist Political Diversity

By 1996, one could identify three types of political regimes in postcommunist Central and Eastern Europe.[1] The first, which included Poland, the Czech Republic, Hungary, Slovenia, Lithuania, and (less perfectly because of some political discrimination against their Russian minorities) Estonia and Latvia, was a democratic order—political arrangements that combine free, fair, and competitive elections that are regularly held; rule of law, or rules of the political game that are accepted by both elites and publics and that are applied consistently across time, space, and circumstances; and extensive civil liberties and political rights guaranteed by law. Because of all these features, democracy in general and in these cases in particular can be understood as a way of organizing politics that rests on accountable government.[2] What is striking about Poland, the Czech Republic, and the like at this time, therefore, was that they managed to move quickly to full-scale democracy.

The second type of regime in the region at this time was authoritarian. In authoritarian states, political arrangements lack the characteristics noted above, thereby producing governments that have neither the incentives nor the capacity to be accountable to their citizens. Authoritarian regimes, in particular, lack the institutionalized competition, individual rights, and procedural consistency that translate individual preferences into public policy through elections and representative government. This combination of traits describes the politics in the 1990s in two of the successor states of Yugoslavia (Croatia and Serbia-Montenegro), though authoritarian rule in both instances, it must be emphasized, was more "patchy" than in Yugoslavia during the communist era. Here, it is interesting to note that, despite the efforts of their dictators, Franjo Tudjman in Croatia and Slobodan Milošević in Serbia-Montenegro, some political pluralism was in evidence—most notably in the capitals of Zagreb and

Photo 2.1.   Václav Havel and Alexander Dubček toast the turnover of power by the communists in Prague in November 1989.
(Source: Peter Turnley/CORBIS)

Belgrade, where oppositions had a presence and where publics, even in the face of fraudulent elections, still managed to deny their dictators decisive electoral support.

Finally, the remaining countries in the region, Albania, Bosnia (but only after the Dayton Peace Accords of 1995 had demilitarized the country and provided a skeletal form of government), Bulgaria, Macedonia, Romania, and Slovakia—a group of countries roughly equal in number to the full-scale democracies at this time—fell in between the extremes of dictatorship and democracy. They were what can be termed hybrid regimes. Hybrid regimes are political arrangements that feature some of the formal characteristics of democracy, such as representative institutions and political competition, but that fall short of the liberal standard as a result of unfair elections, extensive corruption, irregular recognition of civil liberties, significant biases in the media, opposition parties that are poorly organized in comparison with parties representing the former authoritarians, and weak ties between political representatives and the citizenry. Also common in this category are several other characteristics that undermined the development of accountable government—in particular, rapid turnover in governments (a characteristic that Poland also shared), an inability of citizens to counteract the power of the state through associational ties with each other (or what has been termed civil society), and a sharp divide between urban and rural politics, with the latter more consistently supportive of authoritarian rule.[3]

What we find in the first stage of the transition from state socialism, in short, are three characteristics. The first is political diversity. Put simply, the deregulation of the political, economic, and social monopoly of the Communist Party that occurred throughout Central and Eastern Europe from 1989 to 1991 was not followed necessarily by the rise of democratic politics. In this sense, the Central and Eastern Europe of this period presented an important lesson. There can be a substantial lag between two developments that are often assumed to be tightly intertwined: the decline of authoritarian rule and the rise of democratic politics. Second, regime change in this region was largely peaceful, but not invariably nonviolent. The Baltic states' attempts to separate themselves from the Soviet Union invited a short-term violent response on the part of the Soviet leadership. The merger in Yugoslavia between two issues—the future of the regime and the future of the state—produced very different political trajectories among the republics that made up the state. It also engendered a war from 1991 to 1995 that left over 200,000 people dead and that undermined democratization in those successor states that served as the major site of this conflict—Croatia and Bosnia—while shaping in the process developments in their neighbors, particularly Macedonia and Serbia-Montenegro. Moreover, the fall of Ceauşescu in Romania was also violent. These contrasts aside, however, what is striking is that where regime transition was accompanied by violence, the result was either a hybrid regime or dictatorship. Thus, democracy and a peaceful adjudication of conflicts—with the latter often serving as one definition of democratic governance—were closely associated with one another in the Central and East European transitions.

Finally, there were significant differences across the region in the resources, the cohesion, and the political goals of both the communists and the opposition. For example, while the communists were quick to embrace the liberal political and economic agenda of the opposition in the Baltic states, Poland, and particularly Hungary and Slovenia, they were more resistant in the remaining cases. Serbian political dynamics under Milošević are the most extreme example of this resistance. At the same time, oppositions varied greatly. While in the Baltic countries, Poland, the Czech Republic, Hungary, and Slovenia, the opposition was large, sophisticated, relatively cohesive, and committed to liberal politics, in the remaining countries the opposition tended to suffer from a number of problems. For example, Bulgaria saw divisions over the best way to build capitalism and democracy and to become an effective political force, and in both Serbia and Slovakia elite struggles over political power and their manipulation of national tensions to maintain authoritarian control and stave off demands for democracy demobilized the liberals.[4]

Comparative Perspectives: The Puzzles of Diversity

Was the diversity of postcommunist political dynamics and political pathways in the first half of the transformation surprising or predictable? The answer is that for many analysts the political patterns of postcommunism, as summarized above, were in fact unexpected. This was the case whether we refer to specialists on comparative democratization or specialists on postcommunist Europe.

At the time that communism collapsed, there had already been a clear trend, in evidence since the mid-1970s, suggesting that the decline of authoritarian rule led invariably to the rapid and peaceful rise of democratic politics. This was precisely what had happened, for example, in one state after another in both Latin America and southern Europe (though the Portuguese case was an exception). In addition, the

*Photo 2.2.   The Romanian revolution was the only one that was
violent. Here, a Romanian at a demonstration cries over those
killed by the government forces in December 1989. Until Nicolae
Ceauşescu and his wife were killed by a military tribunal, there was
fighting in the streets of Romanian cities.*

(Source: David Turnley/CORBIS)

dichotomous thinking of the Cold War, which had framed political dynamics and,
therefore, political assumptions in the international order for forty-five years, made it
easy to presume that there were only two political choices in the world: democracy
or dictatorship. Thus, if the hegemony of the Communist Party was challenged and
dictatorship rested upon this hegemony and, just as importantly, if the Soviet Union
failed to back up communist rule in its client states and at home and, indeed, failed
in the more profound sense of continuing to function as a regime, a state, a regional

hegemon, and a superpower, then what would necessarily follow in the wake of its collapse, it was widely thought, were democratic revolutions both within the Soviet Union and throughout the Soviet bloc. As we saw replayed in the American debates about Iraq from 2002 to 2007, moreover, many assumed not just that the political world offered only two regime options, but also that if dictators and dictatorships were subtracted from the equation, publics would necessarily rise up to embrace the democratic cause—and be able to translate these preferences in relatively quick order into well-functioning democratic institutions and procedures. Democracy, in short, was natural, and this would be revealed once the distorting effects of dictatorship were removed.[5]

From these perspectives, therefore, the assumption was that the end of dictatorship constituted the beginning of democracy—and full-scale democracy at that. Such an optimistic reading of the future was unusually tempting in the wake of 1989, given the rapid and regionwide character of the collapse of Communist Party control and the dependence of these regimes and their specific economic and political features on that control. It was a position, however, that was as flawed for the postcommunist world as it would be a decade later for Iraq.[6] Oppositions can be fractious; dictatorships invariably have supporters; constructing democratic institutions can be difficult; and publics can care as much about their personal circumstances as about governmental forms.

Scholars specializing in the postcommunist region had different expectations—though these were also inaccurate in some respects.[7] For some scholars, the emphasis had long been on the striking similarities among the communist states—similarities that spoke not just to common ideological texts, but also to the foundational role of the Soviet Union as the "inventor" and then the "exporter" of state socialism. In all of these cases, communist regimes were governed by a single Communist Party that enjoyed a monopoly over power, money, and social status and that was committed to rapid socioeconomic development through control over the allocation of both labor and capital. What is puzzling, therefore, is how the structural and ideological similarities across this region—similarities that were far greater than what one found, for example, among dictatorships in Latin America or southern Europe—could have translated so quickly into such differences, not just in political regimes, as already noted, but also in economic regimes. Thus, capitalism replaced socialism very quickly in Poland, Hungary, the Czech Republic, the Baltic states, and Slovenia, whereas socialist economics—state ownership of the means of production, planning, and closed economic borders—remained in place to varying degrees in the other countries in the region. Commonalities, therefore, in the most basic building blocks of politics and economics—for example, issues of ownership and competition—gave way very quickly to diversity.

For other specialists, there was widespread recognition that these countries entered the transition with variable mixtures of assets and liabilities, such that postcommunism would not produce, especially in the early stages, identical political dynamics—the similarities in the institutional "skeletons" of these systems notwithstanding. In this sense, diversity was expected. However, what was not expected was the range of regimes that appeared, with the most improbable group being those countries that made a quick and thoroughgoing transition to democratic politics. As some observers were quick to note, of the many countries in Central and Eastern Europe that had experimented with democratic politics during the interwar era, only one—Czechoslovakia—had managed to survive until World War II with democratic institutions and procedures intact. Even in that case, however, the inclusiveness of the polity and the extent of political and certainly economic equality among the nations that shared that state at that time were in some question.[8] There was, in short, little of the political past that seemed to be available for recycling in a democratic order. As a result, democracy was assumed to be at best an uphill struggle—in direct contrast, for example, to Latin America, where the norm was redemocratization, not democracy from scratch.[9]

Many analysts also recognized the considerable costs of the state socialist brand of authoritarian rule due to its unusually penetrative and despotic character. These were dictatorships that, while less and less brutal over time in most cases, were nonetheless extraordinarily ambitious. By owning and planning the economy, monopolizing political power, sealing borders, and atomizing publics, these dictatorships seemed to be committed to the destruction of some of the most elementary building blocks of democratic life—for example, interpersonal trust; respect for the law; confidence in political institutions, such as political parties; and participation in associations independent of the state, such as labor unions, clubs, professional associations, and the like. The autonomy of individuals and groups, so important for countering the power of the state in a democratic order, therefore, had been severely limited by the communist experience. Economic decline during the last years of state socialism, moreover, would also seem to have constrained the rise of democracy, especially since the political regime transition in question would be tied to an unusually costly economic transition. Indeed, it is not just that Central and Eastern Europe featured—and still features—a much lower level of economic development than Western Europe, which many have read as undermining democratic governance, but also that Central and Eastern Europe experienced a decline in living standards in the first half of the 1990s that was far greater than what one saw during the Great Depression, when nearly half of Europe's democracies, we must remember, had collapsed.[10]

When we confront the perspectives of specialists in the postcommunist region versus specialists on recent democratization, therefore, we find a clear contrast. While the former tended to underpredict democracy, assuming in effect that there would be many more regimes that fell into either the hybrid or authoritarian camp, specialists on comparative democratization had the opposite problem. They overpredicted democratic rule. In both cases, the political diversity of the region—at least halfway into the transition—was puzzling. How then can we explain why some countries in Central and Eastern Europe were able to move decisively in a democratic direction, others less decisively, and still others in a decidedly authoritarian direction?

Explaining Early Political Pathways

There are a number of plausible factors that would seem to be helpful in accounting for the differences among postcommunist regimes during the early stages of the transition. One could suggest, for example, that a key consideration would be the age of the state. As a number of studies have suggested, in the West, states were built long before the possibility of democratic politics either entered or could enter the political agenda. State building is a nasty process, wherein political leaders, wanting to secure their access to people and economic resources and to deny that access to their competitors, use the military, local allies, and their rudimentary bureaucracies to solidify their political and economic control over a spatially defined group of people. Rather than negotiate each time they need money and troops, they prefer to create more permanent arrangements—what subsequently became known as states. The essence of state building, therefore, to borrow from Charles Tilly, is that wars make states and states make wars.[11]

By contrast, the demand for democracy in the West arose from very different sources and took place after state building. Once people have lived together for some time in a common state and operate within an increasingly integrated and interactive political and economic context, they can learn to define themselves as members of a common political community, or the nation. In the process, they can also embrace a common political project that redefines the relationship between citizens and the state by arguing that states cannot just be coercive or just provide security to citizens. Instead, they are expected to do more—by recognizing citizens as equal, by guaranteeing political rights, and by creating accountable government.

The necessary sequencing of these developments—spatial consolidation of political authority followed by growing pressures for accountable and legitimate governance—would seem to suggest that the key difference in Central and East European political trajectories after communism lies in whether the state is new or better established. If new, it must thereby be committed to the draconian politics and economics of state building. If better established, because of prior integration of the economy, settlement of borders, and membership in the nation, it can be more responsive to political demands for equality and rights. Indeed, it is precisely this contrast that led Dankwart Rustow to argue more than thirty years ago that democracy only enters into the realm of political choice when issues involving membership in the nation and the boundaries of the state have been fully resolved.[12]

The problem here, however, is that the variations in postcommunist political trajectories are *not* predicted by the age of the state. Just as some of the long-standing states in Central and Eastern Europe, such as Bulgaria and Romania, were hybrid regimes in the first half of the 1990s, so some of the newest states in that period—Slovenia, the Czech Republic, and the Baltic states—were in the group of early and robust democracies. Even more interesting is that in the cases of Slovenia and the Czech Republic, the states were in fact completely new formations—in contrast to Estonia, Latvia, and Lithuania, which were independent states during the interwar years.

Might the differences be explained by ethnic and religious diversity? Again, it is logical to assume that democracy is harder to construct when there are many nations sharing the same state, when national differences coincide with differences in economic resources and political power, when previous governing arrangements play diverse groups off one another, and when national minorities spill over into neighboring states, thereby generating tensions about the legitimacy of existing boundaries.

However, this factor does not distinguish well among the Central and East European countries either. There is national homogeneity in both Poland and Albania, for example, despite their very different political pathways immediately after communism, and unusually high levels of diversity in the robust democracies of Estonia and Latvia (with diversity defined by the size of the second largest ethnic community).

This leaves us with two remaining hypotheses. One is that variation in democratization reflects differences in the mode of transition. Put succinctly, transitions engineered by bargaining between opposition and incumbent elites are more likely to produce democratic government than transitions that occurred in reaction to mass protests—a contrast that has been used to explain differences in democratizing dynamics in Latin America and southern Europe. The problem here is that *most* of the transitions in Central and Eastern Europe involved mass—indeed massive—mobilization, and all of the most successful transitions, with the exception of Hungary and to some extent Poland, took place in response to mass protests. The other hypothesis targets differences in the nature of politics during communism. Here, the argument is that the more liberalized regimes during communism would have laid more of the groundwork for democracy after communism—for example, because their communists were reform minded and because opposition forces had more opportunities to expand their support and develop sophisticated political strategies for winning power. However, the strong democracies within our group are divided in fact between those that experienced more hard-line communist rule—as with Czechoslovakia and the Baltic countries—and more reformist regimes—as with Slovenia, Poland, and Hungary.[13]

Explaining Diversity

How, then, can we explain the early patterns of postcommunist politics? We can begin to answer this question by recognizing the importance of the age of the state and the complexity a transition to statehood introduces in terms of adding national and border questions to what is for the established states a simpler choice between democracy and dictatorship. For the well-established states, the key factor seems to have been the outcome of the first competitive election. In particular, where the opposition won handily (Poland and Hungary), we see quick and sustained democratization. By contrast, where power was more equally divided between the communists and the opposition (as in Romania and Bulgaria), the result was a hybrid regime.

But is this argument in fact a tautology, in that when communists win, dictatorships follow; when the opposition wins, democracy follows; and, finally, when they are neck and neck, a synthesis of the two options materializes? Despite the logic of this observation, there are in fact several reasons to be more confident that the argument about initial electoral outcomes is illuminating. One is that this line of explanation also captures variations in economic reform, with a clear victory of the opposition leading to rapid reforms, resistance to such reforms when the communists win, and a pattern of "fits and starts" reforms when electoral outcomes are more evenly divided. Another is that there is no particular reason to assume that if the opposition wins, they necessarily embrace democratic politics—though in every one of the established states they did. Oppositions, after all, can want many things. Third, it is notable that this argument flies in the face of the generalization in the literature on Latin America and southern Europe that "balanced transitions"—or those where the opposition and the authoritarians are evenly balanced in their power and form political pacts with each other as a result—are precisely the ones that lead to the most successful transitions to democracy. With this type of equality, it has been argued, both sides feel secure enough to proceed with regime change. Thus, what seems tautological in Central and Eastern Europe is in fact "counterintuitive" in other regional contexts.[14]

This leads us to a final point, which helps us deal with the problem of what "causes the cause." Initial electoral outcomes in the contest between authoritarians and opposition forces correlate in turn with patterns of protest during the communist era. To put the matter succinctly, one can conclude that, at least in Central and Eastern Europe, rapid progress toward democracy seems to have depended upon a dynamic wherein the development of a strong opposition during communism translated, with the end of the party's monopoly, into an unusually strong political showing in the first elections—which augured well for the future and quality of democratic governance. In this sense, the proximate cause—or variations in electoral outcomes—alerts us to a more distant cause—or variations in opposition development during communism.

We can now turn to the new states in the region—or the Baltic countries, the Czech Republic, Croatia, Macedonia, Serbia-Montenegro, Slovakia, and Slovenia. (Because of the war and its subsequent development as an international protectorate, Bosnia is left out of the comparison.) Here, the key issue seems to be whether the nationalist project connected with a liberal or illiberal political project—or whether defending the nation was understood to require, or at least be consistent with, democracy or dictatorship. For those countries (then republics) that had nationalist demonstrations or movements during communism (Croatia in the early 1970s, Serbia-Montenegro in the early 1980s, and Slovakia in the late 1960s), the resulting dynamics divided the opposition into democrats and nationalists while weakening public support of the communists and pushing them to bear down on nationalism and to resist any political and economic reforms that might expand opportunities for nationalism to reinvigorate itself. As a result, when communism collapsed, either communists became nationalists in order to maintain dictatorial power (as in Serbia-Montenegro and Slovakia), or the nationalists, facing discredited communists, rejected liberal politics in order to take power (as in Croatia). In either case, democracy was poorly served, whether the communists, the nationalists, or some combination of the two emerged triumphant. By contrast, where nationalist mobilization materialized only when communism began to unravel (as in the Baltic countries, Slovenia, and Macedonia), nationalism and liberalism were joined to form a powerful opposition, and communists, not as politically isolated or as compromised as in the first set of cases, had little choice, either in terms of personal preferences or self-interest, but to defect to the liberal cause.

What we find, in short, are two pathways. In the older states, regime change was a product of the balance of power between the communists and the opposition forces and, to push the causal process further back in time, the development of a capable opposition during the communist era. In the new states the key factor seems to have been varying combinations of nationalism, liberalism, and communism, with the particular combination strongly affected by when nationalist mobilization took place and the effects of this timing on the preferences and the popularity of both the communists and the nationalists. Put more simply, one can suggest that patterns of political protest during communism—albeit playing out in different ways in republics versus states and introducing different political options—seemed to play a critical role in either ushering in democratic politics or compromising the democratic political agenda.

Durability of New States and New Democracies

If many observers were surprised by political outcomes in Central and Eastern Europe in the first phase of the transition, they were even more surprised by what transpired in the second phase. What we find from 1996 to 2007 are two political trends, both of which have contributed in distinctive ways to greater stability in the region. The first is that the number of states in the region and the boundaries of the new states that formed from 1991 to 1992 have remained nearly constant, with the important exception of the division of Serbia and Montenegro into two separate states in the late spring 2006. The relative stability of borders in this region since 1992 speaks to several factors. One is that the opportunities for redefining boundaries tend to be fleeting, occurring primarily during the unusual circumstances of a conjoined shift in domestic and international regimes, as happened from 1989 to 1992 when communism collapsed, the Soviet Union was dismembered, and the Cold War ended. Another is that state dissolution during the earlier tumultuous period succeeded to some degree in providing a closer alignment of national and state borders and, with that, an expansion in the legitimacy of both the regime and the state. Finally, powerful actors in the international community tend to resist border changes, because they see an opening up of the question of borders as highly destabilizing for both domestic and international politics. To question existing borders is to invite minority communities throughout the region—and certainly their leaders—to demand states of their own. Such demands are tempting in many cases, because they empower minority leaders, while allowing them to ignore other, more pressing issues, that might challenge their political influence—for example, rising corruption, poor economic performance, and a decline in the quality of democratic life.

However, recent developments in both Montenegro and Kosovo remind us that the borders in southeastern Europe, at least, are still in some flux. Indeed, in sharp contrast to their words and deeds in other parts of the world, including the Caucasus and Russia, major players in international politics, such as the United States and the European Union, were both increasingly unwilling and unable to support the borders of Serbia-Montenegro as they were established during the wars that accompanied the dissolution of the Yugoslav state from 1991 to 1995. Thus, beginning in 1997, the Montenegrin political leadership began to question the value of their federal relationship with Serbia. In 2003, the European Union, eager to keep borders intact, brokered a deal, wherein Montenegro agreed to stay within the larger but quite decentralized state until 2006, when a referendum would be held on the question of Montenegrin independence. In the spring of 2006, this referendum did take place, and a majority (though not an overwhelming one) of Montenegrins expressed their desire to establish their own state. Quickly following the referendum, Serbia and Montenegro went their own ways.

At the same time, a broader array of international actors have consigned Kosovo, a primarily Albanian republic within Serbia-Montenegro—and the site in 1999 of a U.S.-led NATO bombing campaign to protect Albanian inhabitants from Serbian repression and to weaken the Serbian dictator, Slobodan Milošević—to the status of an international protectorate that is neither fully integrated into Serbia nor allowed to become a sovereign state.[15] However, it has become increasingly clear, especially since 2004, that Kosovo is moving slowly but surely to independent statehood. What is less clear is how an independent Kosovo will affect the domestic politics of Serbia. For Serbian publics and politicians, the departure of Kosovo is a good deal more controversial than the exit of Montenegro. The other question is how the international community will manage the departure of Kosovo from the Serbian state. The key issues in this process—or what one can term the standards that Kosovo must meet in preparation for independence—include building a viable state, economy, and democratic order that respects the rights of all the cultural communities that cohabit this province. Thus, while the establishment of the Montenegrin state took place relatively smoothly and quickly, the same is not likely to be the case for Kosovo.

The second trend in the region since the mid-1990s is a pronounced contraction in the political diversity of this part of the world and the emergence of a Central and Eastern Europe composed, for the first time in its history, solely of democratic orders. This development reflects two trends. On the one hand, the first democracies stuck and, indeed, deepened—an outcome that one cannot necessarily have expected, especially in view of the constraints on democratization, noted earlier, as a result of the authoritarian past and the stresses of economic reform. On the other hand, the hybrid democracies of the first stage managed for the most part to shift to the democratic camp in the second stage, while the regimes that were initially dictatorships all moved in a liberal direction, thereby joining the hybrid category and sometimes moving in an even more liberal direction (see table 2.1).

It is safe to conclude, therefore, that the Baltic countries, Poland, the Czech Republic, Hungary, Slovakia, Slovenia, Bulgaria, and Romania fully meet democratic standards and, given their political stability as well as the support of the European Union (for states that either became new members as of May 1, 2004, or, in the final two cases, became members in 2007), are very likely to continue as democratic regimes in the future. At the same time, Albania, Bosnia, Croatia, Macedonia, Serbia, and Montenegro have all made significant progress over the past five years, particularly in building more democratic polities.

A democratic Central and Eastern Europe, therefore, has finally come into being. In this sense, the pessimists were proven wrong, whereas the optimists seem to have been validated—but with one important qualification. As our division of this chapter suggests, democratization in Central and Eastern Europe has come in two stages. The first wave, as already outlined, featured an immediate and sharp break with the communist past, or a process wherein massive demonstrations, a large and unified opposi-

Table 2.1.   Freedom House Rankings for Central and East European States, 2002–2006

Country	2006	2005	2004	2003	2002
Bosnia and Herzegovina	3.5	3.5	4.0	4.0	4.5
Bulgaria	1.5	1.5	1.5	1.5	2.0
Croatia	2.0	2.0	2.0	2.0	2.0
Czech Republic	1.0	1.0	1.5	1.5	1.5
Estonia	1.0	1.0	1.5	1.5	1.5
Hungary	1.0	1.0	1.5	1.5	1.5
Latvia	1.0	1.5	1.5	1.5	1.5
Lithuania	1.0	2.0	1.5	1.5	1.5
Poland	1.0	1.0	1.5	1.5	1.5
Romania	2.0	2.5	2.0	2.0	2.0
Serbia and Montenegro	2.5	2.5	2.5	2.5	3.0
Slovakia	1.0	1.0	1.5	1.5	1.5
Slovenia	1.0	1.0	1.0	1.0	1.5
Ukraine	2.5	3.5	4.0	4.0	4.0

Note: Cumulative average of political rights and civil liberties scores based on a scale of 1 to 4, with 1 considered free and 4 considered unfree.
Source: Freedom House's Freedom in the World (www.freedomhouse.org).

tion embracing liberal politics, and communists who were marginalized (as in the Czech Republic), ideologically sympathetic to the goals of the opposition (as in Hungary and Slovenia), or sufficiently self-interested in the face of a powerful opposition to recognize the logic of defecting from dictatorship (as in Poland and the Baltic countries) combined to end the old order and lay the groundwork for competitive elections that the forces in support of democratic politics then won handily. While this scenario describes what happened with most of the "early democratizers" in the region, there were some variations on these dynamics that should be noted. Thus, in both Poland and Hungary—the two countries that in effect jump-started the collapse of communism in 1989—the critical political turning point was in fact a roundtable between the communists and the opposition forces. The roundtable in Poland followed significant protests in the fall of 1988, and the roundtable in Hungary was strongly influenced by the surprising political outcome of the Polish precedent. In both cases, the roundtable set the stage for subsequent elections, which were semicompetitive in Poland and fully competitive in Hungary. However, in both cases, noncommunist governments were formed, with the predictable impact of deepening the democratic momentum.

The second wave, the developments in Albania, Bulgaria, Croatia, Macedonia, Montenegro, Romania, Serbia, and Slovakia from 1996 to 2006, shared one overarching similarity. Founding elections in all of these cases compromised the transition to democracy—either through the victory of the ex-communists, who were divided in their commitments to democratic politics, or through the victory of nationalist oppositions, who were often more illiberal than their ex-communist counterparts. However, subsequent elections changed the political balance in ways that, in contrast to the earlier period of transition, better served a democratic outcome. In this sense, a key issue in all of these countries was the growth of political competition during the transition—a pattern that we also find in the first democracies and that, because it produced turnover in governing parties and coalitions, contributed to the deepening of democratic politics.

Photo 2.3.   General and former president Wojciech Jaruzelski and former president Lech Wałesa at a debate on Poland's past. Jaruzelski was the head of Poland's martial law government and the leader during the round-tables and Poland's first year after the fall of communism. Wałesa, the former leader of Solidarity, won the first popular election to the presidency after Jaruzelski resigned.

(Source: Rzeczpospolita)

The dynamics of the second round of democratic transitions in Central and Eastern Europe, however, varied in detail. In Bulgaria, Romania, and Slovakia, the key issue was the eventual rise of a more effective liberal opposition that was able to win power and, for the first time, form a durable and effective government. We find a different dynamic in Albania, Croatia, Macedonia, and Montenegro. Here, the key issue was the growing incentives for the ex-communists, reacting to an opposition that was either liberal or illiberal but in both instances highly competitive, to embrace the liberal cause as a means of weakening the incumbents, differentiating themselves, and thereby accumulating political power.

The final dynamic was in Serbia, where we see a replay in effect of the first transitions to democracy in the region, albeit a decade later—a process that also took place, but three years later and informed by the Serbian precedent, in Georgia and in Ukraine in 2004. In Serbia, mass protests in the fall of 2000 in reaction to an attempt by the increasingly corrupt and politically repressive ex-communists to steal the election enabled the opposition—a coalition as broad as what we saw, for example, in Czechoslovakia in 1989—to win power over the long-governing ex-communists. This sharp break with the past, however, was not so sharp, as the subsequent instability of Serbian politics indicated—for example, the continuous squabbling between the Serbian president and the prime minister, the inability of elections to reach the constitutionally required level of turnout, the assassination of Prime Minister Zoran Djindjić in the spring of 2003, and the continued popular support of the antidemocratic Radical Party by a substantial minority of Serbian citizens. The outcome of the presidential election in June 2004, the acceptance of Montenegro's declaration of independence in 2006, and significant progress in both economic reforms and economic performance, however, suggest that Serbia is indeed on the road to democracy—though still facing the likely and highly unpopular departure of Kosovo in the next decade.

These details aside, however, what is interesting about all of these "second wave" democracies is that the shift from either dictatorship to democracy or from hybrid to full-scale democracy took place in response to elections that brought to power governments that had the incentives and the capacity to change the country's political course. But this leaves two obvious questions. Why did the "laggards" in stage one all move in a more democratic direction in stage two? Second, how can we explain, more generally, the recent convergence in regime types in Central and Eastern Europe?

Explaining the Second Wave: Domestic Factors

In contrast to the explanations offered with respect to the first stage of the transition, the explanations of the second stage are much less parsimonious. Indeed, what is striking is the importance of both domestic and international factors, both of which pushed in a similar liberalizing direction. On the domestic side, we can point to two influences. One is suggested by the fact that, if we look at postcommunist Eurasia as a whole (or add to our Central and East European group the remaining twelve Soviet successor states), we find a high correlation between contemporary political arrangements and the duration of Communist Party rule. All of the states of interest in this volume are democratic, and they all became communist after the Second World War. By contrast, the record of democracy in those Soviet successor states where communism was in place since the First World War is far more mixed, featuring, for example, clear-cut dictatorships, as in Belarus, Uzbekistan, and Turkmenistan; low-quality democracies, as with Ukraine prior to the Orange Revolution in 2004; and formerly democratic orders that have moved decisively in a dictatorial direction, such as those in Armenia and Russia. What makes this comparison even more instructive is the durability, albeit continued fragility of democracy in Moldova—the only Soviet successor state, aside from the Baltic countries, that was added to the Soviet Union after World War II. Just as striking, given the Armenian, Russian, and Belarussian cases, is that there have been *no* cases of democratic breakdown in Central and Eastern Europe since the end of Communist Party hegemony (though the period of Vladimír Mečiar's rule in Slovakia after the breakup of the Czechoslovak federation certainly compromised Slovakia's democratic performance in the short term).

Why is the length of Communist Party rule so important? Two plausible factors come to the fore. First, a longer experience with communism means deeper penetration of communist ideology, institutions, and practices—penetration that was secured in part by the number of generations that lived under communist rule. This could make a transition to democracy more difficult, because of the absence of democracy-supporting institutions and values and because of the constraints on the development of a viable political opposition. The second reason is also historical in nature, but asks us to think in broader terms about what this correlation means. The countries of concern in this volume all have a long history of close connections to Western economies, cultures, and political ideas—a history that was abruptly ended by the rise of communism during and immediately after World War II. The geographical proximity to the West, therefore, may have been important in laying the groundwork, once opportunities for political change presented themselves, for subsequent democratic development. The ability of these countries to withstand the challenge of communism, of course, was aided by the brevity of the communist experience—especially, for example, the unusually brief duration of Stalinization, when the most antidemocratic aspects of state socialism were imposed.[16]

The second domestic factor focuses particularly on those countries where illiberal nationalists came to power after the deregulation of the Communist Party's monopoly: that is, Slovakia, Croatia, and Serbia. What happened in all three cases is that the liberal opposition, having been divided and demobilized by the struggle over the national question, finally managed to regroup and remobilize and thereby win elections. The literature on both nationalism and democratic transitions is in fact silent about these kinds of questions, focusing far more on why illiberal nationalist leaders either lose or win during regime change than on why, having won for a time, they then lose power and political agendas are freed to move in a more liberal direction. What is striking about our three cases is that there are in fact two commonalities. One is that the opposition was able to focus on the threats and costs of one leader in particular (Mečiar, Tudjman, and Milošević), and the other is that international actors, including the EU, the United States, and transnational networks of nongovernmental organizations, played an important role in providing support to the opposition—for example, training them in the art of resistance, providing electoral monitors, and helping them organize campaigns to increase voter registration and electoral turnout. International influences, in short, were critical—an explanation that we will now address more systematically.

International Influences

As noted above, geography played a role in the second wave of democratization. However, its impact was also expressed in international dynamics. If the events of 1989, or the regionwide collapse of Communist Party hegemony, indicated the power of diffusion when neighboring states have similar domestic structures, similar historical experiences, and similar external constraints (such as Soviet control), then diffusion, it can be suggested, can still operate after these momentous events. Here, it is important to remember that there was in fact a great deal of interaction among the states of concern in this volume during the communist era. For example, oppositions in Poland, Hungary, and Czechoslovakia were in contact with each other during communism; the rise of the Solidarity movement in Poland in 1980 influenced opposition development in the Baltic states and in Bulgaria before the dramatic developments at the end of the decade; and protests in Central and Eastern Europe during the communist era invariably called for adoption of some features of the Yugoslav alternative model of communism. While this pattern did not guarantee by any means that these countries would all follow identical pathways once the hold of the communists weakened, it did mean that developments in one country had the potential to influence developments elsewhere in the region—for example, demonstrating that democracy was possible in the first stage of the transition and, later, helping weaker opposition forces in, say, Bulgaria, Romania, and Slovakia, to acquire the strategies needed to move their less democratic countries in a more liberal direction. Indeed, changes in Slovak politics in the second half of the 1990s influenced subsequent political changes in Croatia and Serbia—and Georgia and Ukraine, for that matter. In this way, over time the region converged in both its political and economic forms—as it had in the past, only in an illiberal way and then with the additional nudge of a hegemon, the Soviet Union, committed for reasons of security and ideology to dictatorship.

The importance of geography, or the spatial side of politics, also alerts us to several other international factors. One is the global wave of democratization. By the turn of the twentieth century, a majority of the world's population lived in democratic orders—an unprecedented situation and one that contributed to developments in Central and Eastern Europe by rendering democracy perhaps the "only game in town." That Central and Eastern Europe is in Europe, of course, also mattered, especially given the role of the Helsinki Process, beginning in the 1970s, in solidifying a European norm of democracy and human rights and, indeed, in providing the opposition in Central and Eastern Europe during the communist era with greater resources to question the legitimacy and the performance of their regimes.

This leads to a final international variable: the European Union. As numerous scholars have argued, the European Union has had two effects in Central and Eastern Europe.[17] It has provided a clear standard for democratic politics (and capitalist economics), by which both publics and elites in this region can measure regime performance, and it has provided powerful incentives for those countries to meet (and to continue to meet) EU standards—for example, by offering advice on the construction of liberal orders and by holding out the promise of markets, financial support, and the legitimacy that comes from being coded as European and, therefore, part of a prosperous, stable, secure, and, to use the language of many Central and East Europeans, "normal" community. Many scholars and many Central and East European citizens, of course, debate whether the EU has been such a powerful force for democracy. Does the EU, for example, make democracy both possible and doable, or has it merely courted those countries that were already on the road to democratic government? Does the EU secure sovereignty for the postcommunist countries, or does it undermine their newly won sovereignty by reducing domestic policy control? Do the economic benefits of joining the EU outweigh, especially in the short term, the costs of preparing for membership—which include not just meeting a huge number of expensive conditions, but also facing the constraints imposed by EU markets and the protectionism of older members? Has the EU encouraged competition, or has it merely strengthened those already in power, thereby contributing to inequalities in power and money? Finally, does EU membership produce equality among countries through the creation of a single Europe, or has the eastward expansion of the EU created in effect a hierarchy, dividing the rich western members from their poor eastern cousins and dividing the east in turn between countries designated as either current or possible future members versus those countries that, because of geography, have no hope of joining and that may be, as a result, isolated and perhaps because of that locked into authoritarian rule?

While all insightful in certain respects, these concerns must be placed alongside two incontrovertible facts. One is that all the countries that have recently joined the EU or that have applied for candidate status evidence clear improvements over time in democratic assets. Another is that there is a clear correlation between prospects for joining the EU and the width of the domestic political spectrum. Put simply: what we have witnessed in Central and Eastern Europe is a sharp decline (or in some cases the absence from the beginning) of extremist political voices and the convergence around support for the EU (though public support of the EU, it must be recognized, varies over time and across countries).[18] One striking example is the return to power in 2003 of the Croatian Democratic Union (the HDZ), a party that had formerly ruled over Croatia as a dictatorship but that now embraces EU membership and that has made substantial progress in meeting EU standards. Other examples of this dynamic abound, including the return to power of the Socialist Party in Hungary in 1994; the changing political platform of the ex-communists in Montenegro, starting in 1997; and the victory of Boris Tadić in the Serbian presidential elections of 2004. We can, of course, debate whether political moderation, as in most of the second-wave democracies, is a consequence of the EU's influence or a function of purely domestic developments. However, the fact remains that political leaders in Central and Eastern Europe, either early in the transition or later, have come to believe that joining the EU is critical for their own political future and for concerns about identity, money, stability, and security that are critical to voters.

However we want to construe this dynamic, democratic politics benefits. In the rush to embrace the EU, other ways of meeting these goals, as offered by the extreme right and left, have lost political support, either immediately or later. With respect to the latter and the second round of democratization in Central and Eastern Europe, the result has been either that extremist parties have declined or that they have chosen to adapt. Thus, just as political competition increased in *all* of the countries in Central and Eastern Europe that had lagged in democratization, so the structure of competition itself changed through the decline in political polarization. The EU may very well have played a key role in that process.

Conclusions and Some Speculation

In this chapter, I have argued that the transition to democracy in Central and Eastern Europe has proceeded in two stages. In the first stage, from 1989 to the first half of 1996 (with the Romanian presidential elections constituting the turning point), there were variable regime outcomes, with half of the region moving quickly to democracy and the other half either stuck in a dictatorship or perched precariously between the two regime extremes. In this period, the key issue was the development of the opposition during communism and the extent to which they embraced liberal politics and were able to win in the first competitive elections. In the second period, 1996 to 2004 (and continuing through 2007), the "laggards" in democratization all moved in a liberal direction. In this case, the causes were multiple, including diffusion effects within the region, the role of the European Union, the declining capacity of authoritarian leaders to maintain power through exploitation of cultural differences, and limited constraints on democratization because of what was, from a broader regional standard, a shorter history of Communist Party rule. As a result, the pronounced political diversity of Central and Eastern Europe in the immediate aftermath of the collapse of communism and communist states declined. Just as state boundaries tended to endure, so democratization spread. Indeed, even the exceptional case of Montenegro and its secession from Serbia could be construed as an investment in a more authentic democratic politics for both parts of the Serbia-Montenegrin federation.

The patterns of democratization in Central and Eastern Europe, together with their underlying causes, present us with several important questions that are relevant to this region and, more generally, to the study of recent transitions to democratic rule. One is, What do we mean by regime outcomes? Does it make sense to argue that some countries in Central and Eastern Europe succeeded or failed to become democratic orders after communism, or does it make more sense to argue that the countries in this region were differentially situated to build democratic orders, with the result that democratization took longer in some cases than in others? The analysis presented above suggests that the latter interpretation is more compelling. This implies that there are differences in the assets and obstacles to democratization, and that these differences affect how long a transition can take, even after the evident decline of authoritarian rule.

The time horizons we use to evaluate democratization, therefore, are critical—in two ways. We may draw premature conclusions about political pathways after authoritarianism if we rush to judgment. Second, we may need different explanations for these pathways, depending upon when we choose to step back and evaluate political patterns. In this sense, there seems to be no single road to democratic politics, especially if we allow ourselves to recognize fast versus slower transitions.

But does this mean that, given time, democracy is inevitable? Given the region-wide victory of democracy in Central and Eastern Europe by 2004, or fifteen years into the transition, we might be tempted to draw such a conclusion. However, there are ample reasons to be skeptical. One is that there are still significant differences in the quality of democratic governance in Central and Eastern Europe. For example, there were major protests in Macedonia in 2001 that threatened to bring down democracy (but which had the opposite effects, given the subsequent construction of a more inclusive polity); political support for conservative nationalist parties and conservative politicians has increased recently in both Poland and Bulgaria; and the shift to the democratic column in Croatia and especially Serbia is of very recent vintage. In addition, other waves of democratization in the past, while admittedly not as global in their reach as the current wave, have been followed by democratic breakdowns. Moreover, the current global wave reveals a disturbing pattern: that is, the rise of more and more hybrid regimes that could tip in either political direction and that, at the same time, could endure as halfway houses built on political compromises that promote stability but at the cost of corruption and checkered economic performance. Still another consideration is that democratization in Central and Eastern Europe, as I have repeatedly emphasized throughout this chapter, is strongly advantaged by the long connection of this area to Western Europe and, more recently, by the influence of international institutions, such as the European Union. Finally, Central and Eastern Europe is distinctive in another way that has also invested in democratic political outcomes. This is a region that does not force dominant international powers, such as the United States, NATO, or the EU, to choose between security concerns and democracy promotion—a choice that was evident throughout the Cold War and that undermined, as a result, democratic politics. Even after the Cold War, this is a choice that is being made again with regard to American policy toward Russia, Central Asia, and Pakistan.

Democratization in Central and Eastern Europe, therefore, as in southern Europe beginning in 1974, while proceeding in stages, has been, nonetheless, strongly aided in ways that are largely unavailable to many other countries that have participated in the third wave. Unlucky throughout its history, especially in comparison with Western Europe, Central and Eastern Europe at this time—in comparison with other regions undergoing regime change—has become, in these respects, lucky. Domestic and international factors are working together to support democratic rule, whereas both sets of factors in the past had usually pushed these countries in the opposite direction.

These advantages, however, must be judged alongside some constraints on democratization that are likely to become even more apparent in the future, once the "big" issues of the transition—such as the breakthrough to democracy and staying the democratic course, building capitalism, and integrating with the West—give way to other, more concrete concerns. One issue is the declining capacity of the European Union to provide incentives for new members, candidate members, and countries with association agreements to deepen the dynamics of both democratization and economic reforms. The problem here is that the EU is very divided from within; it is perceived by many publics, whether inside or outside the EU, as too bureaucratic and too removed from the citizenry to represent their interests and to speak for them; and it is unlikely in the near future, precisely because of these problems, to expand to include such new, but precarious democracies as Albania, Bosnia, Macedonia, Montenegro, and Serbia. The EU, in short, is less willing and able to invest in the newest democracies than it was in the case of the first and most robust democracies in the region. In this sense, the north-south divide in Eastern and Central Europe is likely to continue.

Second, there is the continuing problem in many of these countries of both growing corruption and expanding socioeconomic inequality—with the latter sometimes highly correlated with cultural cleavages. Both of these developments can contribute to political polarization—as can several other problems in the region that are unlikely to go away in the near future. One such problem is the weakness of political parties—as institutions that structure political preferences of mass publics; that serve as the primary linkages between government and government; and that shape, especially through elections and parliaments, the course of public policy. Another is very high levels of political cynicism (whether citizens focus on the performance of democratic institutions or on specific politicians), often coupled, not surprisingly, with low rates of electoral turnout. What we find throughout the region, therefore, is both continuing weakness in democratic institutions and public disappointment with the democratic experiment. Democracy, therefore, while regionwide, is flawed, and these deficiencies, while unlikely to be fatal to democracy, will necessarily define the boundaries and the consequences of political competition for many years to come.

Suggested Readings

Bunce, Valerie. "Global Patterns and Postcommunist Dynamics." *Orbis* 50 (Autumn 2006): 601–20.

Bunce, Valerie, and Sharon Wolchik. "International Diffusion and Postcommunist Electoral Revolutions." *Communist and Post-Communist Studies* 39 (September 2006): 283–304.

Gagnon, Valere P. *The Yugoslav Wars of the 1990s: A Critical Reexamination of Ethnic Conflict*. Ithaca, NY: Cornell University Press, 2004.

Mungiu-Pippidi, Alina, and Ivan Krastev, eds. *Nationalism after Communism: Lessons Learned*. Budapest, Hungary: Central European University, 2004.

Vachudova, Milada. *Europe Undivided: Democracy, Leverage, and Integration after Communism*. Oxford: Oxford University Press, 2005.

Zielonka, Jan, ed. *Democratic Consolidation in Eastern Europe*. Oxford: Oxford University Press, 2001.

Notes

1. The tripartite political division of the region in the immediate aftermath of communist regimes has been analyzed by several scholars. See, for example, Valerie Bunce, "The Political Economy of Postsocialism," *Slavic Review* 58 (Winter 1999): 756–93; M. Steven Fish, "The Determinants of Economic Reform in the Postcommunist World," *East European Politics and Societies* 12 (Winter 1998): 31–78; Michael McFaul, "The Fourth Wave of Democracy and Dictatorship: Noncooperative Transitions in the Postcommunist World," *World Politics* 54 (January 2002): 214–44.

2. There are many competing definitions of democracy. Perhaps the most helpful summary of these debates can be found in Robert Dahl, *On Democracy* (New Haven, CT: Yale University Press, 1998).

3. Hybrid regimes are, in fact, quite common outcomes of the global transition to democracy since the mid-1970s. See Larry Diamond, "Thinking about Hybrid Regimes," *Journal of Democracy* 13 (April 2002): 3–24 and Steven Levitsky and Lucan Way, "The Rise of Competitive Authoritarianism," *Journal of Democracy* 13 (April 2002): 51–65. Also see Marina Ottaway, *Democracy Challenged: The Rise of Semi-Authoritarianism* (Washington, DC: Carnegie Endowment Press, 2003).

4. On the issues of demobilization of the liberals in these two countries, see Valere Gagnon, *The Yugoslav Wars of the 1990s: A Critical Reexamination of Ethnic Conflict* (Ithaca, NY: Cornell University Press, 2004) and Kevin Deegan-Krause, "Uniting the Enemy: Politics and the Convergence of Nationalisms in Slovakia," *East European Politics and Societies* 18 (Fall 2004): 651–96.

5. See, for example, Samuel Huntington, *The Third Wave: Democratization in the Late Twentieth Century* (Norman: University of Oklahoma Press, 1991); Guillermo O'Donnell, Philippe C. Schmitter, and Laurence Whitehead, *Transitions from Authoritarian Rule*, vols. 1–4 (Baltimore: Johns Hopkins University Press, 1986); and Guiseppe Di Palma, *To Craft Democracy* (Berkeley: University of California Press, 1991).

6. On the unexpected problems encountered after the fall of Saddam Hussein, see Larry Diamond, "What Went Wrong in Iraq?" *Foreign Affairs* 83 (Summer/Fall 2004): 34–56 and Peter Galbraith, "Iraq: Bush's Islamic Republic," *New York Review of Books* 52 (August 11, 2005): 6–9.

7. A useful summary of these arguments can be found in Grzegorz Ekiert and Stephen Hanson, eds., *Capitalism and Democracy in Central and Eastern Europe: Assessing the Legacy of Communist Rule* (Cambridge, UK: Cambridge University Press, 2003).

8. Carol Leff, *National Conflict in Czechoslovakia: The Making and Remaking of a State, 1918–1987* (Princeton, NJ: Princeton University Press, 1988).

9. See, especially, O'Donnell, Schmitter, and Whitehead, *Transitions from Authoritarian Rule*; and M. Steven Fish, *Democracy from Scratch: Opposition and Regime in the New Russian Revolution* (Princeton, NJ: Princeton University Press, 1995).

10. See Nancy Bermeo, *Ordinary People in Extraordinary Times: The Citizenry and the Breakdown of Democracy* (Princeton, NJ: Princeton University Press, 2003).

11. Charles Tilly, *Coercion, Capital and European States, AD 990–1992* (London: Basil Blackwell, 1992).

12. Dankwart Rustow, "Transitions to Democracy: Toward a Dynamic Model," *Comparative Politics* 2 (April 1970): 18–36.

13. See Terry Lynn Karl, "Dilemmas of Democratization in Latin America," *Comparative Politics* 23 (Spring 1990): 28–49 and Valerie Bunce, "Rethinking Recent Democratization: Lessons from the Postcommunist Experience," *World Politics* 55 (January 2003): 167–92.

14. Bunce, "The Political Economy"; McFaul, "The Fourth Wave"; and Valerie J. Bunce and Sharon L. Wolchik, "Favorable Conditions and Electoral Revolutions," *Journal of Democracy* 17, no. 4 (October 2006): 5–22.

15. The International Commission on the Balkans, *The Balkans in Europe's Future* (Sofia, Bulgaria: Secretariat Center for Liberal Strategies, 2005).

16. The importance of geographical proximity to the West has appeared in a number of studies that have attempted to explain variations among postcommunist political and economic trajectories. See, for example, Jeffrey S. Kopstein and David A. Reilly, "Geographical Diffusion and the Transformation of the Postcommunist World," *World Politics* 53 (October 2000): 1–37.

17. See for example, Milada Vachudova, *Europe Undivided: Democracy, Leverage and Integration after Communism* (Oxford: Oxford University Press, 2005); Wade Jacoby, *The Enlargement of the EU and NATO: Ordering from the Menu in Europe* (Cambridge, UK: Cambridge University Press, 2004); and the essays in Ronald Linden, ed., *Norms and Nannies: The Impact of International Organizations on the Central and East European States* (Lanham, MD: Rowman and Littlefield, 2002).

18. The summer 2005 elections in Bulgaria, however, evidenced an unexpected increase in the support of an extremist nationalist party.

CHAPTER 3

Re-Creating the Market

Sharon Fisher

Transforming the economies of Central and Eastern Europe was probably the most complicated aspect of the transition from communism. At the start of the reform process, there was no single model for how the changes should be carried out. The postcommunist transition was unique. Unlike the transitions in Latin America and elsewhere in the world, there was no real market economy on which to build, so the old state economy had to be dismantled as a market economy developed. Thus, reforms happened in a rather haphazard way, and most knowledge of the transition process was formed after the fact.

Defining the "success" of a country's transition can be difficult, as some former communist states gained international recognition for certain reforms (such as privatization) but were laggards in other areas (such as banking reform). Some countries that initially appeared to be on rapid path toward a market economy eventually slowed down, while the opposite occurred in other cases. In most countries, the "success" of reforms was perceived much differently by foreign observers than by the domestic population, and reformist politicians often suffered in elections. Regardless, it is generally agreed that the most "successful" economic transitions in the region were those of the eight countries that joined the European Union (EU) in May 2004.

In retrospect, the two most important factors in determining the economic success of the Central and Eastern European countries seem to have been initial conditions and the strength of commitment of successive governments to reforms.[1] The Central and East European countries began the transition from communism from somewhat disparate starting points. Some, such as Hungary and Poland, had a head start: they had begun reforms during the final years of the communist era. Others, such as the Czech Republic, benefited from a strong manufacturing tradition. The more advanced countries in the region were generally those with close proximity to Western markets, whether because of historical traditions or the ease of trade and investment ties with the EU. This situation made it easier to attract foreign direct investment (FDI) and turn from trade with the "East" (the Soviet Union and Eastern Europe) to the "West." For example, despite being substantially behind the Central European countries at the end of the communist era, the three Baltic states benefited in the transition period from cooperation with their Nordic neighbors. The countries that experienced the bulk of their industrialization during the communist era often had a more difficult economic transition, especially when they were far from Western markets.

The other key factor determining the success or failure of the initial economic reforms was the policy approach of the new governments. While the political developments in each individual country had a substantial impact on the way market-oriented reforms were carried out, the economic situation also had a major effect on politics, as fickle populations frequently shifted their support from government to opposition depending on which side was promising prospects of greater well-being. It is important to keep in mind that frequent changes in government, often brought on by popular dissatisfaction with how the economic reforms worked, contributed to a lack of continuity in the reform process throughout the region.

The way communism ended in the various countries of Central and Eastern Europe also had a significant effect on the approach governments took to economic reforms. Communists initially remained in control in Bulgaria and Romania but were ousted in Poland, Hungary, Czechoslovakia, and the three Baltic states. As a result, reforms were considerably faster in the latter countries in the early 1990s. According to the European Bank for Reconstruction and Development (EBRD), the presence of a noncommunist government in the initial transition period is strongly correlated with the character of reforms in subsequent years.[2] Once the initial pace was set, successive governments generally continued with the reform process, even when the reformed communists came to power. By the mid to late 1990s, prospects for EU accession also helped push them along.

The Demise of Central Planning

Formally, communist economic policy was based on a protection of workers' interests through a "dictatorship of the proletariat." In practice, however, the Communist Party leadership controlled all social and economic organizations and made all major decisions about the economy. All appointments, including the management of enterprises, had to be approved by the party, whether by the central committee or local organs. The party *nomenklatura* were provided with special rights and privileges to motivate them.

One of the key elements of communist economic policy was "collective ownership," or nationalization of the means of production. Private ownership of land and the means of production was abolished without compensation. Agriculture was collectivized with the installation of communist rule. Only in Yugoslavia and Poland was private farming allowed. Another important aspect of communist economic policy was central planning, with a focus on quantity rather than on quality or profit. The measure of success was the level of production rather than personal consumption. Prices in this system were regulated, and fixed prices at both the wholesale and retail levels meant that open inflation was never a problem. In regard to labor, the communist system offered full employment. Those who did not work were considered "parasites." A balanced budget, on the surface at least, was another element of the communist economic program.

Foreign trade was regulated by the Council for Mutual Economic Assistance (CMEA) trading block, which was established by the Soviet Union, Bulgaria, Czechoslovakia, Hungary, Poland, and Romania in 1949, in response to America's offer to some of these states of aid through the Marshall Plan (and the Soviet Union's insistence that they refuse). Within CMEA (also known as Comecon), there was a plan that laid out a system of international specialization so that different goods were produced in different parts of the region to meet Soviet needs (and also those of the bloc as a whole). This policy insured that no state could stand alone economically. It did not work like a common market; instead trade was negotiated and conducted bilaterally, with oversight from the Soviet Union.

The communist economic system was, even at its best, a tragedy of errors. Central planning meant that bankruptcy was not a possibility. State subsidies were used to keep unprofitable firms afloat. Maintaining a balanced budget thus would have been a challenge if there had been an open accounting. Even though most countries' budget deficits were quite small, they created substantial imbalances. The only way to cover deficits was through foreign borrowing or printing more money.

Economic plans focused on production rather than personal consumption; there was little investment in health care, transportation, housing, and services. Moreover, there was a complete disregard for the environmental effects of production. The pricing system encouraged an intentional lowering of quality by producers and contributed to shortages. After all, decisions were made at the Central Planning Commission based on political goals. Citizens relied on their personal connections to obtain goods and services. This meant that corruption was rampant, a trend that has continued to the present day (see table 3.1). Although socialism was supposed to make individuals committed to the common good, most people were focused primarily on providing for their families.

Table 3.1. Transparency International's Corruption Ratings for Central and East European States, 2002–2006

Country	2006	2005	2004	2003	2002
Bosnia and Herzegovina	2.9	2.9	3.1	3.3	—
Bulgaria	4.0	4.0	4.1	3.9	4.0
Croatia	3.4	3.4	3.5	3.7	3.8
Czech Republic	4.8	4.3	4.2	3.9	3.7
Estonia	6.7	6.4	6.0	5.5	5.6
Hungary	5.2	5.0	4.8	4.8	4.9
Latvia	4.7	4.2	4.0	3.8	3.7
Lithuania	4.8	4.8	4.6	3.6	4.0
Poland	3.7	3.4	3.5	2.8	2.6
Romania	3.1	3.0	2.9	2.3	—
Serbia and Montenegro	3.0	2.8	2.7	2.3	—
Slovakia	4.7	4.3	4.0	3.7	3.7
Slovenia	6.4	6.1	6.0	5.9	6.0
Ukraine	2.8	2.6	2.2	2.3	2.4

Note: Based on a scale of 1–10; 10 is the least corrupt.
Source: Transparency International's Corruption Perceptions Index (www.transparency.org)

Because domestic prices were regulated nationally, there was no link between domestic and foreign prices. As a result, currencies were inconvertible. There were official and unofficial exchange rates. An overvalued domestic currency gave little reason to export goods outside of the region as long as countries did not have debts they needed to repay to foreign creditors. By the end of the communist era, some 60–75 percent of trade was conducted with other CMEA members, and many of the goods produced were uncompetitive in the West.

Before long, the communist economic system began to show signs of strain. As these economies faltered, some countries implemented limited economic reforms. Hungary launched its so-called goulash communism in 1968. In Poland, after several failed attempts, market reforms were begun a final time in 1982. In Yugoslavia, the communist system was considerably more liberal and the economy less plan oriented and more "self-managing" than in other countries in the region. In the late 1980s, the Yugoslav regime introduced extensive market-oriented reforms. Other regimes were more reluctant to make any economic reforms. Even after the partial reforms in the USSR were launched under Mikhail Gorbachev during the late 1980s, countries such as Czechoslovakia, East Germany, Bulgaria, and Romania maintained a hardline stance until the fall of communism in 1989.

In those countries that did introduce reforms, there was a clear pattern. The reach of the plan (the number of things it regulated) was cut. Power was delegated from branch ministries to enterprise managers to help decentralize decision making. Economic incentives were promoted. Pricing was made more flexible and market oriented. Inflation was made a fact of life. The establishment of small private enterprises was permitted. Foreign trade was partially liberalized. Since substantial distortions remained, other, new problems emerged. For example, as unemployment was legalized, jobless benefits were introduced, so a higher share of state revenues had to be devoted to social welfare.

By the late 1980s, the communist system was in precarious shape. Most countries experienced severe economic crises with falling output, profound shortages of consumer goods, accelerating inflation rates, widening current-account deficits, and rising foreign debt. Failing to deliver the expected growth, economic reforms instead called into question the legitimacy of the entire communist system with its claim of superiority over capitalism. Countries such as Poland and Hungary were forced to borrow heavily from abroad to spur investment and consumption in an effort to raise growth rates and appease the population. As the debt to foreign lenders increased, debt service also rose and international credits began to dry up by the end of the decade. Many countries in the region were forced to reschedule their foreign debts.

During the last years of the communist era, the only relative "success stories" were Hungary and Czechoslovakia. Hungary had transformed itself into a socialist market economy, while maintaining some degree of economic balance, although foreign debt did rise substantially. Czechoslovakia, on the other hand, managed to steer clear of major imbalances, despite the hard-line approach of its communist system. Both countries avoided the debilitating shortages that plagued other economies in the region.[3]

Macroeconomic Stabilization

As they transformed toward capitalism, most Central and East European countries inherited strong macroeconomic and external disequilibria from the communist system, including budget imbalances based on overarching social welfare systems and high levels of foreign debt. Even countries like Czechoslovakia, which had relatively stable and positive initial macroeconomic conditions at the outset, had to deal with the inflationary impact of price liberalization and the effects of the collapse of trade with the USSR. Across the region, advisors from organizations such as the International Monetary Fund (IMF) gave technical assistance to devise macroeconomic stabilization programs based largely on methods that were applied in developing countries. Even as governments implemented these programs, it was unclear how effective they would be. After all, postcommunist transitions were unprecedented in the scope of the changes required.

Macroeconomic stabilization programs included price liberalization, restrictive monetary and fiscal policies, and foreign trade liberalization, accompanied by a sharp devaluation of the domestic currency, making it weaker against international currencies such as the U.S. dollar. These measures were aimed at stabilizing the economy and allowing for the introduction of structural changes, including enterprise privatization and reforms of the banking sector and social welfare system.

The main debates on the transition focused not on what needed to be done, but rather on how to sequence and pace the reforms. Some argued that de-monopolization of industry was required before prices were set free to prevent firms from simply hiking prices. In the stabilization package, there was also considerable debate over the extent of the currency devaluation and how much interest rates should be shifted. Devaluation helped to improve external trade balances, allowing for international stabilization. Nonetheless, it also raised the price of imports of consumer and industrial goods, thereby contributing to higher inflation. The small or medium-sized open economies in Central and Eastern Europe were particularly vulnerable to these cross-pressures.

In terms of speed, reformers were divided into proponents of "shock therapy" versus gradualism. The gradualists argued for relatively lax monetary and fiscal policies and a slower transfer of assets from the state to the private sector, with the aim of protecting the population from the social consequences of reforms. With time, it became clear that none of the countries that consistently advocated a gradual approach were successful reformers.

PRICE LIBERALIZATION

Among the countries that launched reforms before 1989, only Hungary broadly liberalized prices under the communist regime. Elsewhere in Central Europe, the "big-bang approach" to price liberalization was used after the fall of communism. Poland took the lead in January 1990, and Czechoslovakia followed a year later. When "big bangs" happened, prices for consumer durables and nonfood items were set by market forces, so shortages disappeared since people were less able to purchase goods. But, politicians and consumers were often reluctant to give up fixed prices on essentials such as food (particularly bread and meat) and gasoline because such a step would impoverish a population that expected economic gains under the new capitalist system. In the end, many governments dropped price controls only because of their inability to continue providing subsidies. In most Central and East European countries, rents, public transport, and utilities remained under state control throughout the 1990s and even into the first decade of the twenty-first century. Prices were often set below the real costs because price hikes were seen as politically risky. In Slovakia, for example, consumer prices of natural gas did not reach world market levels until 2004; regulated rents in the Czech Republic remained well below market prices through 2006.

Price liberalization caused inflation to surge throughout the Central and East European region in the initial transition years. Most countries experienced triple- or quadruple-digit price growth after the fall of communism. Those increases were largely a result of filling out the imbalances from the previous regime, particularly where countries printed money to cover budgetary expenditures. The former Czechoslovakia, where the state maintained a balanced budget under communism, had the smallest increase in inflation following the launch of price liberalization, and inflation never reached triple digits. In contrast, countries such as Ukraine and rump Yugoslavia, where macroeconomic stabilization programs initially failed, suffered from hyperinflation.

For price liberalization to be a success in the postcommunist transitions, the first key lesson was that the initial liberalization had to be as comprehensive as possible. Any additional deregulation of prices proved to be extremely complicated, spurring passionate public debates and broad opposition. Second, the greater the distortions of initial price levels, the more comprehensive deregulations were required, even as the distortions made price hikes more difficult for the public to stomach due to the large increase over communist-era levels. Third, populations willingly accepted price deregulation when it was accompanied by a change in the system. In fact, nowhere in the region did price liberalizations stir widespread protest.[4] A final lesson from the Central and East European region is that high levels of inflation are incompatible with economic growth. In contrast, countries that did not experience hyperinflation were able to moderate the declines in gross domestic product (GDP) during the early transition years.

RESTRICTING MONETARY POLICY

The liberalization of prices in Central and Eastern Europe usually involved higher increases in inflation than were initially expected. This inflation resulted in demands for a loosening control over monetary policy. Many countries in the region, in fact, maintained low interest rates in the initial transition years. This discouraged savings and contributed to a low level of trust in local currencies. Although this negatively affected average citizens, it benefited politically connected individuals because they could obtain loans at low real interest rates.

Eventually, monetary authorities shifted from expanding the money supply to restricting it, with the aim of keeping inflation down. Their policies involved, instead, a slow growth in the money supply, even a negative growth in real terms. These were also accompanied by large increases in interest rates to make them higher than the rate of inflation. In Ukraine, for example, real interest rates were set at a high of 200 percent in spring 1996.[5] This policy of high interest rates discouraged domestic borrowing and encouraged saving and investment. Perhaps more important was the impact high interest rates had in reducing risky lending practices. In each country's transition, "success" required that monetary authorities eventually find a balance between the two extremes of high versus low interest rates to support economic growth.

BALANCING FISCAL BUDGETS

Because the main source of financing for budget deficits comes from the printing of money, fiscal policy is closely linked to monetary policy as an important element in stabilizing economies undergoing transformation. The persistence of fiscal imbalances poses serious risks for the sustainability of long-term economic growth because it triggers higher inflation rates. Thus, one of the first steps in the macroeconomic stabilization program in Central and Eastern Europe was a dramatic reduction of fiscal deficits, so that revenues and expenses in the state budget became more balanced. By reducing state expenditures and increasing revenues, the new elites sought to ensure that the fiscal reforms would provide the necessary funds to sustain a radical stabilization program. Balanced budgets were especially crucial in those countries that were very indebted because the financing of fiscal deficits contributed to sustaining inflation and made it difficult to satisfy creditors. A balanced budget became one of the main criteria for receiving IMF financing and other credits from international financial markets. Governments in the region struggled to balance the demands of their constituents against the austere fiscal targets demanded by international financial institutions.

Initially, fiscal deficits were due largely to high expenditures associated with the oversized public sector and the collapse of revenues due to production declines in the transition process. On the expenditure side, the first step transitional governments took was to eliminate consumer price subsidies, especially for basic food products. The second step involved cutting subsidies for state enterprises. This step proved much more difficult to implement because it contributed to higher levels of unemployment. As firms sought profitability, they typically laid off workers. Pressures for more state expenditures emerged through public demands for higher social spending in the form of social welfare programs and pensions. Most countries in the region maintained enterprise subsidies throughout the 1990s in at least a few key but inefficient sectors, most notably in agriculture, mining, and energy. Eventually, direct subsidies were frequently replaced by indirect subsidies, with state companies getting cheap credits from state-owned banks.

On the revenue side, an entirely new taxation system was necessary. Under the new system, personal income and consumption taxes accounted for a larger share of total tax revenues, thereby taking the burden off enterprises and helping them maintain competitiveness. The first step was to replace the communist-era "turnover tax" with the "value-added tax" (VAT), a consumption tax levied at each stage of production based on the value added to the product at that stage. The tax burden ultimately was borne by the final consumer. In contrast, the "turnover tax" was utilized under the previous system on a discretionary basis. Goods that were considered socially necessary were subsidized by negative tax rates. In the new system, VAT rates were typically around 20 percent, with lower rates for necessities such as food and medicines.

The second important element in reforming the revenue side of the budget was the establishment of personal income taxes. Under communism, personal income taxes were insignificant. In the transition period, three alternative models were used: a social democratic approach with high progressive income taxes that went up to more than 50 percent of gross income for the wealthiest citizens (Hungary and Ukraine), a standard model with a progressive system taxing individuals between 12 and 40 percent of their incomes, and the Baltic model (Estonia, Latvia) with a flat personal income tax—the same percentage for everyone.

The third step involved the establishment of a corporate tax system that was legislated rather than being subject to negotiations between managers and their government supervisors, as it had been during the communist era. Most countries initially chose to impose a flat profit tax of 30–35 percent.[6]

The other major concern of the transition countries was the need for an efficient and effective collection system. After all, since "taxes" were not really a part of a state economy, there was no real infrastructure for tax collection and enforcement. Under communism, taxes were automatically transferred to the budget through the state-owned banking system. In the new regimes, there was a need for institutions, people, and funds to manage the new tax system. Most of the Central and East European countries were relatively successful in establishing a strong, relatively unitary revenue service. The countries of the Commonwealth of Independent States (CIS) had more problems. In most cases, the introduction of the VAT proved successful in boosting revenue collection. In regard to personal income tax, the Baltic approach proved to be by far the most successful model in terms of revenue collection because it was simple and easy to enforce. The progressive taxes merely encouraged underreporting and avoidance.

FOREIGN TRADE LIBERALIZATION

Under communism, trade in the Central and Eastern Europe region was handled through the CMEA. That system was disbanded in January 1991. At that time, the USSR began demanding payment for raw materials in Western currencies and at world market prices. Thus, the USSR signaled that it was no longer willing to subsidize the rest of the region by exporting hard goods and importing soft goods in exchange for political loyalty. Similarly, the Central and Eastern Europe countries were no longer willing to accept political domination in exchange for Soviet subsidies. So, while many analysts initially thought that CMEA's demise would significantly increase trade within the region by removing many of the impediments associated with the old structures, the opposite occurred. There were sharp declines in interregional trade caused by the collapse in demand in the Soviet Union. For the Central and Eastern Europe countries, the postcommunist transition required a major redirection of trade. These transitional economies needed to find export products that would be competitive on world markets in order to service their debts.

Trade liberalization was carried out through a shift to tariffs, accompanied by reductions in tariff rates. This was reflected in the abolition of the many administrative restrictions on the import and export of industrial products from the old system. That shift had the advantage of making trade regulation more transparent and compatible with the General Agreement on Tariffs and Trade (GATT) and later the World Trade Organization (WTO). Trade liberalization began in manufacturing and gradually shifted to sensitive areas such as services and agricultural trade. The Central European countries and Estonia initially had the most success in the first phase of liberalization, introducing tariffs and reducing tariff rates in 1990–1991.

Trade liberalization was important for several reasons. Opening the domestic markets to imported products from the West helped satisfy consumption-starved citizens. Moreover, trade liberalization pushed countries forward in their structural adjustment: given the small size of the domestic markets, competition in most countries could only happen from imports. External economic relationships also contributed to stabilizing the economy, by forcing domestic inflation into line with international rates.

CURRENCY CONVERTIBILITY AND EXCHANGE RATE REGIMES

Currency convertibility and the unification of exchange rates were important steps that took place in conjunction with foreign trade liberalization. As already mentioned, communist regimes had no link between domestic and foreign prices, making currencies inconvertible for international payments. Most former communist countries immediately adopted a fully convertible current account, allowing for trade in goods and services. In contrast, convertibility was introduced only gradually on the capital accounts, which govern the transfer of financial assets. The Baltic states emerged in the forefront of the reforms aimed at bringing capital account convertibility.[7]

In regulating the currency, policy makers began the transition with an initial devaluation that accompanied the introduction of a stabilization program. While two or more different exchange rates had existed in communist systems, including the official and black market rates, this could not happen in economies that were joining the world economy. So a single, official exchange rate had to be established. The devaluation was done to improve trade imbalances by making imports more expensive and exports cheaper. After the initial devaluation, governments adopted one of four types of exchange rate regimes: floating rates (in which the currency floats freely without intervention from the central bank), pegged rates (where the currency's value is fixed against that of another currency or basket of currencies to provide a nominal anchor), crawling pegs (a pegged exchange rate regime where the reference value is shifted at preestablished points in time), and currency boards (in which foreign exchange reserves are used to back the currency).

In addition to foreign trade liberalization, currency convertibility, and exchange rate policy, there were two other important aspects of external economic relations: developing new market-friendly institutions to promote economic integration within the region, and gaining access to preferential trading arrangements in the international economy such as the European Union. The Central European Free Trade Agreement (CEFTA) was established in 1992 by Hungary, Poland, and Czechoslovakia. It was soon enlarged to include other countries from the region. In the USSR, all former republics except for the three Baltic states joined the Commonwealth of Independent States in 1991. Most Central European and Baltic countries signed association agreements with the EU by the mid-1990s. These agreements served to boost exports and consolidate the opening of markets. Membership in GATT/WTO also helped to guarantee the maintenance of free trade. In May 2004, eight Central and East European countries took the final step in international economic integration and became full EU members. They were joined in January 2007 by Bulgaria and Romania.

Structural Reforms

The achievement of macroeconomic stabilization paved the way for the launch of structural reforms creating an investment climate that was conducive to the entry of new businesses, including small and medium enterprises (SMEs). In centrally planned economies, all means of production, transportation, and financial intermediation had been owned by the state. As a result, firms had few incentives to produce high-quality goods. Long-term investment was limited. Moreover, in planned economies no consideration was given to profitability. Firms were often grossly overstaffed, with employees working at half capacity because of shortages of inputs for production. Many firms were overextended. They had to make all the components of the production and maintenance process. Thus, the initial path toward transition involved removing barriers to private business. This required the establishment of an institutional framework that was conducive to the development of a market economy. Governments had to develop commercial, labor, and tax codes that provided the base for the creation of new businesses. Of all the institutions that had to be developed, the establishment of a two-tiered banking system was the most critical.

Fiscal reform played a double role in the transformation process of the former socialist countries. In addition to being a key element in the stabilization efforts, it was also part of the structural adjustment program. Under communism, companies had provided social protection to their employees. The state took over that role in the new regime. This required a transformation of the entire social welfare system through a process referred to as "right sizing" government.

PRIVATIZATION

Privatization was a crucial aspect of the restructuring process because most significantly, it improved the efficiency of resource allocation and contributed to stronger budget constraints on enterprises. Private firms divested themselves of unprofitable sectors and laid off excess employees. Privatization also had positive spillover effects throughout the economy. It helped to spur the development of entrepreneurial spirit. Moreover, receipts from privatized enterprises improved the state's fiscal position as it struggled with reforms. Finally, although the privatization process itself was often plagued by corruption, the sale of state-owned firms eventually contributed to a reduction in the power of government policy makers by establishing new, private owners.

The privatization process across Central and Eastern Europe began through the sale of small-scale enterprises, typically through auctions, direct sales, or giveaways, or through restitution schemes that returned properties to their precommunist owners. Restitution was also used with respect to land and housing. While Hungary and Poland had allowed for small private businesses in the 1980s, in hard-line regimes such as Czechoslovakia, 99 percent of the economy remained in state hands up until the fall of communism. Despite these very different starting points, small-scale privatization was accomplished with relative ease and was close to completion within one to two years in most countries.

The sale of state-owned companies became more complicated when countries began selling off medium and large-scale enterprises. Privatization agencies were created to choose which firms should be sold and establish the rules and regulations for the sales. The main methods used were manager-employee buyouts (MEBOs), voucher schemes, direct sales, initial public offerings (IPOs), and public tenders. The strategies varied between countries. Countries would typically choose one main method and combine it with a mix of other approaches.

Manager and employee privatization involved selling the enterprise to the current management and employees at discounted prices or sometimes simply transferring ownership without a cash payment. That is why the approach is often referred to as an "insider" model. While MEBOs are relatively quick, simple, and popular with the workers, they are also inefficient. Use of the MEBO method slowed the restructuring of the enterprise's management and operations; required continued state support, given the dearth of funds the employees and managers had for investment; failed to bring in the required market expertise; and left the state with little or no monetary compensation for the sale of the enterprise. Slovenia is the only country from the Central and Eastern Europe region that had real success in using the MEBO approach, probably because its economy was already well integrated with Western Europe when the transition started.

The voucher or coupon method involved the transfer of shares in state-owned companies to citizens. Citizens are given coupons for nominal sums (or sometimes for free). They trade these coupons for shares in firms or investment funds. The main advantages of the coupon method have been its speed, relative ease of administration, and equitability. In Central and East European countries, coupon privatization was presented as a way of garnering public support to continue market reforms by turning citizens into shareholders. Nonetheless, like the MEBOs, coupon programs failed to bring in the funds needed for enterprise restructuring. Another downside was that the diffusion of ownership translated into weak corporate governance, which narrowly defined refers to the relationship between a company and its shareholders. Both the coupon and MEBO methods allowed for the transfer of property in capital-starved economies but state budgets did not benefit from the temporary boost in revenues that privatization can bring. The coupon method was first launched in Czechoslovakia in 1992 and was soon copied in other countries.

Many Western market analysts see issuing stock on securities markets at a prede-termined price in an IPO as the most transparent way of selling off state corporations. That method can also reap large revenues for the government. However, IPOs were seldom used in the Central and East European region because of the lack of developed financial markets in the transitioning countries.

Direct sales and public tenders were among the most common forms of privatiza-tion in Central and Eastern Europe. These were usually managed by the state privati-zation agency. In theory, direct sales go to the highest bidder. However, corruption can be rampant in practice due to the lack of transparency. Unlike direct sales, public tenders are not based solely on the level of privatization proceeds but rather on the premise of achieving the highest long-term economic growth potential. Thus, sales are negotiated with buyers, who must present a business plan that takes into account such factors as employment issues, investment, and performance guarantees. These schemes require that the enterprises being sold are attractive enough to encourage investors who are willing to make a long-term commitment. The tender method is more diffi-cult in the short term because negotiations can take a long time and revenues from the sales are generally not as high as in the case of direct sales. Another downside is that setting the rules for the tender is up to the discretion of state officials. Nonetheless, the short-term disadvantages are typically more than offset by the long-term benefits. The public tender method has been seen as the most successful privatization method in the Central and East European region.

Regardless of the privatization approach adopted by a government, speed is con-sidered especially important. The private sector's share of GDP has been closely corre-lated with the success of a country's overall reforms. In countries that implemented rapid economic reforms, over 70 percent of the economy was in private hands a decade after the transition began. That share was generally at less than 50 percent in the gradual reformers.[8]

PRIVATIZATION STRATEGIES IN THE VISEGRAD COUNTRIES

The four countries of the Visegrad Group—so named for the Hungarian town of Visegrad, where the meeting that formed the group was held—are the Czech Repub-lic, Hungary, Poland, and Slovakia. These countries approached privatization in radi-cally different ways in the early 1990s. Hungary first focused on creating an institutional and legal framework for the new capitalist system and addressed the prob-lem of limited domestic capital by beginning early with sales to foreign investors. That proved to be a wise approach since the new foreign owners replaced the socialist-era managers and removed what could have become a powerful force with the potential to obstruct market-oriented reforms. In privatizing, the Hungarians stuck to traditional methods such as public tenders and IPOs, largely avoiding experimentation with alter-native forms such as voucher schemes, restitution, or employee buyouts. Most of Hun-gary's lucrative state properties thus were sold off by 1997, allowing deep restructuring to take place earlier than in the other three Visegrad countries.

Czech and Slovak privatization began when the two nations were still part of the same country. The Czech-devised voucher scheme was launched in an effort to transfer property to private hands as quickly as possible. The program compensated for the lack of domestic capital by offering shares to the population for a symbolic price. This move was aimed at broadening public support for reforms. There was an element of nationalism in the Czech scheme. The desire to keep firms in domestic hands was greatest for strategic companies such as banks, telecoms, utilities, and other "family jewels." A major flaw of the coupon program was that, unlike the Hungarians, the Czechs failed to first create an adequate legal and institutional framework. Insufficient regulation allowed for high levels of abuse, including insider trading and asset stripping. Moreover, because most shares were put in investment funds—many of which were controlled by banks that remained in state hands—corporate governance was absent, unemployment remained unnaturally low, and the banking system ended up in shambles. Only after an economic crisis in 1997 did the Czech Republic shift its approach and focus on public tenders and selling key firms in the banking and energy sectors to foreign investors.

After Slovakia gained independence in 1993, the second wave of voucher privatization was canceled. Privatization initially ground to a halt until political elites devised ways of benefiting from the sale of state assets. In 1994–1998, privatization focused mainly on MEBOs and direct sales, usually to political allies at rock-bottom prices. That approach appealed to nationalists, as the ruling parties stressed their aim of shunning foreign investment and instead creating a domestic entrepreneurial class. The result was that many politically connected but incompetent owners led their empires to ruin, causing great damage to the economy. After the change of government in 1998, Slovakia shifted to an approach similar to that in the Czech Republic with international tenders for key firms in the banking, telecom, and energy sectors.

In its approach to privatization, Poland used a mix of different methods, depending on the orientation of the government in power at the time. In the early transition years, Polish privatization was slower than in Hungary or the Czech Republic. But it accelerated in the latter part of the 1990s after the financial and legal framework had been established. While initially not as open to foreign investors as the Hungarians, the Poles were more welcoming than the Czechs and Slovaks.

Despite the different paths taken in the early 1990s, the approaches of all four countries converged by the end of the decade as they prepared for the competitive pressures of EU accession. As demonstrated by the Slovak and Czech cases, it was possible to prevent key firms from coming under foreign control for some years. However, the results were often not positive, as domestic owners frequently appeared more concerned with their personal interests than with those of the firm and its employees. In contrast, foreign investors generally led the economic recoveries throughout the region, providing improved management techniques and know-how, boosting production and exports, and preparing the economies for the shock of full EU membership.

"RIGHT-SIZING" GOVERNMENT

Right-sizing government is a matter of adapting the public sector to the needs of a capitalist economy. While the stabilization programs dealt with such issues as cutting enterprise and price subsidies and introducing a new taxation system, the structural reform programs required that the government take over certain social welfare functions previously performed by state enterprises, including the provision of health care, housing, and kindergartens.

There are several dilemmas involved in this process. First of all, there was no "optimal" size for government in established Western economies. The public sector, after all, accounts for only 30 percent of the gross domestic product in the United States and over 50 percent in Sweden. Secondly, the public sector experienced severe shocks during the transition. As declines in GDP and fiscal pressures reduced funding for social welfare programs, issues of poverty and inequality became more urgent. Right-sizing does not necessarily mean cutting the size of the public sector, however. While the state's declining role is crucial in regard to enterprise development, it must expand in other areas, such as regulatory activities (including antitrust, securities, and bankruptcy mechanisms) as well as unemployment insurance and other labor market policies.

Under communism, central government tax revenues averaged about 50 percent of GDP and reached as high as 61 percent in Czechoslovakia in 1989. That was far higher than warranted by the level of economic development.[9] During the transition, states faced the challenge of taking on more social welfare functions while at the same time reducing budget deficits. In practice, that was especially complicated since people were accustomed to being dependent on the welfare state. During the early transition years, governments set up generous unemployment schemes with long payment periods covering a large share of the former salary. Benefits also applied to new entrants to the labor market. As unemployment rates rose, however, the generosity of the schemes declined. Although the size of public sectors decreased substantially in the early years of the transition, the public sectors remained large: budget revenues accounted for 42–47 percent of GDP in Central Europe by 1995.[10]

Countries adopted a variety of approaches to fiscal reform. Radical reformers such as Czechoslovakia, Estonia, and Latvia started early with balanced budget targets. The record shows this was a wise decision given that delayed attempts at balancing were unsuccessful in Poland, Hungary, and Lithuania. In the latter cases, the habit of generous social spending was difficult to break for political reasons. Despite a favorable starting point in the Czech Republic and Slovakia, fiscal deficits surged in those countries during the latter part of the 1990s, partly due to the high cost of bailing out the banking sector but also because of the soft-budget constraints related to off-budget funds. The official state budget deficit reached about 1.3 percent of GDP in the Czech Republic during 1997–1998; however, the hidden deficit was almost three times that size.[11]

Fiscal reforms became especially important as privatization wrapped up. In the early years of the transition period, some governments used privatization revenues to finance more spending, helping to compensate for the gap between domestic savings and private investment needs. As the countries approached the end of the transition, however, the international financial community discouraged such practices, and called on countries to use privatization revenues to pay off government debts. As discussed below, fiscal reform became particularly crucial once countries had joined the EU, as the Maastricht criteria required that budget deficits remain below 3 percent of GDP.

Macroeconomic Trends

TRANSITION RECESSIONS AND RECOVERIES

Certain elements of the communist economic system had strongly negative implications for the transition process, even for those countries that had already begun reforms. The causes of recession in the transitions can be divided into macro- and microelements. Macroelements include the effects of high inflation; the impact of the stabilization program, with contractionary fiscal and monetary policies spurring reductions in aggregate demand; and the collapse of intraregional trade, which had negative effects on both export demand (reducing aggregate demand) and import supply (reducing aggregate supply). Microelements of the transitional recessions included problems in coordinating production when the collapse of central planning left enterprises unprepared to find new buyers for their output and suppliers for their inputs, since they had poor marketing skills.

The countries that recovered most quickly from the recession generally had favorable initial conditions. It is no accident that the Central European economies were the first to begin recovering, followed by the Baltic states. Other factors helped limit the term of the transition recession, including a rapid reduction in inflation; the implementation of institutional and policy changes at the microlevel to allow for the introduction of competitive market forces; rapid growth in the private sector, without excessive restrictions; a geographic redirection of trade away from traditional markets and toward the EU; and sectoral restructuring, allowing for rapid growth in the service sector.

The countries that faced special difficulties with stabilization were those struggling the most with the legacies of the old system. Many of the countries in Central and Eastern Europe were new, established in the early 1990s after the collapse of the USSR, Yugoslavia, and Czechoslovakia. They struggled simultaneously with state- and nation-building concerns and defining and defending their borders. As a result, economic reform was often not their top priority. Many had no previous experience with macroeconomic management. There were also problems that arose from having been part of dysfunctional currency areas, such as the ruble (former USSR) and dinar zones (ex-Yugoslavia). In Ukraine, as in other former Soviet countries, the initial use of the ruble was a major impediment to macroeconomic stabilization and a significant cause of inflation, as each country in the ruble zone had an incentive to pursue expansionary macroeconomic policies because some of the resulting inflation would be exported to other countries in the region.

Data indicate that all Central and East European economies experienced large declines in GDP (15–70 percent) between 1989 and 1993. After the onset of the recession, Poland was the first to begin to recover (1992), followed by the rest of Central Europe in 1993–1994. Poland, in 1996, was the first to reach its 1989 level of GDP with Slovenia and Slovakia not far behind. In contrast, Ukraine experienced one of the most serious transition recessions in the entire Central and East European region. Its economy did not begin to experience GDP growth until 2000.

It is difficult to compare pre- and posttransition GDP given the different ways of using statistics and the deliberate falsification or omission of unfavorable data under the old regime. GDP statistics exaggerated the true decline in economic welfare that occurred during the transition. In the communist system, output levels were often overreported for the sake of plan fulfillment. On the other hand, once the transition began, enterprises faced incentives to underreport in order to avoid taxes and divert output to the gray economy. Another factor was the so-called forced substitution practice: the lack of substitutes gave buyers little choice but to purchase goods available under the old system that were not really desired. After the transition began, better substitutes were often imported, reducing GDP but, at the same time, increasing consumer welfare.

As with GDP data, official measures of inflation exaggerated the declines in economic welfare associated with postcommunist inflation. Price liberalization only made explicit the hidden inflationary pressures that had existed in the previous system. The higher prices that resulted from liberalization reduced households' real income on paper, but they also allowed households to purchase whatever they could afford without having to wait in line or endure forced substitution. This trade-off—higher prices and lower real incomes in exchange for less waiting and forced substitution—made some people better off and others worse off. It did not, however, connote automatic impoverishment. Moreover, the higher prices that occurred after liberalization were a partial reflection of the higher product quality that resulted from price liberalization and the creation of a buyer's market.

LABOR MARKET TRENDS

Under central planning, unemployment did not exist. Governments introduced identity cards. Each citizen was required to have a place of employment or prove that he or she was legitimately out of the labor force. Factories were built in areas with high levels of joblessness. Collective farms and large enterprises helped to absorb residual unemployment. The maintenance of full employment meant that many workers received wages in excess of their contribution to their firms' revenues. Thus, the full-employment policy functioned as a disguised form of unemployment compensation.

One of the key aspects of the postcommunist transition was to transfer employment from the public to the private sector. In a market economy, companies locate plants where they can maximize profits, not reduce unemployment. Access to transport, electric power, and raw materials are crucial factors and are often more important than labor costs. Delivery times and transport costs are also key, so manufacturers often prefer to have plants closer to clients and markets. Thus, growth has been concentrated near big cities or Western borders. Large plants in out-of-the-way locations are frequently loss makers.

All of the countries in the region witnessed a rise in unemployment in the early years of the transition, although the increase was much greater in some countries than in others. In the Central and East European countries, layoffs were much more prevalent during the 1990s than in the CIS, where less restructuring took place. The wide variations in unemployment rates within Central Europe were based mainly on demographics. The younger populations in Slovakia and Poland meant that jobless rates were considerably higher than in Hungary, for example. Variations among regions

Photo 3.1.   *This wood-processing plant was abandoned in eastern Poland (Ruciana Nida) as a result of the economic transition, leaving hundreds out of work in the area.*
(Source: Hanna Siudalska)

within a given country were also substantial. The labor force was not very mobile due to poorly functioning housing markets. Of the more advanced countries, Poland and Slovakia had the biggest problems with unemployment among youth, again largely because of the higher shares of young people in the total population.

While overall unemployment rates in Central Europe and the Baltic states have rarely reached as high as 20 percent, certain Balkan countries have experienced much higher jobless rates of around 30 percent or more. Albania's unemployment rates reached close to 30 percent in 1992–1993, but subsequently declined. Meanwhile, by 2004, official jobless rates remained at over 30 percent of the labor force in countries like Macedonia, Bosnia-Herzegovina, and Serbia and Montenegro, partly as a result of the Balkan wars and low levels of foreign direct investment. While those figures are unbearably high, jobless rates are thought to be considerably lower in reality because of the strong informal economy in those countries. Still, long-term unemployment remains a serious challenge for policy makers in the Balkan region.

In certain respects, the rise in unemployment during the 1990s can be seen as a healthy development, a sign of the rationalization of production and employment. Enterprises had incentives to shed redundant workers as they faced firmer budget constraints, particularly in industries with declining competitiveness. Meanwhile, farms shed labor as agricultural subsidies fell. Governments fought the layoffs without much success. They did make it more difficult for companies to cut their workforces, however, by imposing high severance pay requirements along the West European model. Financial pressures forced enterprises to utilize other mechanisms to reduce labor costs, such as early retirement schemes and wage arrears, with the latter especially prevalent in the CIS countries.

Solutions for rising unemployment rates include active labor market policies such as public works projects, job retraining programs, and employment subsidies, especially for uneducated groups such as Roma. Active labor market policies are often mixed with passive policies such as changes in taxation laws and regulations that govern the hiring and firing of employees. While active labor market programs are not always effective in the long run, cutting high payroll taxes and approving legislation that makes it easier for companies to hire and fire workers have had a more substantial impact on job growth. Also important are changes in the jobless benefits system aimed at encouraging the unemployed to find work, as benefits are sometimes set too high in relation to minimum wage. Deregulation of rents can help encourage labor mobility, as can improvements in the banking sector that allow for the growth of mortgage lending. One unwelcome development has been a significant brain drain from Central and East European countries to Western countries, especially among young, educated people who speak foreign languages.

Some countries have tried to use foreign direct investment as a way to bring down unemployment rates. Nonetheless, much of the FDI in the region has been related to privatization. Foreign investors who buy existing firms do not always provide more jobs. Governments often require that investors agree to keep employment at a certain level; however, eventually, the workforce has to be cut to raise productivity. Greenfield investment—which entails the construction of a new plant—is much more beneficial in terms of job creation; however, attracting investors is tough, given the stiff competition among countries. Generally, the business environment and market potential are very important so countries that are already in the EU or are expected to join soon are seen as much more attractive.

Hungary is the one Central and East European country that managed to have substantial success in using FDI as a job creation policy. After they reached double digits in 1993–1995, Hungary managed to cut jobless rates to around 6 percent in 2000–2004 by offering incentives to foreign investors, especially those who invested in regions with high levels of unemployment, such as eastern Hungary. By 2000, Hungary was even experiencing a labor shortage in certain areas as the country's population has been declining since 1980.

For most countries, however, the development of small and medium enterprise remains the only real answer to cutting unemployment. Many countries in the region were slow to develop legal frameworks conducive to substantial growth of small business. Moreover, the slow development of the lending market also delayed progress, as banks were hesitant to lend to small enterprises because there was little recourse if they did not pay their debts, as long as courts did not function properly. In contrast, mortgages were a safer bet for banks since property could be used as collateral.

SECOND-STAGE STABILIZATION

In the transition process, it is important to distinguish between first- and second-stage macroeconomic stabilization programs. The first stage occurred in 1990–1993 during the early part of postcommunist transition. Some countries that started out well later showed signs of imbalance and had to implement second-stage programs. This happened in Hungary in 1995 with the Bokros Plan, in the Czech Republic (1997–1999), Slovakia (1998–2000), and Poland (2001).

The justification for second-stage stabilization programs differed depending on the country, and a variety of solutions was implemented. For example, in the case of Slovakia, the country was on the verge of an acute economic crisis by the time of the September 1998 parliamentary elections because of poorly designed structural and macroeconomic policies, particularly during the years 1994–1998. The government's expansive fiscal policy was among the main causes of the crisis. It involved public financing of large infrastructure projects and state guarantees for bank loans to state-owned companies. Another reason for the crisis related to inadequate bank regulation, contributing to serious problems with nonperforming loans. A third cause was the privatization strategy. It favored domestic buyers over foreign ones and thus generated high current-account deficits that were financed by foreign borrowing instead of inflows of foreign direct investment. The impact of those policies was exacerbated by the central bank's attempts to maintain a fixed exchange rate regime. This meant that monetary policy had to be tightened, sending interest rates upward and contributing to increased insolvency among Slovak enterprises. A solution to the credit crunch necessitated intervention in macroeconomic management and in the banking and enterprise sectors. That included austerity measures aimed at stabilizing public finances and reducing the current-account deficit, restructuring and privatizing the state-owned banks, and easing and accelerating bankruptcy proceedings.[12] With stabilization largely achieved by 2002, the country was then able to move on to more advanced reforms.

External Economic Trends

BALANCE OF PAYMENTS

Current-account balances in the Central and Eastern Europe region have fluctuated considerably during the transition period. By the mid-1990s, most countries in the region had balances that were within respectable limits, with deficits of about 5 percent of GDP or less, while some countries even recorded surpluses. However, deficits shot back up in 1996–1998, as access to external financing grew. Current-account gaps generally have narrowed in subsequent years, particularly in countries where second-stage adjustments took place. By 2004, current-account deficits were down to around 5 percent of GDP or less in Central Europe (except for Hungary), but higher in the Baltic states.

The level of the current-account deficit is often closely linked with the gap between exports and imports of goods, particularly in the lesser-developed countries of the region. While foreign trade deficits in the Central European countries have generally remained under control, some Balkan countries such as Bosnia-Herzegovina and Albania have been plagued with very low export-to-import ratios, reaching 31 percent and 26 percent, respectively, in 2004. As a result, those countries must rely on high surpluses on the "current transfers" account (which includes foreign grants and workers' remittances from abroad) to keep overall current-account deficits in line. Even so, Bosnia's current-account deficits have been in the double digits as a percentage of GDP during much of the transition period. Throughout the region, the balance of trade in services, which includes transport, travel, and other services, has generally been in surplus. One factor that has introduced an element of uncertainty into the level of the current-account gap has been the rising income deficits, as foreign investors send their earnings home. Income deficits have been especially apparent in Central European countries that have attracted significant levels of FDI.

Despite frequent warnings about the unsustainability of current-account deficits that surpass 5 percent of GDP, large deficits are not always a sign of an unhealthy economy. Estonia's current-account gap reached about 10–13 percent of GDP in 2002–2004. At the same time, economic growth was strong, inflation was low, and budget balances were in surplus. A negative current-account balance must be compensated for by a positive financial account. This can stem from inflows of foreign direct and portfolio investment as well as long-term and short-term foreign loans. If supported by inflows of FDI rather than by foreign borrowing, high current-account deficits are not overly worrying.

FOREIGN DIRECT INVESTMENT

Privatization deals involving foreign investors were initially unpopular in some Central and East European countries, as people feared that their governments were "selling out." That was particularly true when firms in certain strategic sectors were sold. Nonetheless, experience has shown that all of the Central and East European countries have needed to attract foreign capital in order to provide the investment resources and expertise necessary to fuel growth. FDI brings modern technologies, know-how, new forms of management, and an altogether different corporate culture. Thus, foreign investment is recognized as a way of speeding up the restructuring of companies and helping to improve their overall competitiveness. It also accelerates a country's access to global markets. Foreign-owned companies have often had much stronger export sales than domestic ones, particularly during the early transition years.

Much of the FDI in the Central and Eastern Europe region was initially concentrated in a few manufacturing branches, such as automobiles and automotive components, electronics, food processing (particularly soft drinks, breweries, dairies, and sweets), tobacco, and construction materials. Investments in retail trade were also significant. From the mid-1990s, states began selling their shares in the strategic utilities, telecom, and banking sectors, with foreign investors often gaining significant stakes. FDI in the banking sector has been especially important, bringing in more competition, a greater variety of products, and higher levels of expertise. In countries such as Slovakia and the Czech Republic, there was initially considerable opposition to sales of key banks to foreigners. Nonetheless, by the time the privatizations took place, the banking sectors in those countries were in such poor shape that there were few protests.

Although there are many advantages to investing in the Central and East European region, transition economies are in certain respects risky for foreign investors. Labor regulations and taxes are frequently complex and subject to rapid change,

Photo 3.2.   With the demise of communism and the influx of Western capital, there was a rush of construction in the capitals of the former Central and East European states. Here is the main street of Warsaw with the old train station and new high-rises.
(Source: Corbis)

according to the whims of policy makers. Relatively high levels of corruption and insider trading exist, and many countries in the region have experienced serious problems with corporate governance, as company managers have often felt little responsibility to shareholders. Company registration has also been difficult, with barriers to small business and smaller-scale investors. Privatization negotiations have frequently been long and difficult, with significant political interference. Meanwhile, bankruptcy procedures have been complicated by an inadequate justice system. Finally, exchange rate volatility has added substantial risk.

During the 1990s, most of the FDI in the region went to Poland, Hungary, and the Czech Republic, all of which proved to be good locations for investment due to the rapid liberalization of foreign trade, the proximity to Western markets (resulting in low transportation costs), the relatively large size of domestic markets, high levels of technical education, much lower wages than their West European neighbors, and relatively good infrastructure. Moreover, the fact that the three countries were seen as front-runners in the EU accession process made investment especially attractive.

As it became clear that additional countries would be included in the first wave of the EU enlargement process, FDI also rose rapidly elsewhere. By the end of 2004, cumulative FDI per capita was highest in the Czech Republic, followed by Estonia, Hungary, Slovenia, Slovakia, Croatia, Latvia, Poland, and Lithuania (see table 3.2). It is not by accident that eight of the nine—with the exception of Croatia—were in the first group to join the EU in 2004. Investors in the new EU member states have the advantage of operating in the same legal and regulatory environment as their main markets. Moreover, EU membership is generally seen as a guarantee of a certain degree of political stability as well as the existence of enforceable contracts should problems occur. More risky countries require higher returns to make the investment worthwhile. While Serbia has achieved considerable success in attracting FDI since the fall of Slobodan Milošević in 2000, most investments have been linked to privatization.

Looking Forward

Some ten to twelve years after the transition began, the more advanced countries in the Central and East European region had completed the vast majority of the post-communist economic reforms. That was particularly true in the case of the eight states that joined the EU in May 2004. In recent years, the leading economies have shifted their focus instead to issues that are also being faced by their counterparts in Western

Table 3.2.   Cumulative FDI per Capita, 2004 (in USD)

Country	FDI
Czech Republic	4,100
Estonia	3,600
Hungary	2,600
Slovenia	2,550
Slovakia	2,300
Croatia	2,000
Latvia	1,500
Poland	1,500
Lithuania	1,300
Bulgaria	1,100
Romania	700
Macedonia	500
Serbia	500
Albania	500
Bosnia	400
Ukraine	200

Source: Global Insight

Europe and elsewhere in the world, including taxation, pension, and health-care reform. Other key concerns for the ten Central and Eastern Europe countries that joined the EU in May 2004 and January 2007 are preparation for joining the euro zone and the convergence of incomes with the wealthier West European economies. At the same time, they must deal with the emergence of poverty and growing disparities in income.

ADOPTING THE EURO

The ten Central and Eastern Europe countries that acceded to the EU in 2004 and 2007 are all expected eventually to join the Economic and Monetary Union (EMU), meaning that they will use the euro as their national currency. In order to do so, they must first meet the criteria on inflation, interest rates, fiscal deficits, national debt, and exchange rate stability that were laid out in the EU's 1992 Maastricht treaty. Inflation must fall below the "reference value," with the rate of consumer price inflation not exceeding the average in the three best-performing EU member states (excluding those countries with negative inflation) by more than 1.5 percentage points. Likewise, average nominal long-term interest rates must be no higher than 2 percentage points above the three best-performing member states. The public finance deficit must be less than (or in some cases only slightly above) 3 percent of GDP, while public debt must be below 60 percent of GDP. Prior to entering the euro zone, each country must join the Exchange Rate Mechanism-II (ERM-II), which serves as an EMU waiting room. Upon entry to the ERM-II, a country pegs its currency to the euro, keeping the exchange rate within 15 percent of its central rate. A country must remain in the ERM-II for two years, without a currency devaluation, before being allowed to adopt the euro.

Those criteria are not viewed symmetrically by the EU. A revaluation of the currency against the euro is more tolerable than a devaluation. One criterion that is somewhat flexible concerns public debt, as countries with debt over the 60 percent limit have been accepted to the euro zone in the past, so long as the overall share was declining. In any case, Eurostat data published in April 2007 showed that all ten of the Central and East European member states—including Romania and Bulgaria, which joined in January of that year—fulfilled the public debt criteria as of 2006, with the exception of Hungary. Hungary's public-debt-to-GDP ratio was somewhat above the limit, at 66 percent.

Three of the new Central and Eastern Europe member states (Estonia, Slovenia, and Lithuania) entered the ERM-II in June 2004. All three countries initially hoped to adopt the euro in 2007, which was the earliest possible date for the new member states. Nonetheless, only Slovenia was given approval by the European Commission to join the EMU in 2007, as both Estonia and Lithuania were delayed by inflation rates that were above the Maastricht limit. Inflation has been a particular challenge in the Baltic states because the currency pegs do not allow for exchange rate fluctuations, meaning that real appreciation must occur through inflation. Given their problems in bringing down inflation, it is now assumed that Estonia and Lithuania will not be able to adopt the euro until around 2010–2011. Both countries have maintained currency boards throughout the transition, meaning that accession to the EMU will be a relatively simple process. Still, Estonia's high current-account deficit (at over 10 percent of GDP through 2006) may be cause for some concern. Having joined the ERM-II almost one year after its Baltic neighbors (in May 2005), Latvia's euro zone accession was initially expected in 2008. However, as in Estonia and Lithuania, stubbornly high inflation meant that EMU membership for Latvia was also unlikely before 2010–2011.

At the time of EU accession, the four Visegrad countries all had problems that would prevent them from adopting the euro in the near term. Public finances were seen as the biggest obstacle for Poland, Hungary, the Czech Republic, and Slovakia. In 2004, all four of those countries had deficits that were close to or above the Maastricht limit of 3.0 percent of GDP (see table 3.3). Nonetheless, the challenge of meeting the Maastricht fiscal criteria was eased by March 2005 revisions to the European Council's Stability and Growth Pact that allowed countries to exclude a gradually reduced share of pension reform costs from total public finance expenditures in 2005–2009. Even without those changes, Slovakia appeared to be on track to reduce its public finance deficit to less than the 3.0 percent level by 2007, thanks to extensive reforms that were implemented in 2003–2005. Slovakia joined the ERM-II in November 2005, and euro adoption was widely expected in 2009. Still, the change in government following the June 2006 parliamentary elections presented some risks in regard to both fiscal policy and inflation.

In contrast to the other new EU member states, Hungary, Poland, and the Czech Republic are unlikely to accede to the EMU before 2012–2013 or even beyond. The fiscal situation is particularly worrisome in Hungary, as the government has consistently overshot its budget deficit targets. Although the Czech Republic recorded good fiscal results in 2004–2006, the country was reluctant to implement reforms that would keep deficits under control in the medium to long term. Most notably, the Czech Republic lagged behind others in the region in regard to pension reform.

Even after the larger Central European countries meet the Maastricht criteria, euro zone accession may be pushed back even further for political reasons. It makes sense for small countries such as the Baltic states and Slovenia to accede to the euro zone as soon as possible. Advantages include the reduction of exchange rate risks, lower interest rates, and the elimination of transaction costs associated with maintaining a national currency. Those factors should help attract investment and contribute

Table 3.3. Public Finance Deficit, 2003–2005, as a Share of GDP

Country	2003	2004	2005
EU-15	−2.9	−2.6	−2.3
Estonia	2	2.3	2.3
Latvia	−1.2	−0.9	0.1
Lithuania	−1.3	−1.5	−0.5
Slovenia	−2.8	−2.3	−1.4
Slovakia	−3.7	−3	−3.1
Poland	−4.7	−3.9	−2.5
Czech Republic	−6.6	−2.9	−3.6
Hungary	−6.3	−5.3	−6.5

Source: Eurostat, October 2006

to real economic convergence. Nonetheless, some politicians and economic analysts in the larger Central European countries have been more hesitant, preferring to maintain a national currency as long as possible in order to have more control over domestic economic policy.

TAXATION REFORM

Accession to the EU has spurred a third round of taxation reforms in many of the Central and East European countries, with the aim of raising competitiveness, simplifying the taxation system, and ensuring a reduction in budget deficits. The need to meet the Maastricht criteria for entry into the euro zone was seen as a key impetus for fiscal reforms in Slovakia, for example. Nonetheless, the Maastricht budget requirements are also important in providing a basis for healthy medium- and long-term economic growth. If budget deficits are not brought under control, macroeconomic balance could be threatened, particularly once privatization revenues run out.

There are several justifications for introducing more competitive taxation policies. First of all, transfers from the EU budget have been considerably lower with the 2004 enlargement round than they were in the case of countries such as Portugal and Greece. Thus, the new member states must rely on other factors to spur development. In the new member states, GDP per capita in 2005 ranged from just 47.2 percent of the EU-25 average in Latvia to 80.6 percent in Slovenia (see table 3.4). Strong investment inflows are seen as a prerequisite for the more rapid GDP growth that is needed to help countries catch up with the income levels in Western Europe. Once in the EU, however, member states are limited in the kinds of incentives they can offer to foreign investors. Many of the perks provided by Hungary in the 1990s are no longer permitted. Moreover, the new EU member states are now struggling to attract investments that are not based on low wages alone, given that salaries are rising as the countries become increasingly integrated with the West. Thus, countries must look for other ways of bringing in investment.

Table 3.4.   GDP per Capita, 2005

Country	GDP
Slovenia	80.6
Czech Republic	73.8
Hungary	61.4
Estonia	60.1
Slovakia	55
Lithuania	52.1
Poland	49.8
Latvia	47.2
Croatia	48.8
Romania	34.7
Bulgaria	32.1
Macedonia	25.9

Note: Calculated in PPS terms; EU-25 = 100. PPS is Purchasing Power Standard, which calculates GDP by taking into account differences in prices across countries.
Source: Eurostat, June 2006

In the older EU countries, the so-called European social model makes reforms difficult, given strong labor unions and the need for consensus in social dialogue. In contrast, the new member states have found it easier to implement sweeping changes. Slovakia was the regional leader in introducing a taxation system that was simple and attractive to investors, with very little formal protest. While Estonia introduced a flat income tax in the early years of its transition, spurring several other countries to follow suit, Slovakia became the first to adopt that approach at a more advanced stage of reforms. Slovakia's flat tax took effect in January 2004, just months before the country's EU entry. Slovakia's taxation changes applied not only to individuals, but also to corporations, all at a flat rate of 19 percent. Moreover, the country's VAT rate was unified at a rate of 19 percent, while the government canceled the inheritance, dividends, real estate transfers, and gift taxes. Although considerable doubts emerged before those changes took effect, the impact on tax collection was surprisingly positive in 2004–2005. That was particularly true in regard to the corporate income tax, as the new system helped to reduce tax evasion. There were some negative effects of the taxation reforms, however. In 2005, Slovakia's VAT rate was among the highest in the EU. Although the reforms benefited poor and wealthier citizens, they slightly increased the tax burden on middle-income Slovaks, at least in the short term.[13] The social consequences of the reforms hurt the center-right government in the 2006 elections, as support for left-leaning parties grew.

Slovakia's tax changes have triggered reform efforts elsewhere in Europe, particularly in neighboring countries. In 2004, Poland's corporate income tax rate was reduced to the same rate as in Slovakia, while the rate in Hungary was brought down to just 16 percent. The Czech Republic began to gradually lower its corporate income tax rate starting in 2004, and Austria was forced to lower its rate as of January 2005. Initial reactions from countries such as Germany and France to tax reforms in the new member states were not positive, and Slovakia and other so-called neoliberal states were accused of "tax dumping." France and Germany went so far as to call for the harmonization of taxation rates within the EU to prevent firms from moving eastward to benefit from more advantageous conditions. Currently, taxation and social policy are up to the individual member states, and pressure from new accession countries as well as the United Kingdom and Ireland will likely keep things that way. At just 12.5 percent in 2005, Ireland's corporate income tax rate was still well below that in the EU member states from Central and Eastern Europe.

The tax changes in Central Europe and the Baltic states have inspired other EU hopefuls. Serbia imposed a flat corporate tax rate of just 10 percent in August 2004, the lowest rate in Europe, while Montenegro went one notch further in January 2006, to 9 percent. Romania implemented a flat corporate income tax at a 16 percent rate as of January 2005.

One area that still remains problematic in many Central and East European countries is the high level of payroll taxes that firms are expected to withhold from employees' paychecks. While enterprises have largely been freed of the burden of providing social services, they have not been exempt from paying for them. Payments for unemployment compensation and pensions are largely funded by payroll taxes, which can be very high, at up to 50 percent of the nominal wage rate. High payroll taxes discourage job creation and drive economic activity underground, thus reducing the tax base.

Although in other respects Slovakia's taxation system was seen as a model for establishing a business-friendly environment, in 2005 the country still had one of the highest payroll tax rates in the OECD (Organization for Economic Cooperation and Development) as a share of gross wages, with the Czech Republic close behind. Reducing payroll taxes would help reduce long-term unemployment rates, particularly for low-income workers.

SOCIAL POLICY REFORM

Social policy is one of the most difficult aspects of the reform process, as such changes are extremely unpopular politically. The Visegrad countries inherited very comprehensive social safety nets from the communist period, featuring such perks as free health care, free education through graduate school, extensive paid maternity leave for women, and full pensions even if no contributions had been made. Many of those policies were maintained during the 1990s. Thus, the Central European countries were considered premature welfare states, with levels of social security benefits found in countries with much higher per capita GDPs. By contrast, the CIS countries generally had underdeveloped welfare states during the transition period, given the difficult budgetary constraints.

In carrying out reforms, one of the key concerns was to better target the benefits provided so they would reach the people who needed them the most. Much of the traditional safety net was regressive, with the bulk of the subsidies going to those who were already relatively well off. For example, across-the-board subsidies for household electricity and natural gas were especially beneficial for people with large homes, while

Photo 3.3.   Homeless man in Budapest. The transition to democracy and difficult economic reforms profoundly affected vulnerable segments of the populations, as the governments often had to cut welfare programs to adjust the economy.

(Source: Daniel Nemeth)

those with smaller dwellings received less. Thus, one way of addressing that imbalance was to raise household electricity prices to market levels, while providing subsidies for lower-income people.

Another key question relates to which agencies and levels of government should be charged with administering benefits. Two conflicting principles exist in that regard. First, if policies are made by national governments, statewide standards are established. Thus, a country avoids the situation where regions compete for business by lowering taxation rates and providing fewer benefits. At the same time, however, putting policy making in the hands of regional or local governments may help promote experimentation and provide more accountability. There is no single standard in the EU; France embodies the first alternative and Germany the latter approach. Several of the new EU member states, including Poland and Slovakia, have implemented administrative reforms aimed at achieving decentralization.

The pension system has been one of the key concerns of policy makers in the realm of social welfare reform. That is particularly true in countries such as Hungary, where the aging population would have resulted in a fiscal meltdown if reforms were not implemented. Pension reforms generally include raising the retirement age, taxing working pensioners, shifting the formulas by which pensions are indexed, and moving toward a system that is based on employee contributions. International organizations such as the World Bank urged Central and East European countries to privatize their pension systems, in line with the models developed by Chile and other Latin American countries. Thus, countries were encouraged to shift from a pay-as-you-go system, where today's workers pay the benefits for current retirees, to one with personal accounts. The new approach is often referred to as a "three-pillar system," with the first pillar constituting a downsized pay-as-you-go scheme and the second pillar comprising personal accounts. The third pillar is optional and refers to voluntary private savings accounts. The new approach to pensions was intended to encourage savings, while at the same time improving the long-term health of state finances.[14]

Hungary and Poland were the first countries in the Central and East European region to pursue pension reform along the Chilean model, transforming their pension systems in 1998 and 1999, respectively. They were followed by Latvia (2001), Bulgaria, Croatia, Estonia (all 2002), Lithuania (2004), and Slovakia (2005). The costs of switching from one system to another were quite large. Nonetheless, privatization revenues provided a good source of funding, helping to make the reforms socially acceptable by avoiding large hikes in taxation rates. Participation in the new pension system was generally mandatory for new workers but optional for older citizens. Still, the personal accounts were more popular than expected among older workers, signaling distrust in the old system and expectations of higher yields from private funds.[15]

POVERTY

Countries in the Central and East European region began the transition with one of the lowest levels of income inequality in the world; however, that situation has been changing. While high inflation impoverishes society as a whole, stabilization programs can harm certain groups, particularly those who are living on fixed incomes or who are reliant on the state for transfers. The incidence of poverty also appears to be associated with high jobless rates, particularly when combined with states' increasing frugality in providing unemployment benefits. The loss of a stable income is the main cause of poverty throughout the region.[16] In terms of demographic groups, poverty is generally found more frequently among citizens with low levels of education and skills, those living in rural areas, those with large families, and among women and children.

While poverty and inequality have emerged as a real problem in some CIS countries, they are generally less severe in Central and Eastern Europe than in other transitional societies. That may be partly due to the high levels of literacy in the postcommunist world, the close proximity to Western Europe, as well as better-targeted social benefits. Some citizens supplement their income with household garden plots and occasional employment, while others work in the informal economy. Many urban families depend on relatives in the countryside for certain agricultural goods. Populations in countries such as Albania have survived mainly thanks to foreign assistance and workers' remittances, as citizens move to Greece and Italy in search of work, sending their earnings back home to their families. Despite rising poverty levels in the 1990s, purchases of consumer durables also increased significantly in many countries, partly due to the declining prices of such goods relative to salaries.

While poverty levels may stop growing or even decline once a country's economy strengthens, certain groups have continued to suffer. The situation is particularly severe among Roma, whose share of the total population varies from less than 1 percent in Poland to nearly 10 percent in Slovakia. In absolute terms, Romania has by far the biggest Romani population, at an estimated 1.8 million. Throughout the region, Roma generally have lower levels of education than the rest of the population. For example, an estimated one million Romanian Roma are illiterate. They frequently face racial discrimination in hiring, resulting in jobless rates that are much higher than the rest of the population, at about 70 percent in Slovakia and 85 percent in the Czech Republic. Moreover, the housing of Roma is often poor and sometimes lacks electricity and running water.[17] Although efforts have been made by various governments and international institutions to alleviate poverty among Roma, the obstacles are great, and progress has been slow.

When Is the Transition Complete?

Despite the challenges still faced throughout the Central and East European region, many countries have managed to emerge from the shadow of communism. In economic terms, the transition is deemed complete when soft-budget constraints are eliminated and formerly state-owned companies begin performing like competitive enterprises. Thus, the end of the transition is defined as the point when the wide differential in the productivity of labor and capital among new versus old firms that exists at the start of the transition has eroded. It marks a time when there are no more distinctions between old, restructured, and new companies.[18] Policy makers are no longer focused on issues that are specific to the postcommunist transition, but instead are facing problems shared by more advanced, Western economies.

While most of the new EU member states have reached the end of the postcommunist transition period, at least in economic terms, significant challenges remain in many of the Balkan and CIS countries. Fortunately, the states that are further behind have the advantage of being able to study the various reform models implemented by their counterparts in Central Europe and the Baltics to determine the appropriateness of certain policies in their own countries. That may help the Balkans and CIS to move forward more rapidly, once they adopt a pro-reform course.

Suggested Readings

Åslund, Anders. *Building Capitalism: The Transformation of the Former Soviet Bloc*. Cambridge, UK: Cambridge University Press, 2002.

Bell, Janice. *Unemployment in Transition: Restructuring and Labour Markets in Central Europe* (Economies in Transition to the Market). New York: Routledge, 2000.

Dubrowski, Marek, and Ben Slay, eds. *Beyond Transition: Development Perspectives and Dilemmas*. London: Ashgate, 2004.

Ekiert, Grzegorz, and Stephen E. Hanson, eds. *Capitalism and Democracy in Central and Eastern Europe*. Cambridge, UK: Cambridge University Press, 2006.

European Bank for Reconstruction and Development (EBRD). *Transition Report 2000: Employment, Skills and Transition*. (London: EBRD, 2000).

Frydman, Roman, Kenneth Murphy, and Andrzej Rapaczynski. *Capitalism with a Comrade's Face*. Budapest, Hungary: CEU Press, 1998.

Funck, Bernard, and Lodovico Pizzati, eds. *Labor, Employment, and Social Policies in the EU Enlargement Process: Changing Perspectives and Policy Options*. Washington, DC: The World Bank, 2002.

Kornai, Janos. *The Socialist System: The Political Economy of Communism*. Princeton, NJ: Princeton University Press, 1992.

Lavigne, Marie. *The Economics of Transition: From Socialist Economy to Market Economy*, 2nd ed. New York: Palgrave Macmillan, 1999.

World Bank. *Transition: The First Ten Years*. Washington, DC: The World Bank, 2002.

Notes

1. See World Bank, *Transition: The First Ten Years* (Washington, DC: The World Bank, 2002), chapter 2.

2. European Bank for Reconstruction and Development (EBRD), *Transition Report 2000: Employment, Skills and Transition* (London: EBRD, 2000), 18–19.

3. For more on the communist economic system and its collapse, see Anders Åslund, *Building Capitalism: The Transformation of the Former Soviet Bloc* (Cambridge, UK: Cambridge University Press, 2002), chapters 1 and 2.

4. The first three lessons are noted by Anders Åslund. See Åslund, *Building Capitalism*, 167–68.

5. Åslund, *Building Capitalism*, 238.

6. See Åslund, *Building Capitalism*, 227–32.

7. Åslund, *Building Capitalism*, 171.

8. For a listing by country, see EBRD, *Transition Report 2000*, 14.

9. Åslund, *Building Capitalism*, 222.

10. See EBRD, *Transition Report 2000*, 55, 69.

11. World Bank, *Transition*, 53.

12. Slovakia's second-stage stabilization policies and their causes are discussed in Katarína Mathernová and Juraj Rencko, "'Reformology': the Case of Slovakia" *Orbis* (Fall 2006): 629–40.

13. Peter Goliaš and Robert Kičina, "Slovak Tax Reform: One Year After," April 2005 (INEKO and Business Alliance of Slovakia).

14. World Bank, *Transition*, 81–83; Åslund, *Building Capitalism*, 344–45.

15. World Bank, *EU-8 Quarterly Economic Report* (April 2005).

16. EBRD, *Transition Report 2000*, 106.

17. Arno Tanner, "The Roma of Eastern Europe: Still Searching for Inclusion," 1 May 2005, Migration Information Source.

18. World Bank, *Transition*, xix.

CHAPTER 4

Ethnicity, Nationalism, and the Expansion of Democracy

Zsuzsa Csergo

As Central and East European societies emerged from communism, people throughout the region expressed their preference for democracy, free markets, and the European Union (EU). Many in the West expected the EU to supersede nationalism, with its traditional focus on the establishment of the territorially sovereign, culturally homogeneous nation-states. In earlier centuries, efforts to achieve such congruence between the political and national unit in Europe involved aggressive efforts to change state boundaries, eject or assimilate nonconforming groups to "purify" the nation, or encourage minority populations to repatriate to other countries.[1] By the end of the 1980s, such methods of nation-state creation were no longer acceptable in the western part of the continent. The European Union seemed to offer the best prospect for moving beyond the era of the traditional nation-state.

A lesson that much of the scholarly literature about nationalism drew from Western European development in this period was that, if democratization and marketization could progress unhindered, politics grounded in ethnic and national identity would lose its relevance, and more advanced—rational, individualist, and inclusive—notions of citizenship would take its place.[2] These were the thoughts voiced from within the Iron Curtain during the communist decades by dissident Czech, Hungarian, Polish, and other intellectuals who articulated alternative visions of a free society and spoke poignantly about universal human values and inalienable individual rights and freedoms.

Against the backdrop of such expectations, the story of Central and Eastern Europe after the collapse of the communist regimes is filled with reasons for disappointment. Even after the initial euphoria over the end of communism, the voices expressing themselves most forcefully spoke about "nationhood" and, in the overwhelming majority of cases, exalted the supposed inalienable rights of groups rather than individuals. Ethnically conceived national groups all over the postcommunist countries of Central and Eastern Europe viewed democratization as the opportunity finally to achieve or consolidate national sovereignty over territories they claimed as their "national homelands." All three multinational federations (the Soviet Union,

Yugoslavia, and Czechoslovakia) fell apart as a result of such aspirations. Of the seventeen countries commonly considered to belong to this region, twelve were established or reestablished after 1989 along national lines. Only five countries continued within their existing borders, and of these Bulgaria and Romania began the difficult process of regime change away from communism by first reasserting themselves as "nation-states" against the aspirations of national minority groups.

Clearly, nationalism not only remained relevant after the collapse of communism, but it emerged as the most powerful ideology that most important and popular political elites and parties advanced and that publics in these countries found appealing. At the same time, the desire to "return to Europe" and join Western institutions also were very significant throughout the region. In some cases, aspirations to strengthen national cultures while joining an integrated Europe seemed fully compatible. For instance, people throughout the West cheered the fall of the Berlin Wall and the subsequent reunification of the German state. Although wary of the disintegration of the Soviet state, Westerners also celebrated the reestablishment of the three Baltic states as examples of forward-looking, Western-oriented nationalism. When mass nationalist violence broke out in former Yugoslavia, however, influential public voices in the West began asking whether Central and East Europeans were returning to their violent past rather than transitioning into a peaceful and prosperous future in a common European home. Some argued that ancient hatreds made the rebirth of nationalism inevitable in such places as the Balkans.[3] Others argued that it was the process of democratization that engendered manipulative elites' interests to employ nationalism.[4]

Developments in other parts of the world since 1989 have demonstrated that neither the popular appeal of nationalism nor the problems that this ideology poses for democratic governance are specific to the postcommunist region. Nationalism is a powerful ideology throughout the contemporary world. Wherever political elites and publics design nationalist strategies, the process reveals sources of tension rooted in the "Janus-faced" character of nationalism: as with other political ideologies, nationalism is forward-looking in the sense that it articulates a vision about a national future; at the same time, nationalist strategies almost always call for turning to the past for self-definition.[5] When nationalists claim self-government rights for "the nation" on a "national" territory or "homeland," they usually offer a certain interpretation of history to justify these claims. Whether such a historiography relies on historical evidence is less important for nationalism than the degree to which it can foster a sense of shared history and purpose. To express this idea, "national myth" is the term most often used to describe national stories. Some national myths have been more successful than others in accommodating ethnic diversity. The so-called civic type of nationalism, which builds community on shared political traditions, is potentially more inclusive than "ethnic nationalism," which requires members of the nation to share a common ethnicity. Nonetheless, even countries commonly considered textbook cases of "civic nationalism," such as Britain, France, and the United States, reveal striking similarities to "ethnic nationalism," as schools, churches, the media, the military, and various other state and private or public institutions perpetuate unified national stories and literatures, and mental maps of national homelands.[6]

In many instances, the national myth contains stories about ethnic competition over territory, invoking memories of past ethnic dominance and subordination, which

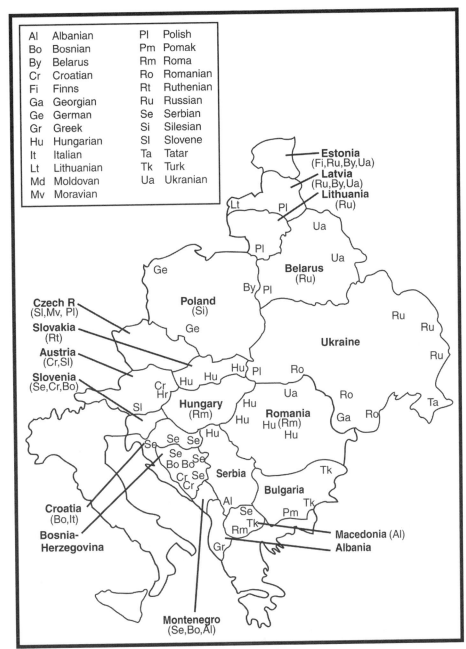

Al	Albanian	Pl	Polish
Bo	Bosnian	Pm	Pomak
By	Belarus	Rm	Roma
Cr	Croatian	Ro	Romanian
Fi	Finns	Rt	Ruthenian
Ga	Georgian	Ru	Russian
Ge	German	Se	Serbian
Gr	Greek	Si	Silesian
Hu	Hungarian	Sl	Slovene
It	Italian	Ta	Tatar
Lt	Lithuanian	Tk	Turk
Md	Moldovan	Ua	Ukranian
Mv	Moravian		

Map 4.1. Ethnic Concentrations in Central and Eastern Europe, 2007

continue to influence current state- and nation-building processes.[7] Yet not all ethnic groups engage in national competition. A key difference between ethnic and national groups is that although ethnic groups aim to reproduce particular cultures, only national groups claim self-government rights on a particular territory. In postcommunist Central and Eastern Europe, the majority and minority groups that articulated competing notions of self-government rights were national groups that defined "nation" on the basis of ethnic markers—most commonly language, in some cases religion. Despite this commonality, significant differences emerged in the ways in which national aspirations were articulated and posed against one another throughout the region. Before offering explanations for these differences, the following pages provide a brief account of state and nation building in the period that preceded democratization and how these processes created the conditions in which postcommunist democratization and nationalism subsequently took shape.

Nationalism before Democratic Competition

The pursuit of modern nation-states by nationalist political elites and counter-elites within the Hapsburg Empire began in the second part of the nineteenth century, and the dynamics of these efforts highlighted the fundamentally competitive character of modern nationalism. Whether in the framework of the multinational Hapsburg state (reconstituted after 1867 as the dualist Austro-Hungarian Empire) or its successor states, the nationalist policies that a dominant ethnic group adopted invariably triggered resentment and engendered conflicting nationalist aspirations from other groups. It was during this process that national literatures emerged in vernacular languages, and that national historiographies were written and became justifications for nationalist demands. Czechs and Hungarians defined their national myths and aspirations in opposition to Austria's Germans. After the creation of the dualist state, the same pattern remained characteristic in both parts of the monarchy. In the Austrian part, Czechs and Slovenes challenged German cultural dominance and articulated unsuccessful calls for national sovereignty. In the Hungarian part, the nationalist movements of non-Hungarians (Slovaks, Croats, and Romanians) encountered similar rejection by Hungarian elites.[8] Besides challenging one another, nationalist political elites also competed for international support and legitimization for their conflicting notions of national power. The complex matrix of these domestic and international interests led Austria-Hungary into the First World War and, at the end of the war, resulted in the dissolution of the monarchy into its successor states.

When the victorious powers agreed to establish the successor states at the end of the First World War, they relied on the Wilsonian principle of national self-determination. The demographic patterns of the region, however, made the delineation of clear "national" borders impossible. The states created to bring justice to previously subordinate national groups of the monarchy also became multinational, with new "titular" nations attempting to establish political and cultural hegemony over national minorities. Although relations of dominance and subordination were reversed after the dissolution of the Austro-Hungarian state, the same pattern of nation building continued, with multiple groups sharing the same state but holding conflicting notions of sovereignty.

Sovereignty is one of the fundamental principles of political organization and also one of the most contested because it takes different forms, and these forms are at times incompatible with one another.[9] As Barkin and Cronin observe, "there has been a historical tension between state sovereignty, which stresses the link between sovereign authority and a defined territory, and national sovereignty, which emphasizes a link between sovereign authority and a defined population."[10] This tension had become particularly apparent in Central and Eastern Europe by the mid-nineteenth century and remained salient throughout the region's history. Yugoslavia, created to provide southern Slav peoples with a common state, in reality comprised a diversity of national groups that maintained strong prejudices and reproaches against one another. A famous expression of Slovene prejudices, for instance, is the 1927 statement by Catholic party leader Korošec: "In Yugoslavia it is thus: the Serbs rule, the Croats debate, and the Slovenes work."[11] Even in Czechoslovakia, where the leadership established the strongest democratic institutions in the region, large national minority populations remained discontented with their status and continued to challenge the legitimacy of the new state.

With the political principle of national self-determination internationally legitimized, competing nationalist aspirations crystallized in the interwar period and formed the basis for strategies that later escalated into some of the atrocities committed during World War II. The Hungarian government focused its efforts on regaining lost territories and population. Wary of this Hungarian policy of irredentism, neighboring governments that had gained significant territories from historic Hungary designed aggressive economic and cultural policies to achieve more effective control over those territories and their inhabitants. Greater Romania, for example, based its institutional policies primarily on reordering the ethnic hierarchy in Transylvania in favor of Romanian dominance.[12] Hungarian organizations forcefully challenged these policies. Similarly, in Czechoslovakia many Germans and Hungarians joined political parties that challenged the legitimacy of the state. These groups felt vindicated when Hitler dismembered Czechoslovakia in 1938, occupied the Czech Lands, and helped to redraw contested political borders throughout the region. The supposed right of the sizable German-speaking population of interwar Czechoslovakia, the Sudeten Germans, to belong to a common German nation-state served as a pretext for Hitler's destruction of the Czechoslovak state. After Germany's show of military might, the governments of Hungary, Romania, and Slovakia (a state that Hitler helped create) each became Hitler's allies at various times of the war, trusting that their participation on the victor's side would help them establish, reclaim, or maintain sovereignty over mutually claimed "national" territories and peoples. As a result of Hitler's policies the Hungarian government was able to reannex two regions with majority Hungarian populations (the southern region of Czechoslovakia in November 1938, and northern Transylvania between 1940 and 1944). These sudden reversals of fortune were as traumatic to the Slovak and Romanian inhabitants of these territories as they had been for Hungarians after World War I. After the defeat of the Axis powers at the end of World War II, the post–World War I borders were reestablished, and the conditions for nationalist policies changed significantly.

Nationalist competition contributed also to the collapse of Yugoslavia in 1941, when Hitler and Mussolini divided the state among Germany, Italy, Hungary, and Bulgaria, and established in the center of the former federation a Croatian state ruled by the fascist Ustaše. In the bloody civil wars that engulfed Yugoslavia in subsequent years, the Ustaša government led a violent campaign against Jews, Roma, Serbs, and other groups; Yugoslav Partisans fought to defend villagers against terror; and the extreme nationalists among Serbian Chetniks engaged in revenge attacks against ethnic Croatians and Muslims. By the end of the war, over a million people were killed, including Serbs, Croats, Bosnian-Herzegovinian Muslims, Danube Swabians (a German-speaking ethnic group), Jews, Slovenes, and Roma.

It was against the backdrop of such violence that many communist leaders in the

Photo 4.1.   Roma refugee camp in Zvecan, north of Kosovo, November 1999. Although the exact figure is unknown, millions of Roma live in often substandard conditions throughout Central and Eastern Europe and often have disproportionately high unemployment rates.

(Source: Lubomir Kotek/OSCE)

region, among whom ethnic minorities were represented in disproportionately high numbers, viewed internationalism as an appealing alternative to nationalism. Although communism provided leaders with unprecedented power to conduct "social engineering," none of these regimes succeeded in creating homogeneity in societies where multiple groups had earlier competed with each other for national rights. There emerged no "non-national" Yugoslav people in Yugoslavia or Czechoslovaks in Czechoslovakia, capable of holding these federations together when the communist regimes began collapsing in 1989. The Soviet state was similarly unable to engender non-national identities and loyalties.

Despite an initial emphasis on internationalism, in practice nationalism remained a key organizing principle during the communist period. In Yugoslavia, the communist leader Josip Broz Tito made the eradication of national antagonisms his primary goal in 1945 and suppressed all overt manifestations of ethnic sentiment. Nonetheless, by the end of the 1960s, Slovenian, Croatian, Serbian, and other national identities were reasserting themselves in literature and arts, and by the mid-1970s these groups achieved self-government in the constituent republics of the Yugoslav federation. In the other part of the region that fell under Moscow's dominance, each of the "brotherly states" of Central and Eastern Europe pursued its own brand of nationalism in domestic politics.[13] The postwar Czechoslovak government, for instance, declared ethnic Germans and Hungarians collectively guilty of having contributed to Hitler's destruction of Czechoslovakia, and gained Soviet approval for the expulsion of these ethnic groups from the country. Based on the so-called Beneš Decrees (named after the state's president, Eduard Beneš), Czechoslovakia expelled the overwhelming majority of ethnic Germans to Germany and a large percentage of the Hungarian population, including much of the Hungarian educated class, to Hungary.[14] Those who remained in the state were denied citizenship rights until 1948. Despite such a drastic policy to achieve an ethnic balance favoring the state's two titular groups, the Czechs and the Slovaks, a significant number of Hungarians remained in the Slovak part of Czechoslovakia. Throughout the communist decades, they were subject to economic, cultural, and educational policies that severely restricted their ability to reproduce their culture and improve their socioeconomic status. The relationship between the Czechs and the Slovaks was also tense from the beginning of cohabitation. Initial notions of a unified Czechoslovak identity were soon replaced by efforts to loosen Prague's control over the Slovak part of the land in a federal structure that better represented national interests.

Compared to Czechoslovakia, the postwar Romanian communist government adopted more minority-friendly policies. Because the ethnic Hungarian party was instrumental in the communist takeover in Romania, Hungarian minority leaders gained Moscow's support in achieving full citizenship rights, participation in the government, and the right to maintain cultural and educational institutions. The same Soviet government that in Czechoslovakia gave its full support to President Beneš's policies to expel the German and Hungarian minorities facilitated the establishment of regional autonomy for Hungarians in Transylvania in 1952 in Romania. Although this autonomous region was short-lived, the first communist-dominated Romanian government was much better disposed toward minorities overall than was the Beneš government in Czechoslovakia.[15] As the influence of ethnic Hungarian leaders in the

Communist Party weakened, however, the government launched a nationalizing strategy that severely weakened the political status and social structure of the Hungarian community in Transylvania. Beginning in the mid-1960s, the government of Nicolae Ceaușescu launched a ruthless strategy to consolidate a centralized unitary national state. Ethnic Germans were offered incentives to emigrate to West Germany, and Hungarians were subjected to administrative, economic, and educational policies aimed at their assimilation.

Of the unitary communist states in the region, Poland and Hungary were the only two that did not have sizable national minority groups. The small ethnic communities that existed in these states presented no systematic challenge to majority cultural dominance. Within the framework of the Moscow-led communist camp, the Hungarian government also indicated little interest in influencing the conditions of ethnic Hungarians living in the neighboring states. Under such circumstances, the significance of the national principle appeared less prominent in either case than it did in the region's multinational states. Yet the absence of internal national minorities did not make nationalist motivations irrelevant in these countries. In Poland, national aspirations contributed to the emergence of Solidarity, the most powerful anticommunist movement in the region in the 1980s. In Hungary, interest in the national principle strengthened by the end of the 1980s, especially with regard to Hungarian minorities living in the neighboring states.

Democratization and Nationalist Competition

With the collapse of communism came the promise of change, and for majorities and minorities alike change brought a chance to redefine old ideas of citizenship and self-government. At the beginning of the process, most societies in the region experienced a unifying spirit of euphoria over the collapse of repressive regimes.[16] Democratization offered unprecedented opportunities for these societies to articulate differences through competitive elections, political parties, and parliamentary debates. The European Union offered a model of political integration and a way of transcending the nationalist competitions of the past. Yet the most influential political actors throughout the region articulated their intentions to achieve both stronger national sovereignty and European integration.

The international institutions that most of the newly elected governments aspired to join (NATO, the Council of Europe, the Organization for Security and Cooperation in Europe, the European Union) insisted on peaceful negotiations about sovereignty issues. In the aftermath of the Cold War, as various majority and minority groups in the region asserted claims for national self-government, Western international institutions reasserted the principle of individual rights, and also began adopting an impressive number of documents calling for the protection of the rights of minority cultures. These documents signaled increased international recognition that many states incorporate multiple nation-building processes, and tensions arising from these situations must find lasting solutions acceptable to all parties involved.[17]

Despite the relative consistency of international expectations and the shared objective of Central and East Europeans to return to a "common European home," the conditions under which this goal could be harmonized with nationalist aspirations varied. Consequently, there were significant variations in the way nationalism manifested itself throughout the region. The differences revealed themselves primarily in the goals that leaders and groups articulated and the strategies they designed to achieve those goals. An overwhelming nationalist goal in the region was to establish national entities by creating new states (in former Yugoslavia and Czechoslovakia) or reestablish precommunist state borders (in the Baltic region). Another form of nationalism pursued national dominance in existing states, despite minority opposition to this strategy (Romania and Bulgaria). A third form aimed at strengthening a common sense of nationhood beyond state borders (Hungary). The pages that follow offer explanations for these differences in nationalist strategy, emphasizing the influence of preexisting state structure (federal or unitary);[18] national composition (whether national strategies involve internal or external national minorities); and the choices of national elites (to what extent majority and minority elites were willing to negotiate their claims within the emerging democratic institutions, employing the prospects of NATO and European integration in the process).

FROM MULTINATIONAL FEDERATIONS TO NATIONAL STATES

The nationalist movements that pursued state formation emerged in the three multinational federations—Czechoslovakia, the Soviet Union, and Yugoslavia. Although each of the three dissolving federal states was ethnically diverse, only a limited number of groups defined themselves in national terms and claimed rights to national self-government. In each case, the titular groups of substate administrative units were most likely to claim such rights. These were the Serbs, Slovenians, Macedonians, Montenegrins, and Croatians in former Yugoslavia; the Czechs and Slovaks in former Czechoslovakia; and the Estonians, Latvians, and Lithuanians in the former Soviet Union. In each case, those engaged in state formation had to answer the following questions: What would be the physical boundaries of the successor states? What would "the nation" mean within those boundaries? Who belonged to the new political community and under what terms? And what should happen to those who did not belong? In all cases, the political elites that led the movements for national independence played a very important role in shaping the debates about these questions. They also had the task of finding the appropriate means for resolving any conflicts associated with national independence. In the great majority of cases, nationalist claims were negotiated peacefully, within the channels of democratic political competition. In other cases, however, democratic forms of parliamentary debate and party competition were unable to contain national conflicts, and these conflicts escalated into devastating wars.

Democratization Derailed: Nationalism in the Balkans

In former Yugoslavia, the substate borders of the republics did not coincide with people's mental maps of "historic homelands." Consequently, national self-determination became a vehemently contested idea in the Balkans, as multiple national groups living in a mixed demographic pattern claimed the same territory as "their own," and each group turned to a different national myth and conflicting interpretation of past relations of dominance and subordination, sacrifice and victimization.

Serbs and Croats comprised the majority of the state's population as well as the overwhelming majority of the three largest republics—Serbia (and its autonomous provinces, Kosovo and Vojvodina), Croatia, and Bosnia-Herzegovina. Approximately 24 percent of Serbs lived outside of the Republic of Serbia, 22 percent of Croats outside Croatia, and tensions between these two groups influenced interethnic relations throughout Yugoslavia. Montenegrins generally identified with Serbs, and Muslims lived intermixed with Serbs and Croats. Only Slovenia and Macedonia, with their very small Serbian and Croatian populations, were not drawn into Serbian-Croatian competition.[19] In such a context, successive unilateral declarations of independence by nationalist elites contributed to a cycle of conflict that marked the entire decade of the 1990s and caused devastation and horror not seen in Europe since World War II.

The unilateral declaration of independence triggered military intervention even in Slovenia, where no other groups had articulated competing national claims for the same territory. The Yugoslav federal military rolled in to prevent Slovenia's independence by force. The fight for independent Slovenia, however, was relatively uneventful compared to the brutal wars that followed it in other parts of the disintegrating state. The Yugoslav army by 1991 had evolved into primarily a Serbian army and, in the absence of Serbian claims for Slovenia as a "national homeland," European mediation was quickly able to convince the Yugoslav army to withdraw and hand over sovereignty to the Slovenian state in October 1991.

In other Yugoslav republics, where majority and minority political elites advanced competing and mutually incompatible claims for the same "national homeland," these claims were able to mobilize large-scale ethnic support that led to violent conflict. The Serb Democratic Party in the Krajina region of Croatia, for instance, immediately challenged the emerging Croatian movement for an independent state by demanding administrative and cultural autonomy for the Serb-majority region. Unable to achieve this goal immediately, the leaders of the four Serb-controlled areas declared the formation of the Serb Autonomous Region of Krajina in January 1991 and added in March the same year that this region would "dissociate" from an independent Croatia and remain within Yugoslavia.

This sequence of unilateral declarations of national sovereignty exacerbated an already existing distrust and hostility among these groups and helped trigger a devastating war in Croatia. The government of Croatia on one side and the Yugoslav state presidency and Serbia on the other employed armed forces to resolve the crisis. In a parallel development, the Croatian and Serbian inhabitants of the region also turned to violence against one another, each side attempting to resolve the sovereignty issue according to its own version of self-government rights. The war ended in 1995 with the help of U.S. and European mediation, and after brutal destruction in Croatian cities and villages, great suffering among the civilian population, and "ethnic cleans-ing" on both sides that resulted in the displacement of more than a half million refu-gees. Today, the independent Croatian state no longer incorporates significant national minority groups.

Competition over national sovereignty became particularly vicious in Bosnia-Herzegovina, a republic in which three groups began their fight for an acceptable state design in April 1992. The Party of Democratic Action, representing the majority Muslim population, advocated an independent and unitary Bosnia-Herzegovina, with no internal territorial division along national lines. The Serb Democratic Party first rejected separation from Yugoslavia and fought for a separate state in the Serb-populated areas—in the hope of future reunification with other Serbian-inhabited ter-ritories of (former) Yugoslavia. The Croat Democratic Union allied itself with the Muslim party against the Bosnian Serbs, but this cooperation remained tense, as the Croats claimed authority over the Croatian-populated regions and were also interested in the prospects of unification of these regions with Croatia. (In 1993, the Croats attempted to establish a Bosnian Croat state. In 1994, the Croat Democratic Union re-allied itself with the Muslim party to form a Croat-Muslim federation.) The war over the fate of Bosnia-Herzegovina lasted from 1992 to 1995, and involved the engagement of the Serbian and Croatian militaries as well as NATO forces. Although all three groups committed atrocities, Serbian troops were responsible for more crimes than their counterparts, and the Muslim population suffered most grievously.[20]

The Dayton agreement, reached through international mediation in 1995, cre-

Photo 4.2.   Croatian refugees fleeing from Bosnian forces in June of 1993 near Trav-nik, when the Herzegovinan Croats turned on the Bosnians creating an interally disas-ter. The Serbs were reported to have sat in the hills laughing.

(Source: Jim Bartlett)

ated a loose confederation that holds the Muslim-Croat federation and the Serb republic in the common state of Bosnia and Herzegovina, dividing the Muslim-Croat federation into separate national cantons and allowing the Bosnian Croats to maintain a close link with the Croatian state. Although the Serb Democratic Party no longer dominates politics in the Republika Srpska of Bosnia-Herzegovina, the main political parties representing the Serb population have continued to articulate desires for an independent state.

The other territory over which some of the most violent nationalist conflict emerged outside of Bosnia-Herzegovina was Kosovo, a region that features prominently in the Serbian national myth. Before 1990, Kosovo was part of the Serbian republic of Yugoslavia but had a majority ethnic Albanian population. In 1990, Kosovo lost its autonomy under the emerging rule of Slobodan Milošević. As a result, the Albanians in this province were systematically excluded from institutions of political and economic power, and their means of cultural reproduction (such as education in the Albanian language) were virtually eliminated from state-sponsored institutions. When the opportunity for democratization presented itself, Albanian members of the Kosovo assembly articulated the Kosovo Albanians' right to national self-determination as early as 1990. In September 1991, they organized a referendum in which an overwhelming majority of Kosovars (99.8 percent) voted for independence. During the same period, Serbian police and the Serb-led military continued to be in full control of Kosovo. The Kosovo Albanian parties had no military resources similar to those of the governments of Slovenia or Croatia to provide support for their independence claims. Instead, these parties continued to rely on parallel institutions of education, health care, and trade unions to provide for the Albanian population.

By 1996, however, the National Movement for the Liberation of Kosovo (KLA) became impatient with this strategy and began a series of violent attacks against Serbs (police officers and civilians) in Kosovo. Serbian authorities responded with a massive offensive in July 1998, forcing the KLA to withdraw into the hills. The Serbs then began a ruthless and systematic process of "ethnic cleansing," which resulted in approximately 700,000 ethnic Albanian civilians from Kosovo being expelled from their villages and forced to flee to Albania or Macedonia. Despite international intervention, including two months of massive NATO bombings against military and industrial targets also in Serbia, the Serbian government refused to agree to an independent Kosovo. When Serb forces finally agreed in a June 1999 peace agreement to withdraw from Kosovo, the agreement guaranteed the continued territorial integrity of Yugoslavia (Serbia-Montenegro), including the province of Kosovo. A mutually acceptable resolution of this conflict over national sovereignty has yet to follow. Kosovo has been under United Nations administration since 1999. After ethnic riots in March 2004, renewed efforts to reconcile the conflicting aspirations of Serbs and Kosovar Albanians resulted in another plan for the redistricting of Kosovo and the creation of Serbian enclaves with special administrative powers. Although the UN chief administrator has adopted this plan, its support among Kosovo's Albanian population is limited, and international discussions continue over Kosovo's status.

Independence and Integration: The Baltic States

The Baltic states of Estonia, Latvia, and Lithuania were reestablished without significant border disputes within the territorial boundaries that these states had had before their forcible annexation to the Soviet Union in 1940. Although Russians had dominated the institutions of power at both the federal and republic levels, and ethnic Russians had settled in these republics in significant numbers, there were no significant disputes over national territorial borders between Russian nationalist politicians and the leaders of independence movements in the Baltics.

An important factor in the absence of territorial disputes was that, although the Russians were the ethnic group closely associated with Soviet federal power structures, the ethnic Russian population in the Baltic republics was composed overwhelmingly of relatively recent settlers whom the native population viewed as colonizers. As the formerly dominant ethnic group in the Soviet Union, the Russians remaining in the Baltic states were the greatest potential losers of independence. Yet ethnic Russians articulated no systematic challenge to nationalist aspirations in the Baltics. The new states, with their prospects for European integration, offered better socioeconomic conditions than neighboring Russia. Rather than demanding self-government, let alone secession and unification with Russia, ethnic Russian political organizations contested the exclusionary aspects of citizenship and language laws and lobbied European institutions to pressure these governments to adopt more minority-friendly policies. Speaking the Russian language did not signify ethnic or national identity in these states the same way that language was the primary marker of Latvian, Estonian, and Lithuanian identities. The Russian-speaking population included people of different ethnicities who had switched to Russian as the language of advancement to higher status. Consequently, no commonly shared national myth existed among Russian speakers in the Baltic states that could have become the grounds for national sovereignty claims.[21] The only sizable historical minority in the Baltic region was the Polish minority in Lithuania. Although of roughly the same size as the state's Russian minority (at the time each comprising roughly 10 percent of the population), the Polish minority articulated a stronger challenge to majority nation building than Russians in any of the three states—including Estonia and Latvia, where Russians composed a much higher ratio of the population.

The policies of the Russian government in Moscow constituted another significant factor accounting for differences between nation-building processes in the Yugoslav and Baltic regions. With over 100,000 Red Army troops stationed in the Baltic republics when the Soviet Union collapsed, many had feared violent Russian opposition to independence. Nevertheless, the Russian government agreed to withdraw these troops with relative ease. In contrast to the Serbian leadership's involvement in mobilizing Serbian minorities in the secessionist republics and providing them with military resources, the Russian government aimed instead to eliminate discriminatory citizenship and language legislation in these countries through indirect pressure on their governments and through complaints brought to European institutions.

In pursuit of national states, however, Baltic governments adopted policies to establish national dominance over the institutions of the new state. After 1990, there was a strong sense among these populations that democratization should bring national justice. Even though they were formally titular ethnicities in their republics during Soviet occupation, the share and status of indigenous ethnic groups had decreased dramatically due to large-scale deportation campaigns against the native population, the emigration of great numbers of Balts to the West, and the massive influx of Russians (see table 4.1).

Table 4.1.   Ethnic Composition of the Baltic States

Ethnic Composition of Estonia (2000 Census)

Nationality	% of Population
Estonian	67.9
Russian	25.6
Ukrainian	2.1
Belarussian	1.3
Finn	0.9
Other	2.2

Ethnic Composition of Latvia (2002 Census)

Nationality	% of Population
Latvian	57.7
Russian	29.6
Belarusian	4.1
Ukrainian	2.7
Polish	2.5
Lithuanian	1.4
Other	2.0

Ethnic Composition of Lithuania (2001 Census)

Nationality	% of Population
Lithuanian	83.4
Polish	6.7
Russian	6.3
Other	3.6

Source: CIA, *The World Factbook 2005*
www.cia.gov/cia/publications/factbook/fields/2075.html

As a result of these changes, Russian became the predominant language in the public domain, especially in urban centers. The relationship between Russian and the titular national languages during the Soviet era remained that of one-sided bilingualism despite language legislation adopted in the final years of Soviet political reform that aimed at "emancipating" the Baltic languages. Non-Russians had to be fluent in Russian in order to function fully and advance socioeconomically, but Russian speakers were not learning the languages of the republics in which they resided.[22]

Decades of aggressive linguistic Russification, however, seemed only to reinforce the Balts' national aspirations. After achieving independence in 1991, each of the three governments adopted citizenship and language policies that established the dominance of the titular language in the state. The policies of nationalist state building were most aggressive in Latvia, where the ratio of the native population compared to the Russian-speaking population was the smallest, and most moderate in Lithuania, where the ratio of the Russian minority was the smallest. In Lithuania, all residents who had lived in the republic before independence obtained citizenship simply by applying. In Estonia and Latvia, only those who were citizens of the interwar Estonian and Latvian states before their Soviet annexation in 1940 and their descendants had automatic right to citizenship. Citizenship laws required other residents to pass a language proficiency test in order to become citizens of the reestablished states, even though during the Soviet era hardly any Russian school taught Latvian. As a result, roughly a third of the population of Estonia and Latvia were excluded from citizenship.[23] Citizenship laws also disadvantaged ethnic Russians in the distribution of resources. The 1991 Latvian privatization law, for instance, excluded noncitizens. In Estonia, property restitution similarly discriminated against Russians.[24] The Lithuanian government was more willing to abandon the pursuit of titular language dominance in favor of a moderate policy that allowed for language pluralism in local administration.[25]

In general, the story of state and nation building in the Baltic region is about harmonizing national sovereignty with European integration. "Returning to Europe" and obtaining protection from future Russian reannexation by joining the European Union were inextricable parts of the pursuit of national sovereignty in this region.[26] Employing the powerful leverage that these motivations provided, European institutions—especially the Organization for Security and Cooperation of Europe's High Commissioner on National Minorities, the Council of Europe, and the European Union—applied strong pressure on the Baltic governments to adopt more inclusive citizenship laws and more pluralistic educational and language policies that complied with "European norms."[27] After 1998, the governments of Estonia and Latvia began adopting amendments to their citizenship laws that made the naturalization of "nonhistoric" minorities easier. International pressure has been somewhat less successful in influencing them to liberalize their language policies. Language legislation in both states also continues to reflect a nationalist state-building strategy, although in most cases restrictive language legislation was only moderately implemented.[28] Tensions over language use continue, especially in Latvia, where a new bilingual curriculum introduced in 2002–2003, requiring that Russian-language (and other minority-language) schools teach certain subjects in Latvian, met with vehement ethnic Russian opposition.[29]

The "Velvet Divorce" and Its Aftermath: The Czech and Slovak States

In contrast with the violent conflicts over national sovereignty in former Yugoslavia and the powerful public support for independence in the Baltic republics, the independent Czech Republic and Slovakia were created after the peaceful dissolution of Czechoslovakia in 1992. Some accounts of the separation emphasized cultural differences between Czechs and Slovaks and assigned a significant weight to Slovak aspirations for a national state.[30] Yet separation was not primarily the outcome of ethnic division between Slovaks and Czechs. Rather than large-scale popular mobilization for independence, similar to the popular movements in the Baltic states, the creation of independent Czech and Slovak states was an outcome negotiated among the political leaders of the two parts of the federation with only limited public support.[31] At the same time, each of these states was established democratically, by elected governing bodies, and in the absence of significant popular opposition.[32]

Like the separation of the Baltic states, a key reason for the absence of violent conflict over the dissolution of Czechoslovakia was that no disputes emerged between the Czechs and Slovaks over state borders, as the two groups did not initiate mutually exclusive "national homeland" claims to the same territory. Before the first establishment of Czechoslovakia in 1918, Slovaks had lived within the Hungarian kingdom for ten centuries, and the old territorial border remained a substate boundary in Czechoslovakia. After decades of coexistence with the prospect of mobility within a common state—first in interwar Czechoslovakia, later in communist Czechoslovakia—no sizable Czech national minority developed on Slovak territory or Slovak historic minority in the Czech Lands that would articulate a substate national challenge to either of the new states. Another important reason why the Czech and Slovak divorce lacked significant controversy was that the Hungarian minority in the Slovak part of the state, a historic minority with competing homeland claims in the southern region of Slovakia, did not challenge the Slovaks' right to independence.

For reasons described earlier in this chapter, at the time of independence the Czech Republic was one of the least ethnically diverse states in the region (see table 4.2). Czech political leaders therefore faced few challenges to pursuing a single, dominant culture in the new state. Of all the ethnicities in the state, the Roma continue to comprise the largest and most distinct cultural group, with a share of the population estimated between 2 and 3 percent. Official policies and popular attitudes toward this minority after the creation of the new state indicated that the national majority had little desire to accommodate Roma culture. Citizenship laws limited the rights of Roma to become naturalized in the new state. On the level of local government, anti-Roma efforts included attempts to segregate swimming pools, construct walls separating Roma and Czech inhabitants, and provide subsidies for Roma willing to emigrate. The relatively small size and fragmentation of the Roma population, however, prevented these incidents from becoming a matter of broader debate about Czech national exclusivism.[33]

National aspirations found a more complex social context in newly independent Slovakia.[34] Before 1993, the primary question of Slovak national sovereignty had been whether an independent Slovak state was necessary to fulfill national aspirations. After the creation of Slovakia, the key question became how a Slovak "nation-state" could materialize on a territory that incorporated a relatively large, geographically concentrated, and politically well-organized historic Hungarian community (see table 4.3). During the first period of independence from 1992 to 1998, the Slovak political parties in power, under the leadership of Prime Minister Vladimír Mečiar, opted for traditional nationalist policies. In an attempt to suppress minority claims for substate institutional autonomy, these policies were aimed at establishing Slovak majority control over all institutions of government and cultural reproduction. Restrictive language legislation adopted in 1995 was designed to strengthen the status of the Slovak literary standard against regional dialects and to exclude minority languages from the spheres

Table 4.2.   **Ethnic Composition of the Czech Republic (2001 Census)**

Nationality	% of Population
Czech	90.4
Moravian	3.7
Slovak	1.9
Other	4

Source: CIA, *The World Factbook 2005*
www.cia.gov/cia/publications/factbook/fields/2075.html

Photo 4.3.   With the expansion of the European Union, West European tourists have come in large numbers into places like this Hungarian village in Transylvania. Many buy "ethnic gifts" at new shops like this one.

(Source: Dana Stryk)

considered most important for the reproduction of national cultures: local government, territory markings, the media, and the educational system. Hungarian minority parties forcefully challenged these policies and pressed for a pluralist Slovak state. Employing the methods of party competition and parliamentary debate, Hungarian minority political elites asked that Slovakia's historic Hungarian minority be recognized as a state-constituting entity. To guarantee the reproduction of Hungarian minority culture in Slovakia, they demanded substate forms of autonomy—at various times emphasizing either the cultural, educational, or the territorial aspects of self-

Table 4.3.   Ethnic Composition of Slovakia (2001 Census)

Nationality	% of Population
Slovak	85.8
Hungarian	9.7
Roma	1.7
Czech	0.8
Ruthenian	0.4
Ukrainian	0.2
Other	1.4

Source: Peter Mach, "Structure by Nationality of Population in the Slovak Republic." Available online at www.czso.cz/sif/conference2004.nsf/bce41ad0daa3aad1c1256c6e00499152/528df706de821624c1256edd0035b3f9/$FILE/PeterMach.pdf

government. Although there were internal debates among Hungarian parties about the best institutional forms, they agreed on the importance of language rights and claimed the right to use the Hungarian language in the southern region of Slovakia in all public spheres and the educational system.

Majority-minority debates over these questions marked the first decade of democratization in Slovakia. The Mečiar government's policies of increasing centralized control over society also created sharp divisions within the Slovak majority. Based on their agreement about the necessity to move Slovakia away from a recentralizing authoritarian regime, the Slovak and Hungarian parties in opposition eventually formed a strategic electoral alliance that defeated the Mečiar government in the 1998 parliamentary elections. This Slovak-Hungarian electoral alliance was able to form a governing coalition that changed the course of Slovak nationalist policies in the following years. Even though debates about minority self-government and language equality continued and often reflected vehement disagreements, the prospects of European integration provided a significant incentive to both majority and minority moderate parties to negotiate peacefully. They managed to design policies that, while preserving the predominance of the majority language throughout the country, gradually included the minority language in ways that satisfied the main aspirations that minority parties had articulated from the beginning of the 1990s.

CONSOLIDATING NATIONAL STATES: NATION-STATE OR PLURALISM?

The unitary states of Bulgaria, Hungary, Poland, and Romania continued their existence within unchanged state borders after the communist collapse. The absence of state collapse and new state creation, however, did not make nationalist ideology irrelevant in these countries. Wherever majority national elites chose to define the post-communist state as the unitary "nation-state" of the majority national group, and the government engaged in aggressive policies to create majority dominance over sizable ethnic and national minority groups, nationalism became a deeply divisive political strategy. The dynamics of the majority-minority conflict over nation building in Romania highlight the difficulties of consolidating a national state under such conditions.

From Nationalist Communism to Democratic Nationalism: Romania

Like other multiethnic societies in the region, the legacies of past relations of dominance and subordination between ethnic groups continued to influence majority and minority perspectives in Romania about what "national sovereignty" should mean. The Romanian population of Transylvania, today constituting the western region of Romania, lived for centuries under Hungarian rule. It was only after the end of World War I that the current border between Hungary and Romania was drawn, against the bitter resentment of the Hungarians who fell under Romanian rule. Ethnic hierarchies were suddenly reversed, and the interwar Romanian government designed aggressive policies to establish Romanian dominance in economic and cultural institutions throughout the new country.[35] Hitler redressed Hungarian resentments in World War II when he returned the majority Hungarian-inhabited northern part of Transylvania to Hungary. With Hitler's defeat, the contested borders were redrawn again, largely along the same lines that had been created after World War I, and Romania fell under the influence of the Soviet Union.[36] Despite the ruthlessness of anti-Hungarian policies enacted during the dictatorship of Nicolae Ceauşescu, members of the Hungarian minority maintained a strong sense of national identity. Only days after the bloody revolution in December 1989 that toppled what was perhaps the most repressive communist dictatorship in the region, the ethnic Hungarians formed a political party that commanded the overwhelming majority of the votes of their population of 1.6 million in every subsequent election, and they became a significant force in the Romanian parliament (see table 4.4).

Rather than discarding the nationalist policies of the Ceauşescu period, however, the government of Ion Iliescu after 1990 designed a new constitution that defined the state as a "nation-state" based on the unity of an ethnically defined Romanian nation. The regime based its power on alliances with ultranationalist Romanian parties of the left and right, and instituted minority policies that in some ways were more restrictive than their counterparts during the Ceauşescu dictatorship. The new constitution affirmed that Romanian was the only official language in Romanian territory. Laws adopted on public administration and public education also severely restricted the use of minority languages and became sources of intense controversy between the Romanian government and the Hungarian minority party. Like their counterparts in Slovakia, the Hungarian minority party demanded the right to Hungarian-language cultural and educational institutions, and the right to use the language in local and regional government. The Hungarians pressed for these demands through bargaining and negotiations with majority parties willing to compromise on national issues. Although all Romanian parties rejected Hungarian claims for substate autonomy, moderate Romanian parties were willing to form an electoral alliance with the Hungarian party, and—similarly to Slovakia—this strategic alliance defeated the Iliescu government in 1996, formed a coalition government, and began to shift Romanian nation-building policies. Even though the Iliescu government returned to power in the 2000 elections, this time the prospect of membership in NATO and European Union became significant enough for the regime to shift to a minority-friendly

Table 4.4. Ethnic Composition of Romania (2002 Census)

Nationality	% of Population
Romanian	89.5
Hungarian	6.6
Roma	2.5
German	0.3
Ukrainian	0.3
Russian	0.2
Turkish	0.2
Other	0.4

Source: CIA, World Factbook, 2006
www.cia.gov/cia/publications/factbook/index.html

approach, and expand the rights of language use in the spheres most important for minority cultural reproduction.[37]

NATION BUILDING ACROSS STATE BORDERS

Besides the cohabitation of national majority and minority groups in the same state, most ethnic and national minorities in this region also have neighboring "kin-states"—that is, states in which their ethnic kin compose a titular majority.[38] A growing interest emerged among such governments to adopt legislation that would grant various forms of preferential treatment to ethnic kin living in other states. The constitutions of several states, such as Albania, Croatia, Hungary, and Macedonia, contain commitments to care for the well-being of kin living abroad. Several governments, such as Bulgaria, Hungary, Romania, Russia, Serbia, Slovenia, and Slovakia, adopted legislation to provide benefits to co-nationals living abroad. Although these constitutional clauses and benefit laws differ in their specific content, ranging from cultural and economic benefits to dual citizenship rights, their common characteristic is that they support the preservation of national identity and aim to contribute to the fostering of relationships between a kin-state and those outside this state who define themselves in some sense as co-nationals.[39]

Hungary and Virtual Nationalism

The Hungarian state's nation-building strategy after 1990 is the clearest example of the transsovereign type of nationalism in the region. This type of nationalism does not pursue a traditional nation-state through territorial changes or the repatriation of co-nationals within its borders. Instead, it aims to maintain and reproduce a sense of common cultural "nationhood" across existing state borders.[40] Close to 3 million ethnic Hungarians live in Hungary's neighboring states. In an integrated Europe, they will comprise one of the largest historical minority groups. After the collapse of communist regimes, Hungarian political elites were aware that revisionism was an unacceptable proposition if they wanted to join an integrated Europe. Instead of pressing for border changes, they created a network of institutions that link Hungarians living in the neighboring countries to Hungary while encouraging them to remain "in their homeland," and in effect withstand assimilation where they are. To complement these cross-border institutions, the Hungarian government expressed support for Hungarian minority demands for local and institutional autonomy in their home states, and they also supported EU membership for Hungary as well as its neighbors. The logic behind these policies was that if Hungary and all of its neighbors became EU members, and the European Union provided a supranational, decentralized structure for strong regional institutions, then Hungarians could live as though there were no political borders separating them.

Although the "virtualization of borders" appeared attractive to many Hungarians, the idea found little appeal among the majority political parties in neighboring countries. Seven states neighboring Hungary include ethnic Hungarian populations, and five of these states were newly established after the collapse of communist federations.

As discussed earlier in this chapter, the majority national elites in both newly created and consolidating national states were highly reluctant to weaken their sovereignty and accommodate multiple nation-building processes in their territories. Thus, Hungarian efforts unilaterally to "virtualize" borders in the region triggered tensions between Hungary and its neighbors.

The adoption of a "Law Concerning Hungarians Living in Neighboring Countries" (commonly known as "the Hungarian Status Law") in June 2001—which defined all ethnic Hungarians in the region as part of the same cultural nation, and on this basis offered a number of educational, cultural, and even economic benefits to those living in neighboring states—triggered significant attention from policy makers in the region, European institution officials, and scholars of nationalism.[41] The competitive dynamics of nation building in the region and its potentially large-scale regional impact made the Hungarian strategy particularly controversial. The governments of Romania and Slovakia, the two states with the largest Hungarian populations, expressed concerns that the legislation weakened their exclusive sovereignty over ethnic Hungarian citizens and discriminated against majority nationals in neighboring countries. Although these neighboring governments themselves had adopted similar policies toward their own ethnic kin abroad, controversy over the Hungarian Status Law brought Hungary's relations with these neighbors to a dangerously low point. The fact that all of these governments were keenly interested in EU membership eventually helped them compromise. Hungary signed a bilateral agreement with Romania and altered the language of the law in response to European pressure in 2003. Yet the controversy over the Hungarian Status Law foreshadows the challenges of reconciling European integration with the continuing power of divergent and competing national aspirations.

Nationalism and the Expansion of Democracy

The continuing appeal of the national principle in Central and East European societies that have successfully acceded to the European Union challenges old assumptions about ethnicity, nationalism, and democratization. In these instances, democratization did not lead to the broad acceptance of liberal-individualist understandings of citizenship; nor did nationalism result in horror perpetuated in the name of ethnic kin throughout the region. Given the dramatic collapse of states and regimes in a region where state and nation building has always involved ethnic competition, the relatively low occurrence of violent conflict associated with these changes in the 1990s was remarkable.

The force and popular appeal of nationalist demands revealed that nationalism constitutes a significant element of continuity in this region. At the same time, the end of the Cold War and the promise of European integration altered the conditions under which nationalist interests could be articulated. Despite the commonality of these external influences, however, the specific goals that nationalist leaders and groups articulated, as well as the means by which they pursued those goals varied across the region. Most of the former titular groups of multinational federations sought national independence. Where substate boundaries within the disintegrating multinational federation had coincided with the territories that titular groups defined as their historic homelands, and secession encountered no significant challenge from other groups, nationalist state building unfolded without significant violence. In these cases, the prospects for integration into Western institutions helped reinforce initial interests in democratization, and state and nation building followed the recommendations of the Helsinki Final Act of 1975—which had only legitimated peaceful border changes. Examples of such nonviolent (or relatively nonviolent) state formation include the reestablishment of the Baltic states of Estonia, Latvia, and Lithuania; the secession of Slovenia and Macedonia; and the creation of independent Czech and Slovak states.

Where the state-building aspirations of a group encountered forceful challenge by another group claiming the same territory as a historic homeland within a dissolving federal state, and the dominant political elites opted for unilateralism over sustained negotiation across ethnic lines, nationalist mobilization led to devastating wars. This was the situation in the former Yugoslav republics of Croatia, Serbia, and Bosnia-Herzegovina. Competing national elites in these cases opted for national sovereignty even at the most horrific costs, and future prospects for European integration did not figure significantly in their calculations—despite the fact that, before the communist collapse, Yugoslavia had been better connected to international institutions than Soviet bloc countries. European integration became an important part of nationalist strategy only in Slovenia, where belonging to Europe constituted an important element of national identity. With no significant national minority within, the issue of national sovereignty was most easily resolved.

Lithuania provides an important lesson about the significance of the choices that majority and minority political elites make in nationalist competition. In the same period that Croatian and Serbian majority and minority elites were fighting a devastating war in the southeastern part of the continent, the leaders of the Lithuanian national majority and the Polish minority opted for a consensual resolution of the tension over mutually claimed homelands. Eager to satisfy European expectations, they engaged in a bilateral and peaceful negotiation over the issues of autonomy and minority rights.

The issues that Lithuanians debated with the new state's Polish minority were similar to those that national majorities and minorities in both continuing and newly created unitary states faced. Governments in Bulgaria, Romania, and all of the multiethnic successor states of dissolving federations had to answer the question of whether the democratic state could pursue the traditional nationalist aim of the political-cultural congruence of the nation or accommodate minority cultures in a more pluralist state. Excepting Croatia, Serbia, and Bosnia-Herzegovina, in all of these states majority and minority political parties remained committed to democratic means of negotiating their competing notions of sovereignty.

To make matters even more complicated, many governments in the region juggle the dual roles of home state (in relation to their titular nation and national minorities living on their territory) and kin-state (in relation to their kin living outside their territory). Such cases have prompted officials in European institutions to begin designing a common set of norms that assures minority protection and permits kin-states to build relations with external minorities, while continuing to uphold the principle of state sovereignty. In an enlarged European Union, harmonizing the principles of state sovereignty and individualism with the practice of multiple nation building within and across state borders will remain a continuing challenge.

Suggested Readings

Barany, Zoltan, and Robert G. Moser, eds. *Ethnic Politics after Communism*. Ithaca, NY: Cornell University Press, 2005.

Beissinger, Mark. "How Nationalisms Spread: Eastern Europe Adrift the Tides and Cycles of Nationalist Contention." *Social Research* 63, no. 1 (Spring 1996).

Brubaker, Rogers. *Nationalism Reframed: Nationhood and the National Question in the New Europe*. Cambridge, UK: Cambridge University Press, 1996.

Gagnon, V. P., Jr., *The Myth of Ethnic War: Serbia and Croatia in the 1990s*. Ithaca, NY: Cornell University Press, 2004.

Hroch, Miroslav. "From National Movement to the Fully-Formed Nation: The Nation-Building Process in Europe." *New Left Review* 198 (1993): 3–20.

———. *Social Preconditions of National Revival in Europe: A Comparative Analysis of the Social Composition of Patriotic Groups among the Smaller European Nations*. New York: Columbia University Press, 2000.

Hutchinson, John, and Anthony D. Smith, eds. *Nationalism*. Oxford: Oxford University Press, 1994.

Karklins, Rasma. *Ethnopolitics and Transition to Democracy*. Washington, DC: The Woodrow Wilson Center Press and The Johns Hopkins University Press, 1994.

Kelley, Judith. *Ethnic Politics in Europe: The Power of Norms and Incentives*. Princeton, NJ: Princeton University Press, 2004.

King, Charles, and Neil Melvin, eds. *Nations Abroad: Diaspora Politics and International Relations in the Former Soviet Union*. Boulder, CO: Westview Press, 1998.

Laitin, David. "The Cultural Identities of a European State." *Politics and Society* 25, no. 3 (September 1997).

———. *Identity in Formation: The Russian-Speaking Populations in the Near Abroad*. Ithaca, NY: Cornell University Press, 1998.

Livezeanu, Irina. *Cultural Politics in Greater Romania: Regionalism, Nation Building, and Ethnic Struggle, 1918–1930*. Ithaca, NY: Cornell University Press, 1995.

Schopflin, George. *Nations, Identity, Power*. New York: New York University Press, 2000.

Snyder, Jack. *From Voting to Violence: Democratization and Nationalist Conflict*. New York: W.W. Norton & Company, 2000.

Tismaneanu, Vladimir. *Fantasies of Salvation: Democracy, Nationalism, and Myth in Post-Communist Europe*. Princeton, NJ: Princeton University Press, 1998.

Verdery, Katherine. *National Ideology under Socialism: Identity and Cultural Politics in Ceauşescu's Romania*. Berkeley: University of California Press, 1991.

Notes

1. Ernst Gellner, *Nations and Nationalism* (Ithaca, NY: Cornell University Press, 1983), 1.

2. For a comprehensive discussion of the literature about nationalism and modernization, see Anthony D. Smith, *Nationalism and Modernism: A Critical Survey of Recent Theories of Nations and Nationalism* (London: Routledge, 1998).

3. Robert Kaplan, *Balkan Ghosts: A Journey through History* (New York: Vintage Books, 1993).

4. Jack Snyder, *From Voting to Violence: Democratization and Nationalist Conflict* (New York: W.W. Norton & Company, 2000).

5. Tom Nairn, "The Modern Janus," in *The Break-Up of Britain: Crisis and Neo-Nationalism*, ed. Tom Nairn (London: New Left Books, 1977).

6. Anthony D. Smith, *The Ethnic Origins of Nations* (Oxford: Blackwell, 1986); Michael Billig, *Banal Nationalism* (London: Sage Publications, 1995).

7. See also Mark Beissinger, "How Nationalisms Spread: Eastern Europe Adrift the Tides and Cycles of Nationalist Contention," *Social Research* 63, no. 1 (Spring 1996): 135.

8. For a historical account, see Hugh L. Agnew, *The Czechs and the Lands of the Bohemian Crown* (Stanford, CA: Hoover Institution Press, 2004). About nationalism and competition, see Anthony W. Marx, *Faith in Nation: Exclusionary Origins of Nationalism* (Oxford: Oxford University Press, 2003). About resentment as an important motivation for nationalism, see Liah Greenfeld, *Nationalism: Five Roads to Modernity* (Cambridge, UK: Cambridge University Press, 1992).

9. Stephen Krasner, ed, *Problematic Sovereignty: Contested Rules and Political Possibilities* (New York: Columbia University Press, 2001), 1–23.

10. J. Samuel Barkin and Bruce Cronin, "The State and the Nation: Changing Norms and the Rules of Sovereignty in International Relations," *International Organizations* 48 (Winter 1994): 107–30.

11. Quoted in Arnold Suppan, "Yugoslavism versus Serbian, Croatian, and Slovene Nationalism," in *Yugoslavia and Its Historians: Understanding the Balkan Wars of the 1990s*, ed. Norman M. Naimark and Holly Case, 126 (Stanford, CA: Stanford University Press, 2003).

12. Irina Livezeanu, *Cultural Politics in Greater Romania: Regionalism, Nation Building, and Ethnic Struggle, 1918–1930* (Ithaca, NY: Cornell University Press, 1995).

13. About national ideology in Romania, see Katherine Verdery, *National Ideology under Socialism: Identity and Cultural Politics in Ceauşescu's Romania* (Berkeley and Los Angeles: University of California Press, 1991). For the national question in Czechoslovakia, see Sharon Wolchik, *Czechoslovakia in Transition: Politics, Economy and Society* (London: Pinter, 1991).

14. Vojtech Mastny, "The Beneš Thesis: A Design for the Liquidation of National Minorities: Introduction," in *The Hungarians: A Divided Nation*, ed. Stephen Borsody, 231–43 (New Haven, CT: Yale Center for International and Area Studies, 1988).

15. Bennett Kovrig, "Peacemaking after World War II," in *The Hungarians: A Divided Nation*, ed. Stephen Borsody, 69–88 (New Haven, CT: Yale Center for International and Area Studies, 1988).

16. Vladimir Tismaneanu, *Fantasies of Salvation: Democracy, Nationalism, and Myth in Post-Communist Europe* (Princeton, NJ: Princeton University Press, 1998).

17. These documents include the Council of Security and Cooperation of Europe's (CSCE) Copenhagen Document (1990, known also as the European Constitution on Human Rights), which included a chapter on the protection of national minorities; the Council of Europe's (CE) European Charter on Regional and Minority Languages (1992); the United Nations Declaration on the Rights of Persons Belonging to National and Ethnic, Religious and Linguistic Minorities (1992); the CE's Framework Convention for the Protection of National Minorities (1995), which is commonly considered a major achievement as the first legally binding international tool for minority protection; the OSCE's Oslo Recommendations regarding the Linguistic Rights of National Minorities (1998).

18. See Valerie Bunce, *Subversive Institutions: The Design and the Destruction of Socialism and the State* (Cambridge, UK: Cambridge University Press, 1999).

19. Aleksa Djilas, "Fear Thy Neighbor: The Breakup of Yugoslavia," in *Nationalism and Nationalities in the New Europe*, ed. Charles Kupchan et al., 88 (Ithaca, NY: Cornell University Press, 1995).

20. Djilas, "Fear Thy Neighbor," 102.

21. Zsuzsa Csergo and James M. Goldgeier, "Kin-State Activism in Hungary, Romania, and Russia: The Politics of Ethnic Demography" (paper presented at the "Divided Nations" workshop at Queen's University, Kingston, Canada, July 2007).

22. On Soviet language policy, see Rasma Karklins, *Ethnopolitics and Transition to Democracy*

(Washington, DC: The Woodrow Wilson Center Press and The Johns Hopkins University Press, 1994), 151–52.

23. Graham Smith et al., *Nation-Building in the Post-Soviet Borderlands: The Politics of National Identities* (Cambridge, UK: Cambridge University Press, 1998) 94.

24. Julie Bernier, "Nationalism in Transition: Nationalizing Impulses and International Counterweights in Latvia and Estonia," in *Minority Nationalism and the Changing International Order*, ed. Michael Keating and John McGarry, 346 (Oxford: Oxford University Press, 2001).

25. Ellen J. Gordon, "Legislating Identity: Language, Citizenship, and Education in Lithuania" (PhD diss., University of Michigan, 1993). Terje Mathiassen, "Regulations and Language Planning in Latvia and Lithuania," in *Language Contact and Language Conflict: Proceedings of the International Ivar Aasen Conference 14–16 November 1996, University of Oslo*, ed. Unn Royneland, 197 (Volda, Norway: Volda College, 1997).

26. Rawi Abdelal, *National Purpose in the World Economy* (Ithaca, NY: Cornell University Press, 2001).

27. Judith Kelley, *Ethnic Politics in Europe: The Power of Norms and Incentives* (Princeton, NJ: Princeton University Press, 2004).

28. Rasma Karklins, "Ethnic Integration and School Policies in Latvia," *Nationalities Papers* 26, no. 2 (1998): 284.

29. Ojarrs Kalnins, "Latvia: The Language of Coexistence," *Transitions Online* 1 September 2004, www.tol.cz/look/TOL/home.

30. See Gordon Wightman, "Czechoslovakia," in *New Political Parties of Eastern Europe and the Soviet Union*, ed. Bogdan Szajkowski, 67 (Detroit, MI: Longman, 1991); Jiri Musil, "Czech and Slovak Society," in *The End of Czechoslovakia*, ed. Jiri Musil, 92 (Budapest, Hungary: Central European University Press, 1995).

31. Sharon Wolchik, "The Politics of Transition and the Break-Up of Czechoslovakia," in *The End of Czechoslovakia*, ed. Jiri Musil, 240–41 (Budapest, Hungary: Central European University Press, 1995). Abby Innes, "Breakup of Czechoslovakia: The Impact of Party Development on the Separation of the State," *East European Politics and Societies* 11, no. 3 (Fall 1997): 393.

32. About negotiated transitions see Juan J. Linz and Alfred Stepan, *Problems of Democratic Transition and Consolidation: Southern Europe, South America, and Post-Communist Europe* (Baltimore: The Johns Hopkins University Press, 1996), 316.

33. Zsuzsa Csergo and Kevin Deegan-Krause, "Why Liberalism Failed: Majorities and Minorities in European Enlargement" (paper presented at the American Political Science Association Annual Meeting, Philadelphia, PA, August 2003).

34. Kevin Deegan-Krause, *Elected Affinities: Democracy and Party Competition in Slovakia and the Czech Republic* (Stanford, CA: Stanford University Press, 2006).

35. Irina Livezeanu, *Cultural Politics in Greater Romania: Regionalism, Nation Building, and Ethnic Struggle, 1918–1930* (Ithaca, NY: Cornell University Press, 1995).

36. For the history of the interwar period, see Joseph Rothschild, *East Central Europe between the Two World Wars* (Seattle: University of Washington Press, 1974).

37. Zsuzsa Csergo, *Talk of the Nation: Language and Conflict in Romania and Slovakia* (Ithaca, NY: Cornell University Press, 2007). Zsuzsa Csergo, "Beyond Ethnic Division: Majority-Minority Debate about the Post-Communist State in Romania and Slovakia," *East European Politics and Societies* 16, no. 1 (Winter 2001).

38. Rogers Brubaker, *Nationalism Reframed: Nationhood and the National Question in the New Europe* (Cambridge, UK: Cambridge University Press, 1996).

39. Iván Halász, "Models of Kin-Minorities Protection in Eastern and Central Europe" (paper presented at the international conference on "The Status Law Syndrome: a Post-Communist Nation Building, Citizenship, and/or Minority Protection" Budapest, Hungary, October 2004).

40. Zsuzsa Csergo and James M. Goldgeier, "Nationalist Strategies and European Integration," *Perspectives on Politics* 2 (March 2004): 26.

41. Zoltán Kántor et al., eds., *The Hungarian Status Law: Nation Building and/or Minority Protection* (Sapporo, Japan: Slavic Research Center, 2004).

CHAPTER 5

Women's Participation in Postcommunist Politics

Marilyn Rueschemeyer

The end of communism in Central and Eastern Europe created new conditions for citizens to participate in politics. Women as well as men gained the opportunity to vote in meaningful elections, run for political office, form independent groups, and pressure political leaders to take action on issues of interest to them. This chapter will address women's interest in and participation in political life, the share of women among elected political representatives, the pursuit of women's issues by women who have been elected, and women leaders' relation to various constituencies, especially women's organizations.

The chapter begins with some reflections on the communist period, particularly on the importance of women's participation in the labor force in preparing them to take part in political life after the end of the communist regime. It then turns to some of the implications of the transition years for women's participation, the consequences different electoral arrangements as well as parties' political positions have on women's representation among elected representatives, and other factors that promote women's success in politics.[1]

Legacies of the Communist Period

The historical background of the Central and East European countries has given a special shape to developments there after 1989–1990, to the situation and the problems of women, as well as to the emerging democratic politics and the role of women in politics. With some variations across countries, the communist systems of Central and Eastern Europe offered their populations comprehensive if austere provisions of social welfare. Motivated by both ideological and pragmatic concerns, within this broader context of support they provided a new role for women that not only allowed but required full participation in the labor force. This policy did not lead to full equality, either in the family or in leading positions in the state or the economy. But it is wrong to dismiss its influence in creating more egalitarian gender relations. The education that women received, their position in the labor force, and their overall status had a special character even with remaining gender differences in professional training, skill, income, and responsibility. Of course it is important to realize that women's education, work, and gender status as well as the policies affecting them differed among the countries of the region (see table 5.1). Even the quota system for women's political representation played itself out in different ways across countries, though women generally comprised between a fifth and a third of legislators at the national level. Women's participation in social and political life, therefore, varied, and so did their assessment of these experiences.

It is also true that huge numbers of women had important experiences outside the household. As a result, "women learned not to derive their status from their husbands, but from their own educational and professional position."[2] The communist model, whereby most women, even those with young children, worked outside the home, also taught women how to combine work and family life without completely interrupting their work lives. This process was made possible by adaptations in employment practices and work legislation concerning employed mothers.[3] But, even so, many women experienced a great deal of difficulty in combining work and home, particularly as the gender division of labor within the home did not change significantly. More broadly, women had, even with limited political autonomy, considerable participatory experience in communist societies—at the workplace, in unions, and especially in work collectives and neighborhoods.[4]

Many of the demands that women in the West enter politics to fulfill were—even if imperfectly—realized in a number of the Central and East European countries under communism.[5] Thus, women had abortion rights, maternal and child-care leave,

Table 5.1. Percentage of Female Students in Tertiary Education

	1980	1990	2000
Albania	48	48	60
Bosnia and Herzegovina*	38	55	—
Bulgaria	56	51	56
Croatia**	49	47	53
Czech Republic	43	44	49
Estonia***	52	51	60
Hungary	50	50	55
Latvia	57	55	62
Lithuania	55	57	60
Poland	56	56	58
Romania	43	48	54
Serbia and Montenegro****	52	52	55
Slovakia	38	44	50
Slovenia	54	56	56
Former Yugoslav Republic of Macedonia	48	52	56

*Data for 1996 instead of 2000.
**Data for 1996 instead of 2000. Including ISCED level 5 and 6.
***Including postsecondary technical education.
****Data for 1996 instead of 2000.
Source: UNSECE Statistical Division, World Education Report

guaranteed employment, and access to education. There has been some continuity in these areas of social policy in the postcommunist period. A number of these policies have been challenged, and many benefits have been reduced or eliminated. Yet their legitimacy is also recognized, at least among significant segments of the population, and they remain in the public arena of political discussion.

Developments after 1989–1990

Given their levels of education and the skills they have developed through work outside the home, many women in Central and Eastern Europe are well prepared to enter political life, yet they do so only in limited numbers. What makes participation difficult in spite of the fact that women may be better prepared for participation than they were earlier in these societies?

A number of women played a significant role in the transitions from communism through their activities in citizen movements, newly formed nongovernmental organizations, and political parties, some of which had a strong focus on the position of women. In the election to the Volkskammer of the then still separate East Germany in March 1990, for example, more than 20 percent of the newly elected representatives were women.[6] Women also served as spokespersons for the umbrella organizations that were formed to negotiate the end of communism and participated in large numbers in the mass demonstrations that toppled the rigid, repressive regimes in the GDR, Czechoslovakia, and Romania. Yet overall, women's political participation in postcommunist Central and Eastern Europe is far from equal to that of men. Women generally vote in numbers equal to those of men, but they are underrepresented among elected representatives in all of the countries in the region, and women's issues are often sidelined.

In lower- or single-house parliaments, women now represent 32 percent of the elected members in Germany (2005), 9.8 percent in Russia (2003), 20.4 percent in Poland (2005), 15.5 percent in the Czech Republic (2002), and 12 percent in Slovenia (2004) (see table 5.2). These are important increases since the early transformation years.

Women's concerns and issues were frequently defined by (male) politicians as secondary to "more important needs." A fundamental problem is that, given the shift to a market economy and political pluralism, many of these societies are now too poor to sustain the old social supports, which, even if characterized by great variation, included virtually free health and educational services, child care, and other benefits that were important for women's participation in the labor force. The expectation was that a new political economy would eventually produce enough to enable all citizens to live well. The early policy directions were created under conditions of real scarcity, as economic constraints were indeed considerable. But, as these economies recover and many in fact prosper, there are still choices involved in making policy, and these choices reflect not only pressures to respond to economic issues but, to a considerable extent, existing power relations.[7]

Unequal power relations characterize political life on all levels of society. Group

Table 5.2.   Percentage of Women in Selected Parliaments During and After Communism

Country	Last Communist Election*	Most Recent Elections (as of Sept. 2006)
Czech Republic	29.4	15.5
Estonia	32.8	18.8
Hungary	8.3	10.4
Latvia	32.8	21
Lithuania	32.8	22
Poland	20.2	20.4
Romania	34.4	11.2
Russia	32.8	9.8
Slovakia	29.4	16
Slovenia	17.7	12
Ukraine	32.8	7.1

*During the communist period, the parliaments had very limited power. In contrast to the high level of women's representation in these largely symbolic bodies, women were barely represented in the apparatus of the party and the state, where power did reside.
Source: For last communist election, Steven Saxonberg, ''Women in Eastern European Parliaments,'' *Journal of Democracy* 11, no. 2 (April 2000). For most recent election, Inter-Parliamentary Union, ''Women in National Parliaments,'' Inter-Parliamentary Union website (www.ipu.org/wmn-e/classif.htm).

interests tend to be articulated from the experience of men who insist that "women's" issues—such as child care, health, and decreased employment opportunities—must wait until other critical issues are resolved.[8] It is clear that the definition of these needs is part of the political game and the expression of particular political interests.

These unresolved concerns constitute significant barriers to women's political participation and activism. Improvements in some areas of the economy and for some segments of the population since the end of communism have meant disintegration and loss for others, and women often found themselves on the losing side. One major factor accounting for women's limited participation in politics is found in the problems women faced in the early transition years, especially in the frequent discontinuation of social supports and unemployment. People who lose economically and socially also lose political voice.

Discrimination against women with children meant that young mothers at home with small children often became responsible for a number of new obligations, such as having to deal with a new health system and a new education system. For some young couples, finding affordable housing became difficult.[9] As the result of the reduction in child-care centers in some areas, many women became full-time parents, making it even more difficult to search for work, much less become involved in political life.

With the shift to market economies, open unemployment increased sharply in most countries. Large numbers of people in Central and Eastern Europe are still unemployed, and some suffer from severe poverty. Even in some of the more successful transitions, a large percentage of the population is without work. In 2005, nearly 18 percent of the labor force in Poland was unemployed. In eastern Germany, the unemployment rate in 2005 was approximately 17 percent. The Czech Republic had low unemployment during most of the 1990s, though by 2000 the rate had increased to 9 percent; in 2005, it was still 8 percent (see table 5.3). In most of the region, the

Photo 5.1.   *Elderly woman begging for change on the street. The economic transition hit older women particularly hard.*
(Source: Peter Turnley/CORBIS)

percentage of unemployed women is higher than that of men, and more women than men work part-time.[10]

There have been changes with respect to women's work even in countries where unemployment was relatively low, as in the Czech Republic.[11] But unemployment clearly aggravates other problems and inhibits social and political participation. Even

Table 5.3.   Total, Male, and Female Unemployment Rates in Central and Eastern Europe

	Total		Men		Women	
	2000	2005	2000	2005	2000	2005
Bulgaria	16.4	9.9	16.7	10	16.2	9.6
Czech Republic	8.7	7.9	7.3	6.5	10.3	9.8
Estonia	12.8	7.8	13.8	8.6	11.8	7.0
Hungary	6.4	7.1	7.0	6.9	5.6	7.4
Latvia	13.7	9.0	14.4	9.1	12.9	9.0
Lithuania	16.4	8.2	18.6	7.9	14.1	8.5
Poland	16.1	17.7	14.4	16.5	18.1	19.2
Romania	6.8	7.7	7.2	8.0	6.3	7.5
Slovakia	18.8	16.4	18.9	15.7	18.6	17.3
Slovenia	6.7	6.3	6.5	5.9	7.1	6.8

Source: Eurostat, Key Figures on Europe—Statistical Pocketbook 2006, http://epp.eurostat.ec.europa .eu/cache/ITY_OFFPUB/KS-EI-06-001/EN/KS-EI-06-0 01-EN.PDF.

with comparatively generous benefits for the unemployed as found in Germany, those without work in eastern Germany often withdraw from friends and former colleagues. Certain groups of women are isolated more generally, for work meant some degree of social integration.

For reasons of past experience as well as economic need, many women in Central and Eastern Europe attempt to remain in the workforce, even with increased obligations.[12] Labor force participation rates have remained high in the region. However, although it gives women skills and interests that might lead to greater political involvement, employment also takes time away from participation in other outside activities.

Women's political participation is also shaped by developments in the arena of organized politics. It takes time for relevant constituencies to become aware of party policies, and unions, women's organizations, and the parties themselves have attempted to educate potential voters. In the Czech Republic, more women than men voted for conservative rather than for leftist parties in 1996, but women moved to the left more than men, regardless of social class and age.[13] In the German federal election of 2002, exit polls showed that 41.5 percent of women gave their votes to the Social Democratic Party (SPD) compared to 38.1 percent of the men; approximately equal proportions (40.6 percent of the men, compared to 38.7 percent of the women) voted for the right-of-center Christian Democratic Party (CDU) or its Bavarian sister party, the Christian Social Union (CSU).[14] In the 2005 elections, women voted as often for the Christian Democratic Party as for the Social Democratic Party; men continued to prefer the Christian Democratic Party. Among men, the CDU/CSU received 34.8 percent of the vote (2.0 percent more than the SPD); among women both the Social Democratic Party and the Christian Democratic Party received 35.5 percent.[15]

The reemergence of nationalism and the politicization of ethnic identification in some of the postcommunist countries has also had a profound effect on women's participation in public life and on the salience of women's concerns in public and political debate. Nationalism and strong ethnic identification are often associated with more traditional conceptions of gender relations. Women's rights to an active life outside the household are challenged, and the primary emphasis is on their support for the family, as mothers, educators, and upholders of national or ethnic traditions. Efforts to restrict abortion and encourage larger families are often related to these ideals. Furthermore, in this context, it is not uncommon to blame and attack the antitraditionalist stance of socialism, officially committed to equality and the social participation of women.[16]

Can we see some pattern in the way political parties represent women's interests? Although it is impossible to take into account all political parties and although some parties combine perspectives that seem incompatible, two groups of parties appear to have more specific agendas than others, though they do not necessarily receive the votes of a majority of women. The Christian Democratic, church-affiliated, and nationalist parties tend to support a return to a strong family and women's traditional role. The reformed communist, socialist, and social democratic parties generally emphasize gender equality, at least with respect to employment practices and social welfare policies. The liberal parties, though their policies vary even more than those of parties to the right and to the left, tend to support women's right to abortion and attempt to be cosmopolitan in their concerns and connections but do not generally push for interference in the labor market on behalf of women or incorporate a women's agenda in their programs. Their lack of support for active measures in this respect reflects an important issue that separates liberals from reformed communists and social democrats: their attitude toward the role of the state.

Both the economic policy constraints and the new ideological landscape of the political system have an important consequence: getting women elected does not necessarily mean that women's issues are advanced. Especially at the beginning of the transition period, many women engaged in politics did not have an agenda that focused on the needs of women. If they did worry about developments that seemed to reduce work opportunities for women or the decline in more general social support that threatened women's overall life situations, they hesitated in many cases to bring up these issues or press for a fair resolution. Many women leaders were also uncertain of how to relate to the new independent women's organizations that were developing in their country. Women have not been very successful in rising to positions of leadership when they have pushed for clearly female causes.[17]

There are frequently differences in how women's groups and women in parliament "Westernize" feminist issues. Some independent women's organizations became politically involved, while others concentrated on addressing the immediate needs of women through direct help, local projects of all sorts, and, in some cases, organizing centers for women. Often, differences in perspective and focus have prevented women's groups from supporting each other. Differences between women's groups in eastern and western Germany, for example, have hindered common actions. One vivid example of these differences occurred during a meeting of women affiliated with or interested in a German political party. The guest speaker was from the west; the meeting was held in the former GDR. Next to the meeting room were the children of those east German women who attended the discussion. After the west German speaker denounced the family as an institution, the east German women took over the meeting and ignored her. Some of these issues continue to be salient today in Central and Eastern Europe. Differences also exist between those women who move in an international feminist environment and those who do not.[18] Many of the concerns of these two groups of women have differed, and there has been little agreement about who is really emancipated. Women's groups also vary in their understanding of the role and the responsibility of the state. Different conceptions of women's interests and more broadly of gender relations have had an impact on the actions of elected representatives, and they are of equal importance for the political participation of women.

It is an often overlooked fact that women's interests are historically constructed. Articulating women's interests in a radically new economic, political, and social situation and making these goals attractive to women in very different life situations is inevitably a slow process. It is complicated by parallel and competing attempts to articulate class interests as well as the interests of religious and ethnic/national groups. Different definitions of women's needs and interests have frequently been connected to competing political goals. Some political actors emphasized cultural expectations for traditional roles for women. Others, often frustrated by the political and economic course of the transitions, tried to put forth an agenda that would include the interests of women seeking to continue to work and engage in other activities outside the home. Finally, a renewed emphasis on national, religious, and ethnic themes entered the formation of competing political interests and affected the ability of women to introduce other items to the political agenda.

Electoral Arrangements and Political Parties

The chances for women to advance in political life depend to an important extent on structural conditions in the political system. While the share of women among elected representations does not simply determine policy making in the interest of women, it is clearly an important aspect of the place of women in political life.

After the end of communism, there was considerable opposition against quotas for women in representative bodies. Quotas were attacked as responsible for the participation of unqualified women under communism and also for going against more traditional roles for women and men. Those who held these views also felt that men were meant to do the work of politics. Proponents of quotas were frequently attacked as communists or as supporting a return to the old system.

Attitudes toward quotas have been somewhat different in Germany and seem to be changing in other postcommunist countries as well. A quota system for women in public positions in the Green Party and the Social Democratic Party of western Germany as well as in the Party of Democratic Socialism (the reformed communist party), the Alliance 90 (Greens), and the Social Democratic Party in the east led to new opportunities for women. In the 2002 and 2005 elections, nearly a third (32 percent) of the representatives elected to the German parliament were women. The Czech Social Democratic Party, the leading party in the Czech Republic in the early 2000s, initiated quotas for women occupying party offices.[19] Women in the Czech Republic were more likely to be supportive of quotas in the late 1990s than in the immediate postcommunist period.[20] Political parties in Poland have also initiated quotas.[21] The

Polish Parliamentary Group of Women proposed a 30 percent quota but did not gain enough support to pass the measure in parliament.[22] In the Polish parliamentary elections of 2001, the Alliance of Democratic Left and the Labor Union, as well as the Freedom Union, accepted a quota of at least 30 percent for women on their list of candidates.[23] These quotas were also in effect in the 2005 elections. After extensive debate, the Hungarian Socialist Party endorsed a quota system that reserved for women and people under thirty-five one-fifth of the party's elected bodies.[24] These are very important developments and a major change in political life in these countries since the beginning of the transition period.

Proportional representation systems are generally associated with increases in women's representation, while only modest gains have been made in majoritarian systems.[25] When a party expects to win several seats, it is more likely to try to balance its ticket by gender, provided that women are effectively organized within the party. With more seats to distribute, gatekeepers will be more ready to divide winning slots on the party list among a number of internal party interests.

Proportional representation systems foster a contagion effect, as parties adopt policies initiated by other political parties. When a party that is dominant in an individual district in a single-member district system is challenged to nominate more women, it may be able to ignore the pressure because it is unlikely to lose the seat. In a proportional representation system, the loss of a few votes may lead to loss for the party.[26] Closed lists, which give parties more control over choice of candidates, are more helpful for women's participation than open lists.[27] Thus, although preferential voting systems in which voters choose individual candidates give voters the opportunity to promote women, they also give them the opportunity to do the opposite. A highly centralized party gives leaders the control to create openings for women if they desire to do so, and if they do not, a central party organization can be held responsible for

Photo 5.2.   Hanna Suchocka, prime minister of Poland between 1992 and 1993. She served as prime minister under the presidency of Lech Wałesa and was the first woman to hold this post in Polish history.

(Source: Grochowiak Ewa/Corbis Sygma)

low proportions of women candidates. Preferential voting, on the other hand, leaves parties free of responsibility for insuring gender balance.[28] If the forces interested in women's representation are not effectively organized, however, the electoral system will probably have only limited effect.[29] It is thus only under certain conditions that proportional representation results in increasing the participation of women.

The way political parties deal with women's issues also has an impact on the number of women elected to parliament. In several countries, such as the Czech Republic, Hungary, and eastern Germany, left-leaning parties tend to have greater female representation than right-leaning parties. This pattern is in line with the broad characterizations of the parties' policy orientations on women's issues discussed earlier. Thus, it came as no surprise that after the 1998 elections in Hungary, after which a more conservative coalition replaced the socialist-liberal government, the number of women in parliament again dropped. In Ukraine, left-wing parties whose revival started in 1994 worked at promoting women candidates. At the same time, women's profile increased in other parties as well.[30] Yuliya Tymoshenko played a major role in the Orange Revolution in Ukraine and served as prime minister under President Yushchenko. The first woman chancellor of Germany, Angela Merkel, from the former German Democratic Republic, was elected in 2005. Her Christian Democratic Party was forced by the election result to form a coalition with the Social Democrats. In both Germany and Poland, the percentage of women in the parliaments elected in 2005 remained the same. The victory of the Polish Conservative Party, Law and Justice, led to policies related to women that are increasingly conservative. There is no discussion about the equal treatment of women; instead, the government's policy is pro-family, and urges women to have and take of care of more children.

Other Factors Affecting Women's Roles in Politics

The education and professional training of women are crucial for their acceptance in political life, especially at the national level. In Czechoslovakia during the communist period, women in both the governmental and party elites were disproportionately drawn from working-class or peasant backgrounds and had lower tenure and higher turnover than their male counterparts. After the end of communism, although the number of women in public office decreased, the qualifications of those women who have attained high political office have greatly improved.[31] Women leaders thus should have better chances of exercising political power in postcommunist parliaments and have a greater impact on policy than they had under communism.

The educational and occupational patterns resulting from policies adopted during the communist era have given women skills and tools useful in political life. Women's higher qualifications are important for their attractiveness as candidates. In several of the countries of Central and Eastern Europe, women attended university in numbers equal to or greater than men. Thus, the professional experience women gained in the past is an important asset for their political potential today. The experience professional women gained in their work groups as well as through activity in unions is also important, even with all the limitations that were involved.[32]

Women's experience in professional and other nongovernmental associations also helps create the skills needed for wider political involvement. Not only do these activities increase women's experience, but the organizations can become a power base for those who are interested in being political candidates; they also give women visibility with the public.[33]

Local political experience may also be the beginning of a political career. In Hungary, as in many other countries, women's political engagement seems to be most prevalent at local levels,[34] and women's organizations tend to concentrate on local politics, where women seem to be more at ease. Many of the early women's organizations tended to concentrate on social issues and assisting women in difficulty.[35] Many women also work in the professional administration of local governments.[36] Approximately equal numbers of all female deputies in the Czech parliament interviewed in the mid-1990s held an appointed or elected office at the local level prior to being elected to parliament.[37] Many women deputies in Romania in the late 1990s had done extensive work in their party organizations; a number also had experience in local politics and government.[38]

Even when involvement in local politics does not lead women to run for higher office, higher levels of women's participation have an impact on policy. Social spending by local governments in Hungary, for example, shows "significantly higher standards" where women represent the majority in decision-making bodies. As Julia Szalai, a Hungarian sociologist, writes:

> Their presence safeguards a sufficient level of expenditures on the modernization of local childcare facilities, day centers, and homes for the elderly. Similarly, welfare assistance reaches more of the needy and gives them more efficient support in those communities in which women determine the orientation of local politics. These socially "sensitive" political bodies are also usually more open to civil initiatives, thus inviting an even larger circle of women into the shaping of community life.[39]

International organizations may play an important role in opening up possibilities for women. European women's sections of trade unions offered lectures and workshops at the invitation of women's groups in Hungary, for example, where working conditions, low pay, and problems after the end of maternity leave were discussed.[40] European and American groups and foundations, as well as governments, have provided funds for numerous women's nongovernmental organizations and sponsored programs.[41] On more substantive issues, international expectations were important for the 1997 bill passed in the Hungarian parliament that criminalized rape within marriage.[42]

The European Union has also had an important impact on the issues that Central and East European members of parliaments address. The Council of Ministers and the European Parliament recently reached agreement on a commission proposal for tight regulations that would combat sexual harassment at work as well as introduce additional changes to the laws on equality between men and women, for example.[43]

After the June 1999 European parliamentary elections, women represented 30 percent of the total deputies in the European Parliament, a substantial increase from 1979, when women's representation was only 17 percent. In interviews with members of the European Parliament, it emerged that despite national and cultural differences, there were clearly certain women's rights issues, such as child care, sexual harassment, and employment that the women parliamentarians thought they could affect positively. They also believed that the high percentage of women in the parliament made it easier to put those issues on the agenda.[44] As part of the accession process, candidate countries have adopted "gender equality machinery," including committees to monitor discrimination against women, and enacted antidiscriminatory legislation.

Women also participate in politics as members of women's groups as well as women's caucuses in unions and parties, and in professional organizations. Challenges to social policies that benefit women and reproductive rights in particular can galvanize large numbers of women. The organization of women against attempts to criminalize abortion can be seen in a number of countries in the region. Poland is the best-known case because of the intense conflict with the Catholic Church, as both women and men organized in protest against new abortion regulations. Poland now has many women's organizations that address a wide variety of issues; some have worked directly with the Polish Parliamentary Group of Women. A large number of women's groups have also emerged in Hungary. Here, there was an effort to address the possible curtailment of reproductive rights, an increase in the retirement age, and decreased support for child care. Although successful with the first two issues with which they were concerned, women's groups were not able to unify their forces sufficiently to prevent reductions in maternity and family benefits.

The possibilities women leaders have to go against the tight control of party decisions vary across countries. In Poland, a women's group formed in parliament that cut across party lines and included a majority of women delegates, but creation of such a group can be very difficult. In most legislatures tight party discipline and parties' control over the recruitment process limit women's cooperation across party lines. In some cases, women parliamentarians see no need to organize themselves as women within parliament.[45]

Women's success in politics also depends greatly on their ability to frame their concerns and policy ideas in ways that are consistent with the dominant values and experiences of their constituencies. To understand and take into account the cultural, social, and political outlook of the people whom they seek to represent is of critical importance, even if—and perhaps especially if—women deputies are introducing innovative ideas or feminist ideologies.

Conclusion

Although there have been recent increases in women's political representation in some countries, women continue to play a secondary role in political life beyond voting in Central and Eastern Europe. Yet, despite the weak participation of women in the national political scene in nearly all postcommunist countries, women in much of the

Photo 5.3. Yuliya Tymoshenko, former Ukrainian prime minister under President Yushchenko and major player in the Orange Revolution.

(Source: This photo was taken through joint efforts of the UNIAN news agency (www.unian.net) and the International Renaissance Foundation (George Soros Foundation in Ukraine, www.irf.kiev.ua).)

region retain an interest in politics equal to that of men. It is the obstacles women encounter in the postcommunist world, not their limited interest, that explain their low participation. Most women attempt to remain active at the workplace outside of the home, thus continuing their education, the use of their professional and vocational skills, and their contact and experience in the outside world. To the extent that they are active in professional associations, unions, and other voluntary organizations, they remain aware of and gain practice in activities that are important preparation for future political engagement. Social policies encouraging such engagement and political mechanisms that insure women's representation are crucial determinants of levels of women's political activism.

Participation in political life on the local level is typically part of the background of women who become active nationally. Women's activity on the local level in government, in women's associations, and in other nongovernmental organizations contributes not only to vital experience for women but also to the creation of decent social policies. In most of the countries discussed, women's groups have been important first, by helping individuals in marginal social groups who are otherwise without sufficient supports and, secondly, by articulating the needs of these groups to the public and to governmental representatives, thus increasing the sensitivity of representatives to important social concerns. Links with international organizations have been helpful in this respect; links with supportive political parties may be even more important. Even with the frustrations of women active politically on the national level, it is clear that in the years since the end of communism in Europe, women, in several of the countries discussed in this chapter, have gained more experience, have filled more important positions, and are more confident in being able to have an impact in the longer run.

Suggested Readings

Fodor, Eva. *Working Difference: Women's Working Lives in Hungary and Austria 1945–1995*. Durham, NC: Duke University Press, 2003.

Funk, Nanette, and Magda Mueller, eds. *Gender Politics and Post-Communism*. London: Routledge, 1993.

Gal, Susan, and Gail Kligman. *Reproducing Gender*. Princeton, NJ: Princeton University Press, 2000.

Jaquette, Jane S., and Sharon L. Wolchik, eds. *Women and Democracy*. Baltimore: Johns Hopkins University Press, 1998.

Kolinsky, Eva, and Hildegard Maria Nickel, eds. *Reinventing Gender: Women in Eastern Germany since Unification*. London: Frank Cass, 2003.

Kollantai, Alexandra. *The Autobiography of a Sexually Emancipated Communist Woman*. New York: Schocken Books, 1975.

Lapidus, Gail Warshofsky. *Women in Soviet Society*. Berkeley: University of California Press, 1978.

Matland, Richard E., and Kathleen A. Montgomery, eds. *Women's Access to Political Power in Post-Communist Europe*. Oxford: Oxford University Press, 2003.

Ramet, Sabrina P., ed. *Gender Politics in the Western Balkans*. University Park: The Pennsylvania State University Press, 1999.

Rueschemeyer, Marilyn, ed. *Women in the Politics of Postcommunist Eastern Europe*. London: M.E. Sharpe, 1998.

Wolf, Christa. *The Quest for Christa T.* New York: Farrar, Straus and Giroux, 1970.

Notes

1. An earlier version of this chapter has been published as "Les nouvelles democraties europeennes de l'Europe de l'Est," in *Femmes et parlements: un regard international*, ed. Manon Tremblay (Montreal, Canada: Editions du Remue-menage, 2004). Parts of the background material used appeared in Marilyn Rueschemeyer, "Frauen und Politik in Osteuropa: 10 jahre nach dem Zusammenbruch des Sozialismus," *Berliner Journal fur Soziologie* 11, no.1 (2001): 7–18. It has been substantially revised and updated for this volume.

2. Marie Čermaková, "Women in the Czech Society: Continuity or Change," in *Women, Work and Society*, ed. Marie Čermaková, 19–32 (Prague, Czech Republic: Academy of Sciences of the Czech Republic, 1995).

3. Hana Havelková, "Political Representation of Women and Political Culture in the Czech Republic" (paper presented at the Conference on Women's Political Representation in Eastern Europe, Bergen, Norway, 1999).

4. Marilyn Rueschemeyer, "The Work Collective: Response and Adaptation in the Structure of Work in the German Democratic Republic," *Dialectical Anthropology* 7 (1982): 155–63 and Marilyn Rueschemeyer, "Integrating Work and Personal Life: An Analysis of Three Professional Work Collectives in the GDR," *GDR Monitor* (1983): 27–47.

5. Jiřina Šiklová, "Inhibition Factors of Feminism in the Czech Republic after the 1989 Revolution," in *Women, Work and Society*, ed. Marie Čermaková, 33–43 (Prague, Czech Republic: Academy of Sciences of the Czech Republic, 1995).

6. Gunnar Winkler, ed. *Sozialreport 1990* (Stuttgart, Germany: Aktuell, 1990).

7. Marilyn Rueschemeyer, ed. *Women in the Politics of Postcommunist Eastern Europe* (London: M.E. Sharpe, 1998).

8. Ann Graham and Joanna Regulska, "Expanding Political Space for Women in Poland? An Analysis of Three Communities," *Communist and Post-Communist Studies* 30, no.1 (1997): 65–82.

9. During the early transition years in some of the countries, there was continuity in a number of the supports people had taken for granted. In the Czech Republic, for example, rent control kept housing expenses low, but young people looking for new housing often found the costs unaffordable. "The impact of the shift to market rates was compounded by . . . a dramatic decrease in new housing . . . but those who had housing did not face immediate evictions or immediate dislocations." See Marilyn Rueschemeyer and Sharon Wolchik, "The Return of Left-Oriented Parties in Eastern Germany and the Czech Republic and Their Social Policies," in *Left Parties and Social Policy in Postcommunist Europe*, ed. Linda Cook, Mitchell Orenstein, and Marilyn Rueschemeyer, 132 (Boulder, CO: Westview Press, 1999).

10. For the latter see UNECE Gender Statistics Data Base: Statistics on Women and Men in the ECE Region, Regional Symposium on Mainstreaming Gender into Economic Policies, 2004.

11. Marie Čermaková "Women in Czech Society: Continuity or Change," in *Women, Work, and Society* (Working Papers of the Institute of Sociology, Academy of Sciences of the Czech Republic 1995), 10; and Marilyn Rueschemeyer, "Social Democrats after the End of Communist Rule: Eastern Germany and the Czech Republic," *Sociological Analysis* 1, no. 3 (1998): 41–59.

12. Hildegard Maria Nickel, "With a Head Start on Equality from the GDR into the Trap of Modernization in the Federal Republic: German Women Ten Years after the 'Wende'" (paper presented at the Center for European Studies, Harvard University, 1999).

13. Rueschemeyer and Wolchik, "The Return of Left-Oriented Parties."

14. "Clearly Visible Gender Gap," *Deutschland* 6 (December/January 2002): 23.

15. Johann Hahlen, "Final Results of the Representative Electoral Statistic on the Election to the 16th Bundestag," Federal Statistical Office of Germany, Press Office.

16. Branka Andjelkovic, "Reflections on Nationalism and Its Impact on Women in Serbia," in *Women in the Politics of Postcommunist Eastern Europe*, ed. Marilyn Rueschemeyer, 235–48 (London: M.E. Sharpe, 1998); and Jill Irvine, "Public Opinion and the Political Position of Women in Croatia," in *Women in the Politics of Postcommunist Eastern Europe*, ed. Marilyn Rueschemeyer, 215–34 (London: M.E. Sharpe, 1998).

17. Sarah Birch, "Women and Political Representation in Contemporary Ukraine" (paper presented at Conference on Women's Political Representation in Eastern Europe, Bergen, Norway, 1999).

18. Olga Lipowskaja, "Sisters or Stepsisters: How Close Is Sisterhood?" *Women's Studies International Forum* 17 (1994): 273–76.

19. Rueschemeyer, "Social Democrats," 49.

20. Sharon Wolchik, "Men and Women as Leaders in the Czech and Slovak Republics" (paper presented for the Conference on Women's Political Representation in Eastern Europe, Bergen, Norway, 1999), 5.

21. Joanna Regulska, personal communication, 1999.

22. Renata Siemienska, "Consequences of Economic and Political Changes for Women in Poland," in *Women and Democracy: Latin America and Eastern Europe*, ed. Jane S. Jaquette and Sharon L. Wolchik, 125–62 (Baltimore: Johns Hopkins University Press, 1998).

23. Renata Siemienska, who has written about the quotas, has also noted a number of other legislative initiatives of the Parliamentary Group of Women, such as a proposal to modify the method of calculating taxes to protect single parents (usually single mothers), involvement in amending the Family and Guardian's Code, and the liberalization of the abortion law (personal communication 2002).

24. Katalin Fabian, "Making an Appearance: Women in Contemporary Hungarian Politics" (paper presented at the annual meeting of the American Association for the Advancement of Slavic Studies, St. Louis, Missouri, 1999), 7.

25. Richard Matland, "Legislative Recruitment: A General Model and Discussion of Issues of Special Relevance to Women" (paper presented at the Conference on Women's Representation in Eastern Europe, Bergen, Norway, 1999).

26. Richard Matland and Donley Studlar, "The Contagion of Women Candidates in Single-Member and Multi-Member Districts," *Journal of Politics* 58, no. 3 (1996): 707–33.

27. Matland, "Legislative Recruitment," 13.

28. Miki Caul, "Women's Representation in Parliament: The Role of Political Parties" (paper presented for the annual meeting of the American Political Science Association, Washington, DC, 1997); and Pippa Norris and Joni Lovenduski, *Political Recruitment: Gender, Race and Class in the British Parliament* (Cambridge, UK: Cambridge University Press, 1995).

29. Matland, "Legislative Recruitment," 15.

30. Birch, "Women and Political Representation," 15.

31. Sharon Wolchik, "Women and the Politics of Transition in the Czech and Slovak Republics," in *Women in the Politics of Postcommunist Eastern Europe*, ed. Marilyn Rueschemeyer, 116–41 (London: M.E. Sharpe, 1998).

32. Marilyn Rueschemeyer, *Professional Work and Marriage: An East-West Comparison* (Oxford: St. Antony's Oxford/Macmillan, 1981), 138–64.

33. Matland, "Legislative Recruitment," 14.

34. Fabian, "Making an Appearance," 5.

35. Fabian, "Making an Appearance," 14.

36. Julia Szalai, "Women and Democratization: Some Notes on Recent Change in Hungary," in *Women and Democracy*, ed. Jane Jaquette and Sharon Wolchik (Baltimore: John Hopkins University Press, 1998).

37. Wolchik, "Men and Women as Leaders," 8.

38. Mary Ellen Fischer, "The Changing Status of Women in Romanian Politics," in *Women in the Politics of Postcommunist Eastern Europe*, ed. Marilyn Rueschemeyer, 168–95 (London: M.E. Sharpe, 1998).

39. Szalai, "Women and Democratization," 200.

40. Fabian, "Making an Appearance," 18.

41. Fischer, "The Changing Status of Women," 186.

42. Urszula Nowakowska, "Violence against Women: International Standards, Polish Reality," *The Journal of Communist Studies and Transition Politics* 15, no. 1 (1999): 41–63.

43. "Equal Opportunities: Parliament and Council Agree on Tough New Equality Rules," *European Social Policy* 128 (April 2002): 31–32.

44. Jane Freedman, "Women in the European Parliament," *Parliamentary Affairs* 55, no. 1 (January 2002): 179–88.

45. Fischer, "The Changing Status of Women," 187.

CHAPTER 6

EU Accession and the Role of International Actors

Ronald Linden

After the extraordinary changes of 1989, virtually all of the newly democratizing states of Central and Eastern Europe made overtures to join the three major organizations of what was generally referred to as "Europe": the Council of Europe, NATO, and the European Union (see table 6.1). They wanted to do so for a number of reasons. Some were practical: to allow the people of the region to partake of the prosperity and security that the EU and NATO, respectively, had afforded the West European states since the end of World War II. Some were psychological and symbolic: to heal the division of Europe and return to where they would have been had the Cold War not

Table 6.1. Membership in European Organizations

Country	Date of Joining Organization		
	Council of Europe	European Union	NATO
Albania	7/13/1995		
Bosnia-Herzegovina	4/24/2002		
Bulgaria	7/5/1992	1/1/2007	3/29/2004
Croatia	11/6/1996		
Czech Republic	6/30/1993	5/1/2004	3/16/1999
Hungary	11/6/1990	5/1/2004	3/16/1999
Macedonia	11/9/1995		
Montenegro	5/11/07		
Poland	11/26/1991	5/1/2004	3/16/1999
Romania	10/7/1993	1/1/2007	3/29/2004
Serbia	6/3/06*		
Slovakia	6/30/1993	5/1/2004	3/29/2004
Slovenia	5/14/1993	5/1/2004	3/29/2004
Ukraine	11/9/1995		

*Continued membership of state of Serbia and Montenegro, dating from 4/3/03.
Sources: Council of Europe (www.coe.int/T/e/com/about_coe/member_states/default.asp); European Union (www.europa.eu.int/abc/12lessons/index3_en.htm); NATO (www.nato.int/docu/update/2004/03-march/e0329a.htm); and (www.nato.int/docu/pr/1999/p99-035e.htm).

cut them off, and to be included among the world's democracies. This chapter will first offer some background on the region's international environment before 1989 and then briefly consider the role of the Council of Europe. Its primary focus will be on the movement of the Central and East European states toward the EU and the process undertaken by that organization to engage and admit these states. Jeffrey Simon's chapter in this volume deals with NATO accession.

Eastern and Western Europe before 1989

After World War II the two parts of Europe moved in different directions, economically and politically. After being prevented by Joseph Stalin from participating in the U.S.-funded Marshall Plan to rebuild Europe, Central and Eastern Europe was absorbed into the Soviet-dominated economic and political system and its organizations. All of the Central and East European states (except Yugoslavia) became members of the Council for Mutual Economic Assistance (CMEA), founded in 1949 to coordinate economic planning and use of resources. They were also brought into the Warsaw Pact, the Soviet-dominated military alliance established in 1955. Most important, they were bound by bilateral economic, political, and militarily ties to the Soviet Union. Trade was sharply curtailed with the West and reoriented toward the Soviet Union (see table 6.2). Five-year plans approved by the respective communist parties ruled the region's economies, and private economic activity was reduced to insignificance or eliminated altogether.

As a result, while Western Europe regained economic vitality, established convertible currencies, and began to participate actively in global trade and investment, Central and Eastern Europe did not. The states of the region did recover from the war and did make progress in providing basic goods and services for most of their populations, especially in comparison to the low level of economic development that had characterized most the region before the war. But the region was cut off from the stimulant of international trade competition; was not open to Western investment; and, in fact, was utilized as an economic support group for the USSR for the first twenty-five years

Table 6.2. Reorientation of Trade: Share of Central and Eastern Europe's Trade with Western Europe by Year

Country	Imports				Exports			
	1928	1989	1995	2002	1928	1989	1995	2002
Bulgaria	61.6	13.7	38.4	51.3	64.5	7.8	38.6	55.6
CZ/SL	54.8	15.4	45.4	62.0	43.9	16.5	45.7	64.2
Hungary	32.4	30.9	61.5	57.5	25.0	24.2	62.8	73.5
Poland	54.5	27.7	64.7	67.5	55.9	30.5	70.1	67.3
Romania	50.2	7.8	50.9	63.9	53.9	17.5	54.5	68.0

Sources: For 1928 and 1989, Susan M. Collins and Dani Rodrik, *Eastern Europe and the Soviet Union in the World Economy* (Washington, DC: Institute for International Economics, 1991), 39, 40. For 1995 and 2002, European Bank for Reconstruction and Development, *Transition Report 2003* (London: EBRD, 2003), 86. Data for 1928 and 1989 reflect trade with European countries that became or were members of the European Community; data for 1995 and 2002 reflect trade with members of the European Union. For 1995 and 2002 the average for the Czech Republic and Slovakia was used.

after World War II. The USSR extracted from the region an estimated $20 billion worth of technology, machinery, skills, and manufactured goods in the first fifteen years after the war.[1]

The region remained a marginal global economic actor for the entire period of the Cold War. All of the Central and East European states together provided only 4.5 percent of the world's exports—equal to about one-third of the amount West Germany alone provided. The typical Central and East European state received from the USSR nearly 40 percent of its imports and sent to the USSR more than one-third of its exports.[2] None of the region's currencies were convertible, even in transactions among themselves. On the other hand, the region was shielded from sharp jumps in the price of internationally traded commodities like oil because these were provided to the region at the CMEA "friendship price" (a periodically adjusted fraction of the global price). Thus the region's economies avoided sharp recession and had little price inflation but also by the late 1970s and 1980s began to show little or no growth.[3] The states of the region also received a substantial trade subsidy from the Soviet Union because they were able to purchase energy and other resources at lower than world prices and did so in exchange for "soft" goods, those not salable in the West.[4] When Mikhail Gorbachev became the leader of the Soviet Union in 1985 he moved to change this "international division of labor" to adjust to economic realities. The revolutions of 1989 intervened, and the Central and East European states found themselves thrown onto the harsh playing field of the global economy without the experience or economic mechanisms to compete.

The Council of Europe

This body was founded in 1949 to bring together Europe's democracies and try to prevent future conflict by establishing certain norms of appropriate state behavior. Its founding principles are enshrined in the European Convention on Human Rights, adopted in 1950, and several other conventions and instruments adopted over the years. In a practice unique for international organizations, the Council of Europe obliges its members to allow themselves to be taken to court, the European Court of Human Rights, by individuals who allege human rights abuses against them. The council's main task is to insure the highest standards of democratic practices, protect human rights—including social and economic rights and those of women and minorities—and ensure the rule of law. Since the council only admits those states that are practicing democracies, the communist-ruled Central and East European states were not members during the Cold War.

After the changes of 1989 all of the Central and East European states applied to join the council. They adopted European norms and practices for elections, freedom of the media and religion, and the rights of individuals to express themselves and be free from discrimination.[5] Most of the Central and East European states were admitted, though the admission of some was delayed. The outbreak of warfare in former Yugoslavia, for example, prevented that country from joining until after the overthrow of Slobodan Milošević (in 2000) and the creation of the new state of Serbia and Montenegro (now separate states and members). Acceptance into the Council of Europe was important on its own but even more significant as a first step toward joining the powerful political and economic group represented by the European Union.

The Courtship of the EU

What is today an organization of twenty-seven countries including more than 480 million people began in the aftermath of World War II as a limited attempt to link key parts of the economies of former enemies France and Germany. In 1951, the European Coal and Steel Community (ECSC) was founded by those two countries, plus Italy, Belgium, the Netherlands, and Luxembourg. In the landmark Treaty of Rome of 1957 the European Economic Community was created to complement the ECSC and a new European Atomic Agency. These three were combined in 1965 into the European Community (EC). The members created a parliament and modified other parts of the organization, but over the next two decades the organization grew slowly both in terms of number of members (adding the UK, Ireland, and Denmark in 1973; Greece in 1981; Spain and Portugal in 1986) and areas of policy responsibility. By the time the Berlin Wall fell in 1989, the EC still had only twelve members, but it had committed itself (through the Single European Act of 1986) to creating the mechanisms for a single European economy. The Treaty on European Union, referred to as the Maastricht treaty after the Dutch town in which it was signed in 1992, renamed the organization the European Union and began to move the members toward more unified economic functioning as well as stronger common political institutions. Austria, Finland, and Sweden joined in 1995, bringing the number of members to fifteen. In 2002 the common European currency, the euro, was introduced in eleven of the member states.

After the overthrow of communism, the Central and East European states moved to try to join the EU as soon as possible. Hungary and Poland formally applied in 1994; Romania, Slovakia, and Bulgaria in 1995; and the Czech Republic and Slovenia the next year. By that time, all had held at least one set of open elections deemed proper by international observers; had created conditions for the exercise of citizens' rights of expression, assembly, and participation; and were seeing the birth—in some cases explosion—of political parties and interest groups. The states of the region also rejected the idea of re-creating the Soviet-era economic or political alliances in any new form in favor of joining the most successful and attractive international organization in history, the EU. That organization had never had to consider such a potentially large simultaneous expansion before. Moreover, in previous enlargements, the candidates for membership were not only functioning democracies but had established capitalist and Western-oriented economic systems. In Central and Eastern Europe, by contrast, the countries seeking membership were only just starting the process of creating such systems; were much more numerous; and, most important, were significantly poorer than even the poorest EU member. Among potential candidates, for example, the GDP per capita of Poland (the largest) was just over two-thirds that of Greece, the poorest EU member, and only 40 percent of the average of all EU members (see table 6.3).

Table 6.3. Gross Domestic Product per Capita of New and Old Members of the EU

GDP in PPS per Inhabitant, 2001 (EU-15 = 100)	
Luxembourg	190
Ireland	118
Netherlands	115
Denmark	115
Austria	111
Belgium	109
Finland	104
Italy	103
France	103
Germany	103
Sweden	102
United Kingdom	101
Spain	84
Cyprus	74
Slovenia	70
Portugal	69
Greece	65
Czech Republic	59
Hungary	53
Slovakia	48
Poland	41
Estonia	40
Lithuania	39
Latvia	33
Bulgaria	25
Romania	24
Turkey	23

Source: Eurostat, *Towards an Enlarged European Union* (Brussels, Belgium: European Commission, n.d.). In this chart gross domestic product per capita is calculated on the basis of PPS, Purchasing Power Standard, which takes into account differences in prices across countries.

It is not surprising, then, that the EU moved somewhat slowly to establish and to implement standard procedures for bringing the Central and East European states into the organization. Along with financial assistance to help these states reform their economies (see below), the EU signed a series of association agreements, called the Europe Agreements, to govern trade with the Central and East European states. At the 1992 European Council at Lisbon, the organization for the first time pledged to help the Central and East European states not just to reform their economies but ultimately to become members of the organization. At the Copenhagen Council in 1993, the EU set forth the basic criteria that the new members would have to meet to be admitted. These criteria were stability of institutions guaranteeing democracy, the rule of law, human rights, and respect for and protection of minorities; the existence of a functioning market economy as well as the capacity to cope with competitive pressure and market forces within the union; and the ability to take on the obligations of membership including adherence to the aims of political, economic, and monetary union.[6]

To fulfill these criteria, applicants were obliged to accept and pass into legislation the codes, practices, and laws in place in the European Union, referred to as the *acquis communautaire*. Starting in 1998, all of the applicant countries were evaluated annually to assess their progress toward establishing democratic practices, including the rule of law, the exercise of political rights by the population, and the protection of minority rights. Economic assessments judged the countries' movement toward establishing a market economy, including privatization, fiscal and monetary control, and openness to foreign investment. Each applicant's ability to undertake the "obligations of membership" was assessed by measuring the adoption of measures laid out in the *acquis*, covering, for example, agriculture, transportation, environmental policy, and justice and home affairs (e.g., the countries' legal systems, including courts, police, rights of accused, use of the death penalty).[7] In all, there were thirty-one chapters of standards by which these countries were judged and only when all chapters had been "closed," or judged satisfactory by the European Commission, were invitations for membership issued. That happened for eight Central and East European states in 2002, leading to their admission in May 2004.[8] Romania and Bulgaria, however, were subject to "enhanced monitoring" by the commission. After several more reports, they were permitted to join as of January 1, 2007, but under an unprecedented "Cooperation and Verification Mechanism" that obliges them to report on their progress on judicial reform, the fight against corruption, and, in Bulgaria's case, the fight against organized crime.[9]

Photo 6.1.   EU Enlargement Day in May 2004. The flags of Cyprus, the Czech Republic, Estonia, Hungary, Latvia, Lithuania, Malta, Poland, the Slovak Republic, and Slovenia are raised at an EU building, marking their accession to the Union.

(Source: European Community, 2007)

Photo 6.2.   Berlaymont building with "Welcome Bulgaria Romania to the European Union." After several delays due to slow conformance with European standards, particularly in the area of anticorruption reforms, Bulgaria and Romania joined the EU on January 1, 2007.

(Source: European Community, 2007)

The Costs of Joining

For most of the Central and East European states, making the transition to democratic practices with regard to individual freedoms, elections, and political institutions and parties was challenging. Although the countries' populations desired such institutions and practices after four decades of Communist Party rule, not all of the states moved equally quickly. In some cases communist-era practices—and people—remained powerful. In its first report on the region, issued in 1997, the European Commission sharply criticized Slovakia for the practices of then prime minister Vladimír Mečiar. Romania's Ion Iliescu, that country's first elected leader after the fall of communism, was viewed suspiciously because of his communist past. It took his electoral defeat in 1996 to improve the EU's opinion and Romania's chances for joining the organization.

For the Central and East European governments, adapting their countries' political and legal processes to European norms involved making adjustments in a variety of policy arenas. Elimination of the death penalty and laws against homosexuality, for example, was required. Improvements in the legal system, including the formation of independent judges and constitutional courts, were needed in most cases. One of the most common areas of pressure lay in the EU's criticism of the countries' treatment of their Roma (Gypsy) minorities. Numbering over 4 million and scattered through-

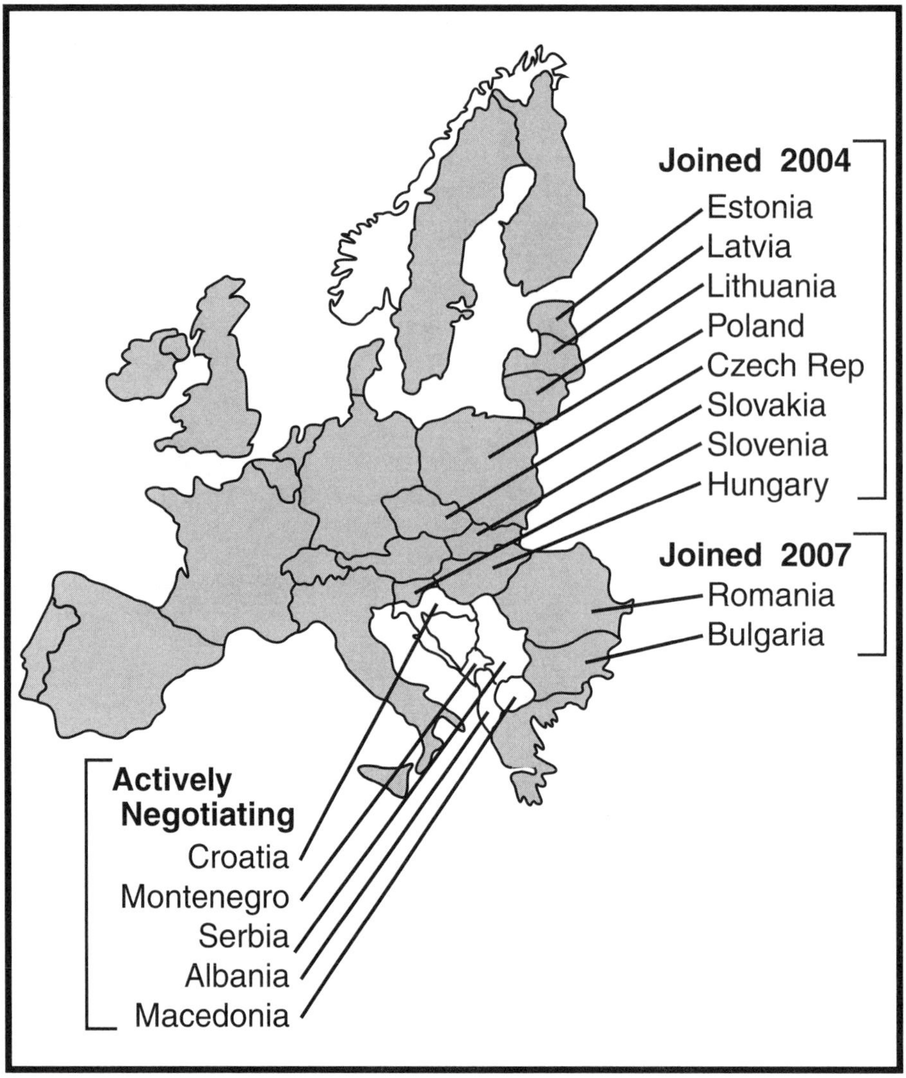

Map 6.1.   European Union

out the region,[10] Roma minorities suffered both legal and economic discrimination, exclusion from employment and political power and, in some cases, actual physical harassment. Even leading candidates for membership such as the Czech Republic were subject to criticism by the EU for restrictive citizenship laws and hostile actions toward Roma.[11]

The EU's involvement in minority issues in the region produced some skepticism even as it provided an opportunity for domestic minority groups and nongovernmental organizations to utilize EU influence on their behalf to secure better treatment from their governments. For example, the EU insisted that the candidate states implement full recognition and guarantees of minority rights that in some cases did not apply in member states.[12]

Setting up appropriate Western-style parliamentary and electoral institutions and getting them running in forms that the EU would approve were relatively simple compared to the process of wrenching the economies into line with EU expectations. These states were not as economically developed, had not traded in a world competitive market, and did not have the resources to make the economic transition without substantial pain. For example, in Central and Eastern Europe on average more than 13 percent of the workforce was employed in agriculture; the figure in Western Europe was just over 4 percent. The Central and East European economies were less productive, used more energy and human resources to produce the same number of goods as in the West, and for the most part produced goods that were not competitive on the world market. To make matters worse, those goods these states could potentially sell globally were precisely those that the EU specialized in—farm products, steel, textiles—and the EU was not eager to open its markets. The Europe Agreements at first put strict limits on Central and East European exports to Western Europe. Within a few years, however, tariff and quota restrictions on Central and East European goods were removed. Given the uncompetitive nature of these economies, it took several years before any could achieve significant positive trade balances (see table 6.4).

With the sharp shift in trade after 1989 and governments getting out of the business of running the economy, production in most of the Central and East European states declined dramatically. In 1991 the six Central and East European states averaged a more than 11 percent fall in their economies, followed by a nearly 4 percent fall in 1992. Growth returned in the Czech Republic and Poland in 1993 and the rest of the region after that, but it remained uneven. It took until the end of the decade for most of Central and Eastern Europe to reach the economic levels of 1989 and even longer for Romania and Bulgaria.[13] Unemployment, which had not officially existed under socialism, soared, reaching more than 12 percent of the workforce on average throughout the region. Part of the adjustment to EU economic policies involved improving the environment for competition, eliminating government support of industries, ending price controls, and allowing bankruptcies. The EU also exerted pressure to allow foreign investment on a nondiscriminatory basis, meaning that experienced, successful Western European companies would be free to buy up valuable assets in these states, now available at bargain basement prices. After 1989 the region attracted more than $170 billion in foreign direct investment (through the year 2004) with the bulk going to the three Central European states, Poland, Hungary, and the Czech Republic.

While proceeding slowly on formal admission, the EU did move to provide the region with substantial economic aid. Through the PHARE program,[14] the organization provided more than $11 billion to Central and Eastern Europe, the Baltic states, and Bosnia between 1989 and 1999. Most of these funds went to infrastructure, education, training, and assisting with privatizing the economies. In 1999 the organization added the SAPARD and IPSA programs,[15] which support rural and agricultural development, and environmental and transportation projects, respectively. Together these programs provided more than $20 billion from 2000 to 2006 for new members in what was termed "preaccession aid" even after they became members.

Perhaps the major challenge to the accession process involves agriculture. Since its formation, the EU has supported farmers by controlling imports, supporting prices, and providing direct payments through the Common Agricultural Policy (CAP). CAP payments constitute the single largest item in the EU budget. With 4 million new farmers added by Central and East European accession to the 7 million already in the

Table 6.4. Balance of Trade between the EU and Central and Eastern Europe

1995	Exports to EU	Imports fr. EU	Trade Balance
Bulgaria	2013	2098	−85
Czech Republic	9273	11679	−2406
Slovakia	3208	3049	159
Hungary	8077.3	9514.6	−1437.3
Poland	16039	18782	−2743
Romania	4388	4811	−423
TOTAL CEE	42998.3	49933.6	−6935.3

1996	Exports to EU	Imports fr. EU	Trade Balance
Bulgaria	1913	1780	133
Czech Republic	12760	16213	−3453
Slovakia	3645	4030	−385
Hungary	8233.8	9684.5	−1450.7
Poland	16248	23739	−7491
Romania	4271	4732	−461
TOTAL CEE	47070.8	60178.5	−13107.7

1997	Exports to EU	Imports fr. EU	Trade Balance
Bulgaria	1942	1628	314
Czech Republic	13557	14021	−464
Slovakia	4540	5133	−593
Hungary	13602.7	13239.6	363.1
Poland	16533	27000	−10467
Romania	4752	5316	−564
TOTAL CEE	54926.7	66337.6	−11410.9

1998	Exports to EU	Imports fr. EU	Trade Balance
Bulgaria	2137	2325	−188
Czech Republic	16976	18361	−1385
Slovakia	5970	6554	−584
Hungary	16781.7	16485.5	296.2
Poland	19285	31030	−11745
Romania	5369	6210	−841
TOTAL CEE	66518.7	80965.5	−14446.8

1999	Exports to EU	Imports fr. EU	Trade Balance
Bulgaria	2035	2611	−576
Czech Republic	18172	18031	141
Slovakia	6076	5852	224

2000	Exports to EU	Imports fr. EU	Trade Balance
Bulgaria	2463	2858	−395
Czech Republic	19905	19926	−21
Slovakia	7015	6246	769

(continued)	Exports to EU	Imports fr. EU	Trade Balance
Hungary	18927.4	17984	943.4
Poland	19338	29829	-10491
Romania	5572	5829	-257
TOTAL CEE	**70120.4**	**80136**	**-10015.6**

2001	Exports to EU	Imports fr. EU	Trade Balance
Bulgaria	2794	3574	-780
Czech Republic	20490	24787	-4297
Slovakia	7569	7351	218
Hungary	22434.6	19378.7	3055.9
Poland	24995	30869	-5874
Romania	7737	8119	-382
TOTAL CEE	**86019.6**	**94078.7**	**-8059.1**

2003	Exports to EU	Imports fr. EU	Trade Balance
Bulgaria	4479.1	5939.31	-1460.21
Czech Republic	41971	36480	5491
Slovakia	17436	17306	130
Hungary	34438	30010	4428
Poland	43299	47031	-3732
Romania	13007	14678	-1671
TOTAL CEE	**154630.1**	**151444.31**	**3185.79**

(continued)	Exports to EU	Imports fr. EU	Trade Balance
Hungary	21117.1	18760.7	2356.4
Poland	22154	29954	-7800
Romania	6630	6727	-97
TOTAL CEE	**79284.1**	**84471.7**	**-5187.6**

2002	Exports to EU	Imports fr. EU	Trade Balance
Bulgaria	3363.63	4377.76	-1014.13
Czech Republic	32327	29221	3106
Slovakia	12657	11944	713
Hungary	27771	23770	4001
Poland	32914	38215	-5301
Romania	10079	10953	-874
TOTAL CEE	**119111.63**	**118480.76**	**630.87**

2004	Exports to EU	Imports fr. EU	Trade Balance
Bulgaria	5321.05	8336.81	-3015.76
Czech Republic	57782	48847	8935
Slovakia	21285	21706	-421
Hungary	43478	42520	958
Poland	58373	60115	-1742
Romania	17170	19276	-2106
TOTAL CEE	**203409.05**	**200800.81**	**2608.24**

Sources: International Monetary Fund, *Direction of Trade Statistics Yearbook 2002, 2005.* (Washington, DC: International Monetary Fund, 2002, 2005). Trade balances calculated as imports of Bulgaria, Czech Republic, Hungary, Poland, Romania, and Slovakia from the EU-15 (for 1995–2004) minus exports to those countries, in millions of U.S. dollars. Data compiled by Kristen Flanagan.

EU, the organization realized that it could not afford to extend to the new members the generous agricultural subsidies it had been providing to farmers in the EU-15 states. Moreover, in global trade negotiations during the 1990s the EU had pledged to reduce the level of its subsidies. Hence, as part of these states' accession, direct payments to Central and Eastern Europe's farmers are at first a fraction of those paid to farmers in Western Europe and will reach the full rate in ten years.[16]

The Politics of Membership

When the European Union was founded, the driving idea was to link continental Europe's major economic powers, France and Germany, so inextricably as to make future wars between them impossible. As other functions became part of common responsibility, such as control of nuclear energy, control of agricultural production, and external trade ties, the organization not only grew in complexity but added members. Great Britain's membership had been vetoed by France in 1963 and was delayed for ten years, but adding democratic Portugal, Spain, and Greece in the 1980s or the relatively rich capitalist countries Austria, Sweden, and Finland in 1995 was not controversial. However, adding eight or ten economically weak states that had operated as one-party dictatorships and state-run economies for four decades was not popular. Public opinion surveys among the members of the EU consistently showed a lack of enthusiasm for enlargement in most of the EU's members. Moreover, some in the union feared that a united Germany—already the organization's largest and most powerful member—would become dominant once several subordinate Central and East European economies were brought in with close ties to Berlin. In part for this reason, France became one of the most ardent supporters of Romania's membership. Despite public ambivalence, movement toward membership proceeded, reinforcing the idea among some that the organization operated with a "democratic deficit," that is, that decisions were being made by distant elites who were not responsible to anyone and reflected bureaucratic imperatives in Brussels more than the desires of their constituents.[17]

In Central and Eastern Europe, though, accession to the EU was very popular. Throughout the 1990s, public opinion polls showed that majorities of the population of the region strongly supported joining the EU. In general, Central and East European populations trusted the EU and saw joining as the right thing to do for their country.[18] Support was not equally high throughout the region, however, as the costs of adjustment and the uneven distribution of such costs among the population became evident. In a 1996 survey, for example, nearly two-thirds of those surveyed felt that private businesses would benefit the most from accession; only one-third felt that farmers and low-income groups would benefit.[19] A curious phenomenon that emerged in public opinion was that, as countries moved closer to joining the EU, public support for doing so fell off.[20] Nevertheless referenda on joining were held in each of the acceding Central and East European countries in 2003 and produced positive—though in some cases, close—votes.[21] By 2006, among the new member-states, public support for membership was at almost the same level as in countries with longer membership, while trust in the EU as an institution was substantially higher and more people in these new members felt their country had benefited from membership.[22]

Apart from accommodating legal, political, and economic systems to the demands of the *acquis*, for several of the new members there were particular issues that provided a challenge to the depth of their commitment to join. Many worried that their inexperienced and weaker economies—especially in the agricultural sector—would not be able to compete with rich and subsidized EU enterprises. People worried that Western Europeans would buy up their countries' low-priced assets and land, leaving local people unemployed and without property. The Polish government, for example, pressed hard to mitigate the impact on Polish land ownership and to secure support for Poland's 2 million mostly small farmers.[23] For their part, politicians in the EU were worried that economic dislocation and the attraction of the more prosperous west would produce a vast labor migration once borders were erased and full EU citizenship—including the right to live anywhere—was extended eastward. In the end, several countries were granted transition periods during which they could retain control over agricultural land purchase. But the "free movement of persons" was also restricted for the new members, with restrictions remaining in place for not less than two and possibly up to seven years.[24]

Border issues will continue to be complicated for several new members. All the new members were obliged to move toward adopting the provisions of the Schengen Treaty (1985) operating among most EU states. This treaty allows for free movement of citizens within the EU but mandates strict enforcement and guarding of the EU's external borders. With that border now pushed eastward, Poles and Hungarians living in Ukraine, for example, find visiting their ethnic kin in new EU member-states more difficult and expensive. Citizens of non-EU states like Ukraine, Russia, and Moldova have to obtain visas to visit places they used to travel to more easily before. This requirement not only presents difficulties in human relations but also depresses the substantial transborder economic activity that had grown up, for example, between Poland and countries to the east. When some countries, such as Hungary, attempted to pass laws giving their ethnic kin in neighboring non-EU countries special rights and privileges, the EU criticized them and obliged them to water down or abandon such acts.[25]

Most of the new members also faced serious issues in terms of compliance with environmental regulations. This chapter of the *acquis* includes extensive regulations affecting power generation, especially nuclear power, water and air cleanliness, and the burning of fossil fuels. Accommodating to EU standards has been enormously expensive for these states and in some cases has obliged them to close down some power plants altogether. To ensure its entry in 2007, for example, Bulgaria agreed to close four of six reactors at the nuclear power plant at Kozloduy, which had produced 40 percent of Bulgaria's power, in return for more than $400 million in aid and loans from the EU.[26]

For the Czech Republic, negotiating the country's entry into the EU brought up issues with origins in World War II. After that war, nearly 3 million German citizens of the newly reborn Czechoslovakia were summarily expelled from the country in retaliation for the German attack on and occupation of the country during the war. Many of these people or their descendents, referred to as Sudeten Germans after the region from which they came, demanded the right to return to their homeland, the right to reacquire the property they lost or be compensated for it, and the retroactive annulling of the "Beneš Decrees" under which they were expelled. In the Czech Republic allowing this to happen was very unpopular but had never been likely until EU membership made it a real possibility. While official Czech-German relations were good and successive Czech governments pushed for membership, many Czechs objected to any "apology" and feared a reverse migration of Sudeten Germans back to the country and a massive loss of property held by Czechs. In the end, the decrees were not annulled, and the Czech Republic was granted a five-year period during which it could control the sale of property.[27]

For all of the Central and East European states, the period after 1989 and before 2004 represented a wrenching shift in both real and symbolic terms. These states had been part of a Soviet-dominated empire for the four decades after World War II as a result of the consequences of that war and the dominant position of the USSR. They had each been ruled by their own Communist Party but always with the Soviet model and, even more important, the level of Soviet tolerance, acting as the key factor determining how far they could deviate from that model. Over the years Moscow had used political and economic ties and Soviet-dominated regional organizations to ensure control. When challenges emerged, as happened in Hungary in 1956 and Czechoslovakia in 1968, the USSR had been willing to use force to keep the countries subordinate. Only in 1989 did the USSR, under Mikhail Gorbachev, refrain from intervening to prevent far-reaching democratic change and the return of full sovereignty to the states of this region.

The irony is that having finally achieved full control over their own affairs, the leaders of the newly democratic Central and East European states, with their populations' agreement, moved relatively quickly to surrender key parts of that sovereignty to a different power center, the EU. By applying for membership and accepting the terms for doing so, the governments of Central and Eastern Europe were obliged to remake virtually all of their institutions and practices in order to conform with standards set, though not necessarily met, by members of the EU. All were willing to do so, and to have their performances judged annually by that organization. Finally, fifteen years after the revolutions that toppled dictatorships in Central and Eastern Europe, and only after the EU was satisfied that national laws and institutions accorded with its norms, the east and west of Europe were formally reunited.

The Case of Ukraine

Ukraine has always been treated differently by the European Union in part because of the slow pace of reform under President Leonid Kuchma (1994–2004) and in part because of the country's close ties to Russia. The country has signed a variety of functional agreements with the EU but, unlike Croatia or Turkey, has not been given the official status of "Candidate Country." Its relations with the EU are governed by a Partnership and Cooperation Agreement (much like the EU's relations with Russia) and are part of the EU's Neighborhood Policy framework.[28] This policy allows for intense cooperation, partnership, and even annual evaluations, like candidate members, but provides for no formal prospect of membership.

During the contested presidential elections at the end of 2004, the EU was very active in mediation efforts and pushed strongly for new and fair elections. The EU did not accept the election of Viktor Yanukovych and in December, just before the new elections, Javier Solana, EU High Representative for Common Foreign and Security Policy, said: "The way the electoral process is conducted will set the framework for future relations between Ukraine and the EU."[29] After the election of Viktor Yushchenko, many hoped that the EU, Ukraine's largest trading partner, as well as the largest donor of technical assistance, would upgrade Ukraine's chances for membership. Instead an ambitious "Action Plan" for further cooperation was adopted and in December 2005 Ukraine was granted the status of "functioning market economy." In September 2006, the EU proposed that a new comprehensive agreement be negotiated to cover all areas of EU-Ukrainian relations, including a Free Trade Area,[30] but in the words of the EU ambassador in Ukraine, "membership is not on the agenda."[31]

Implications for Political Science

A central problem in the study of world politics has always been the question of why states act in certain ways. Do they do so out of considerations of pure power (the realist point of view), because of the nature of their governments (the liberal point of view), because of changes in their identity (the constructivist point of view), or because of the role of international institutions (the liberal institutionalist point of view)?[32] If a state's behavior seems to conform to the dictates of other more powerful states, is that because it has no choice, because it truly associates itself with the behavioral norms of its neighbors, or because it sees gains in acting that way? The case of the Central and East European states accepting and implementing the norms of the EU provides a real-world experiment for such theories, though, like all such experiments, only an approximate one. In the real world, states cannot be put in laboratories with some variables held constant and others allowed to vary. But for the years since the revolutions, the states of Central and Eastern Europe represent an observable "comparative set." Those states, with different cultures and histories and different experiences of conflict, all became democratic and were freed from the dominant power that had ruled their region. They all had strong economic and political incentives to join the EU. Their leaders and populations all claimed to want to adhere to democratic norms, and in most cases they moved to do so.

The question for political scientists and policy makers is twofold. First, why were the Central and East European states so willing to dance to the EU's tune? And second, will they continue to do so now that they are members of the club? Analysts of institutional behavior say that, generally speaking, actors accommodate their behavior either because of "the logic of consequences," that is, they do it because they fear a loss or anticipate a gain, or because of the "logic of appropriateness," that is, they do it because it is the right thing to do.[33] In the case of Central and Eastern Europe, we have seen acceptance and emulation of EU norms across a range of domestic political and economic practices. Has this occurred as a product of rational calculation of cost and benefits? If so, we might expect the new Central and East European members to slide back on democratic practice, for example, once they are members. If they do, what can the EU do to insure compliance? Alternatively, have the changes occurred because there has been a genuine acceptance of the norms of behavior that apply in democracies and market economies? If so, will this persist even after these states' entry tickets have been punched? In that case, the issue of enforcement will be much less important. A definitive answer is not yet evident, for the simple reason that too little time has passed since the first of the Central and East European countries joined in 2004 to see if the changes implanted in the region are genuine. But the answer to this question will tell us a lot, not only about the future of Europe, but about the ability of international organizations to create and foster important global values, like democracy, in parts of the world long deprived of the benefits of that system.

Suggested Readings

Henderson, Karen, ed. *Back to Europe: Central and Eastern Europe and the European Union*. London: UCL Press, 1999.

Ingham, Hilary, and Mike Ingham, eds. *EU Expansion to the East*. Northampton, MA: Edward Elgar, 2002.

Jacoby, Wade. *The Enlargement of the European Union and NATO: Ordering from the Menu in Central Europe*. Cambridge, UK: Cambridge University Press, 2004.

Linden, Ronald H., ed. *Norms and Nannies: The Impact of International Organizations on the Central and East European States*. Lanham, MD: Rowman & Littlefield, 2002.

Mayhew, Alan. *Recreating Europe: The European Union's Policy towards Central and Eastern Europe*. Cambridge, UK: Cambridge University Press, 1998.

Poole, Peter A. *Europe Unites: The EU's Eastern Enlargement*. Westport, CT: Praeger, 2003.

Pravda, Alex, ed. *The End of the Outer Empire*. London: Royal Institute, 1992.

Schimmelfennig, Frank, and Ulrich Sedelmeier. *The Europeanization of Central and Eastern Europe*. Ithaca, NY: Cornell University Press, 2005.

Vachudova, Milada. *Europe Undivided: Democracy, Leverage, and Integration after Communism*. Oxford: Oxford University Press, 2005.

Notes

I would like to thank Kristen Flanagan for her research assistance on this chapter.

1. Paul Marer, "Has Eastern Europe Become a Liability to the Soviet Union? (III) The Economic Aspect," in *The International Politics of Eastern Europe*, ed. Charles Gati, 65 (New York: Praeger Publishers, 1976).

2. James L. Ellis, "Eastern Europe: Changing Trade Patterns and Perspectives," in *East European Economies: Slow Growth in the 1980s*, U.S. Congress, Joint Economic Committee, 99th Cong. 2nd sess., March 28, 1986, 17, 24. Figures are for 1980.

3. Thad P. Alton, "East European GNP's Domestic Final Uses of Gross Product, Rates of Growth, and International Comparisons," in *Pressures for Reform in the East European Economies*, U.S. Congress, Joint Economic Committee, 101st Cong., 1st sess., October 20, 1989, 81.

4. Michael Marrese and Jan Vanous, *Soviet Subsidization of Trade with Eastern Europe* (Berkeley, CA: Institute of International Studies, 1983).

5. For a description of the council and its activities in this area see *Human Rights: A Continuing Challenge for the Council of Europe* (Strasbourg, France: Council of Europe Press, 1995) and *The Challenges of a Greater Europe* (Strasbourg, France: Council of Europe Press, 1996).

6. These criteria can be seen on the website of the EU at http://ec.europa.eu/enlargement/ enlargement_process/accession_process/criteria/index_en.htm.

7. These annual reports can be seen at http://ec.europa.eu/enlargement/archives/key_docu ments/reports_1998_en.htm.

8. In case a Central or East European state fails to fulfill its commitments in certain areas (internal market, justice and home affairs) after accession, "safeguard clauses" are included in the Accession Treaty, allowing for "appropriate measures" to be taken by the European Commission to insure full compliance. The full text of the Accession Treaty can be seen at http://ec.europa.eu/enlargement/ archives/enlargement_process/future_prospects/negotiations/eu10_bulgaria_romania/treaty_2003/ index_en.htm.

9. The "accompanying measures" can be accessed at http://europa.eu/rapid/pressReleasesAction .do?reference = MEMO/06/347&format = HTML&aged = 0&language = EN&guiLanguage = en.

10. Estimates and censuses vary widely on the number of Roma. The best comparative assessment can be found in Zoltan Barany, *The East European Gypsies* (New York: Cambridge University Press, 2001), 157–64.

11. See, for example the 1999 European Commission Annual Report on the Czech Republic, at http://ec.europa.eu/enlargement/archives/key_documents/reports_1999_en.htm. In 1997 the City Council of Usti nad Labem had decided to build a wall separating the Roma area from the rest of the town, an action sharply criticized by the EU and ultimately overturned by the Czech courts. See Lynn M. Tesser, "The Geopolitics of Tolerance: Minority Rights under EU Expansion in East-Central Europe," *East European Politics and Societies* 17, no. 3 (Summer 2003): 483–532.

12. Michael Johns, "Do As I Say, Not As I Do: The European Union, Eastern Europe and Minority Rights," *East European Politics and Societies* 17, no. 4 (Fall 2003): 682–99.

13. Economic data can be found in the annual *Transition Reports* published by the European Bank for Reconstruction and Development, in London.

14. The term PHARE was derived from the French title for the assistance program originally designed for Hungary and Poland and later expanded to all of the Central and East European countries.

15. SAPARD stands for Special Action Program for Agriculture and Rural Development. IPSA stands for Instrument for Structural Policies for Pre-Accession.

16. "Enlargement and Agriculture" available at http://europa.eu.int/comm/agriculture/eu25/ index_en.htm.

17. See Peter Mair, "Popular Democracy and EU Enlargement," *East European Politics and Societies* 17, no. 1 (Winter 2003): 58–63.

18. Public opinion polls can be found on the Europa website at http://ec.europa.eu/ public_opinion/index_en.htm.

19. *Central and Eastern Eurobarometer*, No. 6 (Brussels, Belgium: European Commission, 1996): Annex Figure 33.

20. A Eurobarometer Survey in 2003, for example, showed that among Central and East European states scheduled to join in 2004, 58 percent of the public supported membership; but in Romania and Bulgaria, which were to join only in 2007, support was 74 percent and 70 percent, respectively. European Commission, *Eurobarometer 2003.2: Public Opinion in the Candidate Countries* (Brussels, Belgium: European Commission, 2003), 69.

21. Referenda results can be seen on the website of the Danish EU Information Centre, www .eu-oplysningen.dk/euo_en/spsv/all/21/.

22. European Commission, *Eurobarometer 65: Public Opinion in the European Union* (Brussels, Belgium: European Commission, 2006), 11, 14, 19. Available at http://ec.europa.eu/public_ opinion/archives/eb/eb65/eb65_en.htm.

23. The Polish accession treaty included a provision preventing foreign purchase of land for seven

years in the north and west of the country—territory shifted from Germany to Poland after World War II—and for three years in the rest of the country. See Krzysztof Jasiewicz, "Knocking on Europe's Door," *Problems of Post-Communism* 51, no. 5 (September–October 2004): 37.

24. "Report on Results of the Negotiations on the Accession of Cyprus, Malta, Hungary, Poland, the Slovak Republic, Latvia, Estonia, Lithuania, the Czech Republic and Slovenia to the European Union," available at http://ec.europa.eu/enlargement/archives/enlargement_process/future_prospects/negotiations/eu10_bulgaria_romania/treaty_2003/index_en.htm.

25. Margit B. Williams, "'And the Walls Came Tumbling Down' . . . Or Did They? European Union Accession, and New and Old Borders in Central and Eastern Europe," *Canadian-American Slavic Studies* 39, no. 4 (2005): 421–48.

26. "2004 Regular Report on Bulgaria's Progress towards Accession," available at http://ec.europa.eu/enlargement/archives/pdf/key_documents/2004/rr_bg_2004_en.pdf.

27. "Report on Results of the Negotiations."

28. EU-Ukraine relations are described on the EU website at http://ec.europa.eu/comm/external_relations/ukraine/intro/index.htm#pol. The Neighborhood Policy is described at http://europa.eu.int/comm/world/enp/index_en.htm.

29. "Statement by Javier Solana, EU High Representative for the CFSP, on the Forthcoming Presidential Elections in Ukraine," Brussels, Belgium, 23 December 2004.

30. "Commission Proposes Negotiating Directives for Enhanced Agreement with Ukraine," http://europa.eu.int/rapid/pressReleasesAction.do?reference = IP/06/1184&format = HTML&aged = 0&language = EN&guiLanguage = en.

31. Oksana Bondarchuk, "Ukraine's EU Hopes Far Away," *Kyiv Post*, October 12, 2006; http://www.kyivpost.com/nation/25209/.

32. See James E. Dougherty and Robert L. Pfaltzgraff, Jr., *Contending Theories of International Relations* (New York: Addison Wesley Longman, 2001) for a review of international relations theories.

33. James G. March and John P. Olsen, *Rediscovering Institutions: The Organizational Basis of Politics* (New York: The Free Press, 1989).

CHAPTER 7

Security Issues: NATO and Beyond

Jeffrey Simon

One of the first foreign policy acts of the new postcommunist states was to dissolve their forty-year-old military alliance, the Warsaw Pact. This was the act that, after the fall of the Berlin Wall, marked the institutional end of the Cold War and the end of the division of Europe into two competing blocs, one dominated by the Soviet Union and the other by the United States. In the process, the North Atlantic Treaty Organization (NATO) no longer needed to protect the West from a communist onslaught. Instead, NATO membership became one of the incentives to bring these former communist states to democracy and eventually into membership in their old "enemy."

Initially, NATO's strengths as "a defense cooperation organization" had been used for other purposes, including "creating political/military options for dealing with crises and challenges to the interests of the member states, spreading stability to Central and Eastern Europe, and encouraging cooperation with Russia and other countries."[1]

After 1989, NATO's focus shifted from protecting the division of Europe to bringing the eastern and western parts together, managing conflicts within Europe, and then dealing with terrorist assaults on its member states. To do this, the former states of Central and Eastern Europe are being brought into NATO itself as their military forces are transformed and they are deemed "democratic." NATO forces have been involved as peacekeepers in the conflicts in Bosnia and Kosovo, in conflicts further to the east, and in counterterrorism measures.

The Warsaw Pact and Its Legacy

The inclusion of former members of the Warsaw Pact in NATO was not simply a matter of shifting players on a chessboard. The Warsaw Pact had been formally established in 1955 as a response to the establishment of NATO. It linked the militaries of the Soviet Union and its satellites together under the Soviet Union in everything from weapons production to political and military leadership. The only state in this region that was not a member was Yugoslavia. After the invasion of Czechoslovakia in 1968, Albania withdrew from the Warsaw Pact and Romania pursued its own independent foreign policies.

Warsaw Pact forces shared the same equipment, which fit Soviet specifications and, obviously, not the specifications of NATO forces. From airplanes to guns, that interdependence was further enforced by allowing no single country to produce all the parts for any weapon itself and by giving states specific tasks under the directions of the Warsaw Pact and the Council for Mutual Economic Assistance (CMEA). So no state could be an independent actor militarily. The military control structures also were intertwined. While there were high-level officers from all of the Central and East European states, it was Soviet officers who were in control of planning and military action. The others were vetted and under the command of Soviet generals.

Map 7.1.   Warsaw Pact and NATO States, 1989

For the Soviet Union and its allies, being a defensive and offensive force was not their only critical role. Unlike NATO, these were politicized militaries in which political control was as important as military prowess and professionalism. The only military maneuvers the Warsaw Pact actually carried out were to stop the Prague Spring Czechoslovak liberalization in 1968 and to pressure Poland during the 1980–1981 unrest that resulted in the imposition of martial law. For the conscripts and the professional military, there was a heavy diet of political training to go along with military training. Required military service for men out of school or during their college careers was a time to indoctrinate them, even though the indoctrination was seldom effective. Even military oaths made reference to defending the bloc and the Soviet Union, rather than the homeland.

Warsaw Pact maneuvers and the joint command were ways for the Soviet Union to get one more measure of reliability for these militaries. These were forces whose mission was to protect the Soviet bloc. Their defense lines ranged from the inner German border and Czechoslovakia eastward. In the event of NATO moves, each military had a specific task, and there were clear offensive plans for attacks on the West that had been in place for almost forty years by 1991. Crack troops from the Soviet forces were stationed all along the so-called Iron Curtain border between east and west.

After 1989, however, the Warsaw Pact almost immediately became a vestigial organization as the new democratizers turned to the West for economic and political guidance. The Soviet army's "invasion" of the Soviet Republic of Lithuania in early 1991 to stop popular demands for independence made the Warsaw Pact's existence, even as a historical marker, unacceptable to the new leaders. Soon after the invasion, the foreign ministers of Poland, Czechoslovakia, and Hungary demanded the dissolution of its military structures. In June 1991, the foreign and defense ministers of the Warsaw Pact's members met to declare its military functions over. The Warsaw Pact was no more. Nine months later, the Soviet Union collapsed as well.

The Central and East European leaders who brought down the Warsaw Pact thus forced NATO to develop new ways to include them. Politically, for these countries to become members or partners of NATO meant that the divisions of the Cold War were over and that these states, once "the ideological enemy," had become trusted allies. The logic for large militaries dependent on draftees had to be rethought. The military's political wing no longer had a place. It required a complete restructuring and reconstruction not only of the chain of command but also a complete shift to Western weapons and equipment. Soviet troops in the German Democratic Republic (East Germany), Poland, Czechoslovakia, and Hungary had to return to the Soviet Union and to an economy already unable to meet the demands of its population, and without any clear foreign policy goals of its own.

To join NATO, the Central and East European states had to restructure their militaries and civil-military relations, do away with their old Warsaw Pact airplanes, guns, and other equipment, and invest in new equipment that fit with NATO specifications. Professional high-ranking military officers from Warsaw Pact forces had to become partners, or, at least, Partners for Peace, with their old enemies. For these states, even with support and aid from the West, the cost of retooling their militaries and committing to membership in NATO was extremely high, especially since they were also coping with the other costs of the transition. But this first opportunity to become "official" parts of the West seemed to be worth the price.

From New to Old: NATO and Europe

When NATO was formed in 1949, its members (Belgium, Canada, Denmark, France, Great Britain, Iceland, Italy, Luxembourg, Netherlands, Norway, Portugal, and the United States) agreed that the Soviet Union and its allies were the singular threat to their security. They were committed to defending each other if any one was attacked from outside NATO and to be prepared to defend against a Soviet bloc onslaught. The "security umbrella" NATO provided in the early 1950s extended to vital sea lanes from Greenland to Iceland and the United Kingdom. When NATO did expand, it was to make itself even more able to defend Europe: in 1952, during the Korean War, Greece and Turkey were added in order to contain the Soviet Union on its southwestern border; in 1955, the Federal Republic of Germany was taken in—putting NATO on the Iron Curtain that divided Germany and Europe as a whole; and in 1982, Spain was added explicitly to increase the strategic depth of NATO's reach. In 1978, NATO went further to make sure all of its members were equally committed: all agreed to commit 3 percent of their individual budgets to defense as a part of their Long-Term Defense Plan.

The process of inclusion and of developing "battle plans" and strategic plans in NATO was not nearly as hierarchical as that in the Warsaw Pact. Although an American general always headed NATO and the United States was the largest donor to NATO, its troop involvement was far more limited and separated from the rest of the NATO troops. Joint maneuvers were just that: "joint" rather than being dominated by the leader of the bloc. Nor was there any attempt to meld these armies and the foreign policies of NATO states together at times when there was not an active threat. There was also no political training for troops sent to work on NATO missions. The presence of "occupying" troops in Western Germany gave it the security it needed, because its military was very limited by postwar agreements to prevent German rearming, but these were not forces with a political mission.

Although there were many crises in Europe during the Cold War, no NATO member was ever directly attacked, and NATO was never drawn into an armed conflict. As a result, NATO troops were on high alert during the Cold War crises in Berlin and Cuba but were never fully activated. The presence of Soviet troops in Berlin and close to the Soviet bloc's western borders as well as the crises in Berlin in 1961 and the Soviet-led Warsaw Treaty Organization invasion of Czechoslovakia in 1968 made it impossible for the members of NATO to forget there was a threat that necessitated their standing together. Even after Western policy began to shift in the 1970s to both seeking détente with the Soviet Union and building up the nuclear arsenal to defend against it if necessary, NATO held together, although the United States and Western Europe often differed on whether to use the "carrot" or "stick" approaches and how important the military presence was.

NATO's Redefinition

The collapse of communism first in Central and Eastern Europe and then in the Soviet Union brought with it increasing disagreements within NATO over the nature of the threats the alliance faced and the capabilities necessary to deal with them. After all, the threat that had held the NATO states together no longer existed: communist control in Central and Eastern Europe and the Soviet Union had simply collapsed. This period was also marked by moves to enlarge NATO to include what had been "enemy states" in Central and Eastern Europe. These dual processes were further complicated by the eruption of violence in Yugoslavia—the first such violence within Europe's boundaries since World War II—just as the Cold War was ending and NATO's members were redefining their goals and the critical threats. This conflict was particularly difficult for NATO because several of its members (Germany, France, and the United Kingdom) had very different commitments and concerns in the various segments of Yugoslavia. NATO unity was further complicated by the September 11 attacks on the United States and the division between Europe and the United States over how to respond to the terrorist threat in the long term.

NATO's effort to deal with the new reality in Europe began with the Rome Summit's issuance of a New (soon to be Old) Strategic Concept in November 1991, right after the Warsaw Pact had collapsed. It was an effort to start a new European security policy that included the countries in the former Warsaw Pact, even before any of them were fully transformed. This step was followed by a reorientation of NATO's capabilities at the Brussels Summit in 1994. The groundwork was established there for a post–Cold War role for NATO with the establishment of the Combined Joint Task Forces to support the European Security and Defense Identity. That program was designed to strengthen the Europeans' power to work together and take their own initiatives. The shift, though, was not so simple: the debate over what NATO's role should be went on into the Washington Summit in 1999, which dually celebrated the fiftieth anniversary of NATO's founding and the participation of NATO's three new members—the Czech Republic, Hungary, and Poland.

NATO Expansion: Including the East

At the same time that NATO was searching for a new mission for itself and a better balance between Europe and America, the Central and East European states were pressing to get into NATO both as a sign that they were Westernized and also as protection from the instability in Russia. NATO opted for a policy of inclusion to fulfill its long-term goal of a Europe "free and whole," but was not willing to open its doors immediately. The steps in this process began even before the Warsaw Pact had collapsed. At the London Summit in July 1990, NATO invited the Soviet Union and Warsaw Pact members "to establish regular diplomatic liaison with NATO."[2] Once the Warsaw Pact disbanded, NATO took the next step and launched the North Atlantic Cooperation Council to include the former communist countries, without making

Photo 7.1.   NATO flag-raising ceremony marks the accession of the Czech Republic, Hungary, and Poland to the alliance. They were the first postcommunist countries to join the alliance. In March 2004, Bulgaria, Estonia, Latvia, Lithuania, Romania, Slovakia, and Slovenia also joined.

(Source: NATO Photos, 1999)

any moves to make them members.[3] After the USSR disintegrated, NATO moved to include some of the former Soviet republics in the Cooperation Council.

The goal of the North Atlantic Cooperation Council was to promote dialogue on common security concerns with Central and East European countries and the USSR. The dialogue bridged the former East-West divide and illuminated opportunities for practical cooperation. It also was to help Central and East European politicians understand that defense was best rooted in democratic politics and that national security encompassed civil emergency planning and a broader range of concerns than just military issues.

At the 1994 Brussels Summit, NATO leaders moved toward enlargement by establishing the Partnership for Peace (PfP), which included those countries deemed "able and willing to contribute to European security."[4] PfP included all of the states in this volume except the Yugoslav states that were at war. It also included Finland and Sweden, two established democracies that had maintained neutrality in the Cold War and had stayed out of NATO for the entire Cold War. Although, at first, the more democratized countries of Central and Eastern Europe saw the PfP's establishment as "a policy for postponement," in the end, it did address some of their security concerns and established the norm that partners should (and could) also make contributions to common European security efforts.[5] A core group was involved in planning and coordinating military exercises for search and rescue, humanitarian assistance, and peacekeeping.

Photo 7.2.   NATO summit in Brussels in 1994, where the Partnership for Peace program was established. Bosnia and Herzegovina, Croatia, Moldova, Montenegro, Serbia, and Ukraine are members of the program, which is often considered a step toward full NATO membership.

(Source: NATO Photos, 1994)

In July 1997, Poland, Hungary, and the Czech Republic were invited to join NATO itself because they were deemed far enough along in their transitions to be successful "producers of political, economic, social and military security." In addition, during the Madrid Summit, the Partnership for Peace was restructured to allow its members to be involved in actual military operations with NATO troops. When NATO extended this invitation to Poland, Hungary, and Czechoslovakia, it also made clear that "no European democratic country . . . would be excluded from consideration" in the next expansions.[6]

These initial invitees joined NATO on the fiftieth anniversary of Winston Churchill's 1949 Fulton, Missouri, "Iron Curtain" speech on March 12. As they joined, NATO launched its Membership Action Plan (MAP) to help prepare nine more states (Albania, Bulgaria, Estonia, Latvia, Lithuania, Romania, Slovakia, Slovenia, and the former Yugoslav Republic of Macedonia) for membership in NATO. Membership invitations were dependent not just on military readiness but also on evidence that these countries were well on the road to political democracy and a market economy. Equitable treatment of ethnic minorities, good neighbor relations with

Map 7.2.   European Members of NATO, 2006

surrounding countries, and democratic oversight of the military were also required for countries to be deemed "producers" of security and acceptable members of NATO.[7]

The Membership Action Plan states pressed NATO to fulfill its promises to continue its expansion. In May 2000, in Vilnius, Lithuania, the foreign ministers of MAP launched a political initiative to press NATO "to fulfill the promise of the Washington Summit to build a Europe whole and free . . . [and] at the next NATO Summit in 2002 to invite our democracies to join NATO."

At the Prague Summit in 2002, these demands were partially met. The Baltic states, which had been denied membership in the earlier round in response to Russia's opposition to having NATO on its doorstep, were offered membership, as were Bulgaria, Romania, Slovakia, and Slovenia. They formally joined in 2004. Albania, Croatia, and Macedonia were promised that NATO's door remained "open." After the Rose Revolution in Georgia and Orange Revolution in Ukraine, both countries expressed their desire to join the MAP as NATO turned its focus eastward to respond to the expansion of democracy.

NATO's New Roles: Turning to the East and Outside of Europe

As the work of NATO shifted, the military and strategic boundaries of "Europe" moved dramatically to the east, first to the Balkans, then to the Caucasus and Black Sea region. In the new world that emerged, European and American interests diverged. After September 11, this split, on the issue of how to deal with terrorism and the invasion of Iraq, was a deep divide, with the Central and East Europeans caught between the United States and some Western European allies. This dilemma also had an economic dimension in the competition over whose airplanes and weaponry the Central and East Europeans would buy—American or European.

In the early and mid-1990s, even as NATO debated what its role should be and brought in its first set of new members, its troops (and those of its potential new members in the Partnership for Peace) were engaged on the ground as they had not been during the whole Cold War. In 1996, as a part of the Dayton Peace Accords that ended the war in Bosnia in 1995, NATO troops (both from member states and from the states in the PfP) were directly involved as the Implementation Force (IFOR) for the fragile peace agreement. Their presence would continue in Bosnia as the Organization for Security and Cooperation in Europe (OSCE) governance stabilized and the troops went from implementing the peace to being a Stabilization Force (SFOR). This kind of on-the-ground involvement was replayed in the Kosovo Force (KFOR) deployments to maintain the peace after NATO bombing and international pressure had brought an end to open Serb pressure on the Albanians in Kosovo in 1999. Indeed, it was this seventy-eight-day bombing campaign over Serbia and Kosovo that was the high point of NATO military action.

In reality, NATO's involvement in the battles in former Yugoslavia severely tested the ability of the alliance to stay together. Since the bombing campaign had no outside mandate, there were real difficulties in getting a consensus in 1999 on the intervention

Photo 7.3.   The members of the SFOR (Stabilization Force) Multinational Honor Guard stand on the tarmac at Tuzla Air Base, Bosnia-Herzegovina. SFOR remained in Bosnia and Herzegovina from January 1996 to December 2005, when the European Union's EUFOR took over.

(Source: U.S. Department of Defense, 1997).

in Serbia and Kosovo. The KFOR operation enjoyed the mandate of the United Nations (UNSCR 1244). This search for justification for new actions using old provisions was further complicated by the fact that Yugoslavia was an area where different NATO members had different ties and commitments. All this was made even more complicated by the interests of the new and old members as well as the inclusion of Russia and other nonmember armies in the military action and negotiations. NATO's involvement in Bosnia and then in Kosovo was brought about by the United States' interest in having a military presence to enforce the peace and push the Serbs into retreat without a massive and politically untenable commitment of American troops. It was used by the Europeans to stem the bloodshed that led to an outflow of refugees from what had been Yugoslavia into European states who then had to support them.

As NATO troops were used in Bosnia, Kosovo, and Macedonia, the Balkans became part of NATO's "area of responsibility" long before any of the Balkan states were considered for membership. This fact does not mean that maintaining stability in the Balkans and reintegrating the western Balkans have been easy. The hope was that the 2004 accession of Slovenia, Romania, and Bulgaria would stabilize the region by demonstrating to others in the region—Albania and the battling states that came out of the Yugoslav breakup—that membership is possible. These states inside NATO also could advocate and formulate policy for the rest of the Balkans (Croatia, Albania, and Macedonia, as well as Bosnia-Herzegovina, Serbia, and Montenegro). It also means the United States can use Balkan bases to support its operations in Afghanistan and for the Polish-led multinational division in Iraq even as troops remain stationed in Kosovo and Bosnia to keep the uneasy peace.

Since September 11, 2001, NATO and its members have struggled with the need to reshape their defense capabilities to deal with the new risks of global terrorism. The need to deal with this new terrorist threat resulted in NATO opening up further to include, as participants but not necessarily as members or potential members, states in the Caucasus and Central Asia. It also prompted more cooperation among NATO members in working against terrorism, sharing intelligence, and preparing for possible terrorist chemical, biological, or radiological attacks.

The risks for NATO members of living up to Article V have increased, since the terrorist attacks of September 11 on the United States required other NATO members to take action. Immediately after the attacks in Washington and New York, NATO planes and ships began to protect the continental United States and to patrol the Mediterranean Sea. Some NATO members and Partnership for Peace nations became involved in the war in Afghanistan. In the U.S. operation "Enduring Freedom" in Afghanistan, Poland, and the Czech Republic, among other NATO allies, along with Partnership for Peace members Romania, Bulgaria, Ukraine, and Slovakia were involved. After Saddam Hussein was toppled in Iraq, the Poles led a multinational division, which had troops engaged directly in controlling and stabilizing part of Iraq.[8]

The Prague Summit in 2002 endorsed the military concept for "Defense against Terrorism" that calls for "improved intelligence sharing and crisis response arrangements [and commitment with partners] to fully implement the Civil Emergency Planning Action Plan . . . against possible attacks by . . . chemical, biological or radiological agents."[9] The Partnership Action Plan against Terrorism provides a framework upon which to build necessary cooperation within NATO.

In the long run, however, the attacks of September 11 and the U.S. response have triggered real splits within NATO. These splits have been over what the threat is, what is required to deal with it, when and for how long there should be coalition operations, and what conditions are necessary for further enlargement. Not only have there been significant differences of opinion among NATO members over the U.S.-led war in Iraq, but the other NATO states have been unwilling to increase their defense budgets in spite of the widening gap in the military capabilities and investment between the United States and its allies in what Donald Rumsfeld termed the "old Europe" (what was Western Europe) and the "new Europe." This is true, even though all the states in NATO have committed themselves to a broader set of responsibilities and a wider geographical area of engagement. These divergent views have led to conflict between NATO states over the Iraq War. Of the original NATO states, only Great Britain, Spain, Italy, and the Netherlands have had a substantial presence there. The newer NATO states, particularly Poland and Romania, committed themselves in the early part of the war and sent either troops (Poland), or specialized units to support the effort, despite strong popular opposition.

With Bulgaria and Romania now in NATO, the post–Orange Revolution leadership of Ukraine pushing for NATO membership, and Georgia also aspiring to join, the Black Sea is also being transformed geopolitically from a former Soviet area to a NATO "lake." NATO is openly putting a special emphasis on PfP partners in the Caucasus and Central Asia. The new NATO members of Central and Eastern Europe are models for these potential entrants in their use of military cooperation to build confidence and regional security among wary neighbors like those in the Black Sea and Caucasus region.[10] They are also becoming bridges and barriers for a European force that extends further east, and some are ready participants in parts of the "war against terror."

The Costs of Membership

Membership in NATO was, originally, the fastest road for Central and East European countries to take to arrive at officially being part of the West and shedding communist ties. It was a part of the early 1990s' turning away from each other and the Soviet Union toward the West. It demonstrated, for former communists and new leaders alike, that their countries were "democratic" and "Western." Poland's president Aleksander Kwasniewski, for instance, a former communist, made his leadership and favorable reception in NATO a major symbol of the fact that he was not communist but Western and democratic. Among the original entrants, NATO membership was most popular in Poland because of Poles' long-held fear of a Russian attack, even after the Soviet Union fell. Membership was less significant for Hungarians, Czechs, and Slovaks, due to their greater sense of geographical security and their much smaller armies. But it was a step that could not be ignored by any country. After all, being under the NATO umbrella brought with it proof of change and hopes for protection and also financial gains from investments and outside aid.

All this has come with real costs as well. Although the old Warsaw Pact members had invested, in many cases, far more of their budgets in the military during the communist era, the shift to NATO and NATO membership itself were not cheap. NATO countries gave a significant amount of aid to get the militaries, civil-military relations, and even equipment up to NATO standards. But the restructuring and reequipping of these militaries were very expensive projects that involved scrapping much of the old and purchasing new, Western equipment as well as making financial— limited at first but with guaranteed increases—and troop-level commitments that cut deeply into the budgets of these countries.

The costs and benefits were magnified by the other changes and responsibilities these countries had, as well as the increasingly complicated battles within NATO itself. Membership in NATO became a requirement for being "in the West." It was a guarantee of security and, although they were not officially linked, came to be seen as a key step for entrance into the European Union with its economic promises.

The economic transitions in all of these countries were difficult at best. Converting from the ruble economy, dealing with social welfare needs, and managing the dislocations and costs of privatization would not have been easy under the best of

circumstances. Indeed, as or soon after the first entrants joined NATO, their economies went into a tailspin from the complications of the transitions. All this was magnified by the need to stay within the fiscal budget deficit limits imposed by the European
Union on its new members.

The issue of "guns versus butter," then, has the potential of being a real tradeoff
between funding social programs in areas such as unemployment, education, and
health care; making the necessary infrastructure investments in roads and train lines
to keep up with EU demands; and funding the modernization and meeting of NATO
demands. This, it is true, is happening in a context where the economies, even in their
worst periods, are in far better shape than they were in the communist period, so that
the monies paid for the military can double, as they did in the early years in Poland,
Hungary, and Czech Republic, even as the percentage of the budget going to the
military remained relatively stable. But given the potential of political backlash against
the economies' failure to "fund" the expected lifestyle improvements for large portions
of the population, money for defense is an easy political cause.

Support for operations in Afghanistan and Iraq has also been politically charged.
The prospect of having troops in Iraq seemed to bring with it the promise of being
able to get involved in postwar reconstruction and of aligning themselves with the
prestigious United States. On the other hand, it meant in the eyes of some that their
countries were being used as "Trojan horses" for American interests in the European
Union they were about to join. To date, being a part of the Iraq conflict either, as the
Poles have, in a military capacity or, as others have, in support capacities has resulted
in more public skepticism about NATO membership and the "New Europe."

NATO Tomorrow

In the end, the fate of the new NATO and its impact on its new members is not clear.
None of the newly democratizing states can refuse membership or risk being turned
down. For that matter, NATO needs, if it is to be an all-Europe defense force, to take
in all the states that shift from authoritarianism toward democracy and capitalism as
long as Russia and other states raise the specter of authoritarianism or even the return
of confrontation. On the other hand, the nature of the new threats and conflicts
within Europe and outside can only draw the new members of NATO closer. After
all, those conflicts threaten them as much as or more than they do the old members.
As NATO redefines Europe eastward, the Central and East European countries are no
longer the border states but the bridges or heart of Europe. They need the backing of
NATO as long as there are threats to their security, real or perceived, coming from
the increasingly authoritarian Russia and its unreformed satellites.

Finally, membership in NATO and the European Union is, for all its costs, neces-
sary for being a part of the democratic world of Europe in the twenty-first century.
Even if their politics are not fully stable in the coming decade, the Central and East
European countries will not revert back to communism. Instead, they will become

even more significant players as NATO pushes the boundaries of Europe eastward and they move from being "new entrants" to being new players in the security and stability of Europe as a whole.

Suggested Readings

Asmus, Ronald. *Opening NATO's Door: How the Alliance Remade Itself for a New Era*. New York: Columbia University Press, 2002.

Daalder, Ivo H., and Michael E. O'Hanlon. *Winning Ugly: NATO's War to Save Kosovo*. Washington, DC: Brookings Institution, 2000.

Goldgeier, James. *Not Whether, but When: The U.S. Decision to Enlarge NATO*. Washington, DC: Brookings Institution, 1999.

Kaplan, Lawrence S. *NATO Divided, NATO United: The Evolution of an Alliance*. New York: Praeger, 2004.

Kay, Sean. *NATO and the Future of European Security*. Lanham, MD: Rowman and Littlefield, 2003.

Michta, Andrew, ed. *America's New Allies: Poland, Hungary, and the Czech Republic in NATO*. Seattle: University of Washington Press, 2000.

Serfaty, Simon, ed. *Visions of the Atlantic Alliance: The United States, the European Union, and NATO*. Washington, DC: Center for Strategic and International Studies, 2005.

Simon, Jeffrey. *Hungary and NATO: Problems in Civil-Military Relations*. Lanham, MD: Rowman & Littlefield, 2003.

———. *NATO and the Czech and Slovak Republics: A Comparative Study in Civil-Military Relations*. Lanham, MD: Rowman and Littlefield, 2004.

———. *Poland and NATO: A Study in Civil-Military Relations*. Lanham, MD: Rowman & Littlefield, 2004.

Simon, Jeffrey, ed. *NATO Enlargement: Opinions and Options*. Washington, DC: National Defense University Press, 1996.

Sloan, Stanley R. *NATO, the European Union and the Atlantic Community*. 2nd ed. Lanham, MD: Rowman and Littlefield, 2005.

Yost, David. *NATO Transformed: The Alliance's New Roles in International Security*. Washington, DC: United States Institute of Peace, 1999.

Notes

1. Stanley Sloan, "NATO's Evolving Roles and Mission," *Congressional Research Service* 97-708 F (March 11, 1998).

2. Heads of State and Government, "London Declaration on a Transformed North Atlantic Alliance," meeting of the North Atlantic Council in London, paragraph 7 (July 6, 1990).

3. Heads of State and Government, "Rome Declaration of Peace and Cooperation" meeting of the North Atlantic Council in Rome, paragraph 11, Press Release S-1(91)86 (November 8, 1991).

4. "Declaration of the Heads of State and Government participating in the meeting of the North Atlantic Council in Brussels," paragraph 13, Press Communiqué M-1(94)3 (January 11, 1994).

5. These occurred in the form of Individual Partnership Programs (IPPs), which involved broad cooperation in the Planning and Review Process, peace support operations, moves to insure transparency, and the development of democratic oversight of the military.

6. Heads of State and Government, "Madrid Declaration on Euro-Atlantic Security and Cooperation," meeting of the North Atlantic Council in Madrid, paragraph 8 (July 8, 1997).

7. "The Study of NATO Enlargement" briefed to Partners in September 1995.

8. Those involved directly were Macedonia, Slovakia, Latvia, Lithuania, Estonia, Ukraine, Romania, and Bulgaria, as well as Azerbaijan, Georgia, and Kazakhstan.

9. Heads of State and Government of the Atlantic Council, "Prague Summit Declaration," *NATO Press Release* 127 (November 21, 2002).

10. These include military contacts between Romania and Hungary to improve interstate relations in the early 1990s, the continued deployment of Czech-Slovak battalions in UNPROFOR (UN Protection Force) and UNCRO (UN Confidence Restoring Operation) during and after the January 1993 "Velvet Divorce," and the Polish-Ukraine battalion in Kosovo (and now Iraq).

Part III

CASE STUDIES

CHAPTER 8

Poland

THE POLITICS OF "GOD'S PLAYGROUND"

Jane L. Curry

Poland's transformation out of communism led the way for the transitions of the rest of what had been the Soviet bloc. Polish communists were the first to enter into negotiations to share power with their opponents. Poland was the first Soviet bloc state to hold even partially free elections since the end of World War II. Poland was the first to have a noncommunist government. Months after the first noncommunist prime minister and cabinet took over, this new government, with the support of all the communist deputies in the parliament, put in place the most drastic and rapid economic reform of any of the postcommunist states.

Being the first to reform, though, did not guarantee success. Poles did not get what they expected or wanted from their version of democracy and capitalism. Indeed, being first meant Poles had no road map. They went as far as they thought the Soviet Union and the rest of the bloc would tolerate. Within months, communism collapsed everywhere except the Soviet Union, which was clearly too weak to hold back change in its old allies. So the Poles' calculations as to how much they could democratize proved too restricted.

This early and fast start on democratization and economic reform, as well as reformers' fear of opposition from the Soviet Union or even from the police and military in Poland, created complications that impact Polish politics even today. These complications were magnified by the economic reforms of 1990 and the weaknesses of the old communist system. Poland was, by 1989, over $40 billion in debt to the West[1] and still tightly wound into the Soviet bloc economic system. Its opposition had been the largest in the communist world without even counting the over one-third of the population that had joined Solidarity in 1980–1981. Poles knew how to work together to oppose. They had high expectations for democracy and capitalism because they had been guest workers in the West, had ties to their families in the West, and had an elite that tried to buy them off with its openness to the West. But in the end, the communist-era reforms left them with high hopes, little practice in making policy, and an economy of foreign debt, inflation, and failed factories.

Poland's democratic institutions have been reformed over and over again. Capitalism has worked on a macroeconomic scale. But Poles are some of the least satisfied people in the former communist world; the economic reforms have not worked for many in the population and, for most, have not met their expectations; and Polish politics have been progressively more and more about voting out and punishing "the bad guys" than about building a political elite, party loyalty, or popular trust in democratic institutions. Indeed, by 2006, Poland's politics were marked by the hard line of the party of the president and his twin brother, the prime minister, against anyone who disagreed with them and by more and more right-wing radical nationalism and anti–European Union statements. By 2007, the focus of politics was on the battles within the governmental coalition of "convenience." Charges and countercharges were made by the three parties coupled with threats of the two small parties to bring down the government, but there were no substantive policy discussions. To the extent it could, the coalition held until the summer of 2007 simply because there was no one else who wanted to work with the small parties, one radical populist and one radically religious and nationalist, and there was no other party strong enough to challenge the tattered trio. Early elections were then held on October 24 to break the impasse.

Precommunist History

The largest country in what was "Eastern Europe," or that part of Europe ruled by communist parties until the late 1980s, Poland has had a long history of opposition to the Russians and struggle against outside conquerors. By 1795, Poland had been completely carved into pieces of the Russian, German, and Austrian empires. From then on, Poles fought at home and abroad for Poland to be independent. It took World War I and Woodrow Wilson's commitment to "national self-determination" for Poland to get that independence. Within the boundaries set in the post–World War I peace accord, Poland stretched from Western cities like Poznan that had long been parts of Germany, well into what were lands primarily identified as Ukrainian (Lwów/Lviv) and Lithuanian (Vilnius/Wilno). It was a multiethnic state where one-third of its population was not ethnically Polish. It was burdened by having to establish national structures, deal with a diverse population of peoples with long histories of conflict, and work with an economy and infrastructure that were turned toward Berlin, Vienna, and Moscow, not Warsaw. Democracy and capitalism had a brief period of success in Poland's initial years of independence, only to be practically washed out by the Great Depression. From all of this, though, Poles learned to maintain their culture and nationalism under foreign occupation. The Catholic Church became closely identified with Polish national identity. These lessons served Poles well during the German occupation of World War II and remained with them for the more than forty years of communist rule.

The destruction of World War II began the history and unresolved conflicts that plague Poland even today. During the war, Poland was first divided between the Soviets and Germans, who waged war on Polish territory. In 1941, the Germans turned on the Soviets and took over the rest of Poland. They used it as a base from which to annihilate Jews and Poles. At the end of the war, the Soviet army took control. In the end, one-third of Poland's population was lost, its capital was leveled, much of its industrial base and many of its cities were destroyed, and the factories and infrastructure that survived were taken back to the Soviet Union to rebuild its own infrastructure.

Communist Experience

Soviet troops brought a communist government in as a "baggage-train government" when they marched across Poland and pushed the Germans out. That new leadership was an uneasy alliance between Polish communist officials, who had spent the war in the Soviet Union, and communists who had fought in the small procommunist underground.

The new rulers had to rebuild and impose unwelcome communist rule at the same time. Their task was complicated by the fact that, in postwar agreements, the boundaries of Poland were moved far to the west into what had been Germany. With this shift came a massive population transfer: Germans in what was now western Poland were expelled or went willingly to Germany. Poles and Ukrainians moved west and settled in the areas the Germans had left.

The Communist Party took control of the government, established state ownership of Poland's economy, and tried to control and limit the Catholic Church. With all this came Stalinist terror, eased only by the communist leaders' reluctance to repeat Stalin's prewar destruction of the Polish Communist Party leadership by carrying out the blood purges that happened elsewhere in the Soviet bloc. The leaders were also restrained by the refusal of the Catholic Church to submit totally to the new regime. At the same time, there were those who gained much from the ongoing reconstruction and industrialization: large numbers of new industries were built, young peasants moved to factory work, and a whole new class was educated.

With Stalin's death in 1953 and the death of Poland's Stalinist leader, Boleslaw Bierut, in March 1956, fear and control decreased. In the summer of 1956, Polish workers demonstrated, demanding "bread and freedom" and calling out that "the press lies." Polish troops fired on the demonstrators, killing less than a hundred. Open intellectual protests spread throughout Poland in the fall. Polish United Workers' Party (PUWP) members demanded reforms in the party itself. The party leadership tried to end this Polish October by bringing back Władysław Gomulka, the postwar party leader who had been jailed in the Stalinist period for his independence. He promised to follow "a Polish road to socialism" that would allow private farming, small private enterprises, freedoms for the Catholic Church, and much greater freedom for public discussion. From then on, Poland remained on its own "freer" road.

These events were the first in what would be a series of revolts against communism's failings: student and intellectual demonstrations erupted in 1968, and workers' riots in 1970, 1976, and 1980 were triggered by price increases and economic failures. After each, the communist authorities made concessions in an attempt to maintain their hold and buy support, only to fail to meet their promises. With each uprising, though, opposition grew and became more organized until, after the 1976 workers' demonstrations, the Committee to Protect the Workers (KOR) was formed to aid the workers and their families, to produce an underground press to let people know about their rights and the human rights violations, and to encourage independent thinking. By the end of the 1970s and the early 1980s, this opposition had flowered into a massive underground press empire, human rights organizations, and a whole nonregime cultural milieu, including a "Flying University" that provided courses and instructors not allowed in the communist curriculum.[2] It was from this opposition and the workers who had tried to strike and lost in the 1970s that Solidarity emerged and that the men and women who would take Poland into its transition would come.[3]

When Edward Gierek took over as head of the party after the December 1970 Gdańsk shipyard strikes, he promised Poles their lives would improve. To do this, he tried to jump-start the economy by borrowing from the West to build new factories with Western equipment that were to pay for themselves by exporting products to the West. The plan did not work: much of the money was wasted, Polish goods did not sell, and Poland had to borrow more and more just to pay off the interest on its debts. By the end of the 1970s, the shelves of Polish stores were so bare that essentials had to be rationed.

The struggle for control culminated in the summer of 1980 with the eruption of workers' strikes over a new round of price increases on staples and the virtual collapse of the consumer economy: food and other necessities had virtually disappeared. What little there was on store shelves was rationed or came from individuals' connections. Poles were further emboldened by the fact that Karol Wotyla, the former archbishop of Krakow, had become pope and returned to Poland in June 1980 as a conquering hero feted by communist leaders and the population alike.

By 1980, the government was so desperate to placate Western creditors without touching off demonstrations that it imposed price increases region by region and told local leaders to negotiate pay increases if there were strikes. By August, rolling price increases had been imposed across the country. The last stage was to impose them on the seacoast towns where the 1970 riots had brought down the Gomulka regime. The workers in the Gdańsk shipyards went on strike and refused to simply negotiate pay increases. Under the leadership of dissident worker Lech Wałesa, they occupied the shipyards demanding not just the economic and social welfare benefits communism had promised but also the right to have an independent trade union, the right to strike, and the promise of more media freedom to inform Poles accurately about their situation. Intellectuals joined them. Workers from other places in Poland sent messages of support. Solidarity became a national movement for economic and political change in Poland.

This process was not a simple one. By the end of its first year, more than one-third of the entire population were members of Solidarity. A farmers' Solidarity and a student Solidarity had formed and forced the government to recognize them. Party members had joined Solidarity and sought to bring its openness into the Polish United Workers' Party. Independent press and discussions appeared everywhere. Solidarity elections and a congress were held, and their demands increased. As the economic situation worsened, strikes and demonstrations became the order of the day even as party leaders perceived that the Soviet Union would invade if things got out of hand. Poland's economy simply could not work well enough and was too indebted to put food on the shelves, much less provide the gains the Gdańsk Agreements promised. All the government could do was make more and more political concessions, even as the other Soviet bloc states pressed the Polish government to stop conceding. For them, the potential for chaos and contagion was all too real and threatening.

On December 13, 1981, the freedoms Solidarity had enjoyed for fifteen months ended, not by an invasion but by a Polish military "takeover." Thousands of Solidarity activists, as well as party leaders accused of corruption and mismanagement in the Gierek era, were interned. Polish soldiers were on the streets. Media freedom and free discussion ended. Solidarity and other independent groups were shut down. Military officers supervised factories, schools, and government offices. Most Poles were too shocked to act. Western states imposed sanctions on Poland. But martial law, under General Wojciech Jaruzelski as head of the Polish military and Communist Party, continued formally for more than two years, and Jaruzelski's regime lasted until the end of the 1980s. During this time, Solidarity and the other independent organizations were disbanded, but an active underground movement remained, and dissident publications and activities proliferated. At the same time, the difficulty of daily life in a situation of shortages meant that most individuals focused on feeding and supplying their families rather than engaging in ongoing political activity on either side.

Transition from Communism

By 1988–1989, Poland's economy had failed to rebound and provide what Poles thought they had been promised. The communists' efforts to get popular support had largely failed. Much of Poland's population was alienated from both Solidarity and the communist government. To deal with this alienation, the communist leaders moved to reach out to the opposition while at the same time trying to get the economy moving by decreasing controls on prices and forcing factories to be self-supporting. When none of these maneuvers worked, the government, with the support of the Catholic Church, sought Solidarity leaders' agreement to begin discussions on systemic change. The church leaders helped bring the two sides together and agreed to facilitate the roundtable talks between them.

No one thought communism would end. For the rulers, the roundtables were a way to hold on to power by getting Solidarity to share responsibility for Poland's problems and move toward a new, more open system of government over the next four years. For Solidarity's self-appointed representatives, the roundtables were initially about the relegalization of Solidarity as a trade union. For the population, the hope was that the roundtables would protect the economic guarantees of a social welfare state and that the freedoms of the Solidarity era would be returned. The church wanted the roundtables to stabilize Poland and insure its own position.

After five months of private discussions and nine weeks of public discussions, the two sides agreed to defer decisions on economic reforms and to move ahead with political reforms and elections designed to give the PUWP and its former allies dominance, while giving Solidarity and other nonparty people a reason to join in the new government and share responsibility. The system they agreed upon in the Roundtable

Accords was designed to provide enough concessions for Solidarity to participate in elections but still guarantee the Communists and their allies a majority of seats. In the process, they created a system that broke the taboos but did not violate the Soviet Union's old limits.

The Polish governmental system was redesigned to have a second legislative chamber (the Senate) and a presidency elected by the two houses together. To insure the dominance of the Communists, 65 percent of the seats in the parliament (Sejm) were designated for members of the Communist Party and its two subsidiary parties and 35 percent of the seats were designated for candidates who belonged to no party. This was where the candidates of Solidarity could run. Finally, forty seats were reserved for the so-called National List of the regime's notables and reformers. A majoritarian election system, where those who did not get a majority in the first round had to run against the next closest candidate in a second election, was used for both the "party" and nonparty seats as well as the "National List." The Senate, as a tradeoff, was elected without any constraints.

The results of the elections held on June 4, 1989, defied all expectations. The candidates that Solidarity identified as "theirs" won every nonparty seat in the Sejm and all but one in the Senate. Almost none of the Communist Party candidates, on the other hand, got the requisite majority to "win" in the first round. Their seats all had to be decided in the second round. All but the two men whose names were at the bottom of the National List lost.[4] The presidency went, as had been tacitly promised, to Jaruzelski, the man who had both called for the hated martial law and supported the roundtable talks. His victory was the result of a political compromise Solidarity leaders engineered to placate Communist Party and military hard-liners in Poland and hard-line leaders elsewhere in the Soviet bloc.

The 65 percent majority established for the Communist Party and its old allies did not hold. The smaller parties, long Trojan horses to draw peasants and small entrepreneurs into the system, broke with the PUWP and joined Solidarity. That reversed the percentages the "establishment" and the "opposition" got in the Sejm: people elected as PUWP members now held 35 percent of the seats, and 65 percent of the seats were held by Solidarity and its new allies from the old system. The Soviet Union accepted the new system.

No one knew what would happen next. Solidarity deputies' only platform had been against the Communists. They had no real plan to change Poland. Communist deputies were not prepared to be the minority. They had expected only to share power with nonparty members.

A new, noncommunist government was formed in September 1989. Tadeusz Mazowiecki (a longtime Catholic editor, dissident, and advisor to Solidarity leader Lech Wałesa) was named prime minister on Wałesa's recommendation. He formed a government primarily of dissident intellectuals with three communist ministers to manage the most important ministries for Soviet interests: the police and spy services, military, and transportation. Western-educated economist Leszek Balcerowicz was named minister of finance and deputy prime minister to run the economic reform.

The new government was overwhelmed by the task of "unmaking communist control" and agreeing on concrete policies for the transition. What had been the Solidarity monolith against the Communists dissolved into many factions. Faced with

W SAMO POŁUDNIE
4 CZERWCA 1989

Photo 8.1.   Solidarity poster that covered the streets of Poland the morning of the June 1989 elections, based on a Gary Cooper poster for the film High Noon.

going from a ruling party to a minority party after forty years, Communist Party deputies wanted to have as little to do with the rejected system as possible. They split into factions. By January 1990, the PUWP had dissolved itself and passed its resources on to the new Social Democratic Party of the Polish Republic (SLDRP).

Solidarity and Communist deputies were relatively unified in trying to cut and paste the communist constitution to fit the Roundtable Accords. First, they cut out provisions like the "leading role of the party" and the promise of fealty to the Soviet Union. They also passed bills to allow for "shock therapy" economic reform (the Balcerowicz Plan) to make rapid privatization and foreign investment possible. This program, coupled with the inflation that began when the last communist government freed most food prices, triggered a drop in the purchasing power of the zloty by 40 percent at the end of the plan's first month (January 1990) and brought a rapid end to popular euphoria over communism's end and Poland's "return to Europe."

Parties and Elections

After the elections in 1989, holding elections became politicians' way to solve problems and legitimize the system, even though elections increased fragmentation, parties failed to establish themselves, and the public became more and more negative about elected officials and institutions with each election and change of leaders. The other solution to these problems was to rewrite election laws or change the duties of various offices. Fewer and fewer eligible voters voted. The center disappeared, leaving parties with murky ideologies that were more focused on individual personalities rather than on economic and social policy.

The rush to elections began in the summer of 1990. Local government elections were held before the duties of the various levels of local government were established. Almost at the same time, a campaign by Lech Wałesa and his followers erupted to force Jaruzelski's resignation and the passage of a law to popularly elect the president.

Lech Wałesa won the first popular presidential election, defeating then prime minister Tadeusz Mazowiecki and more narrowly defeating Stanislaw Tyminski, an émigré with no clear platform or qualifications who promised instant wealth for everyone. This election, in the fall of 1990, caused more fragmentation of Solidarity and set the pattern for voters' decisions. Voting for someone new who promised dramatic improvement in living conditions became the standard for electoral decisions. The other permanent feature that began at this point was the regional difference in party support between the prosperous west and big cities that supported those they perceived to be pro-reform and the impoverished east and small towns that supported those who opposed change and promised social welfare.

In the early parliamentary elections of 1991, twenty-nine parties were elected in the Sejm's proportional representation elections. The Senate was equally divided after plurality elections gave sixteen parties at least one seat. In addition to two warring Solidarity-based parties, the Solidarity trade union, and new parties like the half-serious "Friends of Beer Party," there were a number of small right-wing parties that condemned both the former Communists and Solidarity deputies for the losses "caused by" the Balcerowicz Plan. The campaign was marked by nationalist and religious rhetoric. Only the former Communists, the Social Democratic Party of the Polish Republic, remained unified. This was their response to their unaccustomed status as losers and their communist-era experience of party organization.

So divided was this parliament that within two years it was unable to make policy and turned in on itself. The larger of the many parties in the Sejm did push through two laws that have continued to impact party politics. First, to cut down on the fragmentation of the Sejm, political parties were required to win 5 percent of the national vote and coalitions 7 percent, to hold any seats in the Sejm. Second, the Sejm legalized a system allowing for parties in parliament to get ongoing funding and national government funding for parties' campaigns if they had won at least 3 percent in the preceding election. This funding has been paid after the elections on the basis of the number of seats a party wins in the Sejm or Senate.

In 1993, this electoral law resulted in the Social Democrats, with only 20.41 percent of the votes, and their former allies, the renamed Polish Peasant Party, with 15.4 percent of the vote, winning 60.5 percent of Sejm seats. The nine right-wing parties that ran could not form a coalition, so they got no seats even though, together, they polled 34.45 percent of the vote. From the parliamentary elections of 1993 on, there has been a parliamentary seesaw every four years between the "left" and "right" coalitions or parties. Complicating the shifts, right-wing parties and governing coalitions have fragmented, appeared, and disappeared from one election to the next. Party ideologies are confusing at best. The divide on social welfare economy versus a free market state has not been the split between left and right. In spite of the fact that most Poles see the economy as the critical issue, the key divide for voters and parties has been about being positive about the past: communist or not, and being pro-Church or not.[5]

- The political center comes from the anticommunist opposition and professionals who led Poland's reforms from 1989 to 1991. The Democratic Union won only 10.59 percent of the votes and 16.07 percent of the seats in the 1993 election. In 1997, renamed the Freedom Union, it won 13.37 percent of the vote and 13.04 percent of the seats. It joined with the right-wing coalition after this election. Since 2001, it has been unable to make the required 5 percent threshold needed to obtain seats in the Sejm. Its center position was taken by the Citizens' Platform (PO), representing promarket, pro–European Union reformers. They won 12.7 percent of the vote with 14.1 percent of the Sejm seats when they began in 2001 and placed second in 2005 with 24.1 percent of the vote and 28.9 percent of the seats.

  This center has stood for establishing a liberal market economy, democratization, and the "Return to Europe," and against Polish nationalism. Although some of its leaders were lay Catholic opposition leaders during the communist era, this was not a party that supported giving the Catholic Church real power in politics.

- The popularly defined left, the Social Democrats (SLD) who succeeded the Communist Party, steadily increased their support base for postcommunist Poland's first fifteen years, even when they lost the 1997 election. They imploded after returning to power in 2001 with 41.04 percent of the vote and 42.6 percent of the seats. Claims of corruption and mismanagement, as well as the public sense that they had failed to deliver on their promises, haunted them in the years leading up to the 2005 election. As a result, the once monolithic party fragmented. A more liberal, "less corrupt" group broke off and formed an offshoot Social Democratic Party (SDPL). In the 2005 election, the SLD managed to win only 11.3 percent of the vote and 11.9 percent of the seats. Their reformist offshoot won 3.9 percent. Voters, who identified the SLD with the communist social welfare era, had lost faith in them and turned wholeheartedly to populist or right-wing parties.

In the 1995 presidential election, the SLD leader, Aleksander Kwasniewski, defeated former Solidarity leader and then president Lech Wałesa in a close vote. Five years later, he was easily reelected with over 50 percent of the vote in the first election, though he distanced himself from the party.

Although this party was seen by the public as "left" and drew former Communist Party members and those who had "lost" with the demise of communist social welfare, this party supported the end of state ownership and social welfare by maintaining that a more prosperous private sector would "trickle down" resources to the poor. To avoid its communist ties, it also advocated strong involvement with the United States and Western Europe and was circumspect in its open opposition to the power of the Catholic Church.

In the summer of 2007, Kwasniewski returned to the political scene and formed the Left and Democracy Movement, in which the Left Democratic Alliance was the major party and some of the leaders of the old Freedom Union were minor players. It was intended to respond to the popular disgust with the right-wing government that had ruled since he retired and the presidential and parliamentary elections in 2005. It was also committed to adopting the new European Treaty without a referendum and to joining the euro zone—a dramatically more European stance than the nationalist right.

- The Polish Peasant Party, a successor to the communist-era Peasant Party and to the prewar, nonsocialist Peasant Party, has seen its following decrease since 1993 but has remained in the Sejm. By 2005, it lost supporters to the populist Self-Defense Party and other right-wing parties: it won only 5 percent of the vote.

- Sitting on neither the right nor the left is the Self-Defense Party (Samoobrona). The populist Self-Defense Party has had an even more mixed political profile. Its leader is a former state farm director from the communist period who made his name demonstrating against the Polish government and Western Europe. Its platform avoids the visceral anticommunism of other right-wing parties but has an even more simplistic set of social promises. Initially, as a peasant party, it got publicity from dumping grain on the roads and demonstrating in parliament. Its numbers have swelled with members of the lower levels of the old communist bureaucracy and losers in the transition. But it only broke through in 2001 with 10.2 percent of the vote (11.5 percent of the seats in parliament). In 2005, it came in third, ahead of the ruling Social Democratic Party, with 11.4 percent of the vote and 12.1 percent of the seats.

- The self-proclaimed right, after its fragmentation brought defeat in 1993, formed the Solidarity Electoral Action coalition for the 1997 election. The parties that remained in the coalition then garnered only 5.60 percent of the vote in 2001, too few to be allotted Sejm seats as a coalition. In its stead, a number of parties emerged, differing dramatically in their economic and social stands, proclaiming to be the voice of the right. These parties include the Law and Justice Party, an anticorruption and pro-social-welfare party (9.5 percent of the vote in 2001 and 27 percent in 2005 for 33.7 percent of seats); and the League of Polish Families, a Christian-nationalist party (7.9 percent of the vote in 2001 and 8.0 percent in 2005). The strength of these new right parties was clear from the victory of Lech Kaczynski, the presidential candidate for the Law and Justice Party, in 2005. He defeated the centrist Citizens' Platform candidate in the runoff with 54.04 percent of the vote thanks to the support of Self-Defense and the League of Polish Families as well as the peasants.

This right wing emerged in response to Poles' bitterness about their losses in the initial move to democracy and capitalism. They claimed to advocate against an end to social welfare even as they emphasized their anti-communism. They identify as Polish nationalists, most of whom oppose Poland's involvement with both the West and the former Soviet states. Most implicitly or explicitly support Catholic religious values as the core of public policy. They attack communists for communist-era repression, controlling the transition, and using it to their benefit. Therefore, they argue former communists should be punished for the evils of communist rule. Most are, at best, skeptical of the European Union. In the 2005 election, the most powerful of these parties, Law and Justice, led with calls against corruption by government officials and "the elite," promises to end corruption and inequality, and promises to punish and exclude communists and their agents from power.

Polish parties, with the exception of parties from the old communist system, have had neither the incentive nor the resources to do ground-level organization and build an infrastructure. After the era of Communist Party rule, the very word "party" and the notion of being a party member had negative connotations, so most of the groups that ran for elections eschewed the word "party" and suffered from not having the resources to build structures and gain members. Candidates, even from the most established parties, have had to invest their own money in campaigns, and, once in parliament, they receive money for their expenses directly from the parliament's budget. This means that party loyalty gives them nothing.

Only the former Communists (SLD) invested in the infrastructures typical of European parties. The SLD started ahead. It inherited some of the PUWP's buildings, equipment, and membership lists. It also inherited a tradition of members organizing for the party. This process weakened after the 2001 election when the party both sought to expand its leadership and also felt it was without any solid competition.

The other political groups in Poland have been incapable of or uninterested in investing money in increasingly expensive infrastructure and offices. They are "couch parties" focused around individual leaders and existing only during political campaigns. For most, membership is the equivalent of voters in any given election.

In the end, the party battles reflect the personal interests of politicians rather than the interests and values of Poles. For most Poles, their losses in the process of economic reform are far more important public policy issues than issues like Poland's foreign policy, dealing with the communist past, or imposing Catholic values by prohibiting abortion. Public opinion shows that, although Poles believe in democracy, their faith in the way the Polish system has been run, its politicians, and its economic and political policies has declined over the years, even as the economy has stabilized. So too has their involvement in politics and civil society organizations, including the Catholic Church. There is also evidence of a popular nostalgia for the communist days and a dramatic decrease in their faith in elective institutions and in the church as well as Western states.[6]

Civil Society

Unlike the rest of the postcommunist world, Poland had well-established alternative institutions that participated in the transition: the Catholic Church and Solidarity. These institutions have played major roles in politics and also in the emergence of civil society. Professional associations, in the communist period, acted more independently than was allowed elsewhere in the bloc. At the same time, in the communist period, Poles had the experience of being part of elaborate friendship networks that helped them get food and goods that were perpetually in short supply. Also, they had the most extensive and elaborate network of opposition groups of any country in the Soviet bloc. Indeed, many of these groups produced an elaborate and regular set of publications and ran an alternative educational system in addition to providing support for individuals working in the opposition or workers punished for their demonstrations.

Tragically, these institutions did not blossom in the transition but gradually lost out. The informal networks were no longer necessary once the economy was reformed. Professional groups were tainted by their communist-era pasts and did not work in a system where there was competition for jobs within the professions. And the established institutions of the Catholic Church and Solidarity retained their symbolism but lost popular support when they had to be "for something" rather than simply against communism. Where they survived, what they did was seen as "corruption" or self-serving rather than legitimate "surviving around the system" and taking risks to change it.

The Catholic Church had enough power and popular support that the communists had to allow it to function for almost the entire communist period as a religious institution and symbol of the limits of communist rule. In the 1980s, its role was magnified by the election of Karol Wotyla, the former archbishop of Krakow, as the first non-Italian pope in 400 years.

Under his aegis, church officials played a role as the mediators between the government and the opposition and then, after the 1989 election, the church served as the base for the new Poland. From the first elections, local churches and the hierarchy's statements voiced concerns and support for candidates in elections. It pushed though and won required religious education in all schools and, eventually, won strict limits on abortion. In next decade and a half, the church went from Poland's most respected institution to one of its least respected, according to public opinion surveys. It also saw its attendance and donations decline, while the number of Polish children born out of wedlock and the number of abortions continued to increase. So, while Polish politicians were wary of going against the church's wishes, much of the public increasingly claimed to think the church had too much influence in politics and to ignore its directives.[7]

The politics of the Catholic Church were more complicated in the postcommunist period when they no longer had an enemy. Even though church governance was hierarchical, church politics were increasingly split between the church leaders in the curia, the local parish priests, and a liberal Catholic lay intelligentsia. Some priests took and take a far more hard-line stance on what the church and religious people should do than either the curia or the lay intelligentsia. That fragmentation magnified in the 2005 election. Not only had the right-wing, privately owned Radio Marya become so powerful and popular with its xenophobia, racism, and anti-Semitism that the church hierarchy had no way to moderate it or stop it, but also the resurgence of nationalism and its political identification with protecting Catholicism worked to catapult the reactionary League of Polish Families into parliament and the cabinet.

Solidarity was the other major alternative institution in Poland as it made its transition. Even more dramatically than the church, Solidarity has fragmented and lost its public support. By 1989, it had gone from being an active political movement fighting to achieve workers' rights and change politics to being a social symbol of regime opposition after martial law was declared and Solidarity disbanded. In 1989, its leaders were the major negotiators in the roundtable talks and its designated candidates (signaled by pictures with Lech Wałesa) the victors in the 1989 elections. By 2000, Solidarity and its leaders were battling over its legacy and had little or no social support.

Being in the government was problematic for Solidarity as a trade union. Its old unity against communism's failures fragmented rapidly when policy had to be made. First there were the splits between the intellectuals who had advised Solidarity and those who had come to leadership from the working class over who should lead and what policy should be. Solidarity then found itself in the untenable position of being both a trade union that had to reestablish itself and its resources after nearly ten years of being illegal and a political party or the base for a political party. In the end, Solidarity lost. The dual roles of a trade union fighting for workers' rights and a reformist political party dissuaded its supporters.

Beyond this, there was another trade union, OPZZ, that started as the government's substitute for Solidarity, took Solidarity's resources when it was closed down, and grew radicalized in the late 1980s when it fought for worker support as the communist government moved to create a more market economy. These two unions competed for supporters. In the end, membership and faith in both dropped. Workers felt no one represented their interests.[8]

In the end, both Solidarity as a trade union and Solidarity as a political party had so failed to represent workers' interests and to stay together that they now exist almost exclusively as a historical symbol of what once was. As the economic transition reduced the free time and resources of most people, many other civil society institutions failed to fill the void. Initially, Western foundations created civil society organizations in Poland. Most of these have lasted only as long as the funding from the outside. Other organizations have sprung up, but most of these are focused on providing special benefits and privileges for their members or, in the case of what were once parent-run schools, substituting for poor state services.

Photo 8.2.   Lech Wałesa (president of Poland 1991–1995), Tadeusz Mazowiecki (prime minister 1989–1991), and Aleksander Kwasniewski (president
1995–2005).

(Source: Rzeczpospolita)

Political Institutions

For most of its postcommunist history, governance and political battles in Poland
have been more about which institution (president, prime minister and Council of
Ministers, Sejm, Senate, or courts) has which rights to do what about actual policy.
Initially, the Stalinist constitution was revised to add the Senate and a presidency and
to remove the "leading role of the Communist Party" from the constitution. The
additions and deletions did not provide a framework to coordinate and balance what
institutions could and could not do. Elected officials were left to establish the responsibilities of their offices either, if they were legislators, by passing more legislation or, if
it was the president or prime minister, by simply claiming the right to act and setting
precedents.

Poland's constitutional system began as a strong semi-presidential one and transformed, in reaction to Lech Wałesa's attempts to wrest control, to a system focused
on a strong cabinet and parliament. After the roundtable negotiations, the president
was given the right to veto legislation or refer it to the constitutional court for review,
disband parliament and call new elections, call a "State of Emergency," play a role in
selecting the prime minister and cabinet, appoint officials for some supervisory councils and some top judges, and represent the country in international politics and military affairs. Wojciech Jaruzelski, as Poland's first president and a remnant of the
defeated regime, stayed in the background and used virtually none of his presidential
powers unless asked to act by the Solidarity government.

After Lech Wałesa became president, he made claims of powers that were not his. In response, the powers of the presidency were limited by the 1992 and 1997 constitutions, and the powers of the prime minister and cabinet were increased. So, although the presidency retains most of these powers in the final constitution, each of these powers is counterbalanced by the power of the legislature or the prime minister. Until 2005, even in the one period when the president and the government were from the same party (Social Democrats), these checks and balances worked.

In the process, the prime minister and cabinet have seen their constitutional powers increase. The president has the right to step in and name a prime minister only if the Sejm is too divided to agree. The prime minister and his cabinet can be removed only with a vote of no confidence by the parliament. The prime minister has the responsibility to select his cabinet and present it to the Sejm for approval. The government also has the explicit responsibility to lead the policy-making process in domestic and foreign affairs, carry out the laws passed by the parliament, put forth regulations as authorized by the Sejm, and manage the budget of the state. Finally, all laws must be cosigned by the president and prime minister.

The powers of legislation are concentrated in the Sejm. The Sejm also has the right to appoint officials to various public boards and to some seats on the court. The Senate, on the other hand, is primarily a body to review and revise Sejm legislation and serve as a moderator in conflicts.

In reality, the powers of the presidency, the prime minister, and the parliament have been far less matters of what the constitutions have outlined and much more the result of the politics and personalities of the moment. Poland's four presidents have each cut very different profiles for themselves. In the first three cases, they claimed to represent no political party but merely be representatives of the Polish people as a whole.

What they tried to do depended on their own interests and sense of power. Jaruzelski avoided conflict with the new Solidarity government. Lech Wałesa rode in as the leader of the victorious Solidarity movement and the first noncommunist leader for Poland. He attempted an "imperial presidency" for which he claimed greater and greater powers. Most of what he claimed he would do never happened. But by two years into his rule, he was faced with a parliament that was very divided. There were deadlocks with the government, public opposition to and disgust with his style of leadership, and even claims from former supporters that he had been a secret agent. All of this weakened not only his popular support but also his ability to lead. Indeed, after he disbanded the parliament following a vote of no confidence in the government in 1993 and called new elections, he found himself trapped in a continuous conflict with the former Communists' parliamentary majority and their prime minister and cabinet. In the end, the result was that no matter what Wałesa did, he was checkmated by the parliamentary majority.

Aleksander Kwasniewski was very different from his predecessors. Given the public attacks on his party and on him for having communist connections, he focused on disproving the stereotypes of communists. He was a "by-the-book president," taking no more power than was constitutionally mandated. He resigned his membership in the very party he had formed and claimed to represent all Poles. At the same time, he was able to work behind the scenes, in his first term, with the SLD and Peasant Party parliamentary majority to get legislation passed and avoid conflicts and, at the end of his second term, to work against the collapse of the SLD government. After the 1997 election, he worked with the right-wing coalition. In this situation, he focused particularly on acting as a professional who avoided direct conflict. He became the representative of Poland to the world, with a special emphasis on the West and leading Poland to NATO. In the process, he returned prestige and the faith of the public to the presidency.

In 2000, Kwasniewski was so strong that other parties fielded candidates with little hope of winning. His slogan, "Poland: A Home for All," emphasized his apolitical leadership. One year later, the parliamentary elections brought the SLD back as the dominant party balanced against a fragmented right wing. By default, Poland moved back to a semi-presidential state with the president appointing Marek Belka as prime minister when Leszek Miller's 3 percent public support translated into a vote of no confidence by the SLD.

In 2005, Lech Kaczynski of the Law and Justice Party was elected president. His position was strengthened by the fact that his party was the largest in the Sejm and was able to form a government with two very different but small parties (Samoobrona, or Self-Defense, and the League of Polish Families). The possibility of checks and balances was severely compromised by the fact that the Law and Social Justice Party was dominated by the Kaczynski brothers, identical twins who took the posts of president and prime minister and appointed their friends and allies to ministerial posts. The weakness of the rest of the parties on the political scene meant that there was no credible option to rein in this party and its fractious coalition. As the result of changes in the electoral laws for local governments and the leaders' commitment to "cleansing" the system of "agents" from the communist period, the Kaczynski brothers were able to limit the checks on their power. Indeed, their claims that individuals who disagreed with them were agents of the old communist police—along with the real threats that the lustration process would be changed so that all the old secret police files would be public and individuals could be removed from public office on the basis of those files—made opposition to the government's decisions risky. At the same time, the coalition engaged in continual internal battles over charges and countercharges. This brought it to an end in August 2007. Early elections on October 21 turned the tables. More Poles voted (53.8 percent) than had voted in any election since 1991. They voted against the coalition's politics: Law and Justice got 32.16 percent and its "partners" got so few votes that they were out of parliament. The free market Citizen's Platform "won" with 41.39 percent of the votes—enough to have a majority of seats in the Sejm with the Polish Peasant Party (8.93 percent). Left and Democracy won 13.5 percent.

Economic Transformation

In 1988, it was popular disaffection with the Communists' attempts to resolve Poland's economic crisis by moving toward a market economy that forced the Communists to ask Solidarity to join in the roundtable talks. In the elections that followed, under all the rhetoric, the failure of the economy to meet people's expectations and Poles' sense that the political elites were using politics to enrich themselves brought down one government after the other. In 1989, the economic reformers inherited an

*Photo 8.3.   President Lech Kaczynski congratulating his
twin brother, Jaroslaw Kaczynski, on his swearing in as
prime minister in 2005.*
(Source: Rzeczpospolita)

economy distorted by the Communists' attempts to avert disaster and buy off the
population by importing Western equipment and technology in the early 1970s;
exporting all they could to pay back the debt; borrowing to pay off the interest in the
mid- and late 1970s; opening up to small privately owned foreign businesses in the
early 1980s; and, finally, moving to free prices and shift the zloty from its ruble base
to one based on international currency trading.

All this was actually complicated by communist Poland's ties to the West. Poles,
more than any other Central and East Europeans but the Hungarians and Yugoslavs,
had traveled and worked in the West and, as a result, had seen enough to have higher
expectations of democracy and capitalism. Western countries also had more power
over Poland's decisions than they did in the rest of the communist world because
Poland was so heavily indebted to the West. After all, Poland's attempt to jump-start
its economy in the early 1970s by borrowing from the West had failed, leaving it
trapped by its debt. This meant that the Poles' decisions about how they transformed
their economy were very much dependent on the approval of their Western creditors.

Economic reform began with "shock therapy" or the "Balcerowicz Plan," a program designed to curb the high inflation and open the Polish market to competition
with the outside. This plan involved ending price controls, making the Polish zloty

convertible, eliminating trade barriers, eliminating government subsidies for state enterprises so they had to be self-supporting, restricting wage increases, reducing the money supply, and increasing interest rates. This rapid transformation was the most dramatic and rapid in any postcommunist country. It was unanimously ratified by all the members of the Polish parliament to go into effect virtually overnight on January 1, 1990, in the hope that it would jump-start the economy and create the necessary stimulus for privatization.

Its results were disastrous for most Poles. By the end of January, individual purchasing power dropped 43.2 percent. Registered unemployment went from 0.3 percent in December 1989 to 6.5 percent a year later, 11.4 percent in December 1991,[9] and 16.4 percent in 1993. The declines in all the major economic indicators for the next two years were equally dramatic: the gross domestic product dropped over 18 percent. In the first month alone, industrial production dropped 30 percent, and the purchasing power of wages and salaries went down more than one-third. Peasants' incomes dropped by about half. At the same time, a small group of wealthy "owners and consultants" emerged. Polish agricultural goods lost out to better-packaged and heavily subsidized Western goods that were often cheaper than their unsubsidized Polish equivalents.

By 1993, the economy had begun an upswing that lasted through the mid-1990s when it slowed perceptibly. Growth hovered around 5 percent a year in the mid-1990s. Even as the economy grew, however, there were problems. The growth in the economy was only in specific areas where productivity increased, so fewer people produced more. The export sector lagged behind, leaving Poland with a serious deficit. Inflation remained high. For a large percentage of Poles, the new buildings and foreign investments in the major cities meant far less than bankruptcies in the smaller and more rural regions. These triggered significant regional unemployment outside the major cities and a slide into poverty for a majority of the population, even as a smaller but ever-increasing number of people gained from the changes.

The solution for the government was to push privatization. New small firms, largely based on imports and street trade, blossomed. They began by working around the existing rules and paying little or no tax. At the same time, most of the old state cooperatives and private enterprises that had survived the communist era collapsed as a result of mass-produced Western goods and soaring costs for rent, materials, and salaries. Many state stores were simply turned private by their employees. As a result, the share of employment and the national income that was in the private sector grew from less than one-third to more than half of the Polish economy by 1993, even though larger and weaker state firms continued on virtually untouched by privatization.

This next step proved extremely complex. Solidarity leaders advocated moving toward employee ownership and maintaining cooperative enterprises. Leszek Balcerowicz and his supporters wanted simply to privatize state industries as quickly and completely as possible by establishing a stock market and letting those that were weak go bankrupt. Only after eleven draft laws were rejected did this Thatcher-style privatization become law. The conflict remained. When it was passed in June 1990, there were also provisions for employee ownership and the "mass privatization" that gave Poles credits to become stockholders in what had been state firms.

In the end, Poland's privatization was piecemeal, done largely through foreign investment and "mass privatization." For mass privatization, the firms that were salable were consolidated into National Investment Funds. In the process, only 512 of the 8,453 state firms were included, most of them small firms. As a result, only about 2 percent of the total workforce was involved initially. Money that was to prepare the firms for privatization went to the managers rather than to upgrading and reorganizing the firms. Every adult Pole got a share certificate for 180 zloties (about $40) to invest in these funds. For most Poles, this minimal "mass privatization" was far from enticing. There were few options, and most were in minor parts of the Polish economy. Rather than enlivening the market, at the end of the process, the worth of the firms and of the certificates had fallen to less than half their original worth.[10]

Most foreign direct investment involved government and private firms buying up state firms and Western businesses moving in to import products from outside. The bulk of new investments were largely in construction and the opening of huge supermarkets and discount stores. In the end, the Polish economy, 75 percent of which was in private hands by 2000, was a "subsidiary economy" of foreign firms. Their investment decreased dramatically after 2000: between 2000 and 2002, the total direct foreign investment dropped from $9,341 million to $4,131 million.[11]

There were serious political complications in both mass privatization and foreign direct investment. For most Poles, this privatization did not bring with it gains. Wages and work conditions in many foreign firms have been below even Polish standards. Many Poles felt that Poland was being sold off, at bargain prices, to the West because 75 percent of banking services were controlled by Western capital and large parts of other key institutions like the media, part of the postal services, and telephone services were owned by outside interests. The disgust this engendered from a public that was not getting the benefits it expected from capitalism was magnified by the revelations and accusations of corruption in both left- and right-wing governments involved in selling off, with huge tax and price breaks, Polish industry and resources to Western firms and, in early 2000, Russian interests.

Although Poland's economy had one of the fastest growth rates in Central and Eastern Europe, that growth was not matched by the growth of salaries and employment rates. From the late 1990s on, the economy has declined in terms of what it produced for the population. The unemployed population has grown and the worth of most workers' earnings has dropped. To keep the state sector solvent, many (mostly larger) firms that could not easily be sold off were closed down or sold off at low prices. Because so much of Poland's industry had been concentrated in single-industry towns and regions, this meant that, outside the major cities, there were areas of mass unemployment.

Social Conditions

The outcome of Poland's "shock therapy" and its privatization process, built as it was on an economy that had been bankrupt by Western debt and failed production in the communist period, has not been good for most of the Polish population. Indeed, Poland has the highest level of poverty of any country in Central and Eastern Europe: by some government calculations, 58 percent of the population lives below the government-established social minimum (with enough income to cover not only food and housing but also clothes, limited cultural events, and education). Poland also has a significant gap between the rich and poor.[12] Before the 2005 elections, unemployment hovered around 20 percent, with approximately 40 percent unemployment among youth. More than half of those without work then had been unemployed for more than two years. The losses of the peasants were even greater. Until the European Union supports began, the peasant sector grew increasingly impoverished. With those supports, the peasant population has gained far more than anyone predicted.

All this was aggravated by the fact that the economic reforms had a very negative effect on the social welfare that had been a "given" in the communist era—free education, health care, and guaranteed pensions. The privatization of the economy and the shutting down of failing enterprises also increased the level of unemployment. As a result, unemployment support was needed. Yet, from the imposition of the Balcerowicz Plan until the election of 1997, reforming basic social welfare was not on the government's economic agenda—the Balcerowicz Plan and the legislation that followed ignored the whole sphere of social welfare. That, coupled with European Union pressures for a low budget deficit, made either reforming or supporting social services difficult at best. Instead, the doctors and teachers saw their salaries decline; financial support for hospitals, schools, and other social welfare institutions dried up; and the wealthier segment of the population has set up private hospitals and schools for their own use. Many professionals shifted to the new private sector in education and health care, took on multiple jobs, or left the country.

All this was also aggravated by the heightened demand on and costs to the state for health care and education as well as unemployment assistance and pensions. The economic reforms increased the cost of basic necessities dramatically even as privatization and the commitment to an exchangeable currency and meeting European Union requirements decreased the money the state could spend on such services. At the same time, Poland had a high percentage of its population who were either too old or too young to work (64.5 percent in 2000 down to 58.9 percent in 2003).[13]

The results of these social demands and the inability of the state to meet them were dual. Initially, there was a drop in the number of students going into higher education (with the exception of languages and "business") and a dramatic increase in the mortality rate. Women's participation in the economy and politics has dropped along with social supports. The communist ideological commitment to gender equality ended. Unemployment and family support funds were so limited that no one could live on the unemployment benefits or on the family subsidies that the regions gave out. Most of the unemployed drifted away into the gray economy of illegal trade and crime. And, particularly in the rural areas and small towns, poverty became a steady state, destroying the upward mobility opportunities that had been the promise of communism. In the second stage, youth unemployment and the promise of work for those with the right training increased the demand for some form of higher education. This, in turn, resulted in the proliferation of private schools not only at the lower levels but also in higher education. It also resulted in the emergence of an impoverished public health-care system and a parallel private system.

By 2005, the level of unemployment and the weaknesses in the state sector, which traditionally employed the bulk of the professional class, resulted in a dramatic out-migration from Poland. Some estimates for 2005 were of a 2 percent decline in the population as a result of this out-migration for work to the countries in Western Europe that would take Poles and for work where there were national restrictions on citizens from Central Europe working. This has particularly affected the long-underpaid Polish medical profession. In response, the Polish government initiated campaigns for young people to stay in Poland or work abroad and return. They have involved cities like Wroclaw advertising for Polish young people to "see the world and come home to work."

Public policy in these areas was limited at best. After 1989, Jacek Kuron, a long-time member of the opposition and the first noncommunist minister of social welfare, fought for decent unemployment benefits and even set up his own soup kitchens as a model for private action to deal with problems for which there was no governmental money. Only after the 1997 election was there an attempt to create coherent public programs to reorganize the health-care system and pension system and its funding. By 2005, neither the right-wing Solidarity Electoral Action (AWS) government nor its Social Democratic successor had been able to implement effective reforms in these areas. Hospitals had closed down for months at a time because of the lack of funds, and one health-care reform had been declared unconstitutional by the Constitutional Court, leaving the health-care system to function with no legal structure for more than a year until a new law was passed in 2004. The crisis in public services has continued virtually unabated, and has expanded with demonstrations and strikes not only by doctors and nurses but also by policemen and teachers.

Foreign Policy

Poland's foreign policy has tried to bridge three worlds: the United States, Western Europe, and the former Soviet bloc. Given the strength of the Polish lobby and the size of the Polish economy and unpaid debt, American interests were early and powerful players, as were Western European interests.

For all the initial government's interest in "Returning to Europe," it was impossible to turn away from the Soviet Union totally. The Soviet Union was first a player in how the Poles designed the limits of their transition and then a worry and also an opportunity. It was an established market for Polish goods that could not be sold elsewhere. It was also the major source of energy resources for Poland. Former Soviet peoples' desire to go to the West was both a blessing and a problem. On the one hand, Poles first worried that there would be a mass exodus from these poorer states to the West, flooding Poland with refugees. Instead, they got a plethora of skilled laborers from Ukraine and other former Soviet states ready to work at low wages in Poland to cover their expenses in their home countries. On the other hand, Polish foreign policy moguls came to see being a bridge between east and west as the way to give Poland a strong role in Western European foreign policy.

This balancing act was complicated as it was coupled with incentives for both right and left to legitimize themselves by being welcomed by American leaders,

NATO, and the European Union (all of which were courted by and tied themselves to the Social Democrats, the successors to the Communist Party). For all of Poland's former politicians but especially the former Communists, one key way to legitimize the economic reforms was to say that they were required for Poland to be in Europe and a part of the transatlantic alliance. One thing, beyond their loyalty, they could offer their Western counterparts was their experience with and ties to the former Soviet states.

Since the left and the failing center were tied to reforms and turning to Europe (and the United States), it fell to the right wing to emphasize Polish nationalism and the risks and costs of alignment. They were inclined to picture Poland as being sold off to Western (and former Soviet) interests. Hence, the Euroskeptics who dominated in the European Union parliamentary elections in May 2004 were largely from right-wing parties in Poland.

The balancing act that was required was not easy, nor was responding to the demands of membership in the EU and NATO or to America's circle of friends. While Poland was the central geographic corridor for NATO and the European Union's expansion eastward, it lagged in making the required reforms. It also did not always side with the Europeans in economic and political matters. In fact, Poland was called by some "America's Trojan horse." When faced with the choice between American and European producers, it inclined toward American products. Its leadership was ever loyal to American foreign policy. After Britain, Poland was one of the first European states to join the "coalition of the willing in Iraq," with a sizable contingent of troops that both the right and left governments maintained.

NATO membership was an important symbol of Poland's turn to the West. It was, for Poles, a guarantee that they were safe from their eastern neighbors even though there was no commitment on the part of the old NATO forces to protect Poland in the event of an attack. The costs of joining and retooling its military were partially cushioned by the Western aid it had received earlier and the aid targeted to smooth its movement into NATO.

Poland's membership in the European Union was guaranteed by its geographic position in the center between east and west. Even if it lagged in its preparations, it could not be ignored and could not avoid membership. Many in Poland and the West feared the results of Poland's inclusion in the European Union, even as they cheered this visible end to the division of Europe. Since it had one of the highest, if not the highest level of unemployment in Europe, and one of the poorest economies, many feared that Poles would leave en masse to work in Western Europe. Provisions were enacted allowing countries to bar Central and East Europeans from long-term stays to work in most of Western Europe.

In the east, Poland built (with Western European money) one of the most heavily guarded borders in the world to keep emigrants from the east from getting into "Europe" through Poland. Although Poland's neighbors could come with only a visa—given out free at embassies and consulates, this new border had unexpected side effects: it cut off or reduced the barter trade that had been "big business" for eastern Poland, where factories were so poorly developed that they could only make it in trade with the even poorer countries to the east.

European Union subsidies and special provisions eased the major concerns about the domestic impact of entry into the EU. For peasants in Poland, there was a major threat of being submerged by Western Europe in spite of the support monies that were promised by the European Union. This fear proved false. Peasants, in fact, gained. The other major fear of Poles had been that Germans would retake their lands in western Poland. The European Union protected Poland by ruling that, for the first seven years after Poland joined the EU in 2004, Polish land could not be purchased by foreigners.

Poles' enthusiasm for joining the European Union was there in the initial vote for EU membership in May 2003 when 77 percent—lower than any other Central and East European state except Czech Republic and Slovakia—voted "Yes" for membership after an active government campaign in favor. But by the elections for the EU parliament in June 2004 (less than two months after May 1, 2004, when Poland officially joined the EU), only 20.4 percent voted and, of those, 55 percent supported candidates from parties that were, at best, skeptical of the EU.

As a result, Polish policy toward the European Union has been split. On the one hand, the Social Democratic government treated membership in NATO and the EU as its great achievement. The Law and Justice government that began in 2005 has been Euroskeptic, painting Poland's position and role in the EU as being defenders of Polish interests and the traditional Catholic faith. On the other hand, with a majority of Poland's deputies from the Euroskeptical right, Poland has not always gone along with standard EU procedures. So Poland was a leader in the demand that the EU constitution define Europe as a Christian society. They have also advocated for Polish sovereignty against the outside. In 2007, this went so far as to nearly block an agreement on voting provisions for the new EU constitutional document. The Poles demanded that the votes be counted in a way that gave them nearly the same number of votes as more populous Germany. In a last minute compromise, the Poles were placated by a delay in the new voting system until 2012.

As it has moved westward in its foreign policy, Poland has also maintained strong ties to Russia and the former Soviet states. In the process, Polish governments have tried to insure continued access to Russian energy resources and markets. The Polish economy has also benefited from the cheap laborers that have come west to Poland to work. At the same time, Polish foreign policy has, explicitly and implicitly, advocated for democratization in the countries to its east. As Russia under Vladimir Putin has become more authoritarian and popular upheavals have taken place in Georgia and Ukraine, Poland's ability to maintain itself as a bridge between east and west has declined. Indeed, particularly after Aleksander Kwasniewski helped broker the transition in the Ukraine in 2004, Russian-Polish relations, along with Polish-Belarussian relations, have grown colder, with Russia circumventing Poland in building an oil pipeline from Russia to Germany.

And . . .

The grand irony of the Polish transition is that Poland had veered the furthest from Soviet-style communism before the transition began (with the exception of Slovenia), had the most well-developed civil society, and was the first state to begin the transition. Of the former communist states that are new entrants to the EU, Poland is the largest country with the biggest economy. Yet its transition, while clearly toward democracy and capitalism, has been the most troubled, with the public quite willing to change political persuasions and vote out regime after regime; serious economic problems, even as it has the fastest-growing economy in the region; and real popular disaffection. In the end, it was the weakness of Poland's communist regimes and the success of the former communists in returning to power as pro-democracy politicians that not only opened the door for a negotiated transition but also made the construction of a new polity difficult.

As Poland entered the EU, it was old problems that haunted it. The pain of the economic transition for individuals and the gap between their expectations and the realities delegitimized the new system for many. Its failure as well to provide for youth employment decreased young people's excitement about building a "new Poland." The original reformers and the communists who turned democrats have lost credibility, leaving Poland's political system bereft of parties that were a part of the change or that support economic reform and Poland's new position as a part of NATO and the EU. At the same time, Poland's delays in dealing with the past and the secret police files on agents that came to symbolize the evils of communism left them as a political football to shut down opposition and explain away economic failures. The result has been a worsening of the political situation that leaves few clear roads open to "normalcy" in Polish democracy and no real leading parties.

Suggested Readings

Ash, Timothy Garton. *The Polish Revolution: Solidarity*. New Haven, CT: Yale University Press, 2002.

Castle, Marjorie. *Triggering Communism's Collapse: Perceptions and Power in Poland's Transition*. Boulder, CO: Roman & Littlefield, 2003.

Castle, Marjorie, and Ray Taras. *Democracy in Poland*. Boulder, CO: Westview Press, 2002.

Curry, Jane L., and Luba Fajfer. *Poland's Permanent Revolution*. Washington, DC: American University Press, 1995.

Davies, Norman. *God's Playground: A History of Poland* (New York: Columbia University Press, 1982.

———. *The Heart of Europe: The Past in Poland's Present*. Oxford: Oxford University Press, 2001.

Kenney, Padriac. *A Carnival of Revolution*. Princeton, NJ: Princeton University Press, 2002.

Ost, David. *The Defeat of Solidarity: Anger and Politics in Postcommunist Europe*. Ithaca, NY: Cornell University Press, 2005.

Notes

God's Playground is the title of a two-volume history of Poland by Norman Davies (New York: Columbia University Press, 1982). In the title of this definitive history of Poland, Davies makes the point that Poland has been the country most conquered and fought over in Europe and has gone through successive experiments and disasters.

1. David S. Mason, "Poland," in *Developments in East European Politics*, ed. Stephen White, Judy Blatt, and Paul G. Lewis, 45 (Durham, NC: Duke University Press, 1993).

2. Padraic Kenney, *Carnival of Revolution* (Princeton, NJ: Princeton University Press, 2003).

3. Jane Curry and Luba Fajfer, *Poland's Permanent Revolution* (Washington, DC: American University Press, 1995).

4. Those two probably won only because, for the National List, voters could use a single X to mark out all the candidates on the two column National List ballot. The names at the bottom of the two columns often fell below the "X" and so were not counted as being crossed out.

5. Miroslawa Grabowska, *Podzial postkomunistyczny: Spoleczne podstawy polityki w Polsce po 1989 roku* (Warsaw, Poland: Wydawnictwo Naukowe SCHOLAR, 2004).

6. These results come largely from the research of the Center for Research on Public Opinion (CBOS), which publishes its results in English online monthly at www.cbos.pl/EN/cbos_top.htm.

7. Beata Roguska and Bogna Wciorka, "Religijnosc I Stosunek do Kosciola," in *Nowa Rzeczywistosc*, ed. Krzysztof Zagorski and Michal Strzeszewski (Warsaw, Poland: Dialog, 2000)

8. Agnieszka Cybulska, Arkadiusz Sek, Michal Wenzel, and Mariusz Wojcik, "Demokracja w Praktyce," in *Nowa Rzeczywistosc*, ed. Krzystof Zagorski and Michal Strzeszewski, 80–84 (Warsaw, Poland: Dialog, 2000).

9. World Economy Research Institute, *Transforming the Polish Economy* (Warsaw, Poland: World Economic Research Institute, 1993), 6.

10. Barbara Blaszczyk and Richard Woodward, *Privatization and Company Restructuring in Poland* (Warsaw, Poland: CASE, Report No. 18, 1999).

11. *Rocznik Statystyczny 2004* (Warsaw, Poland: GUS, 2005), 597.

12. Tadeusz Kowalik, "Spoleczny Aspekty Nowego Ustroju," 2005 (manuscript).

13. *Rocznik Statystyczny 2004*, 194.

CHAPTER 9

The Czech and Slovak Republics

TWO PATHS TO THE SAME DESTINATION

Sharon L. Wolchik

In November 1989, mass demonstrations in Prague, Bratislava, and other cities caused the hard-line communist system in Czechoslovakia to fall. Preceded by nearly twenty years of stagnation, the Velvet Revolution, as these events came to be called, ushered in a broad process of change designed to reinstitute democracy, re-create a market economy, and reclaim the nation's rightful place on the European stage. It soon became evident, however, that the impact of the transition in the Czech Lands and Slovakia, as well as the perspectives and ambitions of political leaders in the two areas, differed significantly.

After the peaceful breakup of the common state and the creation of two independent states in January 1993, the transition process diverged considerably. Progress in the Czech Republic was recognized by that country's admission to NATO in the first round of NATO expansion in March 1999. In Slovakia, on the other hand, the antidemocratic actions of the government of Vladimír Mečiar and lack of progress in privatization cast doubt on Slovakia's fitness to join the Western club of nations and resulted in the country's exclusion from the first round of NATO expansion. The victory of the opposition in Slovakia in the 1998 parliamentary elections put the country back on track, a fact recognized in Slovakia's inclusion in the second round of NATO expansion in 2004 and its accession to the EU, along with the Czech Republic, Poland, and Hungary, in the same year.

Leaders in both countries continue to face numerous challenges in consolidating democratic governance. Thus, political attitudes and values still reflect an amalgam of precommunist, communist, and postcommunist influences at both the mass and elite levels; civil society remains weak; and the political party systems are still fluid. There are also significant problems in both countries in incorporating minorities, as well as in dealing with the inequalities of opportunity and outcome created by the shift to the market. However, both remain among the most successful cases of transition in the region.

Precommunist History

Many of the differences between the Czech and Slovak Republics date to the precommunist era. Prior to the creation of an independent Czechoslovak state in 1918, both regions were part of the Austro-Hungarian Empire. In contrast to several other states in the region, neither Slovaks nor Czechs, after the Battle of White Mountain in 1620, had a native nobility. However, the Czech Lands were ruled by Austria; Slovakia was part of the Hungarian kingdom for nearly 1,000 years. As a result, the Czechs had greater opportunities to develop a mass-based national movement and participate in politics in Bohemia and in Vienna. The Czech Lands also became the center of the empire's industry.

In Slovakia, on the other hand, efforts to Magyarize, or Hungarianize, the population prevented the formation of a broad-based national movement. These efforts, which were particularly strong after 1878, also kept Slovaks from receiving secondary or higher education in their own language. In contrast to the Czech Lands, which were among the most developed parts of the empire, Slovakia remained predominantly agrarian. Tax codes designed to preserve the political power of the landowning aristocracy in Hungary stifled industrial development, although numerous mining and other centers, largely inhabited by Germans, did develop.

A final difference between the two regions was evident in the sphere of religion. Both peoples were predominantly Roman Catholic, but the population in the Czech Lands was far more secular than that in Slovakia, where levels of religious observance were much higher. There were also important differences in the relationship of Catholicism and national identity and the role of Protestantism in the two areas. Although the Czech national movement that developed in the nineteenth century included Catholic figures and symbols, such as Saint Wenceslas, Protestant figures such as Jan Hus, the fifteenth-century precursor of Martin Luther who called on the church to reform and was burned as a heretic in 1415, were equally if not more important, and Catholicism played a relatively small role in the development of Czech national identity. There was also a small Protestant minority in Slovakia that played an important role in efforts to create a national revival. However, Catholic figures and, in the interwar period, Catholic priests and the church were much more closely linked to the emerging sense of Slovak identity. Slovaks were also much more likely to attend church and turn to church ceremonies to mark major life passages such as birth, marriage, and death.[1]

These differences came to the fore very soon after the formation of the Czechoslovak republic in 1918. The result of efforts by leaders in exile such as Tomáš Masaryk and Milan Štefánik, as well as the need to fill the void created by the end of the Austro-Hungarian Empire at the end of World War I, Czechoslovakia came to include Ruthenia in 1919. The new state brought together regions at very different levels of development populated by peoples with very different experiences.

The impact of these differences was evident throughout the interwar period. The government in Prague was committed to industrializing Slovakia and closing the gap in development levels between the two parts of the country. However, very little progress was made in this respect before the Great Depression plunged Czechoslovakia, as much of the rest of the world, into economic decline. Levels of unemployment sky-rocketed, and emigration increased.[2]

Other policies of the government also fed Slovak dissatisfaction. Faced with the need to staff bureaucratic positions vacated by Germans, the government turned to the generally better-educated Czechs. Czech administrators, as well as Czech business-men and specialists who came to Slovakia as part of the development effort, frequently provoked resentment. The expansion of opportunities for education in the Slovak language that occurred during the interwar period led to a significant increase in the numbers of Slovaks with secondary and higher education, but there were relatively few Slovaks with these qualifications at the beginning of the period.[3] The unitary nature of the state, which was a centralized government based in Prague, also provoked dissatisfaction among many Slovaks, who came to feel that they had merely traded rule from Budapest for rule from Prague.

As a result of these factors, support for nationalist groups grew in Slovakia. Founded by Father Andrej Hlinka, the People's Party (later the Hlinka People's Party) gained an increasing share of the vote in Slovakia. As Hitler gained power in Germany, many leaders and members of the party adopted the trappings of Nazism and looked to Hitler to support their goal of an independent Slovak state.

The German minority in the Czech Lands also became increasingly dissatisfied with the state. Konrad Heinlein's Sudeten German Party received the overwhelming share of the vote of the German minority, and Sudeten German dissatisfaction pro-vided the pretext for Hitler's demand at the Munich conference held in October 1938 that Czechoslovakia cede the Sudetenland to Germany. Faced with the unwillingness of his British, French, and Russian allies to come to Czechoslovakia's aid, President Eduard Beneš acceded to Hitler's demands. This step only temporarily spared his country, however, as the Germans invaded on March 15, 1939, and established the Protectorate of Bohemia and Moravia under German control. Slovak leaders, threat-ened with invasion as well if they did not comply, declared Slovakia to be an indepen-dent state on March 14, 1939.

Czechoslovakia was the only state in the region to retain democratic government until it was ended by outside forces. The interwar democratic system, which is often idealized, was certainly more successful than those in neighboring states in dealing with many of the pressing issues of the day. Progressive labor and occupational safety legislation, and an extensive social welfare system succeeded in incorporating the growing working class and deflecting dissent. Elite political culture, heavily influenced by President Masaryk, also played an important role in supporting democracy, although the country in fact had a dual political culture as evident in the large size of the legal Communist Party.[4] The dominant role of the "pětka," the five-party coali-tion that ruled the country for much of this period and often set policy in discussions among party leaders outside of parliament, resulted in a form of democracy dominated by disciplined political parties and their leaders. The interwar leadership was less suc-cessful in dealing with ethnic issues than with social problems, a weakness that eventu-ally contributed to the end of the interwar state.

Inhabitants of the Czech Lands and Slovakia had rather different experiences dur-ing World War II. Both areas experienced lower levels of human and property loss than states such as Poland or Yugoslavia, which had active resistance groups and which were the scene of heavy fighting. Occupied by the Germans, the Czech Lands were seen as a source of manufactured goods and labor for the war effort. Beneš formed an exile government in Britain and there were sporadic acts against German rule, but there was little armed resistance. Although it had little autonomy, many Slovaks saw the Slovak state led by Father Tiso as the realization of Slovak aspirations for independence. As Hitler's ally, Slovakia was also spared heavy destruction. In May 1945, as Soviet forces approached from the east, Slovak anti-Nazi opposition leaders staged what has come to be known as the Slovak National Uprising against the Germans near the Dukla pass. This action came to be seen after the war as a symbol of Slovak resistance and as a counter to the policies of the Slovak state.

Most of the Jews in both the Czech Lands and Slovakia perished in the Holocaust. Roughly 90,000 Jews lived in the Czech Lands before the outbreak of World War II. In 1942 alone, 55,000 Jews were sent to Theresienstadt; many of these were later deported to Auschwitz and other death camps. An estimated 80,000 Czech Jews, or 90 percent of the community, perished in the course of the war. In Slovakia, only 15,000 of the estimated 90,000 Jews survived.[5]

With the exception of the area around Plzeň, which was liberated by American troops, Czechoslovakia was liberated by the Red Army. After liberation, the country was reestablished according to its interwar boundaries with the exception of Subcarpathian Ruthenia, which became part of the newly expanded Ukrainian SSR. From 1945 until February 1948, the country experienced a modified form of pluralism. The Communist Party enjoyed certain advantages, including control of the ministries of information, the interior, and agriculture, but other political parties existed and were free to participate in political life. In the 1946 elections, which were generally considered free and fair, the Communist Party emerged as the most popular party with 38.6 percent of the vote. Declining support for the party on the eve of the 1948 elections, coupled with changes in Stalin's plans for the region in light of the beginning of the Cold War, led the party to instigate a government crisis in February 1948 over control of the police. The democratic members of the government resigned, and, after President Beneš accepted their resignations, a government clearly dominated by the Communist Party took power.

The Communist Experience

After the February coup, the Czechoslovak communist leadership began implementing the Soviet model in earnest. The few political parties that were allowed to continue to exist were subordinated to the Communist Party, which became the only effective party. The new government also stepped up the nationalization of industry, which had begun under the previous government, and aggressively collectivized agriculture. A central planning board was established to set binding five-year plans based on reorienting the country's economy to focus on heavy industry to the neglect of light industry, the consumer and service sectors, and agriculture. Efforts were also made to industrialize Slovakia, which was much less developed economically than the Czech Lands at the outset of the communist period.

As in other states in the region, the leadership also implemented measures designed to change the social structure by improving the status of previously disadvantaged groups, such as workers and farmers, and remove the privileges of the previous elites. The associational life of the country was simplified. Most voluntary organizations were outlawed and replaced by large, unitary mass organizations under the control of the party. The independent media were disbanded, and a system of strict control of information and censorship was established. The party also asserted its control in the areas of education, culture, and leisure. Political criteria became important for admission to higher education, and the content of education was politicized. The elites also made efforts to use culture and leisure to propagate values and behaviors consistent with Marxism-Leninism.

Since the changes involved in implementing the Soviet model affected almost every area of life and were not chosen by the population but rather imposed from the top down, it is not surprising that the leadership came to rely increasingly on coercion. The purge trials in Czechoslovakia were among the harshest in the region, and numerous high party officials, including the secretary-general of the party, Rudolf Slánský, as well as Vladimír Clementis and several other Slovak party leaders, were executed after highly publicized show trials.[6]

Czechoslovakia remained a model Soviet satellite throughout the 1950s and early 1960s. The regime survived de-Stalinization, which led to the Revolution of 1956 in Hungary, and popular protests and strikes in Poland in 1956, with only modest changes in personnel and lip service to the need to rout out the cult of personality and restore socialist legality. By 1961, however, the previously dynamic economy in Czechoslovkia also began to show the effects of Stalinism. After the economy registered a negative growth rate in that year, party leaders commissioned a team of loyal party economists at the Academy of Science to propose economic reforms. This step, which was followed by the formation of other commissions to examine ways to reform other areas of life, initiated a large-scale process of renewal and rethinking at the elite level. Coupled with growing demands for intellectual freedom on the part of creative intellectuals, particularly writers, it resulted in the elaboration of a new model of socialism that its creators deemed more appropriate to a Western, developed society. The mid-1960s also saw the growth of Slovak dissatisfaction with Slovakia's position in the common state with the Czechs, as well as greater activism on the part of youth and several of the mass organizations.[7]

In late 1967, the reform process spread to the Communist Party, when Alexander Dubček replaced the hard-line Stalinist Antonín Novotný as head of the statewide party. From January 1968, the reform developed an explicitly political aspect. With the end of censorship in March 1968, the movement for change also spread to groups outside the party and its loyal intellectuals. More radical in its demands than those of the reformists within and associated with the party, this mass current kept pressure on Dubček and his colleagues in the party leadership to continue their efforts to create "Socialism with a Human Face," as the model they were elaborating came to be called.

The reformist communist leadership centered around Dubček wanted to pursue reforms within the system. Best expressed in the Action Program the party adopted in April, these demands did not include an end to the Communist Party's monopoly of power or any effort to renounce membership in the Warsaw Pact or separate Czechoslovakia from the Soviet Union and other socialist countries.[8] However, conservative leaders in East Germany and Poland, as well as the Soviet leadership, became increasingly fearful that the reformist spirit would spread to their countries.

Dubček and his supporters were caught between the need to maintain the slowly growing trust of the population and the need to satisfy their allies that socialism was not being threatened. The growth of groups outside the party, including KAN (the Club of Engaged Non-Party People), and Club 231 (a club of former political prisoners), as well as the increasingly radical demands being voiced by some intellectuals,[9] led the reformist leadership to consider the use of force to rein in the reform process, even as they attempted to reassure their colleagues in other socialist states.[10] After several meetings with the Soviet leadership in the summer of 1968 failed to produce the desired results, Soviet and other Warsaw Treaty Organization forces invaded Czechoslovakia on August 21, 1968.

After returning to Prague from Moscow, where they had been forcibly taken during the invasion, Dubček and his supporters attempted to preserve the reform course. It became increasingly difficult to do so, particularly with Soviet forces stationed in the country once again, and in April 1969, when Gustáv Husák, also a Slovak leader, replaced Dubček at the head of the party, it was clear that the reform era was over. Husák presided over the effort to restore orthodoxy in a process known at the time as "normalization." An attempt to reverse the reforms in all areas of life, "normalization" involved the restoration of a clear monopoly of political power by the Communist Party, the restoration of censorship, and the end of economic reform. It was accompanied by a massive personnel purge that removed most of the most talented figures in areas as diverse as culture, education, the economy, and politics from public life. The loss of these approximately 200,000 reformists and the restoration of party control over the mass organizations and media led to an almost twenty-year period of stagnation. During this time, Czechoslovakia once again became a model satellite. All discussion of reform became taboo, and only small numbers of intellectuals, soon labeled dissidents by the regime, engaged in independent activity.

During this period, the regime relied on a combination of material incentives and coercion to gain the population's compliance. The standard of living improved, and many families acquired summer or weekend cottages. Coercion was used primarily against dissident intellectuals who refused to accept the status quo or were active in the small number of independent groups that developed to protest the regime's disregard for human rights and support independent activity. Charter 77, formed in response to the regime's signing of the Helsinki Accords and the prosecution of a group of young rock musicians, the Plastic People of the Universe, in 1977, was the most important of these. Founded by Václav Havel and other intellectuals and writers centered mostly in Prague and other large cities in Bohemia and Moravia, Charter 77 was named for the document to which these intellectuals were signatories, which circulated in samizdat. In the last years of communist rule in particular, the group came to serve as the center of a growing community of independent activists, and many people who remained in good standing with the official world came to rely on their analyses for alternate information on problems that the regime either did not want to discuss or handled in a clearly biased way.[11] In 1989 and the years following, Charter 77 exerted an influence disproportionate to its numbers, as its leaders founded the Civic Forum, and many of its members moved into prominent positions in public life in the early postcommunist period.

On November 17, 1989, the process that came to be known as the Velvet Revolution was set into motion by police brutality during a peaceful demonstration called to commemorate the death of a student during the period of Nazi occupation. Encouraged by the fall of the Berlin Wall and changes in Hungary and Poland earlier that year, hundreds of thousands of citizens participated in mass demonstrations against the regime. As it became clear that the demonstrators were not going to give up and that the Soviet Union would not intervene to preserve communism in Czechoslovakia, leaders of the Communist Party began negotiations with Civic Forum in Prague and Public against Violence in Bratislava—umbrella groups formed by Charter 77 activists—and other dissidents in Prague and members of the paraopposition in Bratislava to coordinate the mass demonstrations. Within twenty-one days, the rigid, seemingly all-powerful, repressive communist system in Czechoslovakia fell. Many of the most conservative, compromised party members were removed from the federal legislature, and new elections were scheduled for June 1990. The election of former dissident playwright Václav Havel as president of Czechoslovakia on December 31, 1989, by a parliament still dominated by Communist Party members symbolized the victory of the Velvet Revolution.

The Transition and the Velvet Divorce

After the end of communism, Czech and Slovak leaders faced many of the same tasks as leaders in other postcommunist states. The highest priority of these was aptly summarized in the election slogans of almost all parties that ran candidates in the June 1990 parliamentary elections: Democracy, the Market, and the Return to Europe. In the political realm, the country's new leaders had to come to terms with the communist past and the need to establish new institutions or reorient the work of existing institutions so that they could function democratically. Other tasks included the recruitment of new leaders to replace the discredited old elite; the repluralization of the political landscape, both in terms of political parties and associational life; and the need to combat the legacy of communism on political values and attitudes, and create a new political culture suitable to a democratic polity.

In the economic realm, the new elites had to enact the legislative basis for the re-creation of private ownership and private enterprise; find a way to privatize state assets, which in Czechoslovakia accounted for over 90 percent of all economic activity at the end of communist rule; encourage the development of new private enterprises; restore economic assets to their rightful owners or their heirs; deal with rising unemployment, poverty, and inequality in a previously very egalitarian society; and address the environmental consequences of the communist pattern of industrialization. With the breakup of the Soviet Union and the Council for Mutual Economic Assistance

Photo 9.1.   Citizens of Prague, Czechoslovakia, turn out by the thousands in November 1989 to protest the Communist regime led by Miloš Jakeš. Just one month later, the regime had toppled, paving the way for the election of Václav Havel as president in December and democratic elections in June 1990.

(Source: David Turnley/CORBIS)

(CMEA), they also were required to reorient the country's trade, which had remained heavily centered in the socialist bloc, to the west.

In the area of foreign policy, the country's new leaders soon reasserted their status as a sovereign state by negotiating the withdrawal of Soviet troops from their territory and began the process of reclaiming their rightful place on the European stage. In the early years after 1989, this process involved discussion about the abolition of NATO as well as the Warsaw Treaty Organization, which was dissolved in 1991. After the breakup of the Soviet Union in 1991, however, Czech and Slovak leaders began a campaign to join existing European and Euro-Atlantic institutions. The EU and NATO were the main targets of these efforts.

In addition to these aspects of the transition, the new leadership of the country, as well as its citizens, had to cope with the social and psychological aspects of the far-reaching changes the transition entailed. In the social realm, these included changes in the social structure, which will be discussed in more detail later in this chapter, as well as the emergence into the open and exacerbation of old social problems, such as juvenile delinquency, alcoholism, drug abuse, crime, and domestic abuse, and the creation of new issues, such as trafficking in persons and organized crime. The widespread dislocations, as well as in many cases, the positive effects of the transition, including the vastly expanded choices available to citizens, also had psychological effects on many members of the population.

Very soon after the end of communism, it became evident that the transition, and particularly, the shift to the market, would be more difficult in many ways in Slovakia. Because Slovakia had industrialized largely during the communist era, it had more of the "monuments of socialist industry," or very large, inefficient factories that could not compete in market conditions. Slovakia had also become the center of the country's sizable arms industry. The shift to the market, with its emphasis on profit and ability to compete on the world market, therefore, created much greater economic disruption in Slovakia, where levels of unemployment were significantly higher than those in the Czech Lands. In 1993, for example, when 3 percent of the population was unemployed in the Czech Republic, close to 15 percent was unemployed in Slovakia.

The nature of the Czechoslovak federation was another irritant to many Slovaks. Although the adoption of a federal system was one of the few changes discussed during the reform period of 1968 that actually was implemented in 1969, the provisions that granted Slovakia a great deal of autonomy in managing its own economic as well as cultural and educational affairs were soon rescinded as the country was "normalized." After 1971, the federation functioned largely as a unitary state. Growing Slovak dissatisfaction with Slovakia's position in the common state was reflected in public opinion polls conducted in the early 1990s that showed that some 80 percent of Slovaks were dissatisfied with the federation.[12] Although most Czechs and Slovaks continued to say that they did not want the state to break up, Czech and Slovak leaders were unable to agree on an acceptable division of power between the republic and federal governments. After the June 1992 parliamentary elections led to the victory of the center-right under Václav Klaus in the Czech Lands and the center-left led by Vladimír Mečiar in Slovakia, the two leaders oversaw the process of dissolving the federation. This step formally occurred in January 1993, when the Czechoslovak Federative Republic, as it was called, was replaced by the Czech Republic and the Slovak Republic.

Initially, political and economic developments diverged markedly in the two independent states. Initial expectations that the transition would be smoother in the Czech Republic were borne out by that country's inclusion in the first round of expansion of both NATO and the EU. Vladimír Mečiar's dominance of political life in Slovakia, on the other hand, and the antidemocratic actions of his government stalled economic reform and resulted in Slovakia's exclusion from the first round of NATO expansion. The victory of OK98 (Citizens' Campaign 98) in the 1998 parliamentary elections brought a broad coalition of parties favoring reform to office. The government of Prime Minister Mikuláš Dzurinda quickly restarted economic reforms, included representatives of the 600,000 strong Hungarian minority in the government and rescinded anti-Hungarian measures adopted by the Mečiar government. It also restored the rule of law, respect for human rights, and political liberties. These steps put Slovakia back on track, and the country was admitted to NATO in the second round of expansion and included in the EU's first round of expansion to the postcommunist world in 2004.

As the pages to follow illustrate, both the Czech Republic and Slovakia have made a great deal of progress in achieving the goals of restoring democracy and the market, and returning to Europe. However, in both, there are still important problems in consolidating democracy and dealing with the economic aftermath of communism.

Photo 9.2.   Václav Havel and Vladimír Mečiar hold a press conference about the future of the country. A month later, the Velvet Divorce was announced, separating the once unified country into the Czech and Slovak republics.

(Source: Czech News Agency)

Political Institutions

The legislature elected for a two-year term in Czechoslovakia in June 1990 was to have been a constitutive assembly: its main task was to revise the country's constitution and reform its legal system so that it would be compatible with democratic government and the creation of a market economy. Although the country's new leaders made a great deal of progress in the latter area, their inability to agree on a division of power between the federal and republic governments was one of the factors that contributed to the breakup of the state.

The two new states that replaced the federation in January 1993 were both unitary states. Their constitutions, adopted in both countries on January 1, 1993, identify them as parliamentary democracies and include provisions guaranteeing their citizens political and civil liberties.

In both states, the government is formed based on the results of parliamentary elections and is responsible to the legislature. The Czech Republic has a bicameral legislature. The lower house consists of 200 members elected for four-year terms on the basis of proportional representation. The upper house, the Senate, which was created in 1996, consists of 81 members who are elected according to the majority principle for six-year terms. One-third of the members of the Senate are elected every two years. Slovakia has a unicameral legislature. Its 150 members are elected to four-year terms according to proportional representation.

In addition to governments headed by prime ministers responsible to parliament, both countries also have presidents who serve as heads of state. The president is directly elected in Slovakia. In the Czech Republic, the parliament elects the president. Officially, the duties of the president are largely ceremonial in both countries. However, in both cases, the office has sometimes been used to counteract or counterbalance actions by the government in ways that go beyond its formal powers. These activities were most evident in Slovakia during the Mečiar period, when President Michal Kováč, formerly a close colleague of Prime Minister Mečiar, came to be seen as an opponent of Mečiar's more authoritarian actions. Václav Havel, who was both the first postcommunist president of the federation and the first president of the independent Czech Republic, exercised influence that far exceeded the powers of his office due to his enormous moral authority and reputation around the world.[13]

Political Parties and Movements

After the end of communism, one-party rule was replaced by a plethora of political parties. The most important of these initially were the broad umbrella groups formed in November 1989 to direct the mass demonstrations and negotiate with the government, the Civic Forum in the Czech Lands, and Public against Violence in Slovakia. Almost immediately, however, other political parties began to form. These included successors to parties that had been active in the interwar period and were later banned under communism, new parties with links to parties in the rest of Europe, nationalist or regional parties and movements, and single-issue groups and parties focused on new issues. Reformed and unreformed versions of the Communist Party also participated in politics in both regions.[14]

As table 9.1 illustrates, the number of political parties and movements that have fielded candidates has in fact increased in both the Czech Republic and Slovakia since 1990. However, many of these were unable to obtain enough votes to pass the threshold of 3 or 5 percent of the vote required to seat deputies in parliament. Thus, four parties gained enough votes to seat deputies in the federal legislature in the Czech Lands and five in Slovakia in 1990; in 1992 six parties crossed the threshold in the Czech Lands and five in Slovakia. Six parties were represented in the Czech Chamber of Deputies in 1996, five in 1998, and four in 2002. In Slovakia, six parties seated deputies in parliament in 1994 and 1998 and seven in 2002. As of the result of the 2006 elections, there were once again six parties in the parliament in Slovakia and five in the Czech Chamber of Deputies.

Although a relatively small and stable number of parties have seated deputies in the legislatures since 1990, the figures in table 9.1 mask an important aspect of politics in the period since 1989. As table 9.2 illustrates, parties continue to appear and disappear with great frequency. Thus, twenty-one of the thirty-one parties that competed in the 2002 elections in Slovakia were new or newly formed combinations of previous political groups, as were two of the seven parties that seated deputies. In the Czech Republic, twenty-five parties fielded candidates in the 2002 parliamentary elections, but seventeen of these parties were either new or reincarnations of previous parties. In the 2006 Czech parliamentary elections, the pattern remained the same, as fourteen of the twenty-six parties that fielded candidates were new. In Slovakia, however, only six of the twenty-one parties that fielded candidates in 2006 were new.

Although they won the June 1990 elections resoundingly, Civic Forum and Public against Violence soon splintered into smaller groups. In the Czech Lands, then finance minister Václav Klaus broke away from Civic Forum in April 1991 to form a

Table 9.1. Ratio of the Number of Parties That Seated Deputies to the Number of Parties Fielding Candidates by Election

	Czech National Council	Czechoslovakia Federal Assembly (Chamber of Nations + Chamber of People)		Slovak National Council
		Czech Lands	Slovakia	
1990	13/4	15/4 + 12/4	17/5 + 17/5	17/7
1992	10/6	20/6 + 21/6	22/6 + 22/5	23/5

	Czech Republic Chamber of Deputies		Slovakia National Council	
1996	17/6	1994	17/6	
1998	13/5	1998	17/6	
2002	17/4	2002	25/7	
2006	26/5	2006	21/6	

Note: In both countries, political parties must receive at least 5 percent of the vote in order to enter parliament. Until the Velvet Revolution, the threshold was 3 percent for the Slovak National Council and 5 percent for the Federal Assembly and the Czech National Council.
Source: Project on Political Transformation and the Electoral Process in Post-Communist Europe, University of Essex (www.essex.ac.uk/elections/)

Table 9.2. Number of Parties That Fielded Candidates and Number of New Parties in the Czech Republic and Slovakia since Independence

	Czech Republic			Slovakia	
	Total # of Parties	# of New Parties		Total # of Parties	# of New Parties
2006	26	14	2006	21	6
2002	25	17	2002	31	21
1998	17	13	1998	14	6
1994	18	14	1996	17	10

Note: New party is defined as one that did not field candidates in the immediate preceding election. Coalition parties are counted as separate parties.
Source: Project on Political Transformation and the Electoral Process in Post-Communist Europe, University of Essex (www.essex.ac.uk/elections/)

political party, the Civic Democratic Party. Those who remained in Civic Forum founded the Civic Democratic Movement and the Civic Democratic Alliance, which succeeded in electing candidates to the Federal Assembly in the 1992 elections, but were no longer viable political entities after that. In Slovakia, Vladimír Mečiar, who was initially part of Public against Violence, broke away in April 1991 to found his own political movement, the Movement for a Democratic Slovakia, which became the single most popular party or movement in Slovakia. Public against Violence was replaced by a variety of other parties on the center-right.

Analysts of politics in both countries have disagreed on how to characterize the political party system that followed the breakup of the initial umbrella organizations. By the mid-1990s, some analysts argued that the proliferation of political parties that followed the demise of these groups was coming to an end and that a simplified party system was emerging. Others argued that, although party labels continued to change, the electorate was sorting itself into two coherent, identifiable large blocs that corresponded in a general way to the left-right division seen in many other European polities.[15] As subsequent elections demonstrated, neither view has been supported by events since that time. Instead, voter support for most parties, with few exceptions, has continued to be fluid, as voters generally have tended to "throw the rascals out" at each election. Both the number of parties and the parties themselves have also tended to change from one election to another. The reelection of a center-right government in Slovakia in the 2002 elections and a center-left government in the Czech Republic in that year, although both with changes in the composition of the coalition, was unusual not only in those countries but in the postcommunist region as a whole.

In the 2006 parliamentary elections, voters in both countries reverted to the more common pattern of defeating the incumbent government. In Slovakia, the Smer, or Direction, movement led by Robert Fico won the largest number of votes, soundly defeating the center-right government of Mikuláš Dzurinda. Fico eventually formed a coalition government with deputies from Vladimír Mečiar's center-left Movement for a Democratic Slovakia and the extreme right-wing Slovak National Party. In the Czech Republic, the center-right Civic Democrats emerged as the strongest party in the June elections but the minority government they lead, which was formed only several months after the election, is a fragile coalition with the Christian Democrats and the Greens that may well face early elections (see table 9.3).

Table 9.3.   Governing Coalitions in the Czech Republic and Slovakia

Party Name	% of Vote	# of Seats
Czech Republic		
2006		
Civic Democratic party (ODS)	35.4	81
Christian-Democratic Union–Czechoslovak People's Party (KDU-CSL)	7.2	13
Green Party	6.3	6
2002		
Czech Social Democratic Party (CSSD)	30.2	70
Coalition of Christian-Democratic Union–Czech People's Party and Freedom Union–Democratic Union (KDU-CSL, US-DEU)	14.27	31
1998		
Czech Social Democratic Party (CSSD)	32.31	74
Christian-Democratic Union–Czech People's Party (KDU-CSL)	9	20
1996		
Civic Democratic Party (ODS)	29.62	68
Civic Democratic Alliance (ODA)	6.36	13
Christian-Democratic Union–Czech People's Party (KDU-CSL)	8.08	18
Slovakia		
2006		
SMER–Social Democracy (SMER-SD)	29.14	50
Slovak National Party (SNS)	11.73	20
Movement for a Democratic Slovakia–People's Party (HZDS-LS)	8.79	15
2002		
Slovak Democratic and Christian Union (SDKU)	15.09	28
Party of the Hungarian Coalition (SMK)	11.17	20
Christian Democratic Movement (KDH)	8.25	15
Alliance of New Citizens (ANO)	8.01	15
1998		
The Slovak Democratic Coalition (SDK)	26.33	42
Party of the Democratic Left (SDL)	14.66	23
Party of the Hungarian Coalition (SMK-MKP)	9.13	15
Party of Civil Understanding (SOP)	8.02	13
1994		
Movement for a Democratic Slovakia and Peasants' Party of Slovakia (HZDS-RSS)	34.97	61
Slovak National Party (SNS)	5.4	9
Association of Workers of Slovakia (ZRS)	7.35	13

Source: Project on Political Transformation and the Electoral Process in Post-Communist Europe, University of Essex (www.essex.ac.uk/elections/)

Irrespective of their views on the nature of the party system that is emerging in Slovakia and the Czech Republic, analysts agree that most parties tend to be weak organizationally. Most have small memberships and poorly defined and staffed local organizations. The unreformed Communist Party in the Czech Republic and the Christian Democratic parties in both countries have larger memberships than most other parties, but their memberships are also relatively small. Levels of party identification, which in more established democracies helps simplify political choices, links

Photo 9.3.   Czech prime minister Mirek Topolánek and Slovak prime minister Robert Fico. Topolánek, head of the Civic Democrats, managed to form a shaky center-right coalition on January 19, 2007, 230 days after the parliamentary elections. Fico raised international eyebrows when he formed a government with Vladimír Mečiar's Movement for a Democratic Slovakia and the ultranationalist Slovak National Party after the June 2006 parliamentary elections.

(Source: Official website of the government of the Slovak Republic, www.government.gov.sk)

citizens to the political system, and moderates conflict, have also remained low. Many citizens do not believe that parties play an essential role in a democratic state, and many continue to hold parties and party leaders in low regard.

In part, these trends reflect the legacy of the communist period. In reaction to the need to be a member of the Communist Party or its youth organization if one wanted to study at university or hold many professional jobs, many people simply have refused to become members of any party. Low levels of party membership may also reflect, however, the trend in much of the rest of Europe for parties to change from being membership organizations that influenced many aspects of their members' lives to electoral parties more along the lines of American political parties. The lack of willingness to become a member of a party or take part in the activities sponsored by parties, as well as negative attitudes toward parties, may also reflect citizens' experiences in the postcommunist era. The tendency of parties to come and go, the similarities in the platforms of many parties, and the frequent change in the party affiliation of political figures all make it difficult and costly in terms of time and attention for citizens to affiliate with particular parties. These trends also appear to reinforce citizens' views of parties as vehicles to advance the personal fortunes of their leaders rather than as mechanisms to aggregate interests and pursue broader policy objectives.

Civil Society

In contrast to the situation in Poland and Hungary, where a strong civil society independent of the government had begun to form prior to the end of communism, there were very few independent groups in Czechoslovakia prior to 1989. Due to the heavy repression and the very real threat of imprisonment, loss of jobs, and other forms of retaliation, the number of independent organizations remained very small even after Gorbachev's reforms in the Soviet Union began to have some impact in Czechoslovakia. Experts estimated that there were approximately 1,500 independent groups in Hungary in the late 1980s.[16] In Czechoslovakia, there were approximately 30 at that time.[17]

Following the end of communism, Czechoslovakia experienced the same resurgence of associations and voluntary organizations that occurred elsewhere in the postcommunist world. As in the case of political parties, some of these groups had ties to groups that had been active in the interwar or immediate post–World War II periods. Some were attached to the newly emerging parties or were branches of international organizations. Still others were new groups designed to further the interests of their members, provide charitable services, or unite citizens with similar hobbies.

Most of these new nongovernmental organizations (NGOs) were funded in the early years after the end of communism by outside funders, and many remained heads without bodies, that is, groups of intellectuals in the major cities with few links to ordinary citizens or members. Domestic philanthropy has increased over time, as has the number of NGOs that no longer rely on foreign funders. Similarly, citizens are more likely to participate in the work of NGOs than of partisan political organizations, and the number of citizens who indicate that they participate in the work of such organizations increased in both the Czech Republic and Slovakia between 1994 and 2004.[18]

The NGO sector was particularly well organized in Slovakia during the mid-1990s when Vladimír Mečiar dominated partisan politics. A coordinating committee known as the Gremium included representatives of the main sectors of the NGO community and sponsored an annual conference to discuss issues of importance to the sector. The Gremium and activists who had participated in NGO campaigns formed the core of those who organized the OK98 campaign of civic actions that increased voting turnout sufficiently to oust Mečiar as prime minister in 1998. The impact of this campaign, which was the first full elaboration of the electoral revolution model in the postcommunist world, was not limited to Slovak politics but served as an inspiration and model for NGO activists in other postcommunist countries.[19]

Once the Dzurinda government was formed, NGO activists articulated their desires to continue to serve as watchdogs of the government and succeeded in passing a freedom-of-information law. With the end of government harassment of NGO activists and the return of respect for democratic procedures, the unity of the sector has diminished. During the 2002 election campaign, individual NGOs sponsored election-related actions. However, there was no repetition of the large-scale NGO campaign to get out the vote that occurred in 1998. Although some NGOs continue to lobby political leaders and monitor their actions, most NGOs have returned to focusing on their particular areas of activity.[20] Others have redirected their activities toward providing assistance to NGOs seeking to promote democracy in other countries.

Political Values and Attitudes

As in many other postcommunist countries, the political attitudes and values of citizens in the Czech Republic and Slovakia continue to reflect a variety of influences. Some of these stem from the precommunist political culture, which contained both democratic and nondemocratic elements in both countries. Others derive from the communist era, and still others have developed in response to the politics and economic policies of the transition since 1989.

The political attitudes of citizens of the Czech Republic and Slovakia differ somewhat from those of citizens in non-postcommunist members of the EU. These differences are most evident in perceptions and levels of trust in government institutions and in citizens' perception of their own political roles. Thus, although citizens' levels of interest in politics in the Czech Republic and Slovakia, as well as in Hungary and Poland, do not differ greatly from those in older EU member states, citizens of postcommunist states have lower levels of trust in government institutions. They also have lower levels of political efficacy, or the sense that they can make a difference at either the local or national level if their interests are threatened.[21]

Surveys conducted in 1994 and 2004 in the Czech Republic and Slovakia found that most citizens in both countries supported democracy. They also held views of democracy that included protection of individual rights and other political liberties as well as the view that democracy should result in a high level of well-being. In the early 1990s, citizens in the Czech Lands were more likely than those in Slovakia to agree with the notion that citizens should be responsible for ensuring their own well-being; they also accepted the idea that a certain level of unemployment was an inevitable element of the shift to the market. As unemployment rates grew in the Czech Republic, however, differences between the two countries in this regard decreased. Popular resistance to the institution of fees for higher education, the introduction of fees for medical services, and other measures that have decreased the government's responsibility for services and welfare are further indications of the extent to which citizens internalized the expectation common during the communist period that the state owes citizens a great deal of material security.[22]

Early studies of levels of tolerance in the two areas found that levels of anti-Semitism were lower in the Czech Republic than in Slovakia, Poland, and Hungary.[23] However, studies done at that time and more recently have documented very high levels of prejudice against the Roma in the Czech Republic as well as in Slovakia.[24]

The Economic Transition

Shortly after the end of communism, Czechoslovakia's new elites began debating the best way to return to a market economy. Early discussions of a more gradual, or third way, to transform the economy soon gave way, under the direction of then finance minister of the federal government Václav Klaus, to the decision to move rapidly and decisively to the market. This decision, which was accompanied by the end of or decrease in government subsides, a rapid increase in prices, and efforts to privatize the economy, which was almost entirely in state hands, led to a steep drop in production and an increase in unemployment, economic hardship, and poverty. The negative effects of the shift to the market were especially evident in Slovakia.

The country's new leaders used a variety of methods to privatize the country's economic assets. These included auctions, sales to foreign investors, and, most distinctively, the use of vouchers or coupons. Under the latter system, citizens were able to buy vouchers, which could then be exchanged for shares in privatizing companies, very inexpensively. This system, which became a sort of parlor game at the time, was designed to compensate for the lack of domestic capital at the end of communism as well as to give most citizens a personal stake in the continuation of market reforms. However, because it was not accompanied by changes in the banking sector or even, until several years later, the adoption of a bankruptcy law, it did little to restructure the economy. As in other postcommunist countries, privatization was also accompanied by massive fraud and corruption.[25]

Political elites also adopted laws to regulate restitution, the return of property that had been seized by the state, to its rightful owners or their heirs and stimulate the development of new private enterprises. The country's trade was also rapidly reoriented to the West, particularly after the collapse of CMEA and the Soviet Union.

Eventually, the shift to the market created more favorable economic conditions in both the Czech Republic and Slovakia. However, in the period soon after the end of communism, policies designed to achieve this goal created greater hardship in Slovakia. They have also affected different groups of the population very differently. Thus, the economic transition created both winners and losers. The former were those who had the skills, contacts, and abilities to benefit from the new opportunities to increase their skills and qualifications, travel abroad for study or work, practice their occupations free of ideological interference, take the risk of working for a private or international corporation, or found a private business. These were primarily those who were young, urban, and well educated. Those lacking such skills and opportunities (those who were older, rural, less educated, as well as families with several or many children and the Roma) experienced primarily hardship as the result of the changes.

As the chapter in this volume on economics indicates, both the Czech and Slovak economies have attracted sizable amounts of foreign investment. In the Slovak case, outside investors began to seriously consider investing in Slovakia after the victory of the liberal opposition in the 1998 elections. Both countries now play an important role in producing many products for the European market, including, most notably, automobiles.

Social Consequences

In addition to poverty and unemployment for some groups, the shift to the market and the broader transition also had a number of social consequences. First among these was the growing inequality that developed. Inequalities in terms of lifestyles, values, and access to higher education existed under communism,[26] but these societies were remarkably egalitarian. Although the communist leadership clearly had many material privileges during communism, Czech and Slovak societies were generally very egalitarian, and those who had greater wealth were fairly circumspect about it. With the return to the market, inequalities increased dramatically. Wage differentials, which had been among the lowest in the communist world, widened significantly, and, with the expansion of availability of consumer durables and goods, it suddenly became clear to many families that they were not living as well as their neighbors.

Czech and Slovak societies have also changed in another fashion. In both cases, they have once again become more complex as the truncated classification of all those employed into either mental or manual workers ended and the return of the market led to the emergence of new occupations and groups, particularly in the rapidly expanding service and financial sectors. Restitution and the growth of the private sector also led to the reemergence of certain previously banned social categories, such as capitalists or entrepreneurs. There were also important shifts in the status and prestige as well as the income of different occupations and groups. At the same time that these changes opened up many new opportunities for some citizens, the situation of members of other groups, such as agricultural workers, unskilled and skilled manual workers, and some members of the party's former apparatus, worsened.

The opening of the borders and decline of tight political and police control also led to the intensification of all forms of social pathology, such as alcoholism, drug use, and abuse within the family, and to the emergence of new issues, such as trafficking in persons, smuggling, and HIV/AIDS. Many of these problems were intensified by the economic transition, as economic hardship took its toll on families.

The end of communism also allowed certain issues, such as ethnic tensions and issues related to sexuality, to emerge into the open and get onto the political agenda. Hungarian activists in Slovakia formed their own political parties and began to make demands for greater respect for minority culture and more attention to minority rights. The positive start to forging new relationships evident in the inclusion of a Hungarian party in the first postcommunist coalition government in Slovakia was interrupted temporarily by Mečiar's government, which enacted a number of laws that restricted the rights of the Hungarian minority to use its language in official dealings, removed dual-language street signs, and required Hungarian women to add the Slavic suffix "ová" to their last names, among others. With the victory of the democratically oriented opposition in 1998, the by now single Hungarian party was once again included in the governing coalitions, and the most offensive legislation of the Mečiar era was reversed. Hungarian leaders continued to press for greater recognition of minority rights, but played a constructive role within the coalition government on many issues. The inclusion of the nationalist, anti-Hungarian Slovak National Party in Prime Minister Robert Fico's coalition after the 2006 elections raised fears that the progress made in this regard would end. There were several isolated incidents of violence in 2006 by Slovaks against ethnic Hungarians who were speaking Hungarian. However, there has not been a return, aside from the occasional inflammatory rhetoric used by some political leaders, to policies that clearly disadvantage ethnic Hungarians in Slovakia.

The status of the Roma community has also become an important issue. Subject to various measures to foster assimilation during the communist era, the Roma continue to face widespread prejudice and discrimination in both the Czech Republic and Slovakia. Education levels among the Roma are very low, and the practice of sending Roma children to special schools for the mentally handicapped continues to be widespread. Unemployment rates approach 85 percent in many Roma communities. The living conditions of many Roma, who live in "settlements" at the outskirts of towns and cities, are very poor, as many Roma communities lack running water, electricity, and other public services. After the end of communism, violence against the Roma also increased.

Unlike the Hungarian minority, the Roma have not developed an effective political organization to raise their claims in the political arena. Both the Czech and Slovak governments have adopted programs, in part at the prodding of the European Union, to improve the status of the Roma, but serious problems, including overwhelmingly negative public attitudes toward them, remain in both countries.[27]

Gender issues have also emerged as political issues since 1989. In part because women's equality was an official goal during the communist era, and in part because the uneven pattern of change in women's roles created great stress for women and their families,[28] many Czechs and Slovaks rejected the idea of women's equality after the end of communism. This backlash was reflected in the view that women should give more emphasis to their maternal rather than economic roles, as well as in reluctance on the part of women to be actively involved in politics. Although most women continued to be employed, women were more likely than men to lose their jobs in the Czech Republic as the result of the transition. They also faced increased competition from men for jobs in areas such as tourism, law, and financial services, that became more attractive under market conditions, and, as did men, new pressure to work productively in both countries. Given the continued traditional division of labor within the home, the task of dealing with the results of declining social services and the need to stretch family budgets to cover necessities also fell most heavily on women during the early part of the transition.

Women's political representation also declined in the early postcommunist period. Many women appeared to share the view of male leaders, including some former dissidents, who argued that politics was too dirty for women or that women had more important tasks than arguing about political issues. This pattern began to change in the late 1990s, as levels of women's representation increased in both the Czech Republic and Slovakia. However, as the chapter on women's issues in this volume indicates, women are still underrepresented among the political elite, and it is still difficult for women leaders to raise issues of particular concern for women.

By the mid-1990s, the backlash against even considering or discussing issues related to women's status began to decrease. Social scientists and women's advocates succeeded in getting certain issues related to women's situation onto the political agenda. Women's groups, particularly the small number of such groups that identify themselves as feminist, have also succeeded in establishing links with a few political leaders and have provided background materials as well as position papers on issues such as same-sex partnerships and legislation prohibiting sexual harassment at the workplace. Public discussion of women's issues in the media also increased. The EU accession process accelerated these trends in both countries, as political leaders were forced to adopt certain laws and establish government institutions to address issues related to women's status as part of that process.

Foreign Policy

As noted earlier in this chapter, foreign policy concerns were a major element in the transition in both the Czech Republic and Slovakia. One of the first steps of the new government was to negotiate the withdrawal of Soviet troops from Czechoslovakia. The country's new leaders also sought to claim their place on the world stage as an independent country once again. Helped by the international stature of then president Václav Havel, Czech and Slovak leaders played an active role in upgrading the status of the Organization for Security and Cooperation in Europe. They also were key players in establishing the Visegrad Group of Czechoslovakia, Hungary, and Poland, which sought to coordinate the three countries' efforts to join NATO and the EU.

After the breakup of the federation, the foreign policies of the newly created Czech Republic and Slovak Republic diverged for several years. The Czech Republic maintained its status as a candidate for inclusion in the first round of NATO expansion, a goal it achieved in 1999, and began negotiations for EU accession. Although the Slovak leadership never renounced the goals of joining NATO and the EU, under Mečiar, Slovakia fell out of the group of countries included in the first round of NATO expansion and was in danger of being excluded from EU expansion as well. The Mečiar government also sought to increase Slovakia's ties with Russia. After the victory of the opposition in the 1998 elections, Slovakia's foreign policy once again emphasized EU accession and NATO membership. Slovakia was included in the second round NATO expansion in 2004 and became a member of the EU, along with the Czech Republic and eight other countries, in that year.

As new members of NATO and the EU, both Slovakia and the Czech Republic have faced often competing pressures from their European and U.S. allies. These became evident almost immediately after the Czech Republic joined NATO in 1999 in the context of the NATO bombing campaign in Serbia and Kosovo in reaction to Milošević's expulsion of most of the Albanian population from Kosovo. The governments of both countries supported this effort, but this step was unpopular with citizens of both.

U.S. actions in Afghanistan and, particularly, the war in Iraq have posed even more starkly the dilemma these countries face in trying to maintain good relations with other EU members and the United States. Both countries sent specialized units to Afghanistan and Iraq. However, as in most of Central and Eastern Europe, citizens in both countries oppose the war in large numbers.

Future Challenges

As the preceding pages have illustrated, both Slovakia and the Czech Republic are among the success stories in the postcommunist world. Although political and economic developments diverged in Slovakia under Mečiar, in the period since 1998, political leaders have successfully achieved many of the objectives set out after the fall of communism in 1989. Thus, both Slovakia and the Czech Republic are now among those countries classified as "free" by Freedom House and other international ranking bodies. Although important problems remain with the party system, as well as with elite and mass political culture, both are widely recognized as functioning liberal democracies.

In the economic realm, both countries' economies are also among the success stories in the region. Economic growth rates have been among the highest in Europe in the 2000s, and foreign direct investment continues to increase. Privatization was successfully accomplished, and the standard of living has reached and surpassed its 1989 level in both countries. Securely anchored in European and transatlantic institutions, both Slovakia and the Czech Republic have also achieved recognition for their roles in supporting pro-democracy movements abroad, particularly in the postcommunist world.

As in other developed, Western countries, numerous problems remain in all of these areas. In the political realm, these include the need to develop a stable system of political parties, and increase linkages between political leaders and citizens and between political leaders and the NGO sector. They also include the need to foster a political culture that supports democracy and includes a greater sense of citizens' responsibility to take action to resolve public problems and actively join with others to address common issues, as well as tolerance. Dealing with corruption in both the political and economic arenas is another area where there is room for improvement in both countries.

In the economic arena, both governments continue to face regional disparities in growth and unemployment, and a host of problems arising from aging and declining populations. They also must address the problem of persistent poverty among certain groups, including most importantly the Roma, as well as other unresolved issues related to the marginal status of the Roma in both societies. Gender issues are another area where greater attention is needed. As their economies continue to grow and the wage differentials compared to more developed EU members that have made both countries attractive to foreign investors change, Czech and Slovak leaders will also need to find other incentives to attract outside capital.

In the area of foreign policy, leaders in both countries will continue to face the need to balance their relations with the rest of Europe and the United States. They also must find a way to play constructive roles as small countries within the EU as well as in regional groupings and define their relations with countries to the east.

As this listing of areas indicates, political leaders and citizens continue to face important challenges in both Slovakia and the Czech Republic. Some of these continue to reflect the legacy of communism and its impact on the transition. Others derive from the transition process itself and its unintended or in some cases seemingly inevitable consequences. Increasingly, however, the problems that dominate the political agenda in both Slovakia and the Czech Republic are those that confront leaders in other developed, Western societies.

Suggested Readings

Fisher, Sharon. *Political Change in Post-Communist Slovakia and Croatia: From Nationalist to Europe-anist*. New York: Palgrave Macmillan, 2006.

Innes, Abby. *Czechoslovakia—the Short Goodbye*. New Haven, CT: Yale University Press, 2001.

Krause, Kevin Deegan. "Slovakia's Second Transition" *Journal of Democracy* 14, no. 2 (April 2003): 65–79.

Leff, Carol Skalnik. *The Czech and Slovak Republics: Nation vs. State*. Boulder, CO: Westview Press, 1996.

Prečan, Vilém. *Prague-Washington-Prague: Reports from the United States Embassy in Czechoslovakia, November-December 1989*. Washington, DC: National Security Archive, 2004.

Saxonberg, Steven. *The Czech Republic before the New Millennium: Politics, Parties, and Gender*. New York: Columbia University Press, 2003.

Skilling, H. Gordon. *Czechoslovakia's Interrupted Revolution*. Princeton, NJ: Princeton University Press, 1976.

Vachudova, Milada Anna. *Europe Undivided: Democracy, Leverage, and Integration after Communism*. Oxford: Oxford University Press, 2005.

Wolchik, Sharon L. *Czechoslovakia in Transition: Politics, Economics, and Society*. London: Pinter Publishers, 1991.

———. "The Politics of Ethnicity in Post-Communist Czechoslovakia." *East European Politics and Societies* 8, no 1 (Winter 1994): 155–88.

Notes

1. Samuel Harrison Thomson, *Czechoslovakia in European History* (Princeton, NJ: Princeton University Press, 1953).

2. Zora Pryor, "Czechoslovak Economic Development in the Interwar Period," in *A History of the Czechoslovak Republic: 1918–1948*, ed. Victor S. Mamatey and Radomír Luza (Princeton, NJ: Princeton University Press, 1973).

3. Owen V. Johnson, *Slovakia: 1918–1938: Education and the Making of a Nation* (New York: Columbia University Press, 1985).

4. H. Gordon Skilling, "Stalinism and Czechoslovak Political Culture," in *Stalinism: Essays in Historical Interpretation*, ed. Robert C. Tucker (New York: W.W. Norton and Company, 1977).

5. Lucy S. Dawidowicz, *The War against the Jews: 1933–1945* (New York: Bantam Books, 1975).

6. See Arthur Koestler, *Darkness at Noon* (New York: Macmillan Press, 1941) for a fictionalized account of the purges.

7. Barbara Jancar, *Czechoslovakia and the Absolute Monopoly of Power: A Study of Political Power in a Communist System* (New York: Praeger Press, 1978); and Golia Golan, *The Czechoslovak Reform Movement: Communism in Crisis, 1962–1968* (Cambridge, UK: Cambridge University Press, 1971).

8. Robin Alison Remington, ed., *Winter in Prague: Documents on Czechoslovak Communism in Crisis* (Cambridge, MA: MIT Press, 1969).

9. Ludvík Vaculík, "2,000 Words to Workers, Farmers, Scientists, Artists and Everyone," in *Winter in Prague: Documents on Czechoslovak Communism in Crisis*, ed. Robin Alison Remington (Cambridge, MA: MIT Press, 1969).

10. Kieran Williams, *The Prague Spring and Its Aftermath: Czechoslovak Politics 1968–1970* (Cambridge, UK: Cambridge University Press, 1997); and Jaromír Navrátil, ed., *The Prague Spring '68* (Budapest, Hungary: Central European University Press, 1998).

11. Sharon L. Wolchik, "Czechoslovakia," in *The Columbia History of Eastern Europe in the Twentieth Century*, ed. Joseph Held (New York: Columbia University Press, 1992).

12. Sharon L. Wolchik, "Institutional Factors in the Break-Up of Czechoslovakia," in *Irreconcilable Differences: Explaining Czechoslovakia's Dissolution*, ed. Michael Kraus and Allison Stanger (New York: Rowman & Littlefield Publishers, 2000).

13. Sharon L. Wolchik, "The Czech Republic: Havel and the Evolution of the Presidency since 1989," in *Postcommunist Presidents*, ed. Ray Taras (Cambridge, UK: Cambridge University Press, 1997).

14. Sharon L. Wolchik, "The Repluralization of Politics in Czechoslovakia," *Communist and Post-Communist Studies* 26 (December 1993): 412–31.

15. Tomáš Kostelecký, *Political Parties after Communism: Development in East Central Europe* (Baltimore: Johns Hopkins University Press, 2002).

16. Rudolf Tokes, "Hungary's New Political Elites: Adaptation and Change, 1989–1990," *Problems of Communism* 39 (November–December 1990).

17. George Schopflin, Rudolf Tokes, and Ivan Volgyes, "Leadership Change and Crisis in Hungary," *Problems of Communism* 37, no. 5 (September–October 1988): 23–46.

18. Tereza Vajdová, *An Assessment of Czech Civil Society in 2004: After Fifteen Years of Development* (Prague, Czech Republic: Civicus, 2005).

19. See Pavol Demeš, "Non-Governmental Organizations and Volunteerism," in *Global Report on Society, Slovakia 2002*, ed. Grigorij Mesežnikov, Miroslav Kollár, and Tom Nicholson (Bratislava, Slovakia: Institute for Public Affairs, 2002); and Valerie J. Bunce and Sharon L. Wolchik, "Favorable Conditions and Electoral Revolutions," *Journal of Democracy* 17 (October 2006): 5–18.

20. Jana Kadlecová and Katarina Vajdová, "Non-Governmental Organizations and Volunteerism," in *Global Report on Society, Slovakia 2003*, ed. Grigorij Mesežnikov and Miroslav Kollár, 605–23 (Bratislava, Slovakia: Institute for Public Affairs, 2004).

21. Zdenka Vajdová and Jana Stachová, "Politická kultura české populace v regionálním rozméru," *Czech Sociological Review* 41, no. 5 (2005): 881–903; and Zora Bútorová, *Political Culture in Slovakia* (Bratislava, Slovakia: Institute for Public Affairs, 1999).

22. See Sharon Wolchik, Jan Hartl, Zora Bútorová, and Olga Gyárfášová, results of "Citizens Political Attitudes and Values in the Czech Republic and Slovakia," in 1994 and 2004, as reported by STEM, Prague, Czech Republic, and FOCUS and the Institute for Public Affairs, Bratislava, Slovakia.

23. Sharon L. Wolchik, *Czechoslovakia in Transition: Politics, Economics, and Society* (London: Pinter Publishers, 1991).

24. Michal Vašečka, Martina Jurásková, and Tom Nicholson, eds., *Global Report on Roma in Slovakia* (Bratislava, Slovakia: Institute for Public Affairs, 2003).

25. Jiří Pehe, *Vytunelování Demokracie* (Prague, Czeck Republic: Academia, 2002).

26. David Lane, *The End of Inequality? Stratification under State Socialism* (New York: Penguin Books, 1971).

27. Vašečka et al., *Global Report on Roma in Slovakia*.

28. Jane S. Jaquette and Sharon L. Wolchik, eds., *Women and Democracy: Latin America and Eastern Europe* (Baltimore: Johns Hopkins University Press, 1998).

CHAPTER 10

Hungary

DEALING WITH THE PAST AND MOVING INTO THE PRESENT

Federigo Argentieri

Hungary's transition out of communism began decades before 1989. The democracy that resulted has been one of the most politically stable and economically prosperous of the postcommunist world. Hungary was also the first country to vote former communists back into power with an absolute majority of parliamentary seats. Its early reforms and the demise of communism opened the door for reform elsewhere in Central and Eastern Europe: it was, after all, Hungary that cut the barbed wire to bring down the "Iron Curtain" in the summer of 1989, starting a chain of events that forced the hand of the East Germans and Czechoslovak leadership.

In large part, the smoothness of its transition was a result of the distance Hungary had traveled in economic reforms and its political liberalization after the repression of the 1950s, as well as the success of reform movements within the party and of intellectual dissent in the late 1980s. From the mid-1960s on, Hungarians had lived with "goulash communism" and its guarantees of satisfactory supplies of food and consumer goods in exchange for the appearance of support for the regime. However, while other systems actively repressed dissidents and questioners of the system, Hungary was renowned for the mantra, "He who is not against us is with us." Not surprisingly then, Hungary's transition was the product of ongoing and overlapping discussions and a series of roundtables that involved reform communists and intellectual groups whose roots were framed by Hungarian historical debates.

Historical Background

Hungary's history has played a major role in its present. Its triumphs and defeats have been a complicated legacy for both the communist rulers and the postcommunist system. Reunified as of 1713 inside the Austrian Empire, Hungarians had far greater cultural independence than the nations that were part of the Ottoman and Russian empires. The "Age of Reforms" triggered a revolution in 1848–1849 in Hungary for freedom and independence. That revolution failed, but changes in the geopolitical realities of Central Europe subsequently resulted in a dual Austro-Hungarian Empire in which Hungarians had separate administrations in every field but military and foreign affairs. As a result, by the end of the nineteenth century, Hungary's economy and culture had blossomed. In the cities, the workers prospered, even as the countryside remained backward and relations with most ethnic and religious minorities remained tense.

All this came to an end when the expansion of the Austro-Hungarian Empire into Bosnia-Herzegovina and its alliance with Germany brought the empire into World War I. As punishment for its defeat, large portions of what had been Hungarian land were occupied by Czechoslovakia and the Balkan states of Romania and Serbia, with the endorsement of Western powers. Meanwhile, a democratic republic was proclaimed, only to be replaced by a Bolshevik "Republic of Councils" in the spring and summer of 1919. Bolshevism in Hungary was a debacle with policies that were both brutal and chaotic. All of this left communism with a very negative image. The Bolshevik experiment ended in a counterrevolutionary offensive by part of Hungary's new military, led by Admiral Miklós Horthy. By August 1919, he and his forces had suppressed the "Red" regime and appointed a new government with Horthy as regent.

To compound the political battles, the peace treaty of Trianon, signed in 1920, resulted in Hungary losing not only the areas that were inhabited by other ethnic groups, but also much of its own historic territory: 120,000 square miles of territory and half its population were taken. Over 3 million Hungarians were cut off from Hungary.

These losses, coupled with the failed "Red" regime and the debacle of World War I, left Hungarians wary of and at odds with both the Soviets and the West. During the interwar years, students began their classes by chanting "*Nem, nem, soha!*" (No, no, never!), meaning that they would never accept the injustice of the treaty. In domestic politics, a semiauthoritarian system emerged that outlawed the Communist Party and limited Jews' access to universities,[1] based on the false assumption that automatically linked Jews to left-wing radicalism.

The combination of the Great Depression and the interest of Hungarians in reclaiming their territory drew Hungary into the orbit of Hitler's Germany. After the Munich Agreements and the dismantling of Czechoslovakia, southern Slovakia and Ruthenia were retuned to Hungary. Then, after the Molotov-Ribbentrop Pact, Hungary regained most of Transylvania. In return, Hungary not only had to increase its restrictions on Jews but it also had to participate in the invasion of Yugoslavia and the USSR in 1941. At the end of World War II, as the German position weakened with the German defeat at Stalingrad and the Allies landing in Italy, Admiral Horthy tried to switch sides. Hitler responded by occupying Hungary in March 1944, and then replaced Horthy (who was arrested in October 1944) with the head of the Arrow Cross Party, the Hungarian equivalent of the Nazi Party. More than a half-million Jews were deported and exterminated. At the same time, the Soviets invaded Hungarian territory, which they occupied by April 1945, after a brutal and destructive fight.

Communist Experiences

Hungary's communist experience proved an even more complicated legacy for its transition than its earlier ones. During the forty-four years between the end of World War

II and 1989, communist rule in Hungary swung back from relative liberalism to very repressive and back again. The memories these shifts left were of a democratic regime that was rapidly co-opted or paralyzed by the communists; a moment of hope for freedom and a return to the West in 1956, followed by the brutal Soviet invasion and years of repression; and then the buying off of the opposition by "goulash communism." The conclusion was that communist rule disintegrated on its own when the economy began to fail in the 1980s. There were, in this history, liberal communists and repressive communists, as well as good memories of economic and social welfare and bad memories of tanks rolling into Budapest and shooting demonstrators and innocent civilians.

The communist takeover of Hungary took almost three years. Churchill and Stalin had agreed in October 1944 that Hungary would be evenly split between the Soviet sphere of influence and the West. Although Hungary was occupied by the Red Army, the first parliamentary elections in November 1945 were free and fair. The Independent Smallholders Party—a centrist, Christian, and anticommunist party—won an absolute majority of over 57 percent of the votes cast but was unable to form a government by itself. But the Allied Control Commission, dominated by the Soviets, forced them to go into a coalition with three left-of-center parties: the Social Democrats, the Communists, and the National Peasant Party. In February 1946, Smallholder Zoltán Tildy was elected president in what would prove to be the last gasp of democracy.

Even as Hungary was establishing a democratic government, albeit in an awkward coalition of anticommunist centrists and left-wing parties, Mátyás Rákosi, the head of the Hungarian Communist Party, was engaged in cutting democracy down through what he called "salami tactics" (using the secret police and other pressures to slice off pieces of the noncommunist parties until there was nothing left). They first pressured the Smallholders to expel their "right wing." Then, as soon as the Paris peace treaty was signed in 1947 and the Allied Control Commission was dissolved, the main leader of the Smallholders was arrested for espionage. Finally, Prime Minister Ferenc Nagy, who had resisted every attempt to nationalize property, was forced into exile. The Social Democrats were then given the choice of merging with the Communists or facing serious consequences. Some accepted the unification. Others refused and were, at the least, forced out of public life. The Hungarian Workers' Party was born of this unification in June 1948, signaling clearly the final victory of the Communists.

Having successfully taken over the political institutions, communist control was openly imposed on all other sectors of society. The economy was transformed: agriculture was forcibly collectivized and the rest of the economy was nationalized. There was a massive industrialization drive that shifted the economy from an agricultural to an industrial one. This meant that there was an exodus from the countryside to the cities and millions of young people suddenly got a chance at education. Religious institutions were attacked. Not only were citizens punished for supporting religion but the then head of the Hungarian Catholic Church, Cardinal József Mindszenty, was arrested, tried, and sentenced to life imprisonment. Terror even hit the Communist Party's own elite. The show trial and execution of Minister of Interior László Rajk for being a Titoist agent in 1949 became the symbol of the spiral of terror that lasted until Stalin's death in 1953.

After Stalin's death, Hungarian politics was manipulated by the different factions in the Kremlin. Control of the state and the party was split between Rákosi, as head of the party, and Imre Nagy, the first Communist minister of agriculture, as prime minister. The Soviet leadership pressed the Hungarian leaders to shift from their attempts at establishing heavy industry to greater production of consumer goods. Nagy pushed reform further, to include a relaxation of the terror and an end to the permanent hunt for "traitors" that had paralyzed Hungarian life since the communist takeover. But, as the balance of power shifted from liberals to conservatives in the Kremlin, Nagy was forced out and Rákosi returned to power.

In 1956, to get an accord with Yugoslavia and follow through on the denunciations of Stalin and his "cult of the personality," Nikita Khrushchev, as the new Soviet leader, forced more change in Hungary. Rákosi, who had boasted of being "Stalin's best Hungarian disciple," was dismissed from office and went into exile in the Soviet Union. He was replaced as head of the Communist Party by equally Stalinist Ernö Gerö. At the same time, there was a renunciation of the trial of László Rajk and a public reburial of his body. This, coupled with the example of liberalization in Poland during the Poznan events and Polish October and the constant shifts in leadership, convinced Hungarians that change was possible.

The Hungarian Revolution[2] would remain seared in the national memory even though it was an officially taboo subject until 1989. It began with student demonstrations on October 23, 1956. Within a few hours, Soviet tanks entered and fired on the demonstrators. Three days later, a new government was brought in with János Kádár as head of the Communist Party and Nagy as prime minister. By this time, though, virtually the entire population was engaged in the struggle for freedom and a genuine pluralist democracy. Parties abolished in 1948 resurfaced and were brought into Imre Nagy's executive. The Hungarian Workers' Party dissolved itself and formed a new Hungarian Socialist Workers' Party (HSWP), and "national committees" and "workers' councils" mushroomed. After briefly withdrawing their troops, the Soviet's intervened a second time on November 4 to suppress the revolution. The Hungarian government, buoyed by the increasingly loud demands of the "freedom fighters" throughout the country, denounced the Warsaw Pact even as Soviet troops killed thousands of demonstrators, jailed thousands more, and sent thousands into exile.

János Kádár went to the Soviet Union and agreed to lead a new government with the support of the occupying Soviet troops. When Nagy refused to resign as prime minister, he and other leaders loyal to the revolution were arrested and deported to Romania. In 1958, they were tried in Hungary. Nagy and other leaders were sentenced to death, executed the next day, and buried in unmarked graves.

As the Rajk reburial had opened the floodgates in 1956, the memorial service and reburial of Nagy and others in June 1989 would signal the end of communist control and was followed by the dissolution of the HSWP.

The repression that accompanied the Soviet occupation and the reestablishment of a one-party system under Kádár's control lasted into the 1960s. In 1963, following negotiations with the UN, some "freedom fighters" and leaders were released from prison and Kádár turned away from repression. The New Economic Mechanism (NEM) was introduced and with it came a real improvement in the Hungarian standard of living and the availability of goods. It provided for "profit" to become a

Photo 10.1.   *A Hungarian resistance fighter carries a gun during the Hungarian Revolution of 1956. Fierce resistance led to death, starvation, and desolation as Russian forces suppressed the anticommunist revolution in Budapest.*

(Source: Hulton-Deutsch Collection/CORBIS)

motive for state enterprises and for open wage differentiation. Although the central planning process remained under the NEM, it no longer dictated the details of what was produced and how. Instead, it set priorities and left decisions about production and pay to factory managers. The agricultural sector remained collectivized, but farms were able to direct their own production and engage in side businesses. Peasants, along with the urban population, also got cradle-to-grave social welfare benefits. In the process, the NEM recognized a range of unions and professional organizations as players in the policy process. Although Hungary remained a part of Comecon and was tied to ruble-based exchange rates and Soviet bloc economic priorities, it opened up to Western investment. In the 1970s that investment brought in some Hungarian refugees from 1956 as well as Western Europeans who set up factories in Hungary and imported and exported goods.

The result was a consumer economy that was vibrant and varied enough to make Hungary "the happiest barrack in the camp" until the 1980s when the forward and backward moves in the NEM and the aging of the economy showed in the failings of the consumer sector.

Politically, communism in Hungary from the mid-1960s was consistently less repressive than elsewhere in the bloc. In part, this difference was due to the fact that the population was both satisfied with what it had economically and wary of trying for political change after the experience of the Soviet invasion. In part, too, it was a result of János Kádár's willingness to allow or inability to stop divisions in the party's leadership and the low level of political pressure that was exerted on the population to do anything more than concede to HSWP rule. Dissident groups, far fewer than in Poland, existed without any real repression or mass popular support. After the mid-1960s, Hungary's borders were continually more open for its own citizens and for émigrés and tourists. Life, for Hungarians, was a tradeoff: political silence for comparative economic prosperity.

By middle of the 1980s, however, the elaborate system of "carrots and sticks" that had held Hungarian communist rule in place was crumbling. The New Economic Mechanism had worn down. The annual growth in gross domestic product decreased from 4.8 percent in the 1970s to 1.8 percent between 1980 and 1985 and continued on a rapid downward trajectory.[3] For workers, tensions over wages grew more acute because the instruments being used to manage the economy did not allow employers to raise wages to improve enterprise performance.[4] Thus, Hungarians' real incomes stagnated and began declining, causing savings out of disposable income to decline.

At the same time, changes in the Kremlin reduced whatever fear remained of Soviet repression. The Soviet occupation troops meant little when Mikhail Gorbachev came to power and made it clear that reform in the Soviet Union would go in ways the Hungarians had not dared and that the Soviet Union would no longer rein in its "satellites." The rise of Poland's Solidarity movement in the early 1980s inspired Hungarian dissidents to publish journals that challenged historical taboos. Repression of dissidents was not an option: Hungary had signed the Helsinki Final Act in 1975. It was increasingly indebted to the International Monetary Fund (IMF) and other Western financial institutions. So it could not risk the kinds of financial sanctions imposed on Poland after martial law if it was going to try and keep its economic bargain with the Hungarian population. And dissent involved only a tiny section of the population.

Kádár himself had aged. While Hungary had changed, he had not. When he did appear in public, his hands shook and his speeches fell flat. The men who had risen up behind him in the party, Károly Grósz, György Lázár, and Miklós Németh began to take the lead in the public eye and behind the scenes. Their postures, though, were increasingly critical of Hungary as it was, and increasingly divided over what should be next and how to deal publicly with the past and present. In 1988, Kádár was forced to retire.

The Transition

As the regime's "carrots and sticks" crumbled, intellectuals in and out of the party began to meet and push the old limits. In June 1985, a good part of Hungary's intellectual elite met just outside of Budapest to discuss the failings of the system since 1956. It happened with no interference from the party or police. In these discussions, the political divide that had characterized Hungarian thinking from the 1930s reemerged. The "people's nationalists" looked on the peasantry as the base of the

Hungarian spirit and wanted to find a "third way" between capitalism and communism. The "urbanists" were secular, not nationalist. The "people's nationalists" pressed for Hungary to intervene to prevent the increasing repression of Hungarians abroad, particularly in Romania where Ceaușescu was engaged in a full-scale assault on Hungarians. The "urbanists," on the other hand, emerged as liberal democrats and defenders of human rights at home, and sponsored NATO and EU membership.

This initial meeting, the crumbling of the economy, and the visible decrease in Soviet power or interest in Central and Eastern Europe triggered the emergence of a plethora of different political groupings that have played a role not only in the transition but also in democratic Hungary. In 1987, the Hungarian Democratic Forum (MDF) formed as a political and cultural movement based on Christian democracy and the traditions of "people's nationalism." They were quite willing to tolerate and even compromise with the reformist wing of the HSWP. In 1988, a group of young lawyers founded the Alliance of Young Democrats (FiDeSz). It was far more outspoken than earlier movements and opposed both the reformist and nonreformist versions of the communist system. Months later, the Committee for an Act of Historical Justice (TIB) emerged, demanding the political, civic, and moral rehabilitation of the veterans of the 1956 revolution and pension benefits for its survivors. Then, the Network of Free Democratic Initiatives appeared and pushed for a reduction in the role of the state and the protection of individual rights, which later transformed into the Alliance of Free Democrats (SzDSz), the third of the key noncommunist parties in democratic Hungary.

These parties and two associations representing the intelligentsia met between March and June 1989 in what was known as the Opposition Roundtable (ORT). Their ultimate goal was to come to a consensus so that they could be monolithic in their negotiations with the regime before it could pass reform legislation and get control of the transition. They agreed to negotiate with the HSWP but only about holding free elections, not about what would follow. In the process, the discussions of the Opposition Roundtable spilled out and further challenged communist control.

As the opposition crystallized into groups and then political parties, the HSWP began to fall apart. After Kádár was forced to resign, Károly Grósz, a relative conservative, took over. But his was not the only faction in the HSWP. Younger reformers like Miklós Németh and Imre Pozsgay, in alliance with older ones such as Rezsö Nyers, struggled within the party. On the outside, the party's position vacillated. Grósz ordered the suppression of the demonstrations on the anniversary of Imre Nagy's execution in June 1988. Then, the younger and more liberal leaders began to reconsider the "1956 events," meet with opposition leaders, and symbolically "cut" the Iron Curtain in May 1989 by cutting the barbed wire fence between Austria and Hungary. As a compromise between the two groups, a "committee of experts" made up of scholars and politicians was established in 1989 to investigate the real causes of the 1956 events. Its report created a major political stir. The Kádárist notion that the 1956 events were a "counterrevolution" was rejected, and the events were designated a "legitimate national uprising."

Preparations began for the reburial of Nagy and the other leaders of the Hungarian Revolution. Kádárist style rule was clearly in its last days. In the spring, the party divested itself of much of its power, even shifting the responsibility for dealing with the politically explosive reburial to the state. Old parties that had been a part of Hungary's moment of democracy and reemerged briefly in 1956 reappeared only to fade away once the transition had happened. Despite the objections of some in the HSWP and leaders in Bulgaria, Germany, Romania, and Czechoslovakia, the funeral was held as a public ceremony in Budapest's Heroes' Square. As more than a quarter of a million people watched in the square and millions more on television, the reform communists stood as honorary pallbearers. New political leaders from the new and old parties gave speeches. The leaders who survived, including Nagy's press spokesman Miklós Vásárhelyi, "spoke of justice, national unity, and the opportunity for 'a peaceful transition to a free and democratic society.'" The young FiDeSz leader Viktor Orbán explicitly demanded the withdrawal of Soviet troops.[5]

With the Communist Party shifting its powers to the state, the history of 1956 rewritten, and the reburial complete, there was no stopping the transition. Negotiations between the ORT and the regime began on June 13, 1989 (the day of the semifree Polish elections). The Hungarian Socialist Workers' Party agreed to focus only on establishing the rules for free elections and amendments to the communist constitution, rather than try to follow the Polish model of negotiating political, social, and economic issues as well. In exchange, the ORT parties had to agree to a triangular table with the Hungarian Socialist Workers' Party's voting power aided by the inclusion of trade unions as minor players in the negotiations. On October 23, 1989, the new Hungarian Republic was proclaimed. A week earlier, the communist HSWP had declared its transformation into a Western-type social democracy, called the Hungarian Socialist Party, and intention to participate in the forthcoming elections.

The final battle of the transition was over whether the president or the parliament should be elected first. For the ex-communists, the best scenario was that the presidential election would come first, because their leader, Pozsgay, was still popular for dismantling the Communist Party and was the most well-known leader. The Alliance of Free Democrats and FiDeSz refused to agree to this and instead organized a referendum on whether the president or the parliament (who would then elect the president) should be elected first. On this issue, the Opposition Roundtable groups split from the Hungarian Democratic Forum, urging abstention rather than changing the roundtable agreement to elect the president and then the parliament. In that referendum, the option of holding the parliamentary elections first won with 50.07 percent. The monolithic opposition split.

Political Institutions

The Roundtable Accords, as they were modified after the referendum and the old parliament's vote for the president to be directly elected, provided for a parliamentary system. After it was elected in March 1990, the initial center-right parliament revised the transitional constitution so that a simple majority was all that was needed to pass most laws and the president was elected by the parliament. These elections were to be held every five years and decided by a two-thirds majority. The single-house parliament selected a prime minister and a president. The parliament was to be elected every four years with a mixed electoral system. The prime minister was responsible for selecting and guiding the ministers, while the president had ceremonial powers and some ability to intervene when there were problems within the system. None of these powers were decisive, however.

Árpád Göncz, elected president by the parliament, created the model for the Hungarian presidency, a model that generated criticism but also garnered his reelection in 1995. His model entitled the president, who represents the country, also to work behind the scenes to get consensus among the various political groups. Through this process, Göncz and his successors have avoided identifying with one side or the other. At the same time, he used the ability to approve the removal of such officials as the heads of radio and television to push the parties away from partisanship in these areas. This is the model his successors, Ferenc Mádl (elected in 2000) and László Sólyom (elected in 2005), have followed.

Dominant coalitions have shifted from election to election. To date, all of the cabinets have been products of coalitions of centrist parties and none has been controlled by a single party. József Antall, Péter Boross, and Viktor Orbán served as conservative prime ministers. There have also been three Socialist prime ministers since 1990: Gyula Horn, Péter Medgyessy, and Ferenc Gyurcsány. But none have carried out real policy shifts.

The stability of Hungary's political system was clear early on when József Antall, the first postcommunist prime minister and founding member of the MDF, died in office in late 1993. He was immediately replaced by another Hungarian Democratic Forum leader, Péter Boross, who served six months until that parliament's term ended. After the Socialist's loss in the 2004 elections to the European Parliament, the socialist party HSP (Hungarian Socialist Party) shifted its leadership to respond to the public's disaffection, which allowed Ferenc Gyurcsány to be the first prime minister to lead two successive terms.

While the ministers have changed with every election, the upper ranks of the state bureaucracy have remained quite stable. Because there was no effective legislation purging the state of workers from the communist era, they have been allowed to remain in their positions if they declared allegiance to the new system. Where changes have occurred, they have been the result of the government's efforts to make Hungary's overall bureaucracy smaller and more professional.

Elections and Political Parties

Elections for the first freely elected parliament since 1945 were scheduled for March 25, 1990, with a run-off on April 8. The electoral system provided for a parliament of 386 seats, of which 176 were to be elected in single-member districts with a French-type, double ballot, majoritarian system and 152 from party lists for each region by a proportional system. The remaining seats (a minimum of 58) were distributed to national party lists to compensate for the "extra votes" that were more than what were needed for a candidate to get elected or were cast for losing candidates in the single-member districts. The goal of this redistribution was to keep the parliament truly representative of the overall national vote. At the same time, any party that received less than 4 percent of the vote nationally was disqualified from having deputies in the parliament. While the system has been responsive to changes in Hungarian public opinion, it has also been extremely stable, with the governing coalitions shifting regularly from right to left but with both sides remaining close to the center and ready to step over ideological divides.

The unquestionable winner of the first election was the MDF, whose president, József Antall, was inaugurated as prime minister in May 1990. Six parties received enough votes to make it into that parliament. Three (MDF, SzDSz, and FiDeSz) were brand-new. They won 277 seats in this first election and would remain the centerpieces of Hungarian politics into the twenty-first century. One (the HSP) could be called both new and old, as it was made up mostly of the reform wing of the old HSWP. The remaining two (the Independent Smallholder's Party and the People's Christian Democrats) were parties of the precommunist period. Together, these two got a total of 65 seats. Among these parties, there was a clear consensus on the direction Hungary should take: toward Europe, democracy, and capitalism. The differences were more on the details of Hungary's move forward and on assessments of the past. These divisions reflected the old Hungarian separation of "people's nationalists" and urbanists. As Bill Lomax has observed:

> Hungarian parties are, almost without exception, elite groups of intellectuals, often long-standing personal friends more like political clubs than representative institutions. Many of Antall's government ministers went to the same school with him. Most of the Free Democrats were together in the democratic opposition. Several of Fidesz' leaders studied law together. . . . The political identities and cleavages they do represent are based neither on social interests, nor political programmes, nor structured belief systems. In fact, to the extent that such cleavages do exist in Hungarian politics, they are found to cut across the parties almost equally—each party has its liberals, its nationalists, its conservatives, its social-democrats, its populists, its radicals.[6]

Initially, the leaders of all the parties (except the Young Democrats [FiDeSz]) were intellectuals from academia and the arts. The Young Democrats were different. They and their constituents were young people. Most of the party leaders had studied law together in the 1980s. As a result, until 1993, they were less bound by ideology and more West European in their thinking and presentations.

In 1994, the Hungarian Socialist Party was the first successor to an old ruling communist party of Central and Eastern Europe to be reelected and returned to power with an absolute majority of seats: yet, in the first of what would be a series of unlikely coalitions, the HSP joined with the Alliance of Free Democrats. Their gains were a reaction to people's initial disappointment with what the transition had brought and also to the weakness in the Hungarian Democratic Forum brought to a head by József Antall's death and the splinter of the Hungarian Life and Justice Party lead by István Csurka. Like the Polish social democrats, they talked not of returning to the old communist system, but of modernization, economic and political reform, and joining Europe. The Alliance of Free Democrats actually lost votes in 1994, but the Hungarian Democratic Forum lost far more and the Alliance of Free Democrats was—in spite of their history of opposition to communism—the largest and most viable partner for the HSP.

In 1998, there was a shift in all the major players' positions and strengths. The Hungarian Democratic Forum had essentially collapsed by 1998. Most of the prewar parties no longer could get enough votes to seat deputies in parliament. In the aftermath of Antall's death and the partnership of the Alliance of Free Democrats and HSP (confirmed by their signing of the Democratic Charter in 1991), the Young Democrats moved to the right. They were able, despite the simultaneous success of the extreme rightist Life and Justice Party, to present themselves as the legitimate successor of the declining MDF. The party leader, Viktor Orbán, when he became prime minister, openly claimed Antall's legacy. Their coalition was made up of the Smallholders and the remnants of the MDF. To further their popularity, they also added "Hungarian Civic Party" to their name.

In 2002, the balance shifted back to the coalition of the Socialists and the Alliance of Free Democrats after a close race with the Young Democrats and the Democratic Forum alliance. The two parties were able to govern with a razor-thin majority. However, when the coalition lost in its first elections to the European Parliament and right-wing and Euroskeptic candidates took a number of districts, Péter Medgyessy (who had been a member of HSWP, a banker in France, and a leader in the private sector in Hungary) resigned. He was replaced by Ferenc Gyurcsány, who had gone on from the Communist Youth Organization to become one of the wealthiest businessmen in Hungary. Under his leadership, the Socialist–Free Democratic Alliance was the first alliance to win two successive elections. This made him the first Hungarian prime minister to serve more than one term, as he led the party to a much clearer victory in 2006.

Until the riots that followed the revelation that Gyurcsány had lied about the status of the Hungarian economy just before the fiftieth anniversary celebrations of the Hungarian Uprising in 1956, political parties and groups in Hungary were quite restrained and remained very centrist. The closeness of the parties ideologically, their ability to form coalitions, and the low turnout rate in Hungarian elections at all levels since the transition began are all reasons for and demonstrations of the lack of engagement of Hungarian voters in particular parties or political battles. In fact, many local government elections have had to be held a second time because less than 50 percent of the population voted in the regular election round. This disengagement changed, at least momentarily, after the Gyurcsány revelation. Budapest and other major cities were rocked by riots of angry and disillusioned voters.

Economic Transition

Economic weakness has been the "Achilles' heel" of Hungarian politics. In the last decade of communism, borrowing money from abroad was the regime's only way to sustain the living standards of its population and keep itself in power. Even with that infusion of foreign loan money, the transition in Hungary was stirred by the stagnation of the economy and its double-digit inflation. The new leaders of Hungary inher-

Photo 10.2.   Riots in Budapest in 2006 after a recording of Prime Minister Gyurcsány admitting to party members that they had lied to the country about the economy was leaked to the public.

(Source: MTI Foto, Olah Tibor)

ited far less debt and a far better economy than their Polish counterparts. But they still faced high popular expectations, a debt of over $20 billion from the Kádár regime's borrowing, and the disaster wrought by the collapse of the Comecon market.

Hungary avoided the Polish "shock therapy" model. Instead, it began by "creating a social market economy" that moved toward private ownership in industries producing consumer goods and providing services. Although legislation promised to begin bankruptcy actions against failing enterprises, few large-scale industries were closed. Instead, foreign investment and ownership was used as a tool to get the economy going.

The transition in Hungary was complicated by its high debt to the West, the collapse of the Soviet market, and the end of cheap Soviet oil and natural gas supplies. Between 1989 and 1992, Hungary's GDP had collapsed by 18 percent, "a decline comparable only to the worst of the Great Depression of the 1930's."[7] Western banks and governments wrote off much of Hungary's debt when they wrote off the Polish debt as part of a package to help both the Hungarian and Polish economies correct themselves. The IMF, the European Community, and the World Bank also provided large loans.

It was only in March 1995 that the "Bokros Plan" for serious economic reform was implemented. In this reform program, privatization was encouraged with monetary incentives and openness to foreign investment. At the same time, state enterprises were allowed to survive and new private enterprises were established alongside of them. The goal was for these private enterprises to edge out the state enterprises. A similar policy governed the reforms in agriculture and social services. The costs of health care and education ballooned as the state continued to provide funds while the wealthy opted out and provided for themselves by creating private health and educational institutions. By 2005, 80 percent of the Hungarian economy was in private hands, and foreign ownership went from about 4 percent in 1990 to 52.1 percent in 1997.

The reforms all seemed to work in the first decade. The population was satisfied. By 1997, the economy had begun to grow by 4 to 5 percent annually. However, the gains came with real hidden costs; many hard economic moves were avoided and the economy depended instead on its Kádár-era base and foreign investment. Keeping costly social welfare programs and encouraging foreign investment by allowing their profits to go abroad meant that the apparent upward course was far from secure. Government accounting only hid the problem. In 2006, as Gyurcsány's leaked statement made to party elites indicated, Hungary's deficit stood at 10 percent. The rhetoric of the demonstrations and the opposition politicians who led them showed that they had no alternative economic proposal. Rather than deal with the social consequences of how Hungary could best deal with its budget deficit and rationalize its economy, the political rhetoric focused on accusations of individuals being "communist" or "anti-Semitic." The promised tax reduction was not to be. Taxes actually had to be raised to pay for increases in government spending and inflation and to placate foreign investors. The plan for Hungary to adopt the euro in 2010 (with its requirement of a deficit below 3 percent) was also put in question. But the anger dissipated when it was clear there were no alternatives to the course Hungary was on.

Social Consequences

The social consequences in Hungary were no different from those in other countries when they began the transformation of their economic and political systems. In spite of the problems in the Hungarian economy in 1989, Hungarians started the transition with higher expectations because they were accustomed to living better than most in the bloc. As Prime Minister Antall detailed in his presentation of the government program after the 1990 elections, the country faced

> declining health and falling living standards of the population. He said Hungarians' life expectancy was the lowest in Europe; that for the past decade the number of deaths had exceeded the number of births; and that because of the polluted environment and the need to work long hours, the health and life expectancy of middle-aged Hungarians were the worst among civilized nations.[8]

The limited economic reforms Hungary undertook at the start of the 1990s left 1 million of Hungary's 10.6 million population living below the subsistence level, and 2 million living at the officially defined "social minimum." Those hardest hit were the pensioners, families with more than two children, and those who found themselves unemployed. Homelessness also appeared because factories closed workers' hostels, citizens were unable to pay the increases in their rent, and people came to Budapest in search of jobs. Roma and illegal aliens—largely ethnic Romanians or Hungarians who "escaped" the more disastrous Romanian economy—added to the numbers of homeless.[9]

In the decade and a half that followed, Hungary's living standards continued to fall. Hungarians, accustomed to rising consumption, have proved less willing than Poles to tolerate a considerable drop in living standards. Also, public opinion has focused on whether consumer goods markets function reasonably well, whether most goods are readily available, and whether there is a "visible" economic crisis.[10] Hence, consumption rose more slowly than incomes and, with real income actually falling, consumption has declined sharply. Increases in consumer prices were exacerbated by subsidy reductions as well as price liberalization.

While some prospered during the 1980s, those lacking the skills needed to access the wealth from the "second economy" and those reliant on state incomes did relatively badly.[11] Job opportunities for unskilled or uneducated people had diminished throughout this time as a result of continuing decrease in the number of vacant jobs and the shift in labor demand toward skilled workers.[12]

Hungary became steadily more polarized and Hungary's ethnic groups, particularly the Roma and illegal aliens, suffered from the economic reforms. While in 1971 Roma males and females had been regularly employed and earned incomes, from the late 1980s onward, they were systematically pushed out of the labor market.[13] By 1993, this trend resulted in shockingly high unemployment figures for the Roma. Less than half of the Roma unemployment rate could be accounted for by factors like the lower educational level and disadvantageous distribution of Roma labor power. The rest was due to discrimination by employers. Thus, the Roma are generally described as major losers in the economic transition. While they make up only 5 percent of the total population, approximately 25 percent of the 2 million poor of Hungary are Roma. Moreover, the Roma in Hungary are discriminated against not only by employers, but also by state or state-controlled institutions like public education, the national health service, the police, and the courts as well.[14]

In its struggle to keep up economic growth and deal with its budget deficit, Hungary has essentially ignored the need to reform its social services. According to the Organization for Economic Cooperation and Development country survey for 2005, Hungary needed to take strong measures to prevent the "failure in the welfare regime change."[15] The problem is that unpopular political decisions must be made to streamline the public health system, limit disability pensions to the really disabled, make labor mobility more effective, and deal with problems in most other state welfare sectors. No political group wants to deal with this directly. Both conservatives and liberal-socialists are separated more by rhetoric than by concrete differences in economic and social policy.

Neither the left nor the right has championed the needs of Hungary's poor. Instead, they have talked about "trickle-down economics." In the early years of the transition, the government gave in when faced with demonstrations by those who had suffered from the economic reforms. The most famous mass scale of these demonstrations were the so-called Taxi Wars, in 1990, when taxi drivers and others blocked the streets of Budapest and roads around the country in response to the government's sudden decision to raise the price of gasoline 66 percent overnight and announced that the price of other energy products would increase in order to deal with shortages caused by decreases in sales by the Soviet Union. In the end, the government backed down.

Until the 2006 demonstrations, other responses to social problems have been far smaller and more subdued. Groups have, when they could, taken matters into their own hands. Some self-help and advocacy groups have been organized and many, like the homeless, have broken the law to provide for themselves.

Foreign Policy

Hungary was a leader in the move toward Europe. It was the first member of the Soviet bloc to become a member of the Council of Europe. On June 4, 1990, the new and free Hungarian parliament marked the seventieth anniversary of the Trianon peace treaty by adopting a resolution which reiterated the acceptance of its existing borders.

Following the dissolution of Yugoslavia, Comecon, the Warsaw Treaty Organization, and the Soviet Union itself (all of which happened between June 25 and December 25, 1991), Hungary attempted to conduct bilateral negotiations with its old and new neighbors and to march resolutely toward membership in NATO and the EU. Its attempts to deal with its eastern neighbors were far more politically problematic. The state treaty with Ukraine, signed in 1991, caused major repercussions in domestic politics. A faction within the MDF, led by the playwright István Csurka, openly rejected the agreement on borders and walked out, eventually forming a new group called Hungarian Life and Justice (or Truth) Party.[16] Further treaties were signed with Croatia and Slovenia (1992), Slovakia (1995), and Romania (1996), which settled Hungarian affairs to the east and left Hungary open to its move toward the EU.

The process of EU membership began with an association agreement with the EU signed in 1994, the former Soviet base of Taszár in southwestern Hungary being transformed into a NATO logistical base in 1996, and full NATO membership was granted in March 1999, on the eve of the Kosovo war. As relations between the United States and parts of the EU deteriorated in 2003 because of the invasion of Iraq, Hungary cautiously supported the Bush administration, while making the point that good relations with all EU members were a priority.

Conclusion

The incredible unity displayed by the Hungarians in 1956 and 1989 did not last for the transition. Yet, although the two political factions have railed at each other rhetorically, the Hungarian parties have never been far apart in their actual policy goals. The reality is that the Hungarian population and the state are well into Europe. Their economy still suffers from the burden of trying to move from "goulash communism" to "goulash capitalism," but the upheavals in 2006 over revelations about the problems of the economy were more about being misled than about the financial restraints that must be imposed. For Hungary, joining the European Union has been a clear benefit. Clearly, there is no interest in turning back or slowing Hungary's move forward.

Suggested Readings

Gati, Charles. *Failed Illusions*. Stanford, CA: Stanford University Press, 2006.

Kornai, János. "Ten Years after 'The Road to a Free Economy': The Author's Self-Evluation." Paper presented at the Annual Bank Conference on Development Economics of the World Bank, Washington, DC, April 2000.

Körösényi, András. *Government and Politics in Hungary*. Budapest, Hungary: Central European University, 2000.

Kun, J. C. *Hungarian Foreign Policy—The Experience of a New Democracy*. The Washington Papers n. 160, Westport, CT, 1993

Lomax, William. "The Strange Death of Civil Society in Post-Communist Hungary." *Journal of Communist Studies and Transition Politics* 13 (1997): 41–63.

Morlang, Diana. "Hungary: Socialists Building Capitalism." In *The Left Transformed in Post-Communist Societies*, ed. Jane Curry and Joan Urban, 61–98. Boulder, CO: Roman & Littlefield, 2003.

Tokes, Rudolf. *Hungary's Negotiated Revolution: Economic Reform, Social Change, and Political Succession*. Cambridge, UK: Cambridge University Press, 1996.

Notes

1. Andrew Janos, *The Politics of Backwardness in Hungary: 1825–1945* (Princeton, NJ: Princeton University Press, 1982), 176–82.

2. For a complete discussion of the Hungarian Revolution and the international actors involved, see Charles Gati, *Failed Illusions* (Stanford, CA: Stanford University Press, 2006).

3. Paul Hare and Tamas Revisz, "Hungary's Transition to the Market: The Case against a 'Big Bang,'" *Economic Policy: A European Forum* 14 (April 1992): 236.

4. Hare and Revisz, "Hungary's Transition to the Market," 241.

5. Rudolf Tokes, *Hungary's Negotiated Revolution* (Cambridge, UK: Cambridge University Press, 1996), 330.

6. Bill Lomax, "From Death to Resurrection: The Metamorphosis of Power in Eastern Europe," *Critique* 25 (1993): 68.

7. Eva Ehrlich and Gabor Revesz, "Coming In from the Cold: Hungary's Economy in the 20th Century," *The Hungarian Quarterly* 41, no. 157 (Spring 2000): 18.

8. Karoly Okolicsanyi, "Prime Minister Presents New Government's Program," *Report on Eastern Europe* (June 18, 1990): 21.

9. Edith Oltay, "Poverty on the Rise," *Report on Eastern Europe* (January 25, 1991): 13–14.

10. Hare and Revisz, "Hungary's Transition to the Market," 230.

11. Hare and Revisz, "Hungary's Transition to the Market," 229.

12. Csaba Halmos, "Political and Economic Reform and Labour Policy in Hungary," *International Labour Review* 129, no. 1: 47.

13. Project on Ethnic Relations, *Roma in Hungary: Government Policies, Minority Expectations, and the International Community* (Princeton, NJ: Project on Ethnic Relations, 2000), 16.

14. Project on Ethnic Relations, *Roma in Hungary*, 8.

15. *A jóléti* rendszerváltás csôdje—Gyurcsány-kormány elsô éve [The Failure of Welfare Regime Change—Gyurcsány's Government First Year] (Budapest, Hungary: Századvég, 2005). This is the third volume of a yearbook on the activity of the executive, sponsored by FiDeSz.

16. *Magyar Igazság es Élet Pártja* (MIÉP). The word *igazság* means both "justice" and "truth."

CHAPTER 11

The Baltic States

REMEMBERING THE PAST, BUILDING THE FUTURE

Daina Stukuls Eglitis

Together, the Baltic countries of Latvia, Lithuania, and Estonia have a population of just over 7 million. Set on the Baltic Sea to the east of the Russian Federation and to the west of Scandinavia, the three countries survived a tumultuous twentieth century. At the dawn of the century, Latvia and Estonia were provinces of the Russian Empire. Lithuania was divided between Germany and Russia. The Baltic countries also saw the turmoil of revolution in Russia, beginning in 1905 and continuing through the end of the empire and the beginning of Bolshevik rule.

Following World War I, the Baltic states were among the progeny of an era that brought into being a host of small independent states. Independence was, however, short-lived, and the nonaggression pact between Nazi Germany and Stalin's Soviet Union sealed their political fate as victims of that era's great powers in Europe. By the end of World War II, a period in which the countries lost a substantial proportion of their populations to war, deportation, political murder, and the flight of refugees, all three were occupied republics of the USSR.

At the end of the century, the ascent of Mikhail Gorbachev helped create opportunities for open discussion and dissent that were unprecedented. The Baltics were among the first to issue challenges and seek changes. The collapse of the Soviet bloc and, subsequently, the USSR itself opened the door to the reestablishment of independence in Latvia, Lithuania, and Estonia, with its accompanying problems, promise, and potential.

Precommunist History

The Baltic countries each had just two decades of experience with independence when they regained autonomous statehood in 1991. In all three cases, independence was declared for the first time in 1918, though formal recognition of independence by the USSR and the international community came later. The Soviet Union recognized the independence of the former provinces in separate peace treaties concluded between February and August of 1920. Between 1921 and 1922, the international community extended its acceptance of the new states: they were welcomed into the League of Nations and given de jure recognition.

The first period of independence was a time of profound challenge and transformation. The three countries were emerging from World War I (1914–1918) and they suffered intermittent fighting that continued through 1920. All were characterized by decimated populations and devastated economies. For instance, Latvia's population plummeted from about 2.5 million in the prewar period to just 1.58 million in 1920. Estonia and Lithuania also lost substantial proportions of their populations to fighting and refugee flight. Agriculture, the key economic sector in all three countries, was deeply damaged by the war, and farmlands lay virtually fallow. The nascent industrial sector, which had taken root in the Latvian and Estonian territories, was in ruins, as most heavy equipment had been moved to the Russian interior during the war. The economic foundation for the new states was tenuous.

In the wake of the devastation, the Baltics undertook massive land reforms, focused on the transfer of land from private estates concentrated largely in the hands of Baltic Germans to the landless peasantry, who had toiled and tilled the soil for generations, but had never owned the land. One goal of reforms was to create a rural economy based on small farms. There was also an interest in transferring more rural land to indigenous populations: in Latvia, most private land was in the hands of non-Latvians, particularly Germans and, in the southeast, Poles. There was some fear in the government of Bolshevik sympathies among the rural peasantry, which compounded the perceived urgency of reform. In fact, land reform was relatively successful in meeting its goals: to complete the Latvian example, by 1925, over 70 percent of rural dwellers, many of them Latvians, were landowners. Though the states regulated some sectors of their economies, the trajectories in all three states seemed to be toward the creation of capitalist societies based on private ownership and entrepreneurship.

Leaders in Latvia, Lithuania, and Estonia quickly laid the foundations for democratic states, putting in place the constitutional and institutional building blocks that would support parliamentary democracies with universal suffrage (they were among the first European states to grant voting rights to women), equality before the law, and guarantees for minority rights. The parliamentary systems entailed weak executive powers and, following the constitutional model of Weimar Germany, proportional representation in the legislative body based on party lists. The fragmented legislatures that emerged from this system, however, contributed to the later rise of authoritarian governments in these states.

In part because the parliaments were populated by a multitude of small parties, Baltic governments were short-lived and political alliances were ever shifting. By 1926, Lithuania was under an authoritarian presidential regime, led by Antanas Smetona. In Estonia and Latvia, democratic parliamentary systems lasted longer, but were also plagued by political problems that were further aggravated by a worldwide economic depression. In Estonia, between 1919 and 1933, the average duration of governments was eight months and, in early 1934, Konstantin Päts rose to rule by presidential decree for the next two years.[1] Later that same year (1934), Latvia's parliament was dismissed and political parties dissolved by President Karlis Ulmanis, who took power in his own hands.

Smetona, Päts, and Ulmanis were relatively benevolent authoritarian leaders. While they placed restrictions on political challengers, they succeeded in bringing about a basic stability that benefited many parts of the economy, including businesses and agriculture, which had responded poorly to the unpredictability of shifting governments. Overall, the cultural and educational sectors flourished, though the nationalist sentiment embraced by the regimes adversely affected opportunities for minority populations to fully realize their aspirations. In Latvia, for instance, the slogan of "Latvia for Latvians" was manifested in policies that, while not coercive or violent, marginalized the interests of minority populations in areas like business ownership and education.

As the Baltic states worked to stabilize their domestic politics and economies, the world around them was erupting in violence. Germany had embarked upon the decimation of its Jewish population, and the Third Reich cast a menacing shadow on its neighbors as well. Stalin's regime in the Soviet Union had already engineered a devastating famine in the republic of Ukraine and conducted murderous purges of enemies real and perceived throughout the country. The partnering of these dangerous governments against the Baltics sealed their fate: the Molotov-Ribbentrop Pact signed by Germany and the Soviet Union in August 1939 contained a "secret protocol" (the existence of which was denied by the USSR until the glasnost era) that divided the Baltic countries into spheres of influence: Latvia and Estonia were "given" to the USSR, Lithuania to Germany (though later Lithuania would be claimed by the Soviets).

Communist Experience

Like the later break from the USSR, the initial annexation of the Baltics into the Union of Soviet Socialist Republics was relatively bloodless. Between September and October 1939, Estonia, Latvia, and Lithuania were forced to accept the terms of mutual assistance treaties with the USSR. The treaties permitted the stationing of Soviet troops on their soil, and tanks rolled across the Baltic borders with no resistance. For decades after, and even today, this "capitulation" has been the source of debate, as many have wondered if resistance could have prevented a half-century-long occupation. In July of the following year, new governments, "elected" from a single slate of Soviet communist candidates in compulsory voting, asked for admission to the USSR. This electoral farce took place on the stage of an increasingly bloody Baltic backdrop: the violence that had been limited during the initial occupation exploded in the early summer of 1940, which initiated what is called the "year of terror" in the Baltics. At least 60,000 Balts, including children under sixteen, were deported in this year alone.[2] Population losses were severely compounded by the tragedies of battleground deaths, civilian war casualties, political killings, and mass migrations of refugees. The Baltics lost a substantial proportion of their populations, including many from the educated professional classes.[3]

Between 1941 and 1944, the Soviet occupation was interrupted by the establishment of German control in the region, but the Soviets had reoccupied most of the Baltic territories by the end of 1944. The years of occupation (1940–1941 and 1944–1990) cannot be uniformly characterized. The Stalin era represented a stranglehold of social control and fear that had begun in the early 1940s. In the late 1940s, the process of collectivization of agriculture gained momentum and was nearly completed by 1952. The process in the Baltics was relatively slow paced, in part because there was rural resistance to collectivization. Resistance was broken by a new round of deportations—the kulak deportations—in 1949, in which about 100,000 rural dwellers, including women and children, were deported from the Baltic republics.[4]

The noose loosened with Stalin's death in 1953. While the persecution of individual dissidents continued under his successor, Nikita Khrushchev, most of the population, if they were willing to abide by Soviet norms and laws, could live in relative normalcy. Restrictions on cultural and social life were less stringent than before, though these areas were still controlled. In terms of economic life, the Baltics were considered among the most "prosperous" republics of the USSR: they had better access to consumer goods and a generally higher standard of living. While, on the face of it, this was a positive development for the Baltic republics, it made them a magnet for more migration from other republics, further shifting the demographics and driving the titular population, particularly in Latvia, closer to minority status. One prominent consequence of this was linguistic: while most Balts learned and spoke fluent Russian, few Russians learned the republic languages. The 1970 census in the Latvian SSR, for instance, showed that over half of Latvians (and a higher proportion in younger generations) spoke Russian; however, less than a fifth of ethnic Russians in the republic could speak Latvian. Russian became an ever more important medium of communication in the public sphere.

Nikita Khrushchev's fall from communist grace in 1964 brought Leonid Brezhnev to power. Brezhnev's regime continued to exercise stringent social control and, in the 1970s, he initiated a concentrated campaign against nationalism: as in Khrushchev's time, the goal was to create the *Homo Sovieticus*, the Soviet Man, free of bourgeois inclinations toward ethnic allegiances. Episodes of dissent were few and far between, though they appeared periodically in the Baltics: the public self-immolation in 1972 of Romas Kalanta, a young Lithuanian, sparked demonstrations in Kaunas. Most opposition remained small and contained, though apparently there was enough concern about simmering discontent that Khrushchev's short-lived successor, Yuri Andropov, a former KGB chief, cracked down hard on dissent, real and perceived.

Discontent in the Baltics, existent but not publicly manifested, was centered in the indigenous populations, the older generations of whom retained the living memory of independence. These populations also feared demographic marginalization. All three, but particularly Latvia and Estonia, had below-replacement fertility rates and aging populations; the two also had large Slavic (mostly Russian) populations, which had increased again in a wave of immigration in the 1970s. Soviet population data showed Latvians approaching the 50 percent mark in their republic, a downward slide that showed few signs of abating. The fear of ethnic extinction, real or perceived, was to become an important issue in the mobilization of civil society when, under Gorbachev, the social controls of several decades were loosened by the policy of glasnost.

Civil Society

In all three Baltic countries, the slow and steady movement toward mobilization of independent civil society and, ultimately, political independence proceeded along similar lines. Prior to 1987, independent mass demonstrations were forbidden in the USSR. The culture of fear wrought by decades of repression also made such collective action highly unlikely. Individual and small-group dissident activities dotted the Soviet historical map, but most citizens were docile, unwilling or unable to oppose the regime. Mikhail Gorbachev's ascent to power in the Soviet Union and his adoption of a policy of glasnost, with the accompanying possibilities for freer expression, opened the door to Baltic social movements that evolved from small demonstrations of discontent to massive manifestations of opposition to the state and regime, the economic and environmental and ethnic policies of the USSR, and the failure of the Soviet government to recognize the illegal occupation of the three countries in the 1940s.

Interestingly, early opposition focused on preservation of folk culture and the environment, issues that were less politically sensitive than independence or Soviet distortions of history. At the same time, the elevation of issues of nature and culture were profoundly symbolic: it can be argued that Soviet destruction of the natural and cultural environments was perceived as symbolic of the destruction of the Latvian, Lithuanian, and Estonian nations themselves. In Latvia, much early independent activity centered upon a proposed hydroelectric station (HES) to be constructed on the Daugava River. The river is central in Latvian history, folktales, and poems: it has been called Latvia's "river of destiny." Opponents of the HES argued that its construction would harm the river and flood surrounding arable lands. The response to an article published in a progressive weekly newspaper, *Literatura un Maksla*, in 1986 was tremendous and gained momentum, as tens of thousands of Latvians wrote to the newspaper to voice their criticism of the project. Notably, in early 1987, construction of the HES was halted by the USSR Council of Ministers. The voices of civil society, long suppressed, achieved a significant victory and set the stage for the coming years of opposition.[5]

In Lithuania, as in the other Baltic countries, indigenous elites played an important role in the early construction of independent civil society. An important part of the active elite included scientists. The focus of widespread discussion and, eventually, opposition focused on the Ignalina Atomic Energy Station (AES), built in the 1970s just eighty miles from Vilnius, the capital of the republic. The environmental and safety standards of the AES were broadly questioned, and the disaster at Chernobyl in Ukraine in 1986 rendered these issues even more critical, though widespread public activism around Ignalina did not really begin until 1988. Leaders of the initially small opposition appealed to the public with science and symbols: the Lithuanian nation was rooted in the earth and Ignalina was a threat to both nature and nation. Although the nascent opposition could not overtly speak out against the Soviet government in 1988, environmental issues provided a platform for civil society to gain a foothold.[6]

Transition from Communism

By 1989, the opposition was openly asking questions about historical distortions, demographic issues, and autonomy for the republics. There was quiet but persistent discussion of secession from the USSR and the reestablishment of independence. Symbolic restoration of nationhood was already under way, as the interwar flags flew over demonstrations and Balts began publicly celebrating national holidays prohibited by the Soviet state. Demonstrations grew into the tens and even hundreds of thousands across the Baltics. The largest demonstration, the Chain of Freedom, took place on September 3, 1989, the fiftieth anniversary of the fateful Molotov-Ribbentrop Pact: on this day, a human chain of nearly a million Balts joined hands across the three countries, stretching from Vilnius in the south to Riga and Tallinn in the north. At the same time, opposition was becoming institutionalized, and changes in some political structures of the USSR and the republics offered new opportunities for challenging the Soviet system from within as well as without.

Competitive elections began in the Baltic countries before those countries regained independence in 1991. In early 1990, the Soviet government permitted (or was no longer in a position not to permit) partially open elections and, in all three Baltic countries, opposition groups fielded candidates for the Supreme Soviets of their respective republics. In Lithuania, which held the distinction of hosting the first multiparty elections in the history of the USSR, pro-independence candidates, some of them members of the Lithuanian Communist Party, which had declared itself independent of the Communist Party of the Soviet Union (CPSU), carried the election. In Latvia and Estonia, which held their elections later, the results were mixed but tilted toward pro-independence candidates. These candidates were favored by ethnic Latvians and Estonians, but a notable proportion of Russian-speaking residents also selected pro-independence candidates.[7]

The legislative activities in the Supreme Soviets of the three republics were important, but the speed at which changes were taking place in the Baltics meant that legislative change, especially within existing Soviet-era political structures, would trail the initiatives of civil society. The civil opposition, already demanding independence, was further radicalized by the events in Lithuania and Latvia in January of 1991. Conservative Soviet forces sought to take over the Vilnius television tower, which was defended by thousands of young Lithuanians. In the violence that followed, Soviet forces killed fifteen protesters and injured hundreds: the graphic images of Lithuanians crushed beneath the treads of a Soviet tank received broad global coverage and signaled a new turn in the political climate. Gorbachev sought to distance himself from both the Vilnius killings and the deaths of five Latvians that occurred when Soviet special forces (OMON) attacked buildings belonging to the ministry of the interior, exacerbating tensions between progressive and conservative forces in the USSR and the republics.

In a widespread rejection of the evolutionary change offered by Gorbachev or the

Photo 11.1.   Independence demonstrations that began in Lithuania in 1989. These culminated with the Chain of Freedom that went through all three Baltic states in September 1989.

(Source: Peter Turnley/CORBIS)

Photo 11.2.   *Vytautas Landsbergis voting in Lithuania's first free elections since World War II. From 1990 to 1992, he held constitutional authority as both the leader of the state and the speaker of the parliament. In 1993, he founded a new political party, the Homeland Union, which won the 1996 parliamentary elections, allowing him to serve as speaker of the Lithuanian parliament from 1996 to 2000.*

(Source: Giedrus Pocius/Sygma/Corbis)

regressive course embraced by conservative elements, residents of the Baltic countries voted in February and March of 1991 in referenda on independence. In February, 90 percent of participants in Lithuania (who were required to be eighteen years of age or older and permanent residents, a category which essentially excluded only Soviet military forces stationed in the republic) voted for independence. In March, 78 percent and 74 percent of the inhabitants of Estonia and Latvia, respectively, voted in the affirmative. Those in favor of independence were not only ethnic Balts, but included substantial proportions of Russian-speaking residents as well.

The hard-line coup that took place in August 1991 did not substantially change the Baltic course, which was pointed toward independence. At the same time, the failed coup effectively destroyed the remaining legitimacy of the CPSU and the Soviet Union itself was left as little more than a formal shell of a country. These developments brought independence more rapidly than had been expected by most people: on September 6, 1991, the USSR recognized the Baltic states as independent entities and, less than two weeks later, they were admitted as full members to the United Nations. On the one hand, Latvia, Lithuania, and Estonia, which had their independence taken by force and deception, had been ready for freedom for the last half century. On the other hand, the foundations for independence in 1991 were somewhat tenuous, as there were no solid institutions of democracy or markets in place, and there was a real and growing tension between opposition forces in favor of charting a new course toward modernity, as represented by the West, and those in favor of turning back the political clock to reestablish interwar norms and institutions.

Political Institutions

Generally speaking, Latvia, Lithuania, and Estonia established their postcommunist political institutions according to what might be described as a "restorationist" principle. That is to say that all three worked from an initial assumption that independence was being "restored" rather than "established" in 1991. Consequently, constitutions, electoral systems, judicial structures, and other key political institutions were initially renewed rather than constructed from scratch. Though the tension between those who wished to follow a more conservative and nationalistic path of restoration (in Latvia, this was rhetorically constructed as the "renewal of the First Republic of Latvia") and those who wished to construct a historically grounded but modern and "European" state (which was rhetorically constructed as the creation of the "Second Republic of Latvia") would grow as time passed, there was an initial inclination in all three states to revert to that which was known and tried and to ground themselves in the foundation of the independent past.

Renewal of states included the renewal of prewar constitutions, which served to underscore the legal continuity of institutions. In Estonia, the post-Soviet constitution of 1992 was based on the constitution of 1938. In Latvia, the 1922 constitution was restored in 1993. This meant, essentially, that basic prewar structures of government and electoral systems were restored. In Estonia, for instance, this entailed the renewal of a parliamentary system of governance in which the government holds executive power and legislative power is vested in the Riigikogu (parliament).

In Lithuania, the 1938 constitution was temporarily accepted, but the leadership of the country opted ultimately to write a new constitution, as the prewar document, despite its symbolic importance to the accepted idea of "restoration" of the country, was declared authoritarian and not well suited to the country.[8] In Lithuania, the Seimas, or parliament, is elected through a mix of proportional representation and direct constituency voting.

The political institutions in Latvia and Estonia maintain continuity with prewar structures in the requirement that seats in the democratic legislatures be filled on the basis of a system of proportional representation. Interestingly, the proportional system was one which, in the interwar states, precipitated problems stemming from the population of parliaments with a multitude of small parties and fragmented interests: in Latvia, for instance, the serious political fragmentation was one of the ways in which President Ulmanis's 1933 assumption of authoritarian leadership was justified. Indeed, the 1993 election in Latvia produced a parliament with eight parties and the 1995 election a parliament with nine parties. At least at the outset, historical continuity held sway over the need to critically evaluate the successes and failures of past political structures. By 2006, some interests consolidated, resulting in the election of a parliament with seven parties.

Photo 11.3.   Former Estonian president Lennart Meri. He served as Estonia's second president from 1992 to 2001. An active leader of the independence movement in Estonia, he was also a writer and film director.

(Source: Erik Peinar)

As in the interwar states, the president in the Baltic countries is titular head of state, but has limited powers. The president is elected by the parliament in a secret ballot for a term of five years in Estonia and three in Latvia (extended to four in 1997). In Lithuania, the president is elected by popular vote, a fact that could, arguably, be used to increase his or her powers if there was evidence of a popular mandate for the person or program. Among the powers of the presidency in Latvia is the power to dissolve the legislature, the Saeima, and to convene and preside over extraordinary sessions of the cabinet, though a good deal of the president's power rests in his or her ability to set a public agenda with a visible presence in the media and society, as Latvia's second postcommunist president Vaira Vike-Freiberga did. Her term in office ended in July 2007. She was replaced by Valdis Zatlers, a physician with little experience in politics.

Photo 11.4.   Federal president of Germany Horst Kohler (L), president of Latvia Vaira Vike-Freiberga, and president of Italy Giorgio Napolitano during their joint press conference at the Fourth Informal Debates of European Presidents on the Future of Europe, in Riga.
(Source: TOMS KALNINS/epa/Corbis)

Another historical continuity between the interwar and postcommunist Baltic states is the relatively short lifespan of governments. In the interwar period, prior to the authoritarian regimes put in place by Smetona, Päts, and Ulmanis, all three countries were characterized by short-lived governments. The period from the de facto end of Soviet rule to the present has been plagued by this dubious legacy: between 1990 and 2003, Estonia had eight governments, Lithuania had seven, and Latvia had ten. All Latvian governments have been coalition governments, four of them multiparty minority coalitions. The multitude of parties and coalitions competing for legislative seats and the low vote threshold (which as been raised over time) required for winning seats in parliament create optimal conditions for shifting allegiances and alliances in the parliaments and, consequently, for unstable support for sitting governments.

Elections and Political Parties

Political parties in the Baltic countries are still in an early state of development. While parties put forth candidates for election, candidates also run on lists associated with political organizations that are not formally political parties. Even most of the parties themselves are not political parties as that institution is understood in the West: few political parties are mass organizations with broad memberships. In Latvia, for example, some of the "parties" are financed by private businesses, which then extend their influence into political appointments and policies. A system by which parties would be at least partially financed by members has not yet developed and, consequently, parties are essentially elite organizations with a narrow base of decision makers and leaders. Muller-Rommel and Norgaard have characterized Latvia as "a new democracy with a low level of institutionalization and a high degree of individual influence by the political elite."[9] Such a description would be no less apt in Latvia's neighboring states, though parties are likely to evolve toward a Western European model.

Political institutions have developed into democratic and at least nominally representative institutions. At the same time, civil society in the Baltics, while it blossomed in the late Soviet period, withered in the transition period. At the end of the 1980s, civil society in the Baltics flourished. In each country, there was a dominant social movement—Sajudis in Lithuania and the Popular Fronts in Estonia and Latvia—leading the mass drive for openness and, later, independence. There was also a revival of older civic organizations such as the Red Cross and the Boy Scouts, and the creation of new groups aimed at preserving the environment and historical sites, protecting young Baltic men from the Soviet military draft, and reviving the folk culture. A nascent free press provided the backdrop for a revived civil society characterized by activism, debates, discussions, and dissent that would have seemed impossible just a few years before.

What is the state of civil society in the Baltics today? Latvian political scientist Artis Pabriks writes:

> The depth of democracy and the strength of civil society frequently depend on the extent to which the individual member of the general public, the ordinary citizen, is willing to devote his or her spare time to public activities. In turn, the willingness to sacrifice one's spare time for public activities depends on how strongly this person believes these activities will make a difference and influence the chosen political cause. A willingness to be active also depends on one's ability to engage other members in the same activity, thus making it a collective effort. In other words, common activities require trust in state institutions as well as solidarity with fellow society members.[10]

It has been lamented in the postcommunist period that "civil society is dead." This grim conclusion is based on the fact that civic activity has declined markedly since the end of the period of opposition, when a substantial proportion of the titular populations, as well as a number of Russian speakers, of the Baltics were involved in social movements: while the dominant movement was ultimately the independence movement, other groups rallied around environmental, cultural, educational, and other causes.

Today, few people are registered for political parties, demonstrations for or against specific government policies or social issues tend to be small, and most inhabitants appear to be too busy pursuing prosperity—or at least struggling to make ends meet—to be active in civic organizations or activities. Even more conventional forms of participation in civic life have declined. In Latvia, over 91 percent of eligible voters cast ballots in the first postcommunist elections of 1993. By 1995, when the next elections were held, the proportion of possible voters opting to participate was just over 72 percent; in subsequent elections (1998 and 2002), the proportion of participants held steady at about 71 percent, but fell to 62.2 percent in 2006. In Latvia, this form of civic participation is further circumscribed by the fact that nearly a half million of Latvia's 2.4 million inhabitants are not citizens. Some of these inhabitants, many of whom are of Russian ethnicity, are not eligible for citizenship because they do not meet residency or language requirements; others are eligible but have opted not to pursue citizenship: as of 2004, just over 74,000 individuals had taken advantage of the opportunity to become citizens of the Republic of Latvia. Whether a lack of confidence in the viability of the state or alienation and apathy are driving the low rate of naturalization will become apparent in the years to come.

Estonia has experienced a similar situation, as it too limited automatic postcommunist citizenship to pre-1940 citizens and their direct descendants: Soviet-era migrants who were permanent residents were to be naturalized within a stringent set of requirements and regulations.[11] In the year 2007, just over a million (or 91.5 percent) of inhabitants were citizens. The remainder were stateless persons or citizens of other countries.

Lithuania extended suffrage broadly to include nearly all inhabitants over the age of eighteen: the relatively low proportion of non-Lithuanians in the country did not make fear of postcommunist Russian political influence a factor in putting citizenship and voting structures in place. The proportion of those citizens opting to participate in elections has, however, declined since the early postcommunist period: while over three-quarters of the eligible electorate opted to participate in the Seimas elections of 1992, fewer than half voted in the parliamentary balloting in October of 2004.

Attitudes and values are an important constituent part of the transition in the postcommunist period. Vilmante Liubiniene cites Lekevicius (1991) in suggesting that "the 20th century revealed the division of the world into two big camps—the West and the East, in one of which the priority was given to individualism and in the other to collectivity. The collectivism of the totalitarian period left a deep imprint in the minds of the people in the post-Soviet countries."[12] This position is notable because while many surveys, including that cited by Liubiniene, highlight the "Western orientation" of the Baltic countries in terms of widespread support for democratic rights and freedoms, as well as a desire for the capitalist market and material wealth, there remains some societal disposition toward the notion that it is the state's responsibility to ensure basic needs and solve basic problems. As might be expected, those who have experienced success in the transition period (younger workers, the well educated, entrepreneurs) express a more positive orientation toward the competitive market system and democracy. Those who have been left behind by the wave of change (pensioners, Soviet-era veterans, farmers, among others) are more nostalgic for the collective values and supports provided by the Soviet state.[13]

Economic Transition

All three Baltic countries have undergone substantial economic changes as a result of the transformation from Soviet-administered command economies to market capitalist economies. The changes have brought economic windfalls and economic displacements, prosperity and poverty, and hope and fear in their wake.

From a comparative perspective, the Baltics have fared better than the other former Soviet republics, though perhaps not as well as Central and East European states such as Hungary and the Czech Republic. Growth rates in the Baltics have largely met or exceeded expectations, with the exception of a period of crisis in 1998, when the crash of the Russian ruble damaged neighboring economies as well. One of the hallmarks of Baltic transformation, in contrast to other former republics, is the speed at which they have privatized former state-owned industries. In Latvia and Estonia, privatization at the ten-year mark of independence was almost complete, with most formerly state-owned small and medium-size enterprises fully privatized. Lithuania has progressed most slowly, though about three-quarters of the economy is linked to the private sector.

All three Baltic countries also have large shadow economies comprised of a variety of activities, including the narcotics and sex trades, both of which have prospered in the more permissive environment of democratic capitalism. Even within the context of legitimate business, there has been corruption and criminal activity, though some of it is well disguised: for example, in Latvia, rackets that sought to squeeze protection money from new businesses have been transformed into registered security firms that provide "protection services."

While the general economic picture in the Baltic countries is positive, the benefits of competitive capitalism have eluded many. Less educated workers who labored in Soviet enterprises have been among those hardest hit. The postcommunist shakeout of the "excess" employment of the Soviet full-employment economy has meant economic dislocation for thousands of workers. The Baltics operated as "middlemen" in the Soviet chain of production, finishing raw materials from other Soviet republics for consumption or use still elsewhere. Consequently, areas that relied on manufacturing plants for employment have been especially hard hit, and unemployment has been quite high in rural areas and small towns.

Though the capital cities of Riga, Vilnius, and Tallinn and a few other areas of the Baltics have enjoyed relatively low rates of unemployment, economic activity, and economic security are by no means invariably partnered. Working people in the Baltics may also be poor people, as wages have remained low since the early postcommunist period. While it is the case that wages were also low in the USSR, the cost of living has risen far faster than wages, creating conditions for widespread economic deprivation. It is notable that while housing prices in state-owned apartment blocks have grown very slowly, the cost of nonpublic housing, food, clothing, automobiles, and many other consumer goods has risen steeply. All three states have large elderly populations and many retirees live on paltry pensions, which put a majority below the poverty line. It is not uncommon to see pensioners begging for money on the streets.

One important symbolic and economic aspect of the postcommunist transformation has been the restitution of property. In theory, laws and practices of restitution were intended to return to prewar owners of private urban and rural property the structures and land of which they were deprived when Soviet occupiers nationalized all property and drove many members of the "ownership class" out of their countries. On the one hand, this move was symbolically significant because it "righted" a Soviet wrong: in the early postcommunist period, nearly any action seen as undoing what the communists did was likely to find a sympathetic constituency. On the other hand, restitution was intended to restore the grid of private property that existed in the interwar period and reestablish an ownership society, the basis of the new capitalism.

While the establishment of private ownership as a foundation for the new market economy was important, the use of restitution as a primary mechanism for achieving the goal yielded mixed results. In Riga, Latvia, for instance, many prewar owners of apartment buildings were able to take possession of the structures, establish rental agreements with tenants, and take over their lost property with few major problems (though improper evictions have been practiced). In rural areas, however, conflicts arose between prewar owners claiming the right to take possession of their land and those who lived upon and, in many cases, farmed that land. In this instance, a fundamental problem arose in balancing the rights of prewar owners with the rights of those inhabiting and working the agricultural space. The laws of restitution favored the former, though local committees overseeing the process in their administrative districts sometimes gave preference to the latter.[14]

The postcommunist economic picture is decidedly mixed. While the changes have brought greater opportunities and prosperity to some, they have brought despair and deprivation to others. A class hierarchy has evolved over the past decade: at the top are young and savvy business entrepreneurs and former communist apparatchiks who used their previous positions as stepping-stones to work and wealth; in the middle are well-educated younger workers pursuing professional occupations; at the bottom are the elderly, the poorly educated, former factory workers, and older workers pushed out of secure Soviet-era jobs.

Social Consequences

Communism embraced an ideology of equality. Capitalism, by contrast, embraces an ideology of competition. In the period of Soviet communism, all citizens were theoretically equal: women and men, Russians and smaller nationalities, professionals and laborers, and so forth. In reality, the situation was more complex. While women were well represented in the workforce, they tended to occupy positions with less power, prestige, and authority. No less importantly, women carried the "double burden" of paid work and primary, if not sole, responsibility for domestic work. Some observers suggested that women bore a "triple burden," the third being the fact that they were usually the ones to wait in long shop lines to acquire needed groceries or other goods that were commonly in short supply in the USSR.

While there was ostensibly ethnic equality, some, to paraphrase George Orwell's *Animal Farm*, were "more equal than others." Russian was the lingua franca of the USSR, and all nationalities were expected to learn the language. Russians living in non-Russian republics, however, rarely learned the local language. Russians were often given priority in acquiring housing while others waited many years for an apartment. Finally, workers in the USSR experienced a general equality, as most had a decent but very modest standard of living. The Communist Party elites, however, had access to special shops that did not run deficits, comfortable holiday accommodations, and decision-making power in an authoritarian society.

In the capitalist and democratic context of postcommunism, there have been both changes and continuities in the forms of inequality in the Baltics. In terms of gender, for instance, women are legally equal to men and have comparable opportunities to gain educational training for the more competitive labor force. In fact, women are more likely than men to be highly educated, and they make up the majority of students in the institutions of higher learning in the Baltics. At the same time, women still suffer a gender wage gap and are less likely to be found in positions of power and authority, particularly in business and politics (though Latvia was home to Central and Eastern Europe's first female president, Vaira Vike-Freiberga).

While women are well represented in the paid labor force, the postcommunist period has also seen a push from some more nationalist political organizations for women to return to home and hearth in order to ensure the creation of new Latvians, Estonians, and Lithuanians. In the demographic and social context of the Baltics, issues of family formation are widely seen as issues of public importance. All three states have pro-natalist policies and social welfare policies intended to encourage childbearing. All three countries have continued programs of social support for mothers, though in the context of rapidly rising living costs, the value of payments like child allowances is paltry.

As noted earlier in the chapter, the sands of ethnic equality have shifted in the Baltics. Whereas in the Soviet period, Russians were the "most equal" of all legally equal nationalities, in the postcommunist Baltics, legal equality is extended to all, but the titular nationalities are preeminent. In Lithuania, citizenship was granted to nearly all inhabitants after independence was won; in Latvia and Estonia, citizenship was initially extended to all who were citizens of the interwar states—while this right was given without regard to ethnicity, in practice most eligible inhabitants were of the titular nationality, as a large proportion of Russian inhabitants had arrived during the Soviet period of occupation. By the turn of the century, most inhabitants were eligible for citizenship though, as noted earlier, many have not opted to complete the process of naturalization.

An ethnic and linguistic issue that has caused some tension in Latvia is education. The government has made the decision to increase the requirements for Latvian language learning in Russian schools and, consequently, to reduce the course work in Russian. This policy has caused dissatisfaction among some Russian-speaking inhabitants, who have become accustomed to having their own Russian-language schools, as was the case in the Soviet period and in the early postcommunist period. The education issue is only a part of the larger "problem" of language that has simmered in the postcommunist Baltic countries: while on the one hand, the Baltic governments have worked to preserve the relevance and expand the usage of the indigenous language, particularly after the marginalization of Latvian, Estonian, and Lithuanian in the public life of the USSR, minority populations have voiced resistance to making Russian a secondary language in the political, economic, and education life of the countries.

The issue of ethnic relations continues to be very important for all three Baltic countries, though perhaps for Latvia in particular, as it has the largest Russian-speaking population and a majority of nontitular inhabitants in most of its cities. On the one hand, the issue has been and will continue to be influenced by state policies and actions: laws about language, education, and equal access to opportunities will help to assimilate or alienate Russian speakers in the Baltics. On the other hand, the issue of language acquisition (of titular languages by Russian speakers) and ethnic relations is powerfully influenced by social, cultural, and economic factors that are not controlled by the state. For example, in Latvia, the rate of ethnic intermarriage is high: consequently, many families are mixed and children learn both languages and bridge both cultures. The practical imperative of profit making in capitalism has also induced young people and other would-be entrepreneurs to learn multiple languages in order to serve more customers more effectively. In sum, while ethnic tensions are present in the Baltics, both state- and microlevel forces help maintain equilibrium and reduce the potential for the ethnic conflict that has torn apart some other states in the region.

Less well known, but no less pressing than other postcommunist social issues are problems of public health, including HIV/AIDS, which is spreading in the region at a significant pace. The spread of HIV/AIDS in Central and Eastern Europe is gaining momentum: a recent report by the United Nations Development Fund suggests that some areas in the region, including Russia, Ukraine, and Estonia, are in the early stages of a potentially dramatic epidemic, having reached an infection rate of 1 percent, a threshold at which it becomes increasingly challenging to halt the momentum of the infection's spread. No less critical is the fact that in this area, 75 to 80 percent of individuals with HIV are under thirty years of age, highlighting the vulnerability of the present and future workforce upon which both household and national economies depend. At this time, about 70 percent of the infected in the region of Central and Eastern Europe are men. This pattern, however, has begun to change, as heterosexual women have become a rising proportion of those infected with HIV.

Drug injection among young men is still the dominant mode of HIV/AIDS transmission, but heterosexual intercourse is a rapidly growing path of infection. While women have, at present, a lower infection rate than men, it is notable that women are three times more likely than men to be infected through heterosexual contact. This signals a growing possibility that HIV/AIDS could move into the general population (rather than being largely isolated in homosexual or drug-using communities), at which point it may grow exponentially, harming not only individuals and their families, but negatively affecting national economic prospects as people die in their most productive years and illness and treatment drain individual and national budgets of resources.

All three Baltic governments are aware of the problem of HIV/AIDS, and both governmental and nongovernmental campaigns have been undertaken to reverse the growth of HIV/AIDS. Educational efforts are under way, though sexual education is still sparsely available in schools and information received by the young on issues such as transmission and testing is spotty and sometimes incorrect.

Public health generally is a serious problem in the region. Aside from the critical issue of HIV/AIDS, problems such as high mortality from heart disease and cancer plague the populations, alcoholism is widespread, and drug use among the young is significant and rising. Depression is also common and, while women are more likely to report being depressed, suicide is more prevalent among men. In fact, men's mortality risk in the Baltics is considerably higher than women's risk: according to the World Health Organization (2006), the probability of dying (per 1,000) population is 301 for Estonian males between the ages of fifteen and sixty and 108 for Estonian females in the same age group. Data for the other Baltic counties are comparable.

Although the Soviet health-care system was plagued with troubles, it was universally accessible and provided basic care to inhabitants, including the provision of vaccinations, a critical component of public health. Though postcommunist governments have sought to keep in place some of the socialist-style universal health services, the shift to a market-based economy has put comprehensive or preventive medical care out of reach of many individuals. Both individual and public health problems are among the critical issues that Baltic governments and societies and communities will face in the coming years.

Foreign Policy

After a half century in the Soviet Union, many in the Baltics embraced the slogan, "back to Europe." For the Balts it meant a "return" to the West and its democratic ideals and capitalist prosperity after five decades under the rule of an occupying power. Almost immediately after formally gaining independence, the Baltics sought seats in the United Nations and all three became members in September of 1991, an important symbolic step that signaled international acceptance of the states.

The accession of the three Baltic countries to the European Union in May 2004 represents another important symbolic and substantive step for those states. In terms of symbolism, the EU's expansion signals the first time since the historical Hanseatic League that nearly the entire Baltic Sea region is part of a single economic and political bloc. In terms of modernity, it brings a geographic part of Europe back into economic and political Europe.

Earlier that year, another major foreign policy goal was realized: in March 2004, the Baltic countries became members of the North Atlantic Treaty Organization (NATO). While there were issues raised in those states about allotting the required defense expenditures in tight budgetary situations, there was no doubt that the Baltics would aggressively pursue membership in NATO. On the one hand, NATO membership represented an important symbolic link to Europe. On the other hand, NATO membership also conferred a right and obligation to mutual defense; in other words, it provided a security barrier against a potential new wave of Russian imperialism.

Relations between the Baltic countries and their neighbors have been marked by both tensions and cooperation. In the early 1990s, there were some significant tensions between the Baltic countries and their eastern neighbor, Russia, over border issues. Latvia, for instance, made a claim on Abrene (now Pitalovo), a small area on the country's southeastern flank that was incorporated into the USSR in 1944, when several substantial border changes were made, including the return of Vilnius to Lithuania and the incorporation into the USSR of a portion of Estonian Narva and Petserimaa. Some rancor was generated by state efforts to claim Abrene and by the printing of a map of Latvia that included Abrene within the borders. Despite symbolic efforts to "restore" the map of the past, borders have remained in place. Cooperation between the Baltics and Russia is fostered largely by trade relations, as there are mutual interests in economic partnerships and profits. At the same time, the Baltics have sought to expand their trade and economic relationships with their western neighbors, particularly after the economic tremors that shook the region when Russia's ruble collapsed in 1998. Membership in the EU will likely mean a further reorientation of trade and economic partnerships toward Western Europe.

Conclusion

The outlook for the Baltic countries of Latvia, Lithuania, and Estonia cannot be characterized with a single adjective. In some respects, the future appears to be bright. Consider that the Baltics have achieved most of the important goals they set in the last decade: the basic mechanisms of democracy and market capitalism have been set firmly in place; membership in those European organizations that would bring them closer to security (NATO) and prosperity (EU) has been secured; and the countries are recognized as postcommunist "success stories" without the violence and upheaval that has cast a shadow over the transition in some other regional states. On the other hand, the countries face challenges both internal and external in the coming years. All three have experienced a potentially destabilizing rise in social stratification, as a segment of the populations expands its human capital, wealth, and power, while other groups are left powerless and poor. This growing wealth gap is one that will need to be addressed if the democratic value of equal opportunity and voice is to be achieved. Further, the serious public health threats posed by diseases like HIV/AIDS must be addressed comprehensively if the Baltics (and neighboring states like Russia and Ukraine) are to avoid the immense losses and challenges faced by African and Asian states that failed to stem the tide of infection in the general population. Responsive, democratic governments and institutions, combined with the active voices of civil society, are the best hope to address societal problems and to foster the positive future progress of three small countries that have experienced a dramatic century of changes and challenges.

Suggested Readings

Eglitis, Daina Stukuls. *Imagining the Nation: History, Modernity, and Revolution in Latvia.* University Park: Pennsylvania State University Press, 2002.

Eksteins, Modris. *Walking since Daybreak: A Story of Eastern Europe, World War II and the Heart of Our Century.* New York: Mariner Books, 2000.

Lieven, Anatol. *The Baltic Revolution: Estonia, Latvia, Lithuania and the Path to Independence.* New Haven, CT: Yale University Press, 1993.

Plakans, Andrejs. *The Latvians: A Short History (Studies of Nationalities).* Stanford, CA: Hoover Institution Press, 1995.

Raun, Toivo U. *Estonia and the Estonians (Studies of Nationalities).* Stanford, CA: Hoover Institution Press, 2002.

Senn, Alfred Erich. *Gorbachev's Failure in Lithuania.* New York: Palgrave Macmillan, 1995.

Smith, David J., et al. *The Baltic States: Estonia, Latvia and Lithuania.* New York: Routledge, 2002.

Notes

1. Romuald Misiunas and Rein Taagepera, *The Baltic States: Years of Dependence, 1940–1990* (Berkeley: University of California Press, 1993), 12–13.

2. Misiunas and Taagepera, *The Baltic States*, 14.

3. Misiunas and Taagepera, *The Baltic States*, 113.

4. Kevin O'Connor, *The History of the Baltic States* (Westport, CT: Greenwood Press, 2003), 126.

5. Daina Stukuls Eglitis, *Imagining the Nation: History, Modernity, and Revolution in Latvia* (University Park: Pennsylvania State University Press, 2002).

6. Jane I. Dawson, *Eco-Nationalism: Anti-Nuclear Activism and National Identity in Russia, Lithuania, and Ukraine* (Durham, NC: Duke University Press, 1996).

7. Anatol Lieven, *The Baltic Revolution: Estonia, Latvia, Lithuania and the Path to Independence* (New Haven, CT: Yale University Press, 1993), 230–42.

8. Thomas Lane, *Lithuania: Stepping Westward* (New York: Routledge, 2001), 132.

9. Ferdinand Muller-Rommel and Ole Norgaard, "Latvia," in *The Baltic States after Independence (Studies of Communism in Transition)*, ed. Ole Norgaard et al., 38 (Northampton, MA: Edward Elgar, 1996).

10. Artis Pabriks, "Ethnic Limits of Civil Society: The Latvian Case," in *Civil Society in the Baltic Sea Region*, ed Norbert Goetz and Jorg Hackmann, 133 (Burlington, VT: Ashgate, 2003).

11. Aleksei Semjonov, "Ethnic Limits of Civil Society: The Case of Estonia," in *Civil Society in the Baltic Sea Region*, ed. Norbert Goetz and Jorg Hackmann, 147 (Burlington, VT: Ashgate, 2003).

12. Vilmante Liubiniene, "Attitudes, Beliefs and Universal Values in Lithuania, Latvia and Estonia," in *Political Representation and Participation in Transitional Democracies: Estonia, Latvia & Lithuania*, ed. Elfar Loftson and Yonhyok Choe, 112 (Stockholm, Sweden: Sodertorn Academic Studies, 2003).

13. Liubiniene, "Attitudes."

14. Eglitis, *Imagining the Nation*.

CHAPTER 12

Bulgaria
PROGRESS AND DEVELOPMENT

Janusz Bugajski

During the course of seventeen years, Bulgaria successfully conducted two historic transformations: from a centrally controlled communist system to a pluralistic market-oriented democracy, and from the closest ally of the Soviet Union in the former Warsaw Pact to a full member of the North Atlantic Treaty Organization (NATO). This dual transformation was neither consistent nor predictable. For much of the early and mid-1990s, the postcommunist Bulgarian Socialists ruled. They resisted full-blown capitalism and a close alliance with the West largely in an effort to preserve their political and economic positions and maintain their traditional ties with Moscow. Sofia's turn toward Western institutions and economic models accelerated after 1998, when a reformist coalition government was elected. In 2004, Bulgaria officially entered NATO and was on track for European Union (EU) membership by 2007.

Precommunist Bulgaria

Bulgaria emerged as an independent state from the Ottoman Empire in several stages. In 1878, following the Russo-Turkish war, the Treaty of San Stefano created a large Bulgarian state stretching from the Danube to the Aegean and including most of present-day Macedonia. The Treaty of Berlin in July 1878 reduced this territory at the insistence of the great powers because of fears of Russian dominance throughout the Balkans. Bulgaria subsequently included the region between the Danube and the Balkan Mountains. The area between the Balkan Mountains in the north and the Rhodope Mountains in the south formed the autonomous Ottoman province of Eastern Rumelia. These border readjustments and Bulgaria's reversion to a semiautonomous Ottoman principality under a German ruler created widespread resentments. However, during the last few decades of the nineteenth century, Sofia adopted the progressive Turnovo Constitution that guaranteed individual rights, and a number of political parties were established including the National Liberal Party and the Bulgarian Agrarian Union.

The country proclaimed its full independence from Turkey in 1908 after several popular revolts, including the Ilinden uprising in August 1903, centered in the Macedonian and Thracian regions. Bulgaria's territorial claims contributed to fueling two Balkan wars in 1912 and 1913. In the first war, the new Balkan states combined their forces to drive the Ottoman armies out of the region. In the second Balkan war, Bulgaria was unsuccessful in its military campaign against Serbia and Greece and once again lost territories in Macedonia and Thrace to its two neighbors. The result left a lasting sense of injustice in Sofia with regard to Bulgaria's rightful frontiers. Sofia retained only a small slice of Pirin Macedonia and a sector of the Thracian coastline. During World War I, Bulgaria allied itself with Germany and Austria, but with the defeat of the Central Powers it was again forced to accept a harsh peace treaty at Neuilly in November 1919 and lost all access to the Aegean Sea.

For most of the interwar period, Bulgaria witnessed political turmoil and economic crisis, particularly after the overthrow of the Agrarian government led by Aleksandur Stamboliyski in 1923. Following a military coup d'état supported by political rivals and nationalist Macedonian activists, Stamboliyski and other Agrarian leaders were murdered. After a decade of political instability and conflict, another coup in May 1934 led by military officers resulted in the formation of a personalistic regime under King Boris III. During World War II, Sofia imposed a royal dictatorship and capitalized on the German occupation of Yugoslavia and Greece to forge an alliance with Berlin to regain parts of Macedonia and Thrace. Sofia also repossessed the region of southern Dobruja from Romania. King Boris died in August 1943. For the rest of the war the country was ruled by a regency, as Boris's successor, Simeon, was only six years old. Bulgaria's territorial advances, including access to the Aegean coastline, were again reversed at the close of World War II, as Sofia found itself once more on the losing side.

Communist Experience

Communist forces, with Soviet military and political assistance, seized power in Bulgaria in September 1944 during the closing stages of World War II. At the end of 1947, they eliminated all organized political and social opposition. They then held falsified elections to legitimize their assumption of absolute power. The former Moscow-directed Comintern (Communist International) agent Georgi Dimitrov returned to Bulgaria from exile and assumed leadership of the Communist Party and the state. A new Stalinist "Dimitrov" constitution was passed in December 1947 that replicated the Soviet prototype. The communist regime, under Soviet supervision, began to place tight restrictions on cultural and political life, conducted a full-scale drive toward state control over the economy, and pursued agricultural collectivization among the peasantry.

Dimitrov died in July 1949 and was replaced by Vulko Chervenkov, another hard-line Stalinist. Chervenkov in turn was replaced by Todor Zhivkov in April 1956 during the slow process of de-Stalinization. However, Zhivkov and his Communist Party maintained tight control over the country for the next thirty-four years until the collapse of the centralized system. Zhivkov's absolute loyalty to Moscow and his ability to thwart any organized domestic opposition to Leninist rule earned him the complete support of the Soviet leadership. There is even evidence that the Bulgarian regime sought to join the USSR as the sixteenth republic. Bulgaria was thus considered to be Moscow's closest and most loyal ally in the entire Soviet bloc.

Transition from Communism

Following a wave of public protests and increasing political pressures against the communist regime, on November 10, 1989, the Bulgarian Communist Party (BCP) Central Committee announced the resignation of Todor Zhivkov as secretary-general and his replacement by foreign minister Petar Mladenov. The new leader promised sweeping political and economic changes to transform Bulgaria into a "modern democratic state." The BCP organized pro-Mladenov rallies, depicting itself as the initiator of progressive reforms, scapegoating the Zhivkov leadership for all of the country's maladies, and trying to deny the reformist initiative to the emerging, but still embryonic, democratic opposition movement.

As head of the Bulgarian Communist Party, Mladenov held meetings with dissident activists in mid-November 1989 and pledged to implement substantive democratic reforms and legalize all types of independent groups and activities. The BCP's subordinate bodies, including the Komsomol youth association, were allowed to be more critical in an attempt to deflate some of the opposition's demands. Reshuffles were conducted in the BCP's governing Politburo and Central Committee, and Mladenov declared himself in favor of free general elections. The regime dropped the BCP's "guiding force" role from the constitution and promised to curtail the repressive role of the security services. These steps paved the way for the creation of a multiparty system. While the BCP endeavored to maintain its political initiative, dozens of new political groups were formed during this time.

Some reform communists demanded the resignation of the entire BCP Central Committee as divisions in the party appeared with the emergence of the Alternative Socialist Association within the party. In early December 1989, a preparatory meeting was held between BCP officials and representatives of some independent groups. Mladenov promised that the authorities would hold a constructive dialogue with all groups "supporting socialism." In order to incorporate leading opposition elements in some workable coalition and to prevent destructive splits within the party, the BCP initiated roundtable discussions with officially sponsored organizations and some of the newly formed opposition groups in January 1990.[1]

The regime continued to be treated with mistrust by most of the opposition, which refused to enter the "Government of National Consensus" proposed by the Communists. At its Extraordinary Congress held in early February 1990, the BCP selected Alexander Lilov as its new secretary-general and replaced the Central Committee with a smaller Supreme Party Council and the ruling Politburo with a new presidency. BCP leaders also initiated steps to separate the party from the state (which they had fully controlled), and the party itself was renamed the Bulgarian Socialist Party (BSP) to distance it from its totalitarian past.

The National Assembly (parliament), controlled by the BSP, elected Andrey Lukanov as the new prime minister. Lukanov attempted to form a more broadly based coalition government, but the initiative was rejected by the Union of Democratic Forces (UDF), which had grown into the chief democratic opposition alliance. The new cabinet became an all-communist body as the BSP's former coalition partner, the Agrarian National Union, refused to join the Lukanov government and purged itself of compromised older leaders. In addition, reformist BSP intellectuals established an Alternative Socialist Party (ASP) and cast serious doubts on the BSP's ability to democratize. Meanwhile, the UDF organized public demonstrations to protest the slow progress in the roundtable negotiations and the limitations on the democratic transition.

By mid-March 1990, the BSP and UDF reached an agreement on the transition to a democratic system and the scheduling of competitive national elections. The BSP won the parliamentary elections held on June 10 and 17, 1990, with 47.15 percent of the vote, giving the party 211 of the 400 parliamentary seats. The UDF obtained a disappointing 36.20 percent (144 seats). The Agrarian Union took 8 percent (16 seats) and the Turkish organization, the Movement for Rights and Freedoms (MRF), 6 percent of the vote (23 seats). The UDF accused the regime of ballot rigging and of maintaining a monopoly over the media. The opposition had insufficient time to organize an effective election campaign and scored particularly poorly in rural areas where the communist-socialist apparatus remained largely intact.

In April 1990, parliament formally created the office of the president, but limited its authority to security matters and ceremonial functions by giving him no veto power over parliamentary legislation. On July 6, 1990, Mladenov resigned as acting president, and the BSP threw its support behind Zheliu Zhelev as the country's new head of state. When the UDF refused to form a coalition to ensure a two-thirds parliamentary majority, the Lukanov government was stalemated. The BSP-led Lukanov government resigned at the end of November 1990 and was replaced a month later by a coalition headed by Prime Minister Dimitur Popov that included the BSP, the UDF, the Agrarians, and independents.

Political Institutions

The unicameral National Assembly also became a constitutional assembly that drafted Bulgaria's new democratic constitution. The document defined Bulgaria as a parliamentary democracy and a unitary state, and prohibited any form of territorial autonomy or the creation of political parties founded on an "ethnic, racial, or religious" basis. Parliament was given legislative supremacy; the president had the right to veto legislation passed by the National Assembly. This constitution was eventually adopted in July 1991 despite opposition from some UDF factions. The parliament or National Assembly is elected every four years in a popular ballot, and the majority party or a coalition that consists of a parliamentary majority forms the new government. The president of Bulgaria is also elected in a general election, but every five years. According to the constitution, his role is more ceremonial and symbolic than substantive in terms of decision making. Any amendments to the constitution require a three-fourths majority in parliament. However, a completely new constitution would need to be adopted by a newly elected Grand National Assembly. Bulgaria's local government consists of twenty-eight provinces named after the provincial capital, with the national capital itself forming a separate province. The provinces are further subdivided into a total of 264 municipalities, which are the main units of local government.

Parties and Elections

Prior to the October 1991 elections, the UDF split because the Union's largest coalition partners, the Social Democratic Party and the Agrarian Union, were refused a more prominent voice in the UDF Council or a greater number of candidates on the UDF electoral list. In addition, the Union was divided between advocates of a moderate line toward the BSP (the "light blues") and a majority who demanded far-reaching de-communization and settling scores with the repressive communist leadership (the "dark blues"). The "light blues" withdrew from the union and formed the UDF-Liberals. The "dark blues," who demanded far-reaching de-communization, became known as the UDF-Movement. They inherited the coalition's organizational network and media outlets.

In the October 1991 elections, the UDF-Movement narrowly won a plurality of votes in spite of declining support for the BSP. The UDF received 34.36 percent of the vote (110 of 240 parliamentary seats). The BSP gained 33.14 percent, thus claiming 106 seats. The only other party to clear the 4 percent threshold and gain parliamentary seats was the Turkish-based Movement for Rights and Freedoms (MRF). Not surprisingly, the parliament became highly polarized, and the UDF had to form a coalition government with the MRF, headed by Prime Minister Filip Dimitrov who was installed in office in November 1991.

One of the top priorities of the UDF-MRF administration was de-communization in all public institutions and the elimination of subversive activities by secret service officers who were trying to obstruct market reform. This task proved difficult because of the entrenched interests that pervaded most state bodies and enterprises. The National Assembly passed a law to confiscate communist property. The prosecution of former communist officials was intensified. About fifty prominent figures were indicted, including Todor Zhivkov. However, the de-communization campaign was depicted by former members of the defunct communist structures as a "witch hunt" that undermined economic progress and failed to do anything for ordinary citizens. The UDF leadership asserted that, without the ouster of communist officials and the elimination of special interests that were parasitical on the Bulgarian economy, the market reform program would not be successful.

The Dimitrov government gave qualified support for Zheliu Zhelev in the indirect presidential ballot in January 1992. Zhelev was a sociologist who had been expelled from the Communist Party in the late 1980s for organizing a group to support political reform. The president was pressured to accept as his running mate Blaga Dimitrova from the UDF-Movement in return for the party's endorsement. Zhelev received only 45 percent of the votes in the first round of balloting and 53 percent in the second round against the BSP candidate Velko Vulkanov. However, there was incessant hostility between the UDF administration and President Zhelev, who represented a more moderate policy line toward the Socialists. Both the government and parliament criticized Zhelev for appointing ex-communists, and both institutions tried to further undercut presidential powers.

By the summer of 1992, the Dimitrov government faced internal splits over such issues as the return of the monarchy, the leadership of the Bulgarian Orthodox Church, and the pace of economic reform. The MRF was particularly disturbed because the decline in the economy seriously affected the Turkish rural population since the land reforms that were implemented favored former Bulgarian owners, and the state was slow to redistribute property to minorities from the state land fund. MRF leader Ahmed Dogan called for a change of policy; but, when this failed in October 1992, the MRF parliamentary delegation joined with the BSP in a vote of no confidence for the UDF government. This motion was supported by Zhelev, who accused Dimitrov of undermining the presidency and alienating the population.

Prime Minister Dimitrov resigned on October 28, 1992, after losing a vote of no confidence. His cabinet was replaced by an "expert" government headed by the Socialist Lyuben Berov that survived until September 2, 1994. It came under mounting criticism for rampant corruption and ties to clandestine business interests. As a result, it was replaced by a caretaker administration under Reneta Indzhova on October 17, 1994, that was to hold power until early general elections were held.

The BSP returned to power in the elections of December 18, 1994, winning 43.5 percent of the popular vote and 125 parliamentary seats. This time, only five parties were able to cross the 4 percent threshold to gain parliamentary representation, compared to the seven parties that entered parliament after the June 1990 elections. BSP leader Zhan Videnov, known as the hard-liner and antireformer, became the new prime minister.[2] Two allied parties, the Bulgarian Agrarian People's Union "Alexander Stamboliyski" and the Political Club Ecoglasnost, which were on the same list as the BSP in the elections, joined the government coalition. The popular swing toward the BSP was confirmed during local elections in October 1994 when Socialist candidates received 41 percent of the votes and the UDF only 25 percent.

The UDF had suffered substantial losses in these elections, gaining only sixty-nine parliamentary seats. It was largely blamed on the preelection economic downturn and on internal squabbling that made a coherent and determined policy line impossible. Following their defeat, the UDF leadership resigned en masse. In early 1995, Ivan Kostov, a liberal reformer and former professor at Sofia's Higher Institute of Economics, was elected to replace Filip Dimitrov as the Union leader. He moved to better coordinate the UDF, to undercut the independence of its constituent parties and factions, and to improve relations with the MRF and other opposition formations.

During its term in office, the Socialist administration under Videnov's leadership, which took power after the December 1994 elections, was accused of maintaining secret connections with business conglomerates siphoning off state funds for the benefit of the old communist apparatus. Failure to follow through on reform measures also led to a rapid downturn of the economy that seriously affected living standards. Policy differences between reformists and conservatives became insurmountable, and the opposition frequently called for votes of no confidence in the administration.

The slow progress of the BSP during 1995 and 1996 in implementing reforms as well as its mishandling of the economy led to a host of financial, social, and economic problems. These reached crisis proportions by the mid-1990s. Meanwhile, the UDF gradually began to regain its popular support by promoting a pro-reform and pro-Western agenda. The UDF had several splits, but it remained the most credible center-right force in Bulgarian politics throughout the 1990s. It operated as a broad anticommunist movement from its inception, with support drawn mostly from among the young, educated, entrepreneurial, and urban populations.

The year 1996 proved to be a watershed in Bulgaria. The country experienced serious economic difficulties caused by the absence of systematic market reforms, widespread corruption, and even outright theft by government officials. Pressures increased for an early parliamentary ballot that could dislodge the former communists from power. However, the BSP and its coalition partners maintained a secure parliamentary majority despite growing pressures from the major opposition bloc, the UDF. The political scene remained polarized between these two formations. Their ideological differences were evident in all major issues affecting Bulgarian society. The Socialists were determined to maintain the economic status quo and stalled the mass privatization program, leading to an even more serious economic decline. Moreover, the government was opposed to NATO membership and strengthened its relations with Russia, despite criticisms from the opposition.

Rifts were also evident within the Socialist Party between the harder-line members linked to Prime Minister Zhan Videnov and reformist elements critical of government policy. These divisions widened after the assassination of former prime minister Andrey Lukanov at the beginning of October 1996. Lukanov had become an outspoken critic of official resistance to reform. Allegedly, he also possessed information on corruption at the highest levels of government that he reportedly planned to make public.[3] Observers contended that Lukanov himself was deeply involved in corruption, and his killing resembled a gangland assassination.

The presidential elections further undermined the Socialist administration. The UDF candidate Peter Stoyanov gained an overwhelming percentage of votes (44 percent) over the Socialist Ivan Marazov (27 percent) in the first round of voting on October 27, 1996. Stoyanov was elected president in the second-round runoff on November 3, 1996, with 59.7 percent of the vote to Marazov's 40.3 percent.[4] Although the post of president was primarily ceremonial, the result emboldened the opposition to push for a no-confidence vote in the Socialist government.

During 1996, Bulgaria faced a major financial crisis. Its hard-currency reserves plummeted, and there were growing doubts that Sofia could meet its critical foreign debt payments. The government continued to prop up obsolete and uncompetitive state-owned industries. Moreover, the former communist apparatus still controlled and exploited much of the economy through shady "economic groups," where corruption was believed to be rampant. An ambitious mass privatization program remained stalled in parliament because of powerful vested interests. As the financial crisis deepened and the currency collapsed, prices soared dramatically. Bread shortages were reported in various parts of the country, and analysts warned of severe food and fuel shortages during the winter months.

Large sectors of the public were angry about the rapid decline in their living standards and the reports of widespread corruption among government officials. Following several months of protests and public demonstrations, the increasingly isolated Socialist government of Prime Minister Videnov resigned in December 1996. The newly inaugurated President Stoyanov called for early parliamentary elections in April 1997 and appointed the mayor of Sofia, the popular and charismatic reformer Stefan Sofianski, as caretaker prime minister.

The Union of Democratic Forces (UDF) participated in the presidential elections in October–November 1996 and in the April 1997 parliamentary elections as part of a broader coalition, the United Democratic Forces (UDF). Its chief allies in the coalition included the Democratic Party (DP) and the Agrarian Party (AP), which formed the People's Union (PU) alliance. The AP was one of about twenty groups claiming to be the successors of the precommunist Agrarians. Most of them were right-of-center formations.

The UDF coalition won the April 1997 election overwhelmingly with 52 percent of the vote and 137 of 240 parliamentary seats. The BSP only got 22 percent of the vote and 58 seats. Ivan Kostov, the UDF leader, was appointed prime minister. The composition of his cabinet reflected Bulgaria's commitment to intensive economic and political reforms and included pro-Western liberal reformers. The new administration benefited from broad public support even though the impact of the planned economic reforms was painful for workers in state industries.

The key priorities of the UDF-led coalition government were stabilizing the economy, combating crime and corruption, and pursuing Euro-Atlantic integration. The UDF-dominated legislature passed a number of important measures to root out the corruption that had become endemic among state officials and industrial managers. A new law was passed in September 1997 that prohibited members of the former communist apparatus from obtaining high positions in the civil service for a period of five years. Parliament also approved the opening up of secret police files to determine which top officials had collaborated with the communist-era security services and engaged in repressive acts. This move indicated that the authorities favored openness and transparency in government operations. Investigations against large-scale corruption were also initiated since some former Socialist officials were believed to have embezzled millions of dollars from state funds.

The authorities were determined to pursue a radical economic reform program to avert a major financial crisis. In consultation with the World Bank, Sofia launched a far-reaching "stabilization program" that lifted most price controls, pegged the national currency to the German mark, and established a Currency Board to control government spending. As a result, the inflation rate decreased dramatically. Parliament also approved a new budget that cut state spending and reduced the subsidies on unprofitable industries. An extensive privatization program was launched that had an impact on the majority of state-owned enterprises. The possibility for social unrest remained since living standards declined sharply as a result of the government's austerity measures and budgetary discipline.

The new government was also determined to pursue Bulgaria's integration into various Euro-Atlantic institutions. President Stoyanov declared that Bulgaria was seeking membership in NATO and was willing to undertake the necessary reforms of its military structure. The previous Socialist administration had been ambiguous about alliance membership and preferred a policy of neutrality and close relations with Russia. The new pro-NATO policy dismayed Bulgaria's traditional ally, Russia. Relations between Sofia and Moscow, as a result, grew tense. Bulgaria's interior minister also accused Moscow of racketeering because of its manipulation of gas prices and control over Bulgarian energy supplies.

The parliamentary majority held by the UDF ensured that the reform program was not seriously challenged by the Socialist opposition. Stoyanov remained very popular despite the painful austerity program imposed by the UDF authorities. However, the local elections in October 1999 were a setback for the UDF, which only narrowly defeated the Socialists in a majority of Bulgarian municipalities. Growing public frustration with layoffs and state spending cuts resulted in a decreased voter turnout of some 50 percent. However, the UDF retained control of the two major cities, Sofia and Plovdiv. Despite the progress achieved by the UDF in securing macroeconomic stability and fulfilling the criteria for international loans, the living standards of the majority of citizens actually stagnated or fell after the elections, especially among pensioners, rural workers, and blue-collar employees, making the population angry.

The Bulgarian political scene changed dramatically in April 2001 with the return of the exiled King Simeon II. The ex-monarch, who was deposed by the communists after World War II, formed his own political group, styled as the National Movement Simeon II (NMS). This was a center-right organization that drew support away from both the UDF and the opposition Socialists. In the parliamentary elections held on June 17, 2001, the NMS scored a landslide victory, gaining 42.73 percent of the vote and 120 seats in the 240-seat legislature. The UDF finished a distant second with 18.17 percent and 51 seats. Two other parties passed the electoral threshold. The Socialist Party captured 17.14 percent of the vote and 48 seats; the Turkish minority-based MRF garnered 7.45 percent and 21 seats.

Simeon II thus became the first monarch to return to power in postcommunist Central and Eastern Europe, although he made no attempt to re-create the monarchy. His party captured the protest vote of impoverished elements of the Bulgarian population, and his selection of young Western-educated professionals as parliamentarians and ministers increased public support for him and his party. The king himself did not run in the elections and, at first, did not even put himself forward as prime minister. He also denied that there were any plans to restore the monarchy and pointed out that the country had far more pressing issues to contend with, such as unemployment, poverty, and corruption.

Critics charged that the NMS message was too populist and insufficiently specific on economic policies. NMS leaders countered that they would continue with the reform program launched by the UDF while paying more attention to combating corruption, attracting foreign investment, conducting reform of the judicial system, and creating new employment opportunities. Moreover, Simeon underscored his government's commitment to the European Union and NATO integration.

What had become an essentially two-party system was jettisoned by the NMS triumph. However, the victors indicated they were intent on creating a coalition government to achieve broader political consensus and ensure effective government during a difficult reform process. The Bulgarian public seemed to reject the continued polarization of public life by voting for this movement that pledged to unify the nation. The MRF was the first party to offer its cooperation, indicating a valuable opportunity for involving the sizable Turkish population in the governing process. In mid-July 2001, Simeon agreed to assume the post of prime minister and proceeded to form a new cabinet.

The NMS electoral base proved diverse. The party's ministers were a mixture of young bankers with Western experience, older Bulgarian lawyers, and representatives of local business groups. However, the NMS government's failure to meet unrealistic popular expectations led to a progressive drop in support for the government and its programs as well as increasing divisions within the NMS itself. By late 2003, 11 MPs had defected from the NMS's initial parliamentary contingent of 120; 10 of them formed the National Ideal of Unity faction that was to the left of the NMS. The New Time group of 22 MPs on the NMS's right also became largely independent. NMS candidates performed poorly in local elections in October 2003, especially as the movement lacked any significant local structures. Although it declared its intention to transform itself into a political party, the NMS lacked cohesion and was principally based around the personality of its leader.

Following its defeat in the 2001 elections, the UDF disintegrated. In fact, by 2004 the center-right splintered into several rival formations, often with weak organizational structures but with charismatic leaders. Some activists were concerned that this development would exclude them from parliament or enable the Socialists to form a workable governing coalition. The mayor of Sofia and former caretaker prime minister, Stefan Sofianski, broke away from the UDF in late 2001 after failing to persuade his colleagues to form a coalition with the NMS. He founded a separate party, the Union of Free Democrats (UFD). Although the party was small, Sofianski benefited from high ratings on a national level. Ivan Kostov resigned as the UDF's leader and created the Democrats for a Strong Bulgaria (DSB) in May 2004, pulling some supporters away from the UDF. Other center-right groupings included the Bulgarian Agrarian National Union (BANU), the St. George's Day Movement (Gergyovden), and the New Times.[5]

The appointment of Nadezhda Mihailova, the former foreign minister, as UDF caretaker leader, in March 2002, provoked intensive criticism and did not improve the UDF's popularity ratings. The UDF's performance in the local elections in October 2003 was disappointing for the party. Mihailova came under increasing attack from Kostov and other UDF leaders at that time. UDF's public support had dropped even further by the 2005 elections.

In 2005, the Bulgarian electorate followed its pattern of always voting out the ruling coalition. This time it was motivated by disappointment that the NMS had not managed to transform the economy enough to benefit the older and less educated part of the population or achieve its promises to control both corruption and organized crime. Beyond this, the "kingmaker" MRF gained from the emergence of a far-right, anticommunist, and xenophobic party, Union Attack, which ultimately got 8.75 percent of the vote. Its attacks stimulated the MRF voters to go to the polls, allowing the MRF to do far better than had been expected.

Photo 12.1.   Ultranationalist party Union Attack members demonstrate against a loudspeaker at a mosque in Sofia. In Bulgaria's 2005 parliamentary elections, Union Attack received nearly 9 percent of the vote

(Source: Nadya Kotseva/Sofia Photo Agency)

This time, both the UDF and the National Movement Simeon II lost to the Coalition for Bulgaria, which centered upon the Bulgarian Socialist Party, the successor to the Bulgarian Communist Party. Its victory was marginal; with only 34.17 percent of the vote for the BSP and 14.17 percent for the Movement for Rights and Freedoms, the two could not form a majority coalition. The Bulgarian Socialist Party, therefore, had to reach out to the NMS (22.8 percent) to join forces for a three-party center-left coalition. This process was facilitated by the BSP's campaign commitment to continuing the economic reforms and maintaining a centrist posture to keep Bulgaria turned toward the West. The resulting government was peopled by men and women in their thirties and forties with Sergey Stanishev, the thirty-nine-year-old BSP leader, as prime minister. The three deputy prime ministers represented the three coalition partners. Economic issues were given to a former member of the UDF. The minister of European affairs, charged with moving Bulgaria toward its 2007 entry into the European Union, continued on from the NMS movement.

Despite all these political splits, by the early 2000s, Bulgaria had developed a relatively stable democratic system with a functioning market economy. The country had held several free and democratic elections, and the political transition between governing parties had been smooth and trouble free. The policies of all the major political forces had been pro-reform and pro-NATO, and even the postcommunist Socialist Party developed a Western and pro-NATO orientation after losing power in 1997.

Most of the BSP social base consisted of pensioners, peasants, some of the technical intelligentsia, and Bulgarians in ethnically mixed areas who veered toward nationalism. The party itself incorporated a spectrum of political trends, from Marxist dogmatists to social democrats. The more market-oriented social democrats began to prevail in the late 1990s after the party's credibility was undermined by the 1996–1997 economic collapse. Georgi Parvanov, elected BSP leader in 1996, pursued a policy of economic reform, social democracy, and pro-Westernism, including support for NATO membership. His position was buttressed by his victory in the presidential ballot in 2001. A young reformist, Sergey Stanishev, was elected to be his successor as Socialist Party leader in December 2001.

During 2003 and 2004, the BSP increased its popularity largely in reaction to falling public support for the incumbent NMS-led government as a result of hard-hitting reforms. This fact was demonstrated in its performance in the 2003 municipal elections. However, the party also has experienced internal divisions. It has endeavored to consolidate its popularity by broadening its appeal among younger citizens. Most of the BSP's political partners are small, center-left formations with limited public support, including the Bulgarian Social Democratic Party (BSDP) and the United Labor Bloc (ULB). A relatively successful center-left formation in the late 1990s called Euroleft formed as a breakaway group from the BSP. It entered parliament in 1997 but failed to gain seats in 2001 and subsequently disappeared from the political scene.

Photo 12.2.   *Georgi Parvanov was elected president in 2001. In 1996, he was elected head of the Bulgarian Socialist Party, where he pursued a policy of economic reform, social democracy, and a pro-Western foreign policy, including support for NATO membership.*

(Source: Website of the president of the Republic of Bulgaria, www.president.bg)

Bulgaria has come a long way in its transformation process, as demonstrated by its accession into NATO and the EU in 2007. However, economic development, structural reform, judicial effectiveness, and public trust are currently still undermined by official corruption and organized cross-border criminality.[6]

These problems are not unique to Bulgaria but instead affect the entire Balkan region. Criminal networks can bribe officials and undermine the stability of democratic institutions by illicitly financing political parties and election campaigns and buying out media outlets. This possibility constrains public trust in officialdom and breeds disillusionment with the reform program in general. According to independent analysts, anticorruption campaigns have registered some success but have not dealt with the structural weaknesses that breed corruption in various segments of society, especially the bribing of magistrates and other public officials.

Some of the most important developments in 2004 included the passing of several amendments by the Bulgarian parliament aimed at improving transparency and decreasing corruption. The government took steps to implement reforms to insure disciplinary action and the removal from office of magistrates involved in corruption. Other initiatives to fight corruption involved the launching of a government website and a review of high-level bureaucrats.

Civil Society

A host of independent groups appeared in the early 1990s, ranging from environmental movements to consumer organizations and public policy institutes.[7] A new nongovernmental organization (NGO) law was adopted in 2000. It introduced the concept of "public benefit organizations." This legislation created special financial and tax incentives for NGOs because they were seen as complementary to the state in dealing with important social issues. Parliament also formed a special standing committee to promote the development of civil society, the Civil Society Committee. It provides NGOs with an opportunity to publicly present their issues. However, because of the diversity of civil society, not all of their important issues are presented at this forum. To increase its legitimacy, the Civil Society Committee has created its own consultative body, the Public Council, with NGO representatives from different fields of expertise and diverse geographic regions to more effectively promote its agenda in parliament.

In some areas, the NGO-government partnership has developed fruitfully, especially in terms of providing social services at the local level. Often, municipalities contract with NGOs to be independent providers of social services. However, NGOs are currently excluded from other potential areas of cooperation, including health care, since hospitals and other health institutions, by law, cannot be organized as NGOs but only as commercial companies or cooperatives. A draft law is pending in parliament to allow NGOs to perform health activities, following an in-depth study of European Union and U.S. legislation and a broad public discussion with NGOs working in the social sphere.

Economic Transition

By the end of the 1990s, Bulgaria had made steady progress in stabilizing its economy under the center-right government elected in 1997. The administration remained focused on privatizing major state-owned enterprises and proved successful in stabilizing the banking sector and reforming social security, health care, and the pension system. Major economic reforms were implemented largely under the auspices of the International Monetary Fund (IMF). These included price liberalization, reduction of tariffs, a balanced state budget, liquidation of unprofitable companies, privatization, removal of state subsidies, a simple taxation system without preferential treatment for any social sector, and the deregulation of the energy and telecommunications sectors.

The Bulgarian economy was stabilized at the macroeconomic level under the UDF government in the late 1990s when it introduced an effective currency board system to control state spending. When the NMS government came to power in 2001, it maintained the commitment to privatization, economic growth, and attracting foreign investment. The country registered a steady growth in gross domestic product (GDP) in the early 2000s, reaching nearly a 5 percent growth rate in 2002, 4.2 percent in 2003, 5.8 percent in 2004, and 4.3 percent in 2005. Agriculture has been steadily declining in Bulgaria in terms of overall economic growth, from just under 17 percent of gross domestic product in 1999 to under 12 percent in 2003 and 9.3 percent in 2005. The most recent indicators show that the service sector contributed some 58 percent of the GDP and industry about 29 percent. Fruits, livestock, tobacco, vegetables, and wine continue to be among Bulgaria's chief exports, while imports mainly include machinery, equipment, technology, mineral fuels, and processed goods. Bulgaria's national debt continued to climb and stood at $13.7 billion in 2003 and €14.5 billion ($17.5 billion) at the close of 2005, an indication that the economy continued to be at least partially reliant on borrowing from overseas sources. Nevertheless, the government was able to meet its debt repayment requirements on schedule.

During the 1990s, Bulgaria diversified its trade and became less reliant on the former Soviet bloc. Trade with the European Union increased steadily, especially with Italy, Germany, and Greece. For example, Bulgaria's exports to the ten new EU member states increased by 10.5 percent in the first quarter of 2004, while imports from these countries grew 29.4 percent. In its trade with the Commonwealth of Independent States (CIS), Bulgaria's exports dropped slightly; imports from the CIS increased 15 percent. Bulgarian exports overall increased to Russia and all neighboring countries except Turkey. As Bulgaria wanted to join the European Union, it increasingly geared its economy toward compatibility with the European market and sought investments from Western countries.

The rate of foreign direct investment (FDI) steadily increased during the term of the center-right governments after 1997 as Western business felt more confident in Bulgaria's institutional, fiscal, and social stability. Anticorruption measures have been implemented, although Western businesses and the European Union have pressured Sofia to pursue more comprehensive judicial and administrative reform to increase investor confidence. According to data from the Bulgarian National Bank (BNB), between 2000 and 2003 Bulgaria attracted around $3 billion in direct business investment from abroad, which was about half of the total investment attracted for the previous eleven years. In 2003 alone, foreign investment was estimated to be $1.32 billion or 7 percent of the country's GDP. FDI inflows in 2005 reached $3 billion and covered a significant portion of the current-account deficit. Bulgaria is poised to outperform Central and Eastern Europe in terms of FDI-to-GDP ratio, according to several international estimates.

Most of the measures adopted by the NMS government after it came to power in 2001 were aimed at supporting business and, more specifically, buttressing certain business sectors. These measures involved the introduction of tax preferences and concessions in public procurement and increased subsidies for agriculture, tobacco growing, and certain state-owned enterprises. At the same time, in order to maintain fiscal discipline, public spending in 2002 was reduced to 39 percent of GDP, compared to 40 percent in 1998 and 44 percent in 2000. The percentage would rise slightly in 2007 as Bulgaria is due to make its first contribution to the EU budget.[8]

The government's involvement in the economy remains significant. By May 2003, about 53.6 percent of state-owned assets were privatized. The public sector constituted 24 percent of GDP. Since then, the privatization process has accelerated, and a number of large enterprises, including the Bulgarian Telecommunications Company; the tobacco industrial complex, Bulgartabak; seven electric-power distribution companies; and thirty-six water electric-power plants have been earmarked for sale. Even with this shift to private industry, the privatization program is being implemented in three ways: capital market offerings, centralized public auctions, and cash privatization. Among the bigger enterprises offered for sale were the Pleven oil and gas prospecting company; the Energoremont companies for power facility repairs in Ruse, Bobov Dol, Varna, and Sofia; and the Maritsa 3 thermal power plant in Dimitrovgrad.

During 2004, the most significant privatization deals were connected with the Bulgarian Telecommunications Company (BTC) and Bulgartabak. The BTC deal was finalized in June 2004; 65 percent of the assets were sold to the Vienna-registered Viva Ventures for €280 million ($338 million). The Bulgartabak process is still under way, after a controversial deal in 2002 was declared invalid. Since then, the government has committed to sell the tobacco holding's twenty-two daughter companies as separate, self-contained units.

The restitution of land and other assets to property owners or their relatives dispossessed by communist nationalization and collectivization proved complicated. Many of the private holdings acquired by farmers after 1990 were small and required owners to band together in some form of cooperative in order to afford mechanized equipment or irrigation. Compensation notes and vouchers were issued in the restitution process to owners who could not recover their actual property for a variety of reasons. Notes and vouchers started to trade on the Stock Exchange in 2003 and since then have appreciated from 13 to 16 percent of their face value to 22 to 24 percent in early 2004.

Although the Bulgarian economy has been growing in recent years, income distribution remains a serious problem. Several parts of the population have not felt any improvements in their living standards. The most deprived groups are those who live in rural communities, ethnic minorities, and unemployed citizens. Large sectors of the population continue to experience low standards of living, long-term unemployment, and low salaries, while the extent of foreign investment has been limited to other postcommunist states such as Poland or Hungary.[9] The unemployment rate remained high throughout the transition. It stood at 16.3 percent of the total workforce by the end of the 1990s and climbed to 17.6 percent in 2002 before falling to 10 percent in 2005. The reasons are common for most postcommunist states: the closure of old loss-making enterprises, the unstable business environment in a fragile market economy, and the slow development of new businesses, which are mostly small or medium sized. The labor market is also relatively rigid; bureaucratic restraints make hiring and firing very costly. In addition, privatization, enterprise restructuring, and military downsizing have left many people jobless.

In a public opinion poll conducted in January 2004, the National Center for the Survey of Public Opinion (NCSPO) found that people identified unemployment as the most significant issue they wanted handled by the government, followed by corruption and crime.[10] Faced with the challenge of high unemployment statistics, the government implemented various reforms aimed at removing some of the bureaucratic restraints, encouraging labor market flexibility, and funding a variety of retraining programs for job seekers. These reforms proved relatively successful, and the unemployment rate has slowly decreased since early 2004. It stood at around 10 percent by the second quarter of 2005.

In addition to the government reforms, the job market has been improved by steady 4 to 5 percent economic growth over the past few years and the increase in foreign investment. Urban unemployment is drastically lower than in rural areas. In Sofia, the rate in May 2004 stood at 3.44 percent, followed by Burgas and Varna with 3.75 percent and 4.86 percent. In comparison, smaller towns like Turgovishte and Montana suffer from 27.29 percent and 22.87 percent unemployment, respectively. EU regional development funds and various government and private initiatives are intended to remedy the situation.

According to a report by the National Statistics Institute (NSI) released in June 2004, the total average personal income in April 2004 reached 157 leva per month ($96.86), while the average income per household per month totaled 406.47 leva ($250.60). Average personal income has increased steadily in recent years and has kept pace with the inflation rate; salaries and pensions continue to account for the main source of income.

Social Impact

In an attempt to bridge the poverty gap, the government undertook a series of initiatives and social welfare programs. It increased the subsidies for agriculture, tobacco growing, and state-owned enterprises. The ratio of subsidies as a portion of GDP increased from 2.1 percent in 1998 to 2.4 percent in 2002; social and welfare spending increased from 11 percent of GDP in 1998 to 14.6 percent in 2002.[11] However, simultaneously under IMF requirements, Bulgaria needed to balance the state budget. Doing so was difficult without increasing the tax burden on the besieged small and medium enterprises, which make up the majority of the economy. Instead of increasing such taxes, the authorities have tried to broaden the tax base and make tax collection more effective. Although the government has faced difficulties in meeting the IMF's budgetary targets in some years, in 2003 it registered a budgetary surplus. A rise in investment, both foreign and domestic, together with education, pension, and health-care reforms are necessary for the long-term improvement of living standards of the population.

An ongoing problem for Bulgaria, as for several other Central and East European countries, is a steady decline in the population, especially as many of the most economically productive, skilled, and educated younger generation have emigrated to find more lucrative employment in Western Europe and the United States. Officials estimate that approximately 50,000 citizens have emigrated annually since 1995. Bulgaria has also experienced falling birthrates. Out of a population of some 8.5 million in the early 1990s, the total declined to 7.5 million by 2003, when the annual growth rate stood at 0.6 percent. Birthrates have registered a continuous decline. For example, there were 9 births per 1,000 people in 2000, but only 8.4 births per thousand by 2003. Families tend to have fewer children in a competitive market economy. Given these trends, the population of pensioners continued to grow, amounting to over 35 percent of the country's total by the early 2000s.

About 85 percent of Bulgaria's population of approximately 7.2 million is Slavic Bulgarian. The country's three largest minorities are the Turks, about 9 percent of the population, the Romas, estimated at around 4 percent, and the Pomaks, or Slavic Muslims, who make up less than 1 percent of the population. Under the communist regime, during the 1980s, there was a policy of forced assimilation directed primarily at the Turkish people, which led to a mass exodus to neighboring Turkey. Since the collapse of communism, Bulgaria has not suffered through any significant ethnic conflicts. After Todor Zhivkov's ouster, Bulgarian officials made strenuous efforts to improve the country's minority policies and to repair the damage suffered by ethnic Turks during the repressive government campaigns in the 1980s. During Zhivkov's assimilation campaign, for instance, Turks had to "Bulgarize" by changing their names to Slavic ones and to give up many of their national customs. Typically, a Slavic suffix was added to a Muslim name, or an entirely new name could be chosen from a list of acceptable Bulgarian names. Over 300,000 Turks fled the country fearing even more severe repression. Their properties were confiscated by the state or sold at low prices to Bulgarians. About half this number of Turks returned to Bulgaria after the democratic changes, but many faced problems in reclaiming their houses and other possessions.

During the summer of 1989, at the height of the Turkish exodus from Bulgaria to Turkey, the bulk of the Pomak (Slavic Muslim) population opposed efforts at forcible integration, and some sought to emigrate. The Pomaks were ethnic Bulgarians who had converted to Islam during the Ottoman occupation; they numbered about 70,000 people. The authorities proved reluctant to allow them to leave the country and denied passports to people residing in predominantly Pomak regions. These policies resulted in several substantial Pomak protests. Pomak regions suffered steep economic decline with the closure of local industries. Observers feared that economic problems would intensify political tensions. Bulgarian officials warned that unemployment and economic deprivations in regions with ethnically and religiously mixed groups were alarmingly high, and minorities complained about increasing discrimination in employment. After 1989, many Pomaks adopted a Turkish identity or demanded Turkish-language education, viewing it as advantageous to associate with a stronger and more influential minority.

The ethnic repression of the Bulgarian Communist regime was one of the first parts of its past that it jettisoned. In December 1989, the BSP (at the time still under the name Bulgarian Communist Party) renounced forcible assimilation, allowing Muslims the freedom to choose their own names, practice Islam, observe traditional customs, and speak their native language. In January 1990, the National Assembly recommended the adoption of a special statute for minority rights. With Sofia's policy reversal, thousands of ethnic Turks returned to Bulgaria and faced new problems of adjustment. Most had lost their jobs and sold their houses for less than their true value. Upon their return, they demanded appropriate reparations. Ahmed Dogan, the political leader of Bulgaria's Turks, demanded a legal resolution that would restore property to victims of the exodus. Turkish deputies in parliament eventually introduced a law that was adopted in July 1992. It stipulated that all Turks were to be given back their property by April 1993 for the low price at which it had been sold. Those who proved unable to buy back their former homes would be given low-interest-rate credits toward the purchase of alternative housing.[12]

In March 1990, the country's major political forces agreed to pass a "Bulgarian Citizens' Names Law" that allowed all victims of forcible assimilation to return to their old names. New birth certificates were issued, and the process of changing names was simplified from a judicial process to a straightforward administrative measure. The process was complicated and costly only for those Muslims who did not act before December 31, 1990.[13]

The issue of minority rights, particularly language use, education, and access to the mass media, generated some controversy. According to the 1991 constitution, Bulgarian was to be the sole official language. Under the Zhivkov regime, ethnic Turks were forbidden to use their mother tongue officially. The legacy of language discrimination persisted in a variety of forms. For example, parliament was reluctant to implement Turkish-language programs in secondary schools for fear of ultranationalist reactions.[14] In January 1991, a consultative council, including the Bulgarian prime minister, decided that the teaching of Turkish as part of the secondary school curriculum was constitutional. The Bulgarian parliament promised to implement a state-controlled Turkish program in all public schools where there was significant minority enrollment. Bulgaria's nationalist opposition claimed that these programs were unconstitutional, so parliament issued assurances that they would not jeopardize the "unity of the Bulgarian nation."[15]

The new Bulgarian constitution prohibits the creation of political parties based on "ethnic, racial, or religious lines" and organizations "which seek the violent usurpation of power." While these stipulations were intended to protect the Bulgarian state, they were frequently cited in efforts by nationalists to undermine the rights of minorities. Nationalist organizations capitalized on Bulgarian fears of alleged Turkish subversion and applied pressure on government organs to outlaw ethnic-based associations on the grounds that they were politically motivated and therefore "antistate."

Even with the regime's repudiation of the old communist-era ways, the Turks have had a hard time advocating for themselves. The main Turkish organization, the Movement for Rights and Freedoms, was singled out for attention. In August 1991, the Sofia City Court decided that a political party formed by the MRF was unconstitutional because it was ethnically based. As a result, it could not participate in any elections. The MRF, in turn, claimed that it was not an entirely ethnic party and harbored no separatist ambitions. In September 1991, the Supreme Court banned the Rights and Freedoms Party (the political wing of the MRF) from participation in general elections on the grounds that it propounded an exclusivist ethnic and religious platform.[16] Nonetheless, the MRF itself and various Turkish cultural and social organizations were not prohibited from functioning, and the MRF legally competed in the second general elections in October 1991. It gained twenty-four parliamentary seats, with 7.55 percent of the popular vote, making it the third strongest party in Bulgaria and a coalition partner for the UDF.

The MRF also became a coalition partner in the government of the National Movement Simeon II in April 2001. The party represents Bulgaria's 746,000 ethnic Turks, although formally there is a constitutional ban on ethnic-based parties. The MRF is a moderate formation. It resisted the demands of separatists within the Turkish community and concentrates on cultural and religious rights and the defense of Turkish economic interests. Smaller, more radical groups have not captured public support. In the NMS government, the MRF had two ministers and several deputy ministers. Its influence has expanded as it has asserted itself on several fiscal and privatization issues by supporting low taxation and transparency in selling state property. In recent years, the MRF also opened itself to non-Turks to increase its membership and voter base. The party has good relations with the Socialists and is now the pivotal party in their coalition with the NMS. It holds the three ministries that most directly affect the agricultural sector.

In some respects, Macedonian groups have been more persecuted than either Turks or Pomaks. The Bulgarian government, together with most Bulgarian political parties, has refused to accept Macedonians as a legitimate minority. Instead they have defined them as Slavic Bulgarians with the same language and history as the rest of the country. They persist in this policy even though Sofia continues to be criticized by the Council of Europe and some human rights groups for its alleged political discrimination against the Macedonian minority.[17] For instance, according to Bulgarian leaders, a Macedonian minority did not exist in the Pirin region in western Bulgaria despite the activities of local radicals who wanted some form of regional autonomy or even unification with the independent state of Macedonia. An openly Macedonian organization styled as Ilinden was established in the Pirin area and applied for official registration only to be turned down in July 1990 by a district court.

Protests by Ilinden supporters were suppressed, and Bulgaria's Supreme Court ruled that Ilinden violated the unity of the Bulgarian nation. Ilinden's statutes promoted the recognition of a sovereign Macedonian minority, a fact that evidently served as evidence that the organization intended to achieve "a united Macedonian state." Ilinden was ordered to disband, but it persisted in a covert fashion, claiming that the decisions of the Bulgarian courts were in violation of international law.[18] In November 1998, the local court in Blagoevgrad reversed its earlier decision and allowed the registration of a Macedonian organization, OMO Ilinden–Pirin with its headquarters in Blagoevgrad.[19]

Nationalist pro-Macedonian groupings were active in Bulgaria in the 1990s and called for closer social, economic, and political links with Macedonia that they hoped would culminate in eventual reabsorption of this former Yugoslav republic by Bulgaria. At the same time, some autonomist Macedonian organizations became active in western Bulgaria, amid suspicions that they were funded by Belgrade and by some militant groups in the Macedonian Republic to sow discord within Bulgaria and press for the separation of the Pirin region from the Bulgarian state.

While Bulgaria addressed its most pervasive ethnic problems during the 1990s and early 2000s, the treatment and position of the large Roma minority remains a problem. Bulgarian officials claim the country's policies have been guided by the Human Rights Charter and the Bulgarian constitution. Clearly, they were in part a response to the tragic treatment of the Turkish population at the end of the communist era. Just as clearly, the outside pressures and aid by international human rights organizations and the European institutions Bulgaria wished to join have influenced the Bulgarian government to develop more coherent legislation that balances concerns over national security and state integrity with full respect for minority rights and ethnic aspirations.

The social and economic position of the large Roma minority and the persistent prejudice and discrimination against it remain a major problem. The Roma themselves are split on what they want and need. Unlike the Turks in Bulgaria, whose leaders perceived the gravest threat as coming from forcible assimilation, Romani spokesmen have been particularly opposed to the segregation and marginalization of the Roma population. Many representatives of the Roma have opposed separate schooling for Roma children because it results in inferior education, insufficient exposure to the Bulgarian language, and stymied career advancement. On the other side, some Roma leaders are pressing for a revival of Romani culture, education, and ethnic identity, fearing gradual assimilation by either the Bulgarian or Turkish communities. In addition, the law on political parties, which prohibited the registration of organizations established on ethnic or religious criteria worked to the detriment of Romani self-organization. After all, even though the Roma clearly do not represent a threat to Bulgaria's "territorial integrity" and the "unity of the nation," or "incite national, ethnic, and religious hostilities," they are barred from forming electoral associations.[20] But their ethnic traditions and their migrant lifestyles make it impossible for them to fit into other parties, which, at best, do not advocate for Romani interests.

A few populist and nationalist groupings have been formed to advocate for "Bulgarian" national interests. Most recently, a party called the "Attack Coalition" managed to win twenty-one seats in the June 2005 parliamentary elections and tried to mobilize anti-Roma sentiments in Bulgarian society. Their program has been opposed by the majority of parliamentary deputies, and they have no impact on government policy. Most nationalist groups are not significant political players. These have included the Nationwide Committee for the Defense of National Interests (NCDNI) and various parties using the designation of the Internal Macedonian Revolutionary Organization (IMRO). IMRO has campaigned for Bulgarian "national interests" on issues such as the rights of Bulgarian minorities abroad. It has attracted some support in a few regions and posts in local government. IMRO and Gergyovden stood together for parliament in 2001, narrowly missing the 4 percent threshold.

Foreign Policy

After the end of World War II, Bulgaria became part of the Soviet bloc. Its security revolved around membership in the Warsaw Pact, dominated by the Soviet Union, which ensured communist rule in each of the Central and East European countries. Bulgaria was largely isolated from the West and even from its Balkan neighbors, such as Yugoslavs. Its economy was tied into the Moscow-centered Council for Mutual Economic Assistance. During the past fifteen years, after the collapse of the Soviet bloc, Bulgaria has made substantial progress in developing relations with all of its Balkan neighbors. It has also succeeded in joining NATO and became a member of the EU in 2007.

Bulgaria was one of the few countries to recognize Macedonia immediately after the republic declared its independence from Yugoslavia in early 1992. At the same time, the Bulgarian authorities were not willing to recognize the existence of a separate Macedonian nation and refused to recognize the Macedonian ethnic minority within Bulgaria. Sofia and Skopje ended a period of political deadlock concerning Bulgaria's recognition of a separate Macedonian language with the signing of a joint declaration and a number of accords on February 22, 1999. Bulgarian prime minister Ivan Kostov and his Macedonian counterpart Ljubco Georgievski signed an agreement to settle the language dispute and to open the way to normalize relations. The joint declaration, signed in both Bulgarian and Macedonian, stipulated that the two countries would not undertake, incite, or support unfriendly activities against each other, including territorial claims or pressures for ensuring minority rights. Seven other bilateral agreements were signed at the same time to promote cooperation, trade, and investment.

Bulgaria has played a leading role in a number of regional cooperation formats, including the multinational South-Eastern Europe Brigade (SEEBRIG), which promoted military interoperability between participating states, and has hosted its headquarters in the city of Plovdiv. Sofia has participated in the regional security initiative SEDM (South-East Europe Defense Ministerial). Bulgaria has also contributed to democratic developments in Serbia following the ouster of Serbian president Slobodan Milošević in October 2000 by assisting nongovernmental organizations and local authorities in Serbia.

The crisis in Yugoslavia posed one of the most difficult foreign policy problems for postcommunist Bulgaria. Bulgaria's relations with Yugoslavia deteriorated under the Milošević regime in the 1990s, and NATO's war with Serbia worsened these relations. Sofia was outspoken about the culpability of Milošević for Balkan instability and supported NATO in its efforts to restore security to Kosovo despite some opposition to this policy inside the country. Bulgaria suffered from a loss of trade as a result of the Yugoslav wars, primarily because of the United Nations sanctions on Yugoslavia and the blockage of traffic along the Danube River.

On the other hand, Sofia has continued to develop good relations with both

Greece and Turkey by balancing its ties with the two Balkan rivals. The government has also been active in developing regional initiatives to enhance security and cooperation across Balkan borders. In July 1999, finance ministers from Bulgaria, Macedonia, and Albania negotiated a common approach to infrastructure projects in southeastern Europe. At a trilateral meeting of the Bulgarian, Albanian, and Macedonian foreign ministers the same month, Bulgaria proposed that it become the host for an Information Center for Democracy, which would work toward the establishment of civil society in southeastern Europe.

In its relations with Russia, its old "leader," Bulgaria has had to deal with significant pressures from Moscow. Moscow considers the Black Sea states of Bulgaria and Romania strategically significant for several reasons. Traditionally, after all, Russia sought to keep open the Bosporus Strait between the Black Sea and the Mediterranean for its navy and raw materials. This goal was accomplished in the late nineteenth century at the expense of the independence of all the states in the region, including Bulgaria and Serbia, which became Russian quasi-protectorates. Why this continued concern? First, control over these countries is critical to projecting Russian influence throughout southeastern Europe and to keeping the Black Sea itself as a zone of Russian dominance. Second, they can provide the infrastructure and energy linkage between Europe and the Caucasus-Caspian regions. And third, Bulgaria is viewed as a historic ally that can help restore Russia's outreach. Currently, Russian strategic ambitions primarily mean the unhindered flow of Russia's energy supplies westward, not necessarily through the Bosporus. Moscow intends to secure alternative routes across the Balkan Peninsula as a shield against potential blockages in Turkey. This goal places Bulgaria in a strategically important position.

In the early 1990s, politicians in Moscow hoped they could draw Bulgaria into a closer political orbit, through membership in the CIS (Commonwealth of Independent States) or in alliance with the pro-Russian quadrilateral inner core of the Commonwealth (Russia, Belarus, Kazakhstan, Kyrgyzstan). These proposals by President Boris Yeltsin were viewed with dismay in Sofia, leading President Zheliu Zhelev to declare them an "insult to Bulgarian sovereignty and national dignity."[21] Moscow concluded a bilateral treaty with Bulgaria during Yeltsin's visit to Sofia in August 1992. Nevertheless, relations did not develop smoothly, and there was no agreement on the repayment of Russia's debt to Bulgaria, which stood at $38.5 million by the end of 2004. Russia vowed to repay the bulk of this debt in military equipment and other goods. Trade between the two countries declined, largely as a result of disputes over the price of Russian gas sold to Bulgaria. Russia has continued its efforts to use Bulgaria as an outpost for its strategic penetration into the Balkans and has relied on the country's cultural and historic links with Russia and its value location. The disintegration of the Soviet bloc raised the question of how Sofia could protect its independence and promote economic development while maintaining balanced relations with Moscow.[22] Russia continued to display a superiority complex toward the smaller Slavic state and expected Bulgaria to remain part of the post-Soviet political, economic, and security space. Instead, Bulgaria elected a pro-NATO reformist government in April 1997 and its progress toward NATO entry generated political tensions with Moscow.

President Vladimir Putin's policy proved more focused and politically active than

Yeltsin's. It was also less direct. It relied on Russian businesses to sponsor public relations campaigns aimed at redirecting Bulgaria's national strategy toward Moscow. However, Russian leaders were perturbed once again when they "lost" Bulgaria in the parliamentary election victory of the King Simeon movement in June 2001. This result prevented the Bulgarian Socialists from regaining power and potentially redirecting the country toward Moscow, as they did in the mid-1990s. The new Bulgarian authorities made it clear that they would seek NATO membership even after Socialist Georgi Parvanov was elected president in November 2001.

Despite Bulgaria's NATO entry, Putin repeatedly sought to revive the Russian-Bulgarian relationship, which had floundered during the administration of the Union of Democratic Forces. During a visit to Bulgaria in March 2003 to mark Bulgaria's liberation from the Ottoman Empire and the 125th anniversary of the Russo-Turkish war, Putin stressed that Russo-Bulgarian collaboration "will significantly contribute to the development of a prosperous and self-determining Europe."[23]

Bulgaria considers itself a partner and ally of the United States. There is overall agreement on major decisions related to Bulgaria's contribution to NATO and the antiterrorist campaign. As a nonpermanent member of the UN Security Council during the 2002–2003 period, Bulgaria supported U.S. positions more consistently than several of America's Western European NATO allies. The center-right government elected in 2005 backed Washington in the Iraqi war despite verbal criticism by the Socialist president Georgi Parvanov and the Socialist opposition in parliament. Although the Socialists are supportive of NATO membership, some of their leaders have also maintained close links with Russian authorities, who seek to diminish America's global role. These ties have weakened over the past decade, so it is clearly in the U.S. interest to limit Moscow's political interference in Bulgaria's domestic and foreign policy.

To join NATO, Bulgaria has had to transform its military and its weaponry to fit NATO standards and consolidate democratic civilian control over the armed forces. The government has restated its commitment to downsizing and modernizing the armed forces in line with its Defense Plan 2004. Sofia plans to transform the army into a fully professional force by 2010.

There was comprehensive political and public support for Bulgaria's NATO membership despite the country's financial constraints, with a firm commitment to allocate approximately 3 percent of the GDP to defense spending over the coming years. The government calculated that the benefits of NATO membership, in terms of military modernization, downsizing, and international interoperability, outweighed the high costs of maintaining an obsolete military structure. There is a high level of protection of classified information in compliance with NATO standards, and the government has tightened controls over the export of possible dual-use weapons and technologies.

Bulgaria supported U.S. and NATO military operations in both word and deed. It granted airspace for the NATO "Allied Force" operation in Serbia in March–June 1999. Bulgaria played an important role in avoiding a possible crisis in relations between NATO and Russia in June 1999 by denying Russian forces overflight rights during NATO's intervention in Kosovo. Sofia facilitated NATO's actions, when Kosovo-bound forces were allowed through. Bulgaria has also participated in two

NATO-led peacekeeping operations: in SFOR (Stabilization Force) in Bosnia-Herzegovina) and in KFOR (Kosovar Force) in Kosovo.

In the U.S.-led antiterrorist and anti-rogue-states campaign since September 11, Bulgaria has allowed air, land, and sea transit to coalition forces and the temporary deployment of U.S. aircraft for refueling and cargo-lifting purposes in both the Afghanistan and Iraq operations. It has allocated military units to the International Security Assistance Forces (ISAF) in Afghanistan and dispatched an anti–nuclear, biological, and chemical (NBC) unit to Iraq.

Moreover, Bulgaria has consistently supported the U.S. position toward the Iraqi question in the UN Security Council and dispatched a contingent of troops to the country after the American-led military invasion. Although several Bulgarian soldiers have died in Iraq, Sofia has remained steadfast in its involvement in the peace-enforcement coalition. It has also been supportive of plans to construct small U.S. bases on Bulgarian soil that could be valuable for America's strategic access to areas of potential future crises in the Middle East, the Caucasus, and Central Asia.

In April 2005, Bulgaria signed an Accession Treaty with the European Union and became a full member of the EU on January 1, 2007. The government had successfully completed the implementation of all thirty-one chapters of the EU's voluminous *acquis communautaire*, which stipulated the reforms that needed to be enacted in various areas of the economy and administrative structure for Bulgaria to meet EU standards. Brussels also included a clause in the treaty that could have led to a delay in Bulgaria's entry if the remaining reforms in the judicial system and in combating corruption were not implemented.

EU membership itself closed an important chapter in Bulgaria's post–Cold War history, as it signaled that the country had successfully completed its transformation from a communist dictatorship to a capitalist democracy. However, EU entry could also bring some turbulence into Bulgarian-American relations at a time when transatlantic divisions on a number of issues are pronounced. Sofia and other Central and East European capitals will certainly seek to strengthen the transatlantic link within the EU. At the same time, they will be subject to increasing pressures from Brussels and various West European capitals to coordinate their policies with the EU's emerging security and foreign policy even if the latter is sometimes at odds with Washington.

Future Challenges

As Bulgaria integrates into the European Union over the coming years, it will face several new domestic and foreign policy challenges and opportunities. It will take many years for Bulgaria to achieve the economy level of its Western European partners, but EU membership also means access to the union's structural funds, which will help to develop the country's economy. The government will seek to attract greater volumes of investment from Western Europe and to reverse the outflow of the most educated sectors of society.

The European Union itself is undergoing a major transformation as a more integrated international actor. Bulgaria will seek to have more influence in EU decision making, and it will need to achieve a beneficial balance in its relations with Washington and Brussels. Similar to other new democracies in the "new Europe," Bulgaria wants the EU to become a united and effective organization. At the same time, it wants to develop close relations with the United States and maintain a prominent role for the NATO alliance in international security.

For this to happen, though, Bulgaria must move forward in developing its infrastructure and stopping the illegal drug trade that goes though Bulgaria. It must also prepare its economy and legal structures to meet minimal European Union standards. To date, though, Bulgaria has moved forward enough to be a popular place for foreign investment and a trusted partner in Europe. Finally, given the reluctance to expand the European Union to include Turkey, Bulgaria has become the geographic link to this strategically located country. At the same time, the positive role its ethnically Turkish party has played cannot help but weaken the sense of Turkey's exclusion as being simply anti-Muslim.

Suggested Readings

Anguelov, Zlatko. *Communism and the Remorse of an Innocent Victimizer.* College Station: Texas A&M University Press, 2002.

Bell, John D. *The Bulgarian Communist Party from Blagoev to Zhivkov.* Stanford, CA: Hoover Institution Press, 1986.

———. "Democratization and Political Participation in 'Postcommunist' Bulgaria," in *Politics, Power, and the Struggle for Democracy in South-East Europe,* edited by Karen Dawisha and Bruce Parrott, 353–402. Cambridge, UK: Cambridge University Press, 1997.

Brown, J. F. *Bulgaria under Communist Rule.* New York: Praeger, 1970.

Crampton, R. J. *A Short History of Modern Bulgaria.* Cambridge, UK: Cambridge University Press, 1987.

Groueff, Stephane. *Crown of Thorns: The Reign of King Boris III of Bulgaria, 1918–1943.* Lanham, MD: Madison, 1987.

McIntyre, Robert. *Bulgaria: Politics, Economics and Society.* London: Pinter, 1988.

Neuburger, Mary. *The Orient Within: Muslim Minorities and the Negotiation of Nationhood in Modern Bulgaria.* Ithaca, NY: Cornell University Press, 2004.

Simsir, Bilâl N. *The Turks of Bulgaria (1878–1985).* London: Rustem & Brothers, 1988.

Notes

1. For a valuable account of postcommunist Bulgaria, see John D. Bell, "Democratization and Political Participation in 'Postcommunist' Bulgaria," in *Politics, Power, and the Struggle for Democracy in South-East Europe,* ed. Karen Dawisha and Bruce Parrott, 353–402 (Cambridge, UK: Cambridge University Press, 1997).

2. Stefan Krause, "Socialists at the Helm," *Transition* 1, no. 4 (March 1995): 33–36.

3. Ivo Georgiev, "Indecisive Socialist Party Stumbles into Crisis," *Transition* 2, no. 26 (December 1996): 26–28.

4. Stefan Krause, "United Opposition Triumphs in Presidential Elections," *Transition* 2, no. 26 (December 1996): 20–23.

5. For an overview of the center-right, see Dilyana Tsenova, "SDS to Have Golden Moment in 40th Parliament," *24 Chasa* (April 2004).

6. Center for the Study of Democracy, *Corruption, Contraband, and Organized Crime in Southeast Europe* (Sofia, Bulgaria: Center for the Study of Democracy, 2003) and *Corruption Assessment Report, 2003* (Sofia, Bulgaria: Coalition 2000, 2004).

7. For more details, see Luben Panov, "NGOs and the State in Bulgaria: Towards Greater Cooperation," *Social Economy and Law Journal* (Winter 2003–Spring 2004): 42–43

8. For useful economic statistics, see "Economic Structure: Annual Indicators," *The Economist Intelligence Unit*, Country Report Subscription, October 1, 2006; www.seeurope.net/?q = node/1447; and www.novinite.com/view_news.php?id = 71935.

9. For more details, see Institute for Regional and International Studies, *Country Report: Bulgaria, State of Democracy, Roadmap for Reforms, 2001* (Sofia, Bulgaria: Institute for Regional and International Studies, 2002).

10. Results of survey published in *Dnevnik* (Sofia), February 6, 2004.

11. Krassen Stanchev, "Bulgarian Economic Policy Is Not Rightist." A study by the Institute for Market Economics, published in *Capital Weekly*, July 19, 2003.

12. Stephen Ashley, "Migration from Bulgaria," Radio Free Europe/Radio Liberty Research Institute, *Report on Eastern Europe*, December 1, 1989; Stephen Ashley, "Ethnic Unrest during January," RFE/RL, *Report on Eastern Europe* 1, no. 6, February 9, 1990; Kjell Engelbrekt, "The Movement for Rights and Freedoms," RFE/RL, *Report on Eastern Europe* 2, no. 22, May 31, 1991.

13. For a discussion of cultural assimilation and the Name Change Law, see "Minority Problems Persist: Elections Set for June," in *News from Helsinki Watch*, "News from Bulgaria," March 1990. On the new law on names, see "Deep Tensions Continue in Turkish Provinces, Despite Some Human Rights Improvements, in *News from Helsinki Watch*, "News from Bulgaria," August 1990.

14. Goran Ahren, "Helsinki Committee on Turkish Bulgarians: Continued Political Oppression," *Dagens Nyheter* (Stockholm), December 24, 1989, *JPRS-EER-90-009*, January 24, 1990.

15. Mitko Krumov, "New Deputies Yuriy Borisov and Vasil Kostov Replace Dobri Dzhurov and Georgi Velichkov Who Resigned," *Duma* (Sofia), January 10, 1991, *FBIS-EEU-91-013*, January 18, 1991. For a discussion of the major strikes in Kardzhali see Bulgarian News Agency (BTA), February 26, 1991, *FBIS-EEU-91-038*, February 26, 1991.

16. "Second Yilmaz Letter Is Unprecedented and Greatly Alarms Nationwide Committee of Defense of National Interests," *Duma* (Sofia), August 30, 1991, *FBIS-EEU-91-172*, September 5, 1991; Kjell Engelbrekt, "The Movement for Rights and Freedoms to Compete in Elections," RFE/RL, *Report on Eastern Europe* 2, no. 91 (October 4, 1991).

17. See the January 2004 report on Bulgaria on the website of the Council of Europe's Committee against Racism and Intolerance, www.coe.int.

18. See Duncan M. Perry, "The Macedonian Question Revitalized," RFE/RL, *Report on Eastern Europe* 1, no. 24, August 24, 1990; Evgeni Gavrilov, *Duma* (Sofia), November 14, 1990, *FBIS-EEU-90-223*, November 19, 1990; Bulgarian News Agency (BTA), September 23, 1991, *FBIS-EEU-91-185*, September 24, 1991.

19. *State Gazette* (Sofia), February 23, 1999, and March 14, 1999; and Bulgarian News Agency (BTA), November 3, 1998.

20. See Helsinki Watch, *Destroying Ethnic Identity: The Gypsies of Bulgaria* (New York: Human Rights Watch, 1991).

21. President Zhelev quoted in Bulgarian News Agency (BTA) April 2, 1996. Bulgaria's Foreign Ministry called Yeltsin's "invitation" to Bulgaria "a cause for concern." Leaders of the opposition UDF claimed that Russia's ultimate aim is the restoration of the Soviet Union in which Bulgaria would be a constituent element. In 1963, Bulgaria's Communist Party leader had offered to make Bulgaria the sixteenth republic of the USSR; the Kremlin seemed to believe that such offers were still valid. The incident mobilized the pro-NATO opposition against the Russian-oriented Socialist government led by Prime Minister Zhan Videnov and backfired against Moscow's policy.

22. Ognyan Minchev, "Bulgaria and Russia," in *Bulgaria for NATO* (Sofia, Bulgaria: Institute for Regional and International Studies, 2002). Even though Bulgarian-Russian friendship has a long pedigree, relations have also been marked by conflicts, as Russia's tsars demanded that the newly

liberated Bulgarian state in the late nineteenth century demonstrate "total economic and political dependence on Russia" (p. 120).

23. "Putin Expresses Aspirations for Russia and Bulgaria Together in a Self-Determining Europe," Mediapool.bg (March 3, 2003). Mediapool is an influential electronic news portal in Bulgaria.

CHAPTER 13

Former Yugoslavia and Its Successors

Mark Baskin and Paula Pickering

It is impossible to compress the story of the Socialist Federative Republic of Yugoslavia (SFRY) and its successor states into a neat and simple story of transition. Its succession twists and turns through pathways of war, reconstruction, and reconstitution into national states—a process not yet completed. In this contentious tale, observers sharply differ on the sources of dissolution, the causes of war, and the current state and future prospects of the post-Yugoslav governments.[1]

The tragedies that occurred are all the more painful since it seemed, in 1990, that the SFRY was on the verge of joining the European Community. It had long ago done away with many of the overtly repressive trappings of Central and East European socialism. Since the 1950s, Yugoslav leaders had been experimenting with liberalizing economic and political reforms, and Yugoslavia had been broadly integrated into international economic, political, and cultural developments. Yugoslavia's socialist regime was more open, transparent, and accepting of non-Marxist ideologies than any in Central and Eastern Europe. And since the 1960s, its citizens had massively enjoyed the opportunities to travel, study, and work abroad.[2] Literature and culture forbidden in the east, from George Orwell's *1984* to punk rock and neoliberal economics, were long prominent in Yugoslav stores.

By 1989, Yugoslav efforts to find a "third way" between Western capitalism and Soviet socialism had clearly run into a dead end. A burgeoning civil society, a business-oriented prime minister, and the popular Slovenian cry, *"Europa Zdaj!"* or "Europe Now!" appeared to move Yugoslavia toward an evolving Europe. But Yugoslavia's other republics and provinces did not share Slovenia's relatively smooth ascension to the EU and have remained outside the "European Home."

This chapter will explore the causes and consequences of the SFRY's demise. It will suggest that the agenda for the dissolution of multinational Yugoslavia was set by a series of incomplete economic and political reforms that left Yugoslavia without the institutional resilience to overcome increasing interregional differences. The national revivals that unevenly swept across Yugoslavia in the 1980s enabled the rise of the uniquely talented leader Slobodan Milošević, who advanced Serbian interests in the name of preserving Yugoslavia. The "Wars of Yugoslav Succession" were the outcome of unequal bargaining in the absence of compelling central authority, the failure of ambitious republican leaders to find a basis for future common existence, and the initial disinterest of Europe and the United States. Yugoslavia's violent dissolution led to a delayed international intervention, settlements that have helped to define the newly independent states, the prominence of international agencies in domestic developments, and transitions that have lasted far longer than had been foreseen in the early 1990s.

Precommunist History

The extraordinarily heterogeneous cultural, social, and political precommunist traditions in the lands of former Yugoslavia stem from their location amid the divisions in Europe between the eastern and western Roman empires; eastern Orthodoxy, western Catholicism, and Islam; the Ottoman Empire, the Republic of Venice, and the Hapsburg Monarchy; and the Warsaw Pact and the North Atlantic Treaty Organization (NATO).[3] Nineteenth-century national movements appeared on the heels of wars, invasions, population movements, shifting boundaries, and religious conversion.

Many current national leaders have focused intently on the historical antecedents to the post-Yugoslav, national states. The medieval Croatian, Serbian, and Bosnian states were relatively brief preludes to their integration into larger, imperial state structures. An agreement with the Hungarian throne in 1102 led to a separate but unequal existence for Croatia within the Hungarian Kingdom until 1918, which put them under the Hapsburg Monarchy after 1526. The battle on a Kosovo field in 1389 between Serbian and Ottoman forces led to the ultimate end of medieval Serbia in 1459. By the time that Serbian power again controlled this area in the early part of the twentieth century, Serbs were greatly outnumbered by Albanians in Kosovo. The Ottoman forces conquered independent Bosnia in 1463 and Herzegovina in 1483. The Slovenes lost their political independence in the eighth century and were incorporated into the Hapsburg Monarchy by the fourteenth century. Macedonia did not enjoy independence during the medieval era and fell under Byzantine, Bulgarian, Ottoman, and Serbian rule in the period before World War I. The departure of the Serbian state northward after 1389 enabled the development of a Montenegrin state, where the bishops of the Orthodox Church became rulers after 1516.

The legacies of imperial rule continue to be felt in these lands. The Ottomans imposed a centrally controlled regime of land tenure, tax collection, and native religious rights that gave extensive autonomy to religious communities. Large-scale conversions to Islam took place only among Bosnians and Albanians, but the forced conversion of young boys to Islam for the Ottoman officer corps remains a potent anti-Islamic symbol. The Ottomans twice advanced to the gates of Vienna and the Hapsburg court and administration: in 1529 and 1682. In response to the Ottoman threats, the Hapsburgs established a military border populated largely by Orthodox Serbs on the Croatian side of Bosnia-Herzegovina. The aspirations of the Hapsburg Monarchy in the eighteenth century to impose enlightened absolutism and bureaucratic uniformity did not succeed in providing a unifying link within the empire—

especially as the Croatian lands did not constitute a single administrative entity in the pre-Yugoslav period. Similarly, Ottoman efforts at internal reform throughout the nineteenth century did not provide a basis for reviving the authority of the center in these far-flung parts of the empire. By the eve of World War I the Austro-Hungarian Dual Monarchy was neither a vital nor an authoritative state, and in the first Balkan war in 1912–1913, the Ottoman Empire had been pushed out of the Balkans by an alliance consisting of Bulgaria, Greece, Serbia, and Montenegro.

This imperial decline was made possible by the spread of ideas of the enlightenment and the romantic movements and Napoleonic revolution of the early nineteenth century, which led to the emergence of modern national movements among the peoples of former Yugoslavia that were rooted in the language and culture of the common people. As discussed below, contending notions of the Yugoslav state combined with the uneven appearance of national movements in the nineteenth century. Serbia was the first state to emerge in a series of uprisings against the Ottomans that began in 1804 and that culminated in formal independence at the Congress of Berlin in 1878. It gained experience in administration, in exercising influence in the region, and in its difficult relations with the government of the Hapsburg Dual Monarchy. The small and poor state of Montenegro also gained international recognition in 1878 in Berlin as a separate government under Russian tutelage. Independence movements in the different parts of Croatia and Slovenia were constrained by their relative weakness within the Hapsburg state and by a shifting set of goals that were rooted in some form of pan-south-Slav federalism, liberalism, integral nationalism, and an enhanced position within the Hapsburg Monarchy. At the Congress of Berlin, the Dual Monarchy took over the administration of Bosnia and, to great Serbian protest, formally annexed it in 1908. In the first Balkan war, the Ottomans lost both Kosovo to Serbia and Macedonia to a larger coalition. But the second Balkan war saw Serbia annex a great deal of Macedonia from Bulgaria. The end of World War I created conditions for the formation of a common state for Serbs, Croats, Slovenes, Bosnian Muslims, and Montenegrins, but that would also house significant numbers of Albanians, Hungarians, Turks, Italians, and others, as well.

The decline of the Ottomans and the Hapsburgs set an agenda that did not favor the emergence of democratic institutions following World War I because of many unanswered questions in economic development, administration, cultural policy, and foreign policy. In his magisterial work, *The Yugoslav National Question*, Ivo Banac suggests, "The national question permeated every aspect of Yugoslavia's public life after 1918. It was reflected in the internal, external, social, economic, and even cultural affairs. It was solved by democrats and autocrats, kings and Communists. It was solved by day and unsolved by night. Some days were particularly bright for building, some nights particularly dark for destroying. One horn of the dilemma was that a single solution could not satisfy all sides. Was the other that a firm citadel could be maintained only by human sacrifice?"[4]

The Communist Experience

The felicitous title of Dennison Rusinow's superb *The Yugoslav Experiment* effectively captures socialist Yugoslavia's policy of permanent political improvisation.[5]

The Communist-led Partisans' seizure of power during World War II, with minimal assistance from the Soviet Union, began a search for a governing formula that would combine an efficient and equitable strategy of economic development with an approach to governance balanced between the leadership of a Leninist party and the broad inclusion of mass organizations. The Communists' capacity to mobilize mass and external support during World War II provided the new regime, led by Josip Broz Tito, with the resilience that was absent in other Central and East European socialist regimes to resist the domination of their internal political and policy agendas by the Soviet Union. This toughness was essential for the experiments in governance that were conducted in an unusual international environment, and that addressed economic decision making and organization, and the evolution of national communities within the Yugoslav federation.

In the first element of the experiment, socialist Yugoslavia found itself in a unique international environment in which it was a member neither of the Warsaw Treaty Organization nor NATO, where it was viewed as a communist country by the West and as a capitalist country by the Soviet bloc. Stalin's expulsion of Yugoslavia from the Communist Information Bureau, or Cominform, in 1948 provided a context to search for a legitimizing formula that would leave Yugoslavia both independent and socialist.[6] Military spending increased from the necessity to maintain a Yugoslav National Army (JNA) that could deter attack. While the top officer corps was ethnically balanced, the middle and noncommissioned officer corps was dominated by Serbs and Montenegrins—a matter of great significance, as most Yugoslav military assets fell to the Serbs during the wars of succession in the 1990s.

By the early 1960s, the Yugoslav government under Tito had adopted an "open" foreign policy between the two Cold War blocs and the newly independent countries in the developing world in which it came to play a prominent role in the movement of nonaligned countries.[7] Tito's Yugoslavia actively pursued an independent political course within the United Nations. It simultaneously traded extensively with communist-bloc countries and developed relations with multilateral financial institutions, such as the International Monetary Fund. It opened up its borders so that by the early 1970s, over a million Yugoslav citizens lived and worked abroad. From the early 1950s, in other words, an increasingly diverse set of foreign relationships helped maintain Yugoslav independence and came to shape the character of internal policy choices.[8] However, by the fall of the Berlin Wall in 1989, Yugoslavia had ceased to represent a daring experiment that commanded Western and Soviet support.

The second element of the experiment lay in a strategy of economic development that was socialist but non-Soviet. Abandoning central planning early on, Yugoslav leaders adopted "self-management" decision making within firms as the regime's central economic symbol. From the early 1950s onward, Yugoslav leaders engaged in a series of partial economic reforms that fell short of creating a market economy similar to those in Europe or North America. These reforms included the de-collectivization of agriculture; the decentralization of economic decision making; the establishment of workers' councils in firms; liberalization of foreign trade; banking reforms; the creation of a Fund for the Development of Underdeveloped Regions; efforts to simulate or create financial, commodity, and labor markets; efforts to remove the party from everyday decision making in the economy; the redesign of the economy in the mid-

1970s into a "contractual economy"; and a policy of liberalizing "shock therapy" in 1990.[9]

The reforms did not work very well over the medium term, mainly because they neither fully embraced the implications of liberalizing reforms that would lead to significant privatization of economic assets nor ensured that the economy would remain "socialist." They did not provide stable economic growth based on a productive agriculture. Instead of narrowing intra-Yugoslav inequality, they were associated with increased economic inequality across and within republics. They appeared to increase Yugoslav dependence on the international economy and led to significantly increasing unemployment and the wholesale departure of labor to jobs in the West. They also continued political meddling in production. By 1990, Yugoslav debt to Western banks had grown to $20 billion. Unemployment reached 15.9 percent and, in the least developed region, Kosovo, was 38.4 percent.[10] At one point in 1989, inflation had grown to 1,750 percent. In the best of political times the Yugoslav government might have overcome these difficulties, but by 1991 it was the worst of times.

The final element of the experiment lay in political reforms that were embodied in large-scale efforts to define new constitutional orders in 1946, 1954, 1963, and 1974. Among other things, these constitutions attempted to devolve power away from the Communist Party of Yugoslavia (CPY) to mass organizations that were more sensitive to diverse popular aspirations. Signs of this devolution included renaming the party the League of Communists of Yugoslavia (LCY) at its sixth congress in 1952, taking the party out of a command position in the mid-1960s by investing more authority in the regional organizations, and purging the hard-line secret police. The LCY leadership attempted to enhance the authority of nonparty governmental and administrative institutions, but stopped short of divorcing the party from power. The purges of liberal party leaders throughout Yugoslavia in the early 1970s led to the re-Leninization of party organizations, which became incubators of the fractious nationalism they were meant to eliminate. This party-led regionalism provided the context for the end of the Yugoslav experiment in brotherhood and unity, the dissolution of the state, and war.

The idea of "brotherhood and unity" was central to the Yugoslav experiment. Yugoslavia was an "unmelted pot" of Muslims, Eastern Orthodox, and Catholics; Serbs, Croats, Slovenes, Bosniacs,[11] Macedonians, and Montenegrins; Albanians, Hungarians, Italians, Slovaks, Czechs, Turks, and others. These peoples had acquired their modern national consciousness within the Hapsburg Monarchy and the Ottoman Empire. Their modern national movements began at different times throughout the nineteenth century and with different degrees of success. The idea of creating some sort of state of South Slavs, or Yugoslavia, was also in the mix. But even the nineteenth century saw tensions between the idea of creating an overarching, primordial common identity and that in which a Yugoslav identity would merely bind together national groups sharing a common political space. This tension characterized political debates between centralizing "unitarists" and decentralizing "federalists" in both royalist and socialist Yugoslavia. And there was nothing inevitable about the creation of the "Kingdom of Serbs, Croats, and Slovenes" at the end of World War I, an entity that became known as Yugoslavia in 1929, whose Serbian royal dictatorship tried to push a common cultural Yugoslav identity that was in practice Serb-dominated. Serb-Croat political conflicts wracked the country right up until its dismemberment by the Nazis in 1941 into puppet regimes in Slovenia, Croatia, and Serbia, and the annexation of Kosovo, Macedonia, and parts of Croatia by neighboring countries with their own claims to these regions. The Communist-led Partisans won the civil war that took place during World War II in good measure because the symbol of Yugoslav "brotherhood and unity" was a supranational appeal to reason and survival.

To recognize and balance national interests, the SFRY was a federation of six republics: Serbia, Croatia, Montenegro, Slovenia, Macedonia, and Bosnia-Herzegovina. Bosnia-Herzegovina, the only republic without a titular nation, was a "community of Moslems, Croats, and Serbs." There were two autonomous provinces within Serbia: Vojvodina, which was home to large numbers of Hungarians, and Kosovo, which had been predominantly Albanian since the end of the World War II.[12] Croatia's population was 12 percent Serb in 1991. Many Serbs in Croatia lived in compact settlements in areas that comprised the Hapsburg military border from the sixteenth century and others in large urban settlements. The Serbs were the SFRY's most dispersed nationality; more Serbs lived outside of their nominal republic than any other ethnic group.

Successive constitutions defined a series of increasingly complex power-sharing arrangements between federal, republican, and regional governments that came to resemble consociational institutions theorized to build stable democracies in culturally plural societies.[13] By 1974, the pattern of representation in all federal-level decision-making bodies was carefully allotted to individuals from each republic (with attention paid to the intrarepublican nationality composition of such delegations), in order to insure the formal picture of federal multinationalism. There was an intricate pattern of interrepublican decision making, wherein republican and provincial representatives in state and government institutions held a virtual veto over each stage of federal decision making.[14] All federal-level institutions were guided by the ethnic key. The presidency, parliamentary delegations, and cabinets included representatives of all republics and autonomous provinces. Under the 1974 constitution, the republics became the SFRY's most significant centers of power. But decentralization of politics left the LCY as "the one ring to bind them all," in Rusinow's phrase, despite the party's loss of political coherence.

Tito also tried to ensure that the country would remain unified by establishing a collective state presidency in 1971. Thus, each republic seat had a member to serve as part of the collective head of state. The president of the state presidency, which Tito held until his death, rotated among the republics and provinces each May according to a predetermined arrangement.

With Tito's death in 1980, the fragility of this house of cards became increasingly apparent. As the winds of change began sweeping through socialist Europe, official Yugoslav politics remained committed to the methods of economic and political half reforms of the earlier socialist era. The bankruptcy of politics-as-usual could be seen in the suppression of demonstrations calling for republican status in Kosovo, in trumped-up show trials of Bosnian Muslims for ostensibly advocating an Islamic republic, and in a series of other public "political cases" that were meant to demonstrate the strength of the political center against disloyal enemies. But the absence of an authoritative political center was exposed in the failure of successive federal governments to identify an effective strategy of economic development and in the failure of republican oligarchs to agree on amendments to the 1974 constitution. The loss of a central vision was clearest in the failure of the Yugoslav presidency to act with any independent authority and the minor role relegated to Federal Prime Minister Markovic in the political drama of succession. The torch had passed to republican leaders who were unable to reach agreement on a constructive course forward.

Most ominously, this political impasse led to the rise of Slobodan Milošević in Serbian politics in a 1987 coup against his close friend and political patron, Ivan Stambolic. Milošević revolutionized Yugoslav politics as the first party leader to depart from a convoluted and ideological public language to simple and direct rhetoric that was comprehensible to the broad masses. He explicitly integrated Serbian national goals into an "antibureaucratic revolution" that was supposed to preserve socialist Yugoslavia. Aside from taking over the Serbian media, Milošević employed sophisticated techniques of mass mobilization to make credible threats against the socialist governments in Slovenia and Croatia after he had put his loyal minions in power in Kosovo, Vojvodina, and Montenegro, thereby giving him political control over four of the eight Yugoslav political units. This tactic made him the single most influential political force in late socialist Yugoslavia, but he lacked both Tito's goal of inclusion and his command of the levers of power. Still, he was the commanding force in Serbian politics until his electoral defeat in autumn 2000 and arrest by the International Criminal Tribunal for the Former Yugoslavia—a decade after the first window of democratic transition closed.[15]

The silver lining to this political cloud might have been the opening up of civil society throughout Yugoslavia in the middle and late 1980s. This process involved publicly confronting previously suppressed conflicts and official excesses, and beginning multiple processes of reconciliation. In theory, a new democratic politics would be inclusive and strive to integrate all citizens and groups into a series of nested political communities that began locally and grew outwards to the federation. In practice, it opened a Pandora's box and sometimes resulted in such inflammatory programs as the Serbian Academy of Sciences' "Memorandum" of 1986 that gave a cogent critique of economic mismanagement alongside a nationalist program aimed at protecting Serbs throughout Yugoslavia. The increasing openness of Yugoslav society meant that former officials and political prisoners could gather at meetings of UJDI—the Association of Yugoslav Democratic Initiative—to search for common ground for the future. It meant the return of *gastarbeiteri*, or Yugoslav guest workers who had been working abroad, and the entry of political émigrés into a rapidly evolving political mainstream. It meant coming to terms with the transnational character of ethno-political communities in the 1980s and 1990s—whether in the selection of an American citizen, Milan Panic, as the Serbian prime minister in 1992, the prominent role played by overseas Croats in Croatian domestic politics in the 1990s, or in the substantial support of Albanian émigré communities for political and military action in Kosovo.

Greater pluralism combined with mounting economic problems to deepen the antagonism between political and economic development strategies pursued in the more economically developed regions (Slovenia and Croatia) and the less economically developed regions.[16] Slovenian and Croatian elites favored a looser, asymmetrical federation together with liberal political and economic reforms. Serbian leaders countered with reforms calling for a recentralization of the state and political system together with a streamlined self-management system. Each of these plans suited the self-interest of the regionally rooted elites who proposed it. Forces for compromise—federal prime minister Ante Markovic and leaders of the less developed and ethnically diverse republics of Bosnia and Macedonia—were easily drowned out. Already disgruntled over having to foot what they considered more than their fair share of the bill for central government and economic development in poorer regions of the country, leaders in Slovenia and Croatia in the late 1980s balked when asked to contribute to Serbia's strong-arm tactics over restive Kosovo. Fearing they would lose the battle with Belgrade over reform of Yugoslavia, the Slovenian party elite in 1989 saw the benefit of "giving in" to the increasing demands of republic youth and intellectuals for pluralism and sovereignty. The pursuit of liberal reform was more contentious in Croatia, where 12 percent of the population was Serb and reformers only gained the upper hand at the end of 1989.

By 1989, the pressure for comprehensive change was great. The federal LCY ceased to exist in January 1990 when the Croat and Slovene delegations walked out of the Fourteenth Extraordinary Congress of the LCY after the Serbian bloc rejected all Slovene motions—e.g., to confederalize the party, to ban use of torture, to provide clearer guarantees of the right of dissociation—without any meaningful discussion. Most former republican LCY organizations soon morphed into Social Democratic Parties (SDPs).[17] This development did not auger a happy outcome to the intense, interrepublican political bargaining about Yugoslavia's future architecture. For the first time since World War II, nationalist ideas were viewed as legitimate, and nationalist "enemies" of socialism became centrally important actors in Yugoslav politics. By 1991, few political or institutional constraints were commonly accepted throughout Yugoslavia. There was also a sense that the window of political opportunity would not remain open long. The Serbian government viewed itself as the protector of Serbs throughout former Yugoslavia, and Croatian president Franjo Tudjman would soon make the error to try to extend Croatia into Bosnia.

State Formation and War

The Yugoslav government barely paused at the precipice of dissolution and war in 1990 and 1991. As described in more detail below, elections throughout the federation in 1990 selected republican leaderships who were accountable to ethnically based republican constituencies. These leaders failed to reach consensus on the shape of a democratic Yugoslav federation. Slovenian and Croatian leaders held well-orchestrated referenda on independence and began transforming their reserve forces into armies. European mediators failed to prevent a war at this "hour of Europe," and the U.S. government was not sufficiently interested at this early moment to act.[18] Five interconnected armed conflicts took place that still cast long shadows on developments in the successor states. It has been difficult to establish precise figures, but estimates of people killed for the entire conflict range from 200,000 to 300,000 people. Over 4.5 million people were displaced at some point in the conflicts. As of the end of 2002, the United

Nations High Commissioner for Refugees estimated that over a million refugees and internally displaced persons (IDPs) were still seeking durable solutions by returning home.[19]

SLOVENIA

The Slovene government declared independence on June 25, 1991, following careful preparations for defense that effectively stymied an ill-prepared JNA (Yugoslav People's Army) offensive. By June 30, Serbian leaders ordered the JNA to prepare to abandon Slovenia. There were eight military and five civilian deaths among the Slovenes, and thirty-nine members of the JNA died. Slovenian independence was formally acknowledged on July 18.[20]

CROATIA

The Croatian government declared independence on June 26, 1991. Following its initially artful invitation to the leader of the Serb Democratic Party to become a vice president in the Croatian government in spring 1990, the Tudjman government awkwardly began firing Serb administrators and police throughout Croatia in the name of achieving ethnic balance in official employment. Armed conflict began in 1990 with a series of skirmishes and the Serbs' consolidation of control in the illegally constituted Serb Autonomous Regions with the aid of JNA officers and arms by mid-March 1991. Croatian Serbs largely boycotted the Croatian referendum on independence. The war featured sieges of Croatia's Danubian city of Vukovar and the Adriatic city of Dubrovnik. Former U.S. secretary of state and United Nations negotiator Cyrus Vance devised a plan that allowed 13,500 UN troops to deploy to oversee the reintegration of the one-third of the republic's territory controlled by Serbs into Croatia.[21] An estimated 20,000 people died during the war. Despite European Community (EC) concerns over the Croatian government's treatment of its Serb minority, Germany recognized Croatia's independence in early 1992; the United States and other European governments soon followed.

International negotiators from the UN, the EC, the United States, and Russia presided over three years of inconclusive negotiations between the Croatian government and rebel Serbs, who repeatedly refused to begin talks concerning the reintegration of Serb-held territory into Croatia in accordance with the Vance Plan. The Croatian government launched two offensives to regain control of most Serb-held territory in May and August 1995, after which approximately 300,000 Serbs fled Croatia.[22] As part of the larger process of ending the war in Bosnia-Herzegovina, UNTAES (UN Transitional Administration in Eastern Slavonia) mediated the formal return of territory by early 1998. The Organization for Security and Cooperation in Europe (OSCE) has remained to monitor aspects of policing, media, and return of refugees. The Croatian government's reassertion of control over its entire territory by 1998 was a turning point that removed the issue of Serb occupation; allowed for the rise of issues of corruption, abuse of power, and economic development; and set the stage for a second wave of democratization.

BOSNIA-HERZEGOVINA

By autumn 1991, a delicately balanced coalition government among Muslim, Serb, and Croat parties broke down with disputes over Bosnia's relationship to rump Yugoslavia and the departure of the Serb Democratic Party delegation, led by Radovan Karadžić, and the formation of multiple Serb Autonomous Regions with JNA support. Croatian president Tudjman had already discussed the partition of Bosnia-Herzegovina with Serbian president Slobodan Milošević by March 1991, in an initiative that would betray Croatia's image as a victim of aggression, strengthen the hand of radically nationalist Croats in Herzegovina, and establish the "territorial integrity of the Croat nation in its historic and natural borders" in a way that would expand the Tudjman government's influence in Bosnia.[23]

The Bosnian government's declaration of independence was recognized by several Western governments on April 6, 1992. Initial Serb campaigns in 1992 rapidly led to the capture of about 60 percent of Bosnia's territory, gains that remained basically intact until the fighting ended in autumn 1995. In an attempt to homogenize Bosnia's ethnically complex social geography in order to control territory, the Serb military engaged in ethnic cleansing[24] and created prison camps. The radical Croatian Defense Council (HVO) subsequently launched offensives in Herzegovina and central Bosnia. Radicalized by foreign Muslim volunteers, a Muslim brigade in central Bosnia also committed crimes, while both Serb and Croat forces destroyed Islamic cultural monuments.[25] The war generated 2.5 million refugees and internally displaced persons.

The international community proved to be ineffective at ending the war. The United Nations Security Council passed over 100 normative acts that established an arms embargo that de facto favored the well-armed Bosnian Serb Army against the poorly equipped Army of the Republic of Bosnia-Herzegovina, created six poorly defended "safe areas" for civilians, and addressed daily crises in the provision of humanitarian assistance and protection of civilians. Concurrently, diplomatic negotiators from the EC, UN, United States, and others drafted a series of peace plans, but took few steps to compel the parties to reach agreement and did not intervene in support of the elected Bosnian government. The UN Security Council deployed 26,000 lightly armed troops in the UN Protection Force (UNPROFOR) scattered throughout Bosnia-Herzegovina during the fighting in support of humanitarian efforts. But these troops were not in a position to compel compliance with the UN mandate and were, in effect, at the mercy of the strongest party on the ground—the Bosnian Serb Army. International negotiators succeeded in compelling Croat forces in Herzegovina and the Bosnian government to cooperate against Serb forces by forming a federation in early 1994. By mid-1995, Serb forces became increasingly assertive, culminating in their conquest of Srebrenica in the largest single post–World War II European massacre. Immediately afterward, NATO air intervention and a Bosniac-Croat offensive ended the fighting and led to U.S.-led negotiations in Dayton, Ohio, in November 1995. Most estimates hold that between 200,000 and 300,000 people died in the conflict.

The U.S.-led negotiations in Dayton resulted in peace accords that created a Bosnia that largely recognized the "facts" created on the ground by the war. Dayton Bosnia consists of an unwieldy configuration of two entities: Republika Srpska (RS) (49 percent) and the Bosniac-Croat Federation (51 percent), each with its own police and army. The RS is relatively centralized, while the Federation is composed of ten cantons with substantial autonomy. Two cantons are explicitly mixed, three are dominated by Croats, and five are dominated by Bosniacs. A large NATO military implementation force and complex civilian intervention began in early 1996, and its work is continued by a force led by the European Union. The High Representative oversees efforts to implement the Dayton Peace Accords by the United Nations, the European Union, the OSCE, the World Bank, and a host of nongovernmental organizations. The High Representative won extraordinary powers at a meeting of the Peace Implementation Committee in Bonn in December 1997, which enables him to override Bosnian institutions to pass legislation and remove domestic officials from office.[26]

KOSOVO

Kosovo has long been an area of discord between Serbs and Albanians. It served both as the center of the medieval Serbian state and as the birthplace of the modern Alba-

Photo 13.1.   *Signing of the Dayton Peace Accords. Leaders of six other nations look on as the presidents of Serbia, Croatia, and Bosnia sign the Peace Accords at the Elysee Palace.*

(Source: Peter Turnley/CORBIS)

nian national movement in the nineteenth century. In the period immediately after World War II, the Serbian-dominated secret police imposed a harsh anti-Albanian order in Kosovo; in the 1950s the situation was so bad that many Albanians declared themselves Turks and emigrated to Turkey. The pendulum swung in the other direction after the fall of Secret Police chief Rankovic in 1966, and by 1974, Kosovo had become almost an equal member of the Federation and Albanians were the leading ethnic group in the province. But beginning with demonstrations in 1981, the pendulum again began swinging back against Albanian interests. Between 1988 and 1990, the Serbian government took steps to limit Kosovo's autonomy. It forced the province's two top leaders to resign; forced the legislature to adopt amendments reducing the province's autonomy; suppressed the Assembly and the Executive Council; terminated Albanian-language instruction in the schools; caused well over a 100,000 Kosovo Albanians to lose their jobs in the administrative, education, and health sectors; and changed street names in the capital, Priština, to Serbian ones. These measures led to large-scale emigration from Kosovo and were accompanied by official efforts to resettle Serbs (including refugees from Croatia) into Kosovo.[27]

In response to these developments, a peaceful movement for autonomy and then for independence developed, headed by the Democratic League of Kosovo (LDK) under the leadership of Ibrahim Rugova. In parallel elections, the LDK won the broad support of Albanians in Kosovo. It established a parallel administration in education and health care that was widely used and supported by Albanians. However, Rugova did not succeed in winning a place at any international negotiating table beyond that of an observer, partly because international negotiators viewed Milošević as essential in ending other conflicts. This failure created the conditions for a more militant phase to the national movement when the Kosovo Liberation Army (KLA) took the initiative in support of independence for Kosovo. Beginning with terrorist activities against Serbian police stations in December 1997, the KLA began more sustained operations, which elicited increasingly harsh responses from Serbian forces. International diplomatic efforts to establish an OSCE Verification Mission in the autumn of 1998 did not succeed in deterring further violence. The failure of the Rambouillet negotiations in France in early 1999 led to a seventy-seven-day NATO air campaign against Serbia and Serb positions in Kosovo and to more intense ethnic cleansing of Albanians from Kosovo. The campaign ended on June 10 with UN Security Council Resolution 1244, which created an interim administration for Kosovo meant to provide a framework for a political settlement of the crisis.

The UN Mission in Kosovo, or UNMIK, had some initial success in deploying in Kosovo, but has not succeeded in establishing institutions that are effective at providing security or the rule of law; brokering an agreement between the authorities in Kosovo and in Serbia over Kosovo's future status; providing guarantees to minorities concerning security, education, and economic opportunity; and meeting a generally accepted level of good governance.[28] The failure of the authorities in Belgrade to negotiate realistically about the future of Kosovo contributes to the continued uncertainty and violence in the province that results in the continuing departure of active Serb populations from Kosovo.

MACEDONIA

The enduring sources of the "Macedonian question," including Bulgarian, Greek, and Yugoslav claims to the region, have not figured into the ethnic conflict between Macedonians and Albanians in the period since 1990.[29] Albanians constitute 25 percent of the population of Macedonia and inhabit the area in the northwest bordering on Kosovo and Albania and in the capital, Skopje.[30] A "policy of half-hearted, half-reluctant ethnic cohabitation" in a series of multiethnic coalition governments since the early 1990s helped maintain a fragile peace but did not provide a basis for integrating the two groups into a common community.[31] Nor did the international presence of the UN Preventative Deployment (UNPREDEP) Serbia and Macedonia, the EC, or the Council of Security and Cooperation of Europe in the mid-1990s lead to political integration. These delaying actions led to a series of skirmishes in 2001 in northwest Macedonia between Albanian guerillas supported by Kosovar irregulars and Macedonian forces. After several months, international diplomats brokered the Ohrid Agreement, which provides for constitutional amendments and reforms to improve the status of Albanians while maintaining the unity of the Macedonian state. NATO briefly deployed in Macedonia in order to collect weapons, and an OSCE mission remains in place.

The failure of the international community to act in a timely fashion in the late 1980s and early 1990s, then, contributed to the uncertainty that permitted stronger and more aggressive forces to gain strength and undermined efforts to move toward peace and the construction of normal political systems. The wars of Yugoslav succession have made the transition from socialism in the countries of former Yugoslavia significantly more complicated than transitions in other parts of Central and Eastern Europe. The influence of the wars becomes clearer when we survey domestic developments, including elite transformation, party politics, the development of civil society, attitudes toward politics, and economic development and policies.

Political Transitions and Political Institutions

The wars of Yugoslav succession have left a deep imprint on the patterns of elite transformation in the successor states. Old and new leaderships easily blended together. Many former communists, such as Serbian president Milošević, Croatian president Tudjman, and Macedonian president Gligorov, became nationalist leaders in the new regimes. Many former democratic dissidents also became nationalist leaders and ideologues. Some former nationalists became liberal, democratic human rights advocates. Returning political émigrés blended effectively with former communists in nationalist parties. Among the older generation, former communists were able to work easily with former nationalist "enemies." Younger able and politically nimble politicians and administrators rose quickly to prominence in all parties and states. A careful examination of elite transformation in Croatia, Serbia, Bosnia-Herzegovina, and

Kosovo would certainly show how nationalist leaders employed the wars to deepen their hold on power and expand political machines that limited significant interparty electoral conflict. The wars thus delayed political democratization and economic liberalization.

The international community also contributed in some ways to this delay. The command systems that were established during the wars facilitated alliances between external agencies and the warring parties at the expense of the citizens for whom the assistance was intended. For example, during the war in Bosnia-Herzegovina, the warring parties took a cut from all humanitarian aid intended for civilians as part of their war effort.[32] After peace agreements, "peace-building" international agencies tacitly helped to buttress the authority of corrupt ethnic leaders simply by dealing with them. The peace accords in Kosovo and Bosnia-Herzegovina have not settled disputes about sovereignty or provided a road map to stable and democratic institutions. The failure to resolve open issues—for example, the status of Kosovo, the capture of indicted war criminals, the return of refugees and displaced persons, or the relationship between Republika Srpska and Serbia—ensured that recalcitrant leaders would find little reason to commit to the implementation of the peace accords. Finally, many important domestic functions were taken over by international officials from the UN, OSCE, Office of the High Representative, and the EU. These individuals generally spoke none of the languages of the region, knew little about the region, and often had little experience in working in postconflict zones. As a result, their actions have often made the transition even more difficult.

By 2006, all the former Yugoslav regions had adopted proportional representation (PR) electoral systems, and all but Bosnia and Kosovo could be described as parliamentary democracies with largely symbolic presidents. However, most did not start the postcommunist period that way. Domestic and international forces helped alter the distribution of power between the president and the parliament, as well as the electoral systems of the former Yugoslav states. For example, as indigenous democratic forces gained strength in Croatia and Serbia, they weakened their countries' presidencies, which had been abused to undermine democracy, by building up and increasing the independence of nonpresidential political institutions. In Croatia, they also jettisoned the single-member district system and adopted the more inclusive and representative PR system.

Institutional engineering was the most elaborate in those regions of former Yugoslavia that experienced significant international intervention. There, international diplomats compelled the adoption of sophisticated power-sharing arrangements that they hoped would ensure members of all ethnic groups a stake in the postconflict political systems. At the end of war in Bosnia, international institutional designers developed an incredibly complex and rigid set of multilayered political institutions that enshrined ethnic power sharing in the collective presidency as well as in most other political and administrative institutions. International engineers induced the adoption of PR systems in Macedonia and Kosovo, as well as the redrawing of electoral district lines in Macedonia, to give better chances to candidates from minorities and small parties. In addition to drafting Bosnia's elaborate rules for representation of all major ethnicities, international officials compelled Kosovo to reserve parliamentary seats for minorities. The pull of the EU encouraged dedicated seats for minorities in Montenegro and in

Slovenia, though the latter does so only for its autochthonous minorities. Germany helped convince Croatia also to reserve seats for minorities. In addition, Croatia reserved seats for representatives chosen by the Croatian diaspora. Electoral engineers also added gender quotas in Macedonia, Bosnia, and Kosovo to ensure the representation of women in political offices. Despite all the attention to crafting political institutions in Bosnia and Kosovo, these domestic institutions are so far overshadowed by international officials, whose powers in practice make these countries international protectorates.

Elections and Political Parties

The countries of former Yugoslavia have often been left out of the bulk of comparative literature on political competition in the postcommunist region. Yet these countries share characteristics of their Central and East European neighbors, including weak party systems, a rather amorphous ideological spectrum, and party fragmentation. These countries are characterized by intensive international involvement in domestic politics, as well as by entrenched ethnic party systems. Valerie Bunce suggests that the victory of a liberal, anticommunist opposition in the first multiparty election permits a decisive break with the authoritarian past and a launching of a liberal program. In contrast, the victory of an ethnically exclusive opposition can obviate democratization and lead to challenges to state boundaries.[33] Communist parties can also adopt nationalist agendas in order to maintain their holds on power.

By these criteria, only Slovenia experienced a relatively smooth democratic transition and process of state formation in its first post-Yugoslav election, the founding parliamentary election. The noncommunist coalition DEMOS won. The leader of the reformed Communist Party won the presidency. This new government enacted pluralist and market reforms and declared Slovenia's independence from Yugoslavia. After the movement-based DEMOS disintegrated, the fragmented party system consolidated into four strong parties: the left-oriented United List of Social Democrats, the moderate-left Liberal Democracy of Slovenia, the center-right Slovenian Democratic Party, and the Christian Democratic Party. These four parties have consistently captured the bulk of the seats in the National Assembly. Broad agreement among Slovenia's elite that their future was tied to European and Euro-Atlantic institutions helped the country achieve early membership in the EU and NATO. In addition, the absence of substantial minorities allowed Slovenia's significant illiberal forces to remain relatively harmless during its march into Europe.[34]

By contrast, the first post-Yugoslav elections in Croatia and Serbia opened the door to nationalist forces that succeeded in advancing narrow ethnic agendas and undermined democratization by wars in Croatia and Bosnia-Herzegovina. The end of war provided a context in which opposition coalitions could overcome their own bickering to win elections in second transitions and begin reform programs that contributed to more normal political competition.

In Serbia, Milošević weathered several waves of antiregime demonstrations and intraparty conflict to remake the League of Communists Serbia into a nationalist authoritarian party with its own satellite, the United Yugoslav Left (JUL), headed by Milošević's wife, Mirjana Marković. In the founding election in 1990, his Socialist Party of Serbia (SPS) ensured that it would dominate the parliament. The SPS's program appealed to socialist conformists as well as to Serbs who had criticized Tito's "weakening of Serb interests" in Yugoslavia in the 1980s.[35] The party was strongest outside Belgrade and in the Serbian heartland. Milošević used existing structures to retain power, acquire wealth, distribute patronage to his family and allies among his criminalized support structure,[36] and manage "Serb" territories outside Serbia. War and a monopoly over politics, effective propaganda through government-directed media, and control of the security forces allowed Milošević to demobilize political opposition and eliminate political alternatives.[37]

With the end of the war over Kosovo, the SPS could no longer label oppositionists as traitors. Ordinary Serbs increasingly attributed their poverty to the SPS's poor governance. Milošević's supporters among the criminal class had become independent of his patronage. The leaders of the liberal opposition finally set aside personal antagonism to unite, and the youth organization Otpor (Resistance) effectively led civic mobilization. These forces overturned Milošević's plans to rig the 2000 presidential elections and helped secure the victory of Vojislav Koštunica, who was supported by an eighteen-party opposition coalition, the Democratic Opposition of Serbia (DOS). The DOS coalition convincingly won the December 2000 parliamentary elections, selecting the Democratic Party's (DS) Zoran Djindjić as prime minister. However, differences between Koštunica and Djindjić over a bargaining strategy with the West on reform led to the disintegration of the coalition. Not long thereafter, war profiteers assassinated Djindjić in response to his plans for reform of the security sector and prospects of closer cooperation with the war crimes tribunal in The Hague.

In the 2003 and 2007 parliamentary elections, Vojislav Seselj's extremist Serb Radical Party (SRS) received more votes than any other party, gaining popular support from dissatisfaction with incumbents, popular sacrifices connected to economic reform, and resentment against Western demands for closer Serbian cooperation with The Hague and with relinquishing Kosovo. However, pressure from the West led Koštunica to form center-right coalitions after both elections that denied the SRS a formal role but allows it influence.[38] Current policies and the popularity of nationalist parties[39] mean that the second transition and movement toward the EU is ongoing, but far from complete in Serbia. This is particularly clear in the Skupstina's quickly and nontransparently drafted constitution that was unanimously adopted in September 2006. This first postcommunist constitution placed Kosovo as an integral part of Serbia in clear opposition to the desires of Albanians in Kosovo, who played no role in drafting or voting on it. Koštunica has struggled to balance demands within his broad coalitions. Koštunica's liberal partners, G17 Plus and President Boris Tadić of the DS, have pushed for the reforms needed to resume talks with the EU on a Stabilization and Association Agreement (SAA), while their powerful and populist supporters remain distrustful and resentful of EU pressure on Serbia. Formation of a government in May 2007 that excluded the SRS, the Serbian security services' help in capturing several high-profile ICTY indictees in June 2007, and EU leaders' desire to cushion the blow of Serbia's anticipated loss of Kosovo induced the EU to resume SAA talks with Belgrade in June 2007.

Photo 13.2.   *Funeral procession for Serbian prime minister Zoran Djindjić, who was assassinated by Serbian radicals in 2003. Djindjić had made many enemies for his pro-Western stance, reformist economic policies, and clampdown on organized crime. He also arrested Milošević and relinquished him to the International Criminal Tribunal for the Former Yugoslavia at The Hague.*

(Source: Website of the Serbian Government, www.srbija.sr.gov.yu)

In Croatia, the nationalist movement was led by the Croatian Democratic Union (HDZ) under the leadership of former Partisan general and political dissident Franjo Tudjman with substantial support from political émigrés. The HDZ won power in 1990 on the basis of its anticommunist expression of Croatian identity. It was viewed as the most serious alternative to the atheistic socialism of the ex-Communists or Party of Democratic Change (SDP, later called the Social Democratic Party).[40] A majoritarian electoral system turned the HDZ's 46 percent of the popular vote into 67.5 percent of the seats in parliament. The losing Coalition of National Accord, which was composed of former Communists and liberals, fragmented and formed a series of smaller parties. A majority of Serb SDP members chose to leave the evolving Croatian SDP. Regional parties in Istria have demonstrated considerable staying power. The war began in 1990–1991 with the refusal of the Serb Democratic Party (SDS) leadership to join the broad governing compact led by HDZ in 1990. This refusal strengthened exclusivist tendencies within the HDZ and reinforced its image as the most serious defender of Croatia against Serb aggressors. As long as Serbs occupied Croatian territory, Tudjman's HDZ was able to monopolize power in Croatia. It tolerated and supported moderate Serb groups in Croatia in an effort to demonstrate its political openness, but its real monopoly of power provided a context for corrupt practices among the HDZ political and administrative elite.

With the return of all Serb-held territory and changes in the electoral laws, the diverse opposition to the HDZ made significant electoral gains in a number of cities and regions on platforms of good governance and political change. After Tudjman's death in the run-up to elections in early 2000, a moderate six-party opposition coalition headed by the SDP won control of parliament on a campaign that included accession to the EU. Their governing program included cutting the purse strings of the hard-line HDZ in Bosnia and cooperation with the International War Crimes Tribunal. However, a governing coalition whose connecting bond lay mainly in beating the HDZ in power would not prove authoritative itself. Its inability to improve economic performance and its cooperation with The Hague's efforts to capture Croatian generals for trial at The Hague led to their defeat in elections in 2004 by a more compact and reformed version of the HDZ. Following its loss of power in 2000, the HDZ splintered and adapted its own electoral appeal to pursue integration into the EU. Its increased cooperation with ICTY in 2006 helped convince EU leaders to begin talks on accession.

Leaders in the tiny, multiethnic, and poor Yugoslav republics of Bosnia-Herzegovina and Macedonia sensed the impending danger that the disintegration of Yugoslavia could lead to the dissolution of their own republics, and they attempted to forge compromises among competing political forces in their areas to respond to the designs of their more powerful and covetous neighbors. Electoral rules, social structure, and anticommunist sentiment worked to establish ethnic party systems. Only the rejection of their compromise proposals in negotiations over Yugoslavia's future led Macedonian and Bosnian leaders to pursue independence. Both countries have lived through external interventions that drastically rewrote domestic political rules.

A 1990 court decision striking down Bosnia's ban on ethnic parties and an electoral rule that mandated that the results of the elections not deviate more than 15 percent from the ethnic distribution in the census contributed to the victory of ethnically based parties, the Muslim Party of Democratic Action (SDA), and the Bosnian branches of the HDZ and SDS in the founding elections. During the campaign, all three party leaders committed to protecting ethnic interests and to interethnic cooperation.[41] Although twice jailed in socialist Yugoslavia (in 1946 and 1983) for Islamic activities, SDA leader and president of Bosnia-Herzegovina Alija Izetbegovic opposed an ethnically based state in favor of a constitution that recognized Bosnia as a state of three constituent peoples and others. However, interparty cooperation deteriorated over the formula for the ethnic distribution of positions within the government administration. A majority of Bosnian citizens supported the referendum on independence, although Serbs boycotted the vote just as they did in Croatia. Leaders in Serbia and Croatia egged on and armed their co-ethnic parties in Bosnia on the pretext that the republic was dominated by radical Muslims.

Ethnic cleansing, international intervention, and institutional engineering created a break with the Yugoslav tradition of "brotherhood and unity." The Dayton Accords included an unwieldy constitution with ineffective state institutions dominated by the ethnically based SDA, HDZ, and SDS in the name of institutionalizing power sharing.[42] Electoralism—or the idea that holding elections will jump-start the democratic process—has actually heightened interethnic tensions in Bosnia.[43] Since ethnically based parties rarely win votes from other groups, party leaders have strong incentives to make radical appeals to insure greater turnout of their own group.[44] Nonetheless, nationalists won increasingly narrow victories until the 2000 elections when international officials convinced diverse social democratic forces to unite behind the Social Democratic Party–led "Coalition for Change." The coalition's efforts at comprehensive reform failed due to internal bickering and to opposition from exclusivist groups, forged during the wars. In the Republika Srpska, the Party of Independent Social Democrats is a regionally based Serbian party that was willing to enter into meaningful dialogue with Bosniac and international officials in the early 2000s, though since 2006 it has turned increasingly obstructionist and focused on maintaining Republika Srpska's privileges, even at the expense of integration into the EU. But international intervention has undermined political accountability in Bosnia. Just after Dayton, international officials did not act against exclusivists who illegally strengthened ethnic partition; the subsequent use of "Bonn powers" undermines the authority of Bosnian officials elected under Dayton's rules.[45] As noted above, the Bonn powers enable the international High Representative to override Bosnian institutions to pass legislation and remove domestic officials from office.[46]

In Macedonia, nationalists and reformed communists (soon becoming the SDSM) split the vote during the founding elections. Although the nationalist Internal Macedonian Revolutionary Organization (later, VMRO-DPMNU) won the most parliamentary seats in 1990, its government fell in a vote of no confidence in 1991. The reformed communists then formed a four-party coalition government that included the Albanian party. The party's leader, Vladimir Gligorov, was elected president by the parliament and served as a bridge between the communist past and pluralist future. The coalition supported interethnic cooperation by including four Albanian cabinet ministers in the government.[47] Although no Macedonian government has been able to break decisively with the past, all coalition governments—including that led by VMRO-DMPNU in 1998—have been multiethnic.

External pressure has actually enhanced multiethnic cooperation in Macedonia, as it has always ensured a European, U.S., or UN commitment to support some sort of power-sharing agreement. The Ohrid Agreement, which ended the fighting in 2001, has provided Macedonians with strong incentives to form an inclusive government of national unity and adopt ethnic power-sharing arrangements in the constitution. In contrast to the outcome in Bosnia, Macedonia's first election following the violence resulted in a multiethnic coalition government led by SDSM and other parties most committed to the peace agreement. Members of various multiethnic coalitions have largely managed to work together to formulate policy and divide the spoils of power. But Macedonia faces serious problems of organized crime, deepening ethnic separation, corruption, and economic development that cannot be so nimbly resolved.

In sum, there is uneven progress in the development of party systems across former Yugoslavia. In Slovenia and Croatia, movement parties that won the founding elections have dissipated and given way to party systems that range from conservative to social democratic parties, with a set of parties in the middle. These systems seem to be on the way to institutionalizing themselves and providing a range of proven policy programs.

Bosnia-Herzegovina and Macedonia, on the other hand, have developed entrenched ethnic party systems that inhibit any other basis of political competition, although ethnically based Social Democratic parties have enjoyed some electoral suc-

Photo 13.3.   July 2006 rally in Macedonia held by the then ruling coalition led by the Social Democratic Alliance of Macedonia during the parliamentary elections campaign.

(Source: Paula Pickering)

cess and have demonstrated their willingness to negotiate constructively across ethnic lines. The absence of a comprehensive second transition in Serbia, Montenegro, and Kosovo means that their political parties remain mired in basic status and constitutional dilemmas and have not moved into interest-driven politics. Enduring and meaningful regional parties as well as smaller liberal and green parties have appeared during these countries' difficult transitions. Although these minor parties have little hope of winning elections, they have facilitated the formation of coalitions that support democratic reform. The durability of these smaller parties might demonstrate that, in the proper circumstances, the post-Yugoslav party systems can resemble those of more settled political systems that lack the daily drama of crisis and war and their legacies.

Civil Society

It is often held that voluntary organizations produce social capital that will strengthen democratization in the successor states. However, the actual impact of such organizations depends on the type of social capital they build and the rootedness of the organizations in local society. Advocacy organizations that link citizens to policy makers can help hold political leaders accountable. Those groups that disperse authority horizontally, rather than concentrate authority, are best at cultivating the repeated interdependent interaction that builds interpersonal trust. Groups that look outward, beyond the interests of their own members toward benefiting the larger community are better at solving broader social problems than those that focus only inward. Finally those groups that link together people of different cultural backgrounds are better at helping integrate a diverse society than those that bring together and provide social support only to those of the same cultural background.[48]

The developments described in this chapter leave little doubt that many civil society organizations in the region are monoethnic. The many voluntary associations that focus on strengthening bonds within single ethnic groups contributed to conflict in Yugoslavia's multiethnic republics. For example, it is difficult to see how many of the religious organizations that were revived in the late 1980s could provide a basis for reconciliation and moderation when many religious leaders directly participated in exclusivist nationalist appeals.[49] Some monoethnic local organizations, which were linked to nationalist parties, crowded out a range of moderate groups that opposed violence.[50] Other organizations are inward looking, hierarchically structured, and willing to use violence to realize their exclusivist goals. These include paramilitary groups such as Arkan's Tigers and Seselj's Chetniks in Serbia.[51] The International War Crimes Tribunal has indicted many leaders of such groups that display the "dark side" of social capital.

Some local, multiethnic organizations that grew out of the war produce social capital that bridges ethnic divisions. Medica Zenica, for example, is a voluntary organization formed by local women residents of all backgrounds in Zenica, Bosnia, to aid female victims of the war.[52] Other groups include displaced persons, veterans, and families of missing persons. Victims' groups in Bosnia and Kosovo can adopt different strategies: either to return as minorities to their homes of origin or to rebuild new lives in areas where they are among the ethnic majority. Veterans associations, which are split along ethnic lines and are inward looking, resent their marginalization in the postconflict period and tend to support nationalist groups.[53]

Western agencies have generously supported nongovernmental agencies (NGOs) that produce "good" social capital that contributes to the democratization of postcommunist states, but overlook NGOs that emerge from local traditions of informal networks of mutual help rooted in everyday life, such as in the neighborhood and the workplace.[54] From their own experiences, donors have favored NGOs that have engaged in advocacy—even where they have shallow roots in society—and whose formation is driven largely by donors' needs. It is encouraging that leaders of advocacy groups, such as legal aid and human rights groups, are making progress in forming networks to monitor and influence government. For example, Sarajevo's Serb Civic Council (SCC) was established during the war by intellectuals to assist Serbs choosing to live in Bosnia's federation. After Dayton, the SCC successfully cooperated with Bosniac and Croat opposition intellectual groups to ensure that Serbs, Croats, and Bosniacs were all legally constituent nations throughout Bosnia. In diverse societies nationalist leaders tend to use conflict to discourage the formation of civic organizations that unite diverse peoples around common interests and thus help keep intercommunal peace.[55] More often, efforts to improve interethnic relations have been mounted by monoethnic groups that are committed to interethnic cooperation.

The long-term character of building tolerant civil societies in Yugoslavia's successor states is clearer to local activists and some international implementers on the ground than to donor agencies that demand immediate results. A recent USAID study concluded that many NGOs in southeastern Europe "still have tenuous links with their communities" because of their orientation toward international donors.[56] Ordinary citizens remain disaffected and often view local NGOs as promoters of Western agendas and sources of support for opportunistic leaders. To be sure, some domestic activists have made progress in strengthening organizations that embrace civility, responsiveness, and democratic principles. However, the successor states' civil societies remain dominated by organizations that promote narrow group interests rather than focusing on crosscutting problems, such as social integration or the political accountability of the government. International donors could be more successful by learning to work with domestic groups by adopting locally determined agendas as key elements in empowering local communities.

Citizens and Politics

As in most postcommunist systems, the significant gap between elites and ordinary citizens that persists in most successor states results from a one-party-system legacy, relatively weak party systems, and corruption. The willingness of citizens to participate in politics has varied according to timing, political context, and economic situation. Voter turnout was high during the euphoria of the founding elections and then tapered off with the realization that the end of one-party rule would not solve problems with political responsiveness. Citizens also quickly discerned the self-serving behavior of political elites working in the new political institutions. In all countries, voter turnout for parliamentary elections has declined since 1990. It slipped from 84.5 percent in 1990 to 61.6 percent in 2003 in Croatia; from 71.5 in 1990 to 58.7 in 2003 for Serbia; from 80 percent in 1990 to 55.4 percent in 2002 in Bosnia; and from 78 percent in 1990 to 73.5 percent in Macedonia in 2002.

Elections for the president of Serbia were invalidated three times when less than 50 percent of voters bothered to turn out in 2002 and 2003. Only amending the law allowed the elections to succeed. The heavy hand of the Office of the High Representative in Bosnia-Herzegovina has further depressed citizens' reported efficacy. Of those who did not vote in the last elections, 43 percent explained that they stayed home on election day because "Bosnia and Herzegovina's politicians cannot change anything."[57] It appears that low levels of participation result from the general perception that parties do not offer meaningful political alternatives, are not responsive to citizens' concerns, or have little power compared to the High Representative.

It is interesting to note that levels of participation in a range of political activities in the former Yugoslav states are roughly the same as the modest level of political participation for the Central and East European region as a whole (see table 13.1).

Citizen mistrust of political organizations is widespread in postcommunist societies and also leads to low levels of membership in political parties.

During wartime, exclusivist leaders succeeded in deflecting the effect of citizen-initiated protests that had become common in the late 1980s through 1991 in Slovenia, Croatia, and Serbia. We saw above that Milošević used demonstrations of unemployed and embittered Serbs to change regional leaderships. Large nonviolent demonstrations—for political reform in Belgrade in 1991 and peace in Sarajevo in 1992—were met with violence by the JNA and SDS snipers, respectively. The Tudjman and Milošević governments easily deflected antiwar protests by committed activists—often women—and could enlist rural-based and nationalist victims groups in support of national goals. But from the mid-1990s onward, antiauthoritarian protests in Zagreb and Belgrade grew larger and bolder. An estimated 100,000 people protested their leaders' attempts to silence popular opposition radio stations, for example.[58] Most significantly, the youth organization Otpor took advantage of low-key U.S. aid and a weakened SPS to mobilize citizens successfully against Milošević in the fall of 2000. A relatively high percentage of respondents in Serbia reported participating in such demonstrations. In Bosnia and post-Milošević Serbia, citizens are more willing to engage in protests if they involve economic rather than political issues.[59] This preference reflects the priority citizens in all of the former Yugoslav states give to economic concerns, as well as the continuing poor performance of the economies in the region.[60]

It is not unusual for protests to become violent. Nationalist protests continue to take place in Kosovo and Bosnia, sometimes with the assistance of ruling parties and the tacit support of local police. Developments that threaten entrenched nationalist leaders can lead to violent protests—against returning refugees and internally displaced people, the normalization of relations in the divided communities of Mostar (Bosnia) or Mitrovica (Kosovo), campaign rallies by minorities, or rumors of interethnic crime. Two days of cross-Kosovo violence in March 2004 that saw Albanian extremists attack Serbs, Roma, and UN and NATO forces were the most significant of these. It is also not unusual for intraethnic political competition to become violent in Serbia, Kosovo, or Bosnia, especially over control of power and wealth that flows from the black market.

Table 13.1. Modes of Political Participation (Percentage Engaged in Activities)

	Unofficial Strike	Membership in Political Party	Lawful Demonstration	Signed Petition
Slovenia	3.0	32.4	9.8	3.7
Serbia	7.5	5.8	24.0	32.4
Croatia	3.2	5.0	7.8	37.4
Bosnia	3.6	7.1	3.6	22
Macedonia	5.0	11.7	17.8	26.6
Central/East European Region*	4.7	6.0	15.5	31.8

Note: N for Slovenia = 1,006; N for Serbia (minus Kosovo) = 1,200; N for Croatia = 1,003; N for Bosnia = 1,200; N for Macedonia = 1,055; N for East European region = 14,004. For each question, "don't knows" were deleted from the sample, resulting in slightly smaller Ns.
*The "Central/East European region" includes all countries of the former Yugoslavia, Bulgaria, the Czech Republic, Hungary, Poland, Romania, and Slovakia. Albania was not included in the survey.
Source: European Values Study Group and World Values Survey Association 2004

Political Values and Attitudes
toward Politics

Some political scientists hold that the political culture of the nations of former Yugo-slavia tends to be a "subject" political culture, in which citizens sit back and expect the government to provide for them.[61] But it is just as easy to argue that citizens are rationally disaffected with a political system whose parties present them with few meaningful choices, especially when patronage networks do not deliver benefits to ordinary citizens. In deeply divided societies with ethnic party systems, citizens tend to vote for parties that represent ethnically defined interests. But ordinary citizens also avoid involvement in politics because it is considered dirty. Some citizens also believe that political parties contribute to ethnic tension.[62]

Surveys indicate that citizens of most of successor countries lack confidence in their political institutions (see table 13.2). The low level of confidence in domestic political institutions runs against the general aspiration for a democratic political sys-tem. The percentage of respondents who agree that "though democracy has its prob-lems, it is the best political system" ranges from a high of 96 percent in Croatia to a low of 81 percent of respondents in Macedonia.[63] These findings are consistent with opinions across postcommunist Europe. When asked to identify elements of democ-racy they consider extremely important, citizens from Serbia, Vojvodina, Kosovo, Croatia, Bosnia, and Macedonia all ranked "a justice system treating everybody equally," "economic prosperity in the country," and "a government that guarantees meeting the basic economic needs of all the citizens" as their top three associations with democracy.[64] These priority associations reflect concern over arbitrary rule, the absence of prosperity, and the prevalence of corruption during the periods of socialism and the wars of succession. They also display an enduring preference for the state to provide for basic needs. The exclusion of political elements of democracy, such as civil liberties and political pluralism, is consistent with the views of citizens in Romania and Bulgaria.[65] The percentage of respondents satisfied with the way democracy is developing in their country ranged from a high of 45 percent in Slovenia and Serbia to a low of 18 percent in Croatia and Macedonia.[66] This result may reflect citizens' interpretations of their country's economic performance: citizens throughout the suc-cessor states identify unemployment as the most important problem facing their coun-tries.[67] Poverty and corruption vie for second place.

Citizens express moderate levels of tolerance for other ethnic groups. As expected in areas that are experiencing interethnic brutality, levels of tolerance toward other ethnic groups worsened during and in the immediate wake of violence. In Croatia, individuals who experienced a personal tragedy expressed lower levels of ethnic toler-ance than those who did not.[68] But this pattern varies. Although Bosnia experienced much higher levels of violence than Macedonia, Bosnian citizens express higher levels of tolerance than do Macedonian citizens. In 2001, 11 percent of a Bosnian sample expressed unwillingness to live next to someone of another religion. Twenty-six per-cent of a Macedonian sample expressed a similar unwillingness.[69] As war's memory recedes, ethnic tolerance in Bosnia has significantly increased, which suggests that

Table 13.2.   Levels of Confidence in Political Institutions (%) (2001)*

	Political Parties	Parliament	Church	Police	Army
Slovenia	19.0	25.3	35.4	47.4	41.6
Serbia	31.3	23.4	52.9	47.4	74.2
Croatia	NA	20.7	61.6	46.4	62.2
Bosnia	14.6	20.2	49.7	63.6	60.7
Macedonia**	9.5	7.0	46.1	51.0	54.5
Central/East European Region	15.9	24.2	49.9	46.6	57.2
2003 EU Members	15.0	35.0	42.0	64.0	64.0

*For the countries of the former Yugoslavia and the Central and East European region, the table shows the percentage of respondents who expressed a "great deal" or "quite a lot" of confidence in particular institutions. For the 2003 EU members, the table shows the percentage of respondents who "tend to trust" particular institutions.

**The degree of disaffection reflected by Macedonian citizens reflects the fact that Macedonia had just experienced months of interethnic violence when the survey was conducted in 2001. Many citizens expressed deep disgruntlement that their politicians and political institutions were incapable of preventing such violence.

Source: For data on Eastern Europe: European Values Study Group and World Values Survey Association 2004.

For 2003 EU members: European Opinion Research Group, *Eurobarometer 60: Public Opinion in the European Union* (Brussels, Belgium: European Opinion Research Group, 2003). Available at http://europa.eu.int/comm/public_opinion/archives/eb/eb60/eb60_en.pdf.

interethnic relations have made greater progress at the grass roots than at the elite level.[70] We find the lowest levels of ethnic tolerance—including coexistence in the same entity—in Kosovo.[71]

In response to policies primarily formulated by a dominant national group, ethnic minorities express significantly less pride in the nationality of their state and trust in political institutions than do members of the predominant group. For example, 92 percent of majority-group respondents in Bosnia express pride in their nationality, while only 56 percent of minority respondents in Bosnia express such pride. The corresponding figures in Macedonia are 90 percent and 42 percent.[72]

The extent to which political values vary according to socioeconomic status depends partly on the political environment. For example, in the immediate wake of Milošević's ouster, voters in Serbia with some university education overwhelmingly (65 percent) supported the DOS opposition coalition, while only 5 percent supported SPS in 2001.[73] With the breakup of DOS, the difficult economic transition, and disputes with the EU over war crimes and Kosovo, there appeared no strong correlation between values and socioeconomic status by 2004.[74] However, generational differences over values are still reported. Relatively liberal young Bosnians have abstained from voting in larger percentages than older age cohorts.[75] Surveys also reveal that urbanites resent the rural residents who have fled from their villages to cities because of violence and poverty—even within the same ethno-national group.[76]

The transformation of values into those that support democratic principles and processes is necessary for democratic institutions to take root and to prevent a reversion to authoritarianism. In particular, tolerance toward other ethnic groups is essential for transition toward more normal political competition and stable states that promote regional stability. The good news is that citizens express levels of confidence in new political institutions and values that are largely consistent with the rest of West-leaning Central and Eastern Europe. They are broadly supportive of democratic ideas but lack confidence in those political institutions that have often failed to deliver benefits to ordinary citizens.

Economic Transition and Social Change

The wars of the 1990s significantly complicated the already challenging transformation of the mixed economics of the Yugoslav successor states. Wars in Croatia and Bosnia in the early 1990s and in Serbia and Kosovo at the end of the 1990s created a series of pariah economies that have been unable to attract substantial foreign investment. The economies suffered physical destruction of infrastructure and productive capacity, as well as the emigration of young, highly educated, and skilled labor. Serbia suffered under sanctions throughout the decades for its support of the Serb war effort in Bosnia. Macedonia suffered from a Greek boycott of its economy in the early 1990s and from the cutoff of Yugoslav markets that had been easily available before 1990.

Even Slovenia, whose EU accession process accelerated its market reforms and whose per capita gross national income rivals that of Greece, has privatized the banking sector slowly. As table 13.3 indicates, the war dramatically slowed the economic development of all successor states, particularly in the first half of the 1990s. In a period of increasing unemployment, these economies uniformly experienced great inflation and decreasing production and GDP. These trends have been particularly significant in Kosovo, where unemployment is as high as 60 to 70 percent.[77]

The wars also significantly curtailed already decreasing interrepublican trade. Those countries with more advanced economies—Slovenia and Croatia—were able to capitalize relatively quickly on their advantageous status by better integrating into the European and global economy than were the less well-developed republics (see table 13.4). For Serbia, Montenegro, Bosnia, and Macedonia, trade tends to be split among former Yugoslav successors and the EU. Deepened political commitment to integration with the EU has accelerated economic reform and improved economic performance—albeit to varying degrees—of those countries still seeking entry into the EU.

The war in Bosnia, Croatia, and Kosovo provided fertile soil for the development of gray economies and corruption—especially the golden goose of international reconstruction aid. Corruption significantly hampers economic development and democratization in all successor states but Slovenia. In terms of Freedom House's measure of corruption from 1 (least corrupt) to 7 (most corrupt), Slovenian garners a score of 2.25; Bosnia and Croatia hover around 4.5; and Serbia-Montenegro and Macedonia score at 4.75.[78] Only the Central Asian states and Belarus score worse. Leadership circles around Serbian president Milošević and Croatian president Tudjman were especially prone to personalizing the public trust, but this phenomenon was also evident elsewhere.[79] Estimates of the size of Bosnia's gray economy range from 30 to 40 percent of unadjusted, official GDP.[80] Control over the gray market has also enabled the leading nationalist parties in Bosnia to maintain power and undermine implementation of the Dayton Accords. Attempts to prosecute war profiteers in Serbia cost Zoran Djindjić his life. Criminal networks among Macedonia's Albanians contributed

Table 13.3.   Main Economic Indicators for the Successor States, 1991–1998

	FRY*	Croatia	Slovenia	Macedonia	Bosnia-Herzegovina
1998 GDP per cap (at current prices)	$1,340	$4,458	$9,860	$1,764	$1,147
1990 GDP = 100 1992	64	71	87	89	NA
(real indices) 1994	45	68	92	65	18
1996	51	77	98	63	31
1998	57	85	104	65	42
Real average GDP (%)					
1991–1993	–21.9	–11.4	–4.1	–15.7	NA
1996–1998	5.6	4.5	3.5	1.7	3
Industrial Production (%)**					
1991–1993	–25.2	–16.3	–9.7	–14.4	NA
1996–1998	8	4	1.7	3.1	22.4/NA
Consumer Price Index (%)**					
1991–1993	94,734	600	92.5	721	NA
1996–1998	471	4.3	8.9	2	0/54***
Unemployment (%)****					
1991–1993	23	16.3	13	19	NA
1996–1998	28	17	14.5	40 (est.)	40 (est.)

*Federal Republic of Yugoslavia (Serbia and Montenegro)
**average annual change
***first for federation, second for Republika Srpska
****annual average of active population
Source: John Lampe, *Yugoslavia as History: Twice There Was a Country*, 2nd ed. (Cambridge, UK: Cambridge University Press, 2000), 398.

to armed violence in 2001.[81] These phenomena are linked to transnational trafficking networks in people and commodities that will not be easily eradicated.

The war significantly slowed economic reform and the privatization of property. The social implications of the war are no less severe. A higher percentage of women than men are unemployed. Young adults are unemployed at higher levels than are other age cohorts. This fact leads young and educated labor to emigrate, a brain drain that affects future economic development. In Kosovo, Bosnia, and Croatia, minorities' unemployment is higher than that of majorities. Widespread poverty in Bosnia, Serbia, and Montenegro has led to social atomization and political demobilization.[82] These economies continue to wait to embark on the process of reform and modernization.

International agencies have attempted to address these problems as part of larger peace accords. They have donated over $5 billion to the Bosnian economy after the signing of the Dayton Accords, and donors' conferences have generated substantial amounts of income for Croatia and Kosovo. While this aid has contributed significantly to the repair and reconstruction of housing and infrastructure, it has been unevenly distributed and kept away from those groups—especially in Republia Srpska and among the Serb community in Kosovo—who have not explicitly supported the

Table 13.4. Increasingly Divergent Economies in 2003

	GNI per capita 2003 (current US$)	GDP growth 2003 (annual %)	FDI, net inflows 2003 (current US$)	Trade in goods as share of 2003 GDP (%) & major export partner (2002)	Unemployment (2002 (as % of labor force)
Slovakia	1,920	2.5	337.0 mil	95.9 (Germany –23.1)	6.1
Croatia	5,370	4.3	1.1 bil	70.5 (Italy –26.4)	14.4
Serbia and Montenegro	1,910	3.0	1.4 bil	48.5 (Bosnia –15.8)	13.8
Macedonia	1,980	3.2	94.6 mil	77.0 (Serbia – 22.1)	31.9
Bosnia	1,530	2.7	381.0 mil	83.7 (Croatia 17.1)	41.1

Source: For GNI per capita, GDP growth, FDI, and trade in goods as a share of GDP, World Bank: www.worldbank.org/data/countrydata/countrydata.html. For index of economic freedom for major export partner, Heritage: www.heritage.org/research/features/index/countries.cfm. For unemployment in all but Slovenia, European Union: www.europa.eu.int/pol/enlarg/index_en.htm; for unemployment in Slovenia, EURO Stat: http://epp.eurostat.cec.eu .int/portal/page?_pageid = 1996,45323734&_dad = portal&_schema = PORTAL&screen = welcomeref&open = /&product = STRIND_EMPL OI&depth = 2.

implementation of the peace accords. A great deal of effort remains to provide a proper legal framework for the economic transition that will enable these countries to benefit from trade and foreign investment. It will be no easy task for international agencies to find an effective balance among goals of recovery, reconstruction, and reform.

Critical Issues

There is no shortage of critical issues facing governments in Yugoslavia's successor states as they look toward accession to the EU. If Slovenia has largely succeeded in leaving the Balkans for Central Europe and EU membership, the other governments face stiffer hurdles to "normalcy." The "pull" of the EU's SAA process has helped induce meaningful reform in Croatia and Macedonia; it has achieved far spottier success in Serbia and Bosnia.

The Croatian government's increased cooperation with the International War Crimes Tribunal's demands to hand over indicted war criminals has been generally taken as a sign of its desire for accession to European institutions. It must also continue to convince its European partners that it has taken all necessary steps to provide for the return of Serb refugees. Croatian policy makers appear to be addressing serious issues in economic reform and improving the rule of law in a political system that is increasingly flexible and whose parties increasingly share consensus on some basic values and norms of behavior. The trends are a source of hope for its future in Europe and at home.

An underlying consensus across factions seems more illusive in the region's other governments, which must still move beyond the war's zero-sum politics. To different degrees, these governments must establish security and the rule of law, find a way to resolve interethnic tensions, find durable solutions for a good many internally displaced persons and refugees, eradicate public corruption and organized crime, undertake economic reform, and expand employment.

In many places, political leaders and nongovernmental organizations must still resolve the basic issues of political status and the constitutional order. The successful implementation of the Ohrid Agreement will go a long way toward creating a functioning political system in Macedonia that can join the community of southeast European countries. The resolution of Kosovo's status would end the uncertainties that provide fertile soil for continuing violence and the absence of reform. Compelling efforts to integrate Republika Srpska into Bosnia will allow Bosnians from all groups to move into a more hopeful future. The narrow victory for Montenegrin independence on May 21, 2006, and Belgrade's willingness to recognize the newly independent state has put to rest the tensions between Serbia and Montenegro and could provide the basis for the emergence of normal politics in Montenegro. These successes would help to lower costs of external deployments in this impending "hour of Europe" in the Balkans.

The Serbian government continues to exercise influence over many of the region's dilemmas. No government has more to gain from a constructive approach to these dilemmas than does Serbia's—a government whose finest traditions were hijacked in the interest of obscurantist nationalist goals that looked to a distant, mythical past rather than to a future of progress and prosperity. This assessment does not relieve political leaders throughout the other successor states from their own responsibilities to contribute constructively to end the fractious fighting. Finally, no solution to these constitutional problems will be found without constructive assistance from the international community, the same community that neither acted to preserve Yugoslavia nor intervened to end aggression. International agencies have been deeply involved in developments in Yugoslavia since 1991 and have overseen the often flawed implementation of peace accords throughout. Their greatest test will be in how adroitly they assist governments in the successor states in managing the transition from war to peace.

Suggested Readings

Brown, Keith, ed. *Transacting Transition: The Micropolitics of Democracy Assistance in the Former Yugoslavia*. Bloomfield, CT: Kumarian Press, Inc., 2006.

Burg, Steven L., and Paul S. Shoup. *The War in Bosnia-Herzegovina*. Armonk, NY: M.E. Sharpe, 1999.

Cohen, Lenard J., *Broken Bonds*. 2nd ed. Boulder, CO: Westview Press, 1995.

Dawisha, Karen, and Bruce Parrott, eds. *Politics, Power, and the Struggle for Democracy in South-East Europe*. Cambridge, UK: Cambridge University Press, 1997.

Demetrijevic, Nenad, and Petra Kovacs, eds. *Managing Hatred and Distrust: The Prognosis for Post-Conflict Settlement in Multiethnic Communities in the Former Yugoslavia*. Budapest, Hungary: Open Society Institute, 2004.

Donais, Tim. *The Political Economy of Peacebuilding in Post-Dayton Bosnia*. New York: Frank Cass, 2005.

Gagnon, V. P. *The Myth of Ethnic War: Serbia and Croatia in the 1990s*. Ithaca, NY: Cornell University Press, 2004.

Gow, James. *Triumph of the Lack of Will: International Diplomacy and the Yugoslav War*. New York: Columbia University Press, 1997.

Judah, Tim. *Kosovo: War and Revenge*. New Haven, CT: Yale University Press, 2000.

Lampe, John. *Yugoslavia as History: Twice There Was a Country*. 2nd ed. Cambridge, UK: Cambridge University Press, 2000.

Naimark, Norman, and Holly Case, eds. *Yugoslavia and Its Historians: Understanding the Balkan Wars of the 1990s*. Stanford, CA: Stanford University Press, 2003.

Ramet, Sabrina Petra. *Balkan Babel: The Disintegration of Yugoslavia from the Death of Tito to the Fall of Milošević*. 4th ed. Boulder, CO: Westview Press, 2002.

Ramet, Sabrina Petra, and Vjeran Pavlakovic, eds. *Serbia since 1989: Politics and Society under Milošević*. Seattle: University of Washington Press, 2005.

Woodward, Susan. *Balkan Tragedy*. Washington, DC: The Brookings Institution, 1996.

Notes

1. To get a sense of differences, see essays by Sabrina Ramet, "Anti-Bibliography: Reviewing the Reviews," in *Balkan Babel*, ed. Sabrina Ramet, 391–404 (Boulder, CO: Westview Press, 2002); Gale Stokes, John Lampe, Dennison Rusinow, and Julie Mostov, "Instant History—Understanding the Wars of Yugoslav Succession," *Slavic Review* 55, no. 1 (1996): 136–60; and Sarah Kent, "Writing

the Yugoslav Wars," *American Historical Review* 102, no. 4 (1997): 1085–1114; and Ivo Banac, "Historiography of the Countries of Eastern Europe: Yugoslavia," *American Historical Review* 97, no. 4 (1992): 1084–1102.

2. William Zimmerman, *Open Borders, Non-Alignment and the Political Evolution of Yugoslavia* (Princeton, NJ: Princeton University Press, 1986).

3. It is impossible to do justice to the diverse cultural, social, economic, and political background of the lands of former Yugoslavia in so short a space. For a general introduction, see Ivo Banac, *The Yugoslav National Question* (Ithaca, NY: Cornell University Press, 1984); Barbara Jelavich, *History of the Balkans*, 2 vols. (New York: Cambridge University Press, 1983); Charles Jelavich and Barbara Jelavich, *The Establishment of the Balkan National States, 1804–1920* (Seattle: University of Washington Press, 1977); Joseph Rothchild, *East Central Europe between the Two World Wars* (Seattle: University of Washington Press, 1974); Jozo Tomasevich, *Peasants, Politics and Economic Change* (Stanford, CA: Stanford University Press, 1955); John Lampe, *Yugoslavia as History: Twice There Was a Country*, 2nd ed. (Cambridge, UK: Cambridge University Press, 2000); Gale Stokes, *Three Eras of Political Change in Eastern Europe* (New York: Oxford University Press, 1997); and Mark Mazower, *The Balkans: A Short History* (New York: Random House, 2002).

4. Banac, *The Yugoslav National Question*, 415–16.

5. Dennison Rusinow, *The Yugoslav Experiment, 1948–1974* (Berkeley: University of California Press, 1978).

6. See Ivo Banac, *With Stalin against Tito: Cominform Splits in Yugoslav Communism* (Ithaca, NY: Cornell University Press, 1988).

7. See Zimmerman, *Open Borders*; and Alvin Z. Rubinstein, *Yugoslavia and the Nonaligned World* (Princeton, NJ: Princeton University Press, 1970).

8. Zimmerman nicely makes this argument. Also see Susan Woodward, *Socialist Unemployment: The Political Economy of Yugoslavia, 1945–1990* (Princeton, NJ: Princeton University Press, 1995).

9. Woodward, *Socialist Unemployment*; Lampe, *Yugoslavia as History*.

10. Woodward, *Socialist Unemployment*, 384.

11. The term "Bosniac" is used to describe the Slavic Muslims who live mainly in Bosnia-Herzegovina, but also in Serbia, Montenegro, and Kosovo. They had been known as Muslims in a national sense since 1971, but the Congress of Bosniac Intellectuals officially adopted "Bosniac" as the name for the people in 1993, and it has been generally accepted among all Slavic Muslims. See Mustafa Imamovic, *Istorija Bosnjaka* (Sarajevo, Bosnia: Preporod, 1998), Francine Friedman, *The Bosnian Muslims: Denial of a Nation* (Boulder, CO: Westview Press, 1995), and Banac, *The Yugoslav National Question*.

12. Kosovo became an "autonomous province" in 1974 enjoying almost all of the perquisites of republican status, but with fewer representatives on the state presidency and without the formal right to secede. It had earlier been an "autonomous region" within Serbia. See Mark Baskin, "Crisis in Kosovo," *Problems of Communism* 32, no. 2 (March–April 1983): 61–74.

13. Arend Lijphart, *Democracy in Plural Societies* (New Haven, CT: Yale University Press, 1980); Paul Shoup, *Yugoslav Communism and the National Question* (New York: Columbia University Press, 1968); Pedro Ramet, *Nationalism and Federalism in Yugoslavia, 1963–1983* (Bloomington: Indiana University Press, 1984); and Steven Burg, *Conflict and Cohesion in Socialist Yugoslavia: Political Decision Making since 1966* (Princeton, NJ: Princeton University Press, 1983).

14. Burg, *Conflict and Cohesion*, 346.

15. Lenard J. Cohen, *Serpent and Bosom: The Rise and Fall of Slobodan Milošević* (Boulder, CO: Westview Press, 2001).

16. Lenard J. Cohen, *Broken Bonds: Yugoslavia's Disintegration and Balkan Politics in Transition*, 2nd ed. (Boulder, CO: Westview Press, 1995), 47.

17. Lampe, *Yugoslavia as History*, 354–55; Sabrina Petra Ramet, *Balkan Babel: The Disintegration of Yugoslavia from the Death of Tito to the Fall of Milošević*, 4th ed. (Boulder, CO: Westview Press, 2002, 54–55.

18. Jacque Poos, foreign minister of Luxembourg at the time of Luxembourg's presidency of the

European Community Council of Ministers in 1991, famously declared that "this is the hour of Europe" during his shuttle diplomacy between Belgrade, Zagreb, Ljubljana, and Brioni. See International Commission on the Balkans, *Unfinished Peace: Report of the International Commission on the Balkans* (Washington, DC: Carnegie Endowment for International Peace, 1996), 56; and Dan Smith, "Europe's Peacebuilding Hour? Past Failures, Future Challenges," *Journal of International Affairs* 55, no. 2 (Spring 2002): 441–60, quote on p. 442.

19. See the estimates at the United Nations High Commissioner for Refugees' Balkan website: www.unhcr.org/cgi-bin/texis/vtx/balkans?page = maps.

20. Lampe, *Yugoslavia as History*, 370.

21. See www.un.org/Depts/dpko/dpko/co_mission/unprof_p.htm for basic information on UNPROFOR.

22. An estimated 900 Serbs were killed in the Croatian offensive against Serb-held Krajina in 1995. See "Croatia: Three Years since Operations Flash and Storm—Three Years of Justice and Dignity Denied," Amnesty International, EUR 64/005/1998, 4 August 1998, available at http://web.amnesty.org/library/Index/ENGEUR640051998?open&of = ENG-HRV (accessed on 4 August 2007).

23. Quoted in Branka Magas, "Franjo Tudjman, an Obituary," *Independent* (London) December 13, 1999, reprinted in *Bosnia Report* (December 1999–February 2000), at www.bosnia.org.uk/bosrep/decfeb00/tudjman.cfm.

24. Ethnic cleansing is a campaign in which authorities, acting according to a premeditated plan, capture or consolidate control over territory by forcibly displacing or killing members of opposing ethnic groups. Human Rights Watch/Helsinki, *Bosnia and Hercegovina: Politics of Revenge—the Misuse of Authority in Bihac, Cazin, and Velika Kladua* (New York: Human Rights Watch/Helsinki, 1997), 6.

25. For example, the HVO destroyed the beautiful sixteenth-century bridge that united east and west Mostar, and Serb forces destroyed the Ferhadija Mosque in Banja Luka, the largest in Europe, among the many objects.

26. The Bonn meeting of the Peace Implementation Council in December 1997 concluded that the "High Representative can facilitate the resolution of difficulties by making binding decisions on . . . interim measures to take effect when the parties are unable to reach agreement . . . [and] actions against . . . officials . . . found by the HR to be in violation of legal commitments under the peace agreement." See website for the Office of the High Representative: www.ohr.int/pic/default.asp?content_id = 5182#11.

27. See, for example, Tim Judah, *Kosovo: War and Revenge* (New Haven, CT: Yale University Press, 2000).

28. See, for example, Mark Baskin, *Developing Local Democracy in Kosovo* (Stockholm, Sweden: IDEA, 2005). Available at www.idea.int/publications/dem_kosovo/index.cfm; and Conflict Security and Development Group, *Kosovo Report* (London: International Policy Institute, 2003). Available at http://ipi.sspp.kcl.ac.uk/rep005/index.html.

29. See, for example, Banac, *The Yugoslav National Question*, 307–28.

30. Republika Makedonija Drzavni zavod za statistika, *Popis 2002* (Skopje, Macedonia: 1 December 2003). Available at http://www.stat.gov.mk/pdf/10-2003/2.1.3.30.pdf.

31. See, for example, International Crisis Group, "Macedonia: Not Out of the Woods Yet," (February 25, 2005). Available at www.crisisgroup.org/home/index.cfm?id = 3295&l = 1.

32. Mary Kaldor, *New and Old Wars: Organized Violence in a Global Era* (Palo Alto, CA: Stanford University Press, 1999).

33. Valerie Bunce, "The Political Economy of Postsocialism," *Slavic Review* 58 (Winter 1999): 756–93. See also Vernon Bogdanov, "Founding Elections and Regime Change," *Electoral Studies* 1 (1990): 288–94, and Valerie Bunce, "Rethinking Recent Democratization: Lessons from the Postcommunist Experience," *World Politics* 55 (January 2003): 189.

34. Sabrina Petra Ramet, "Democratization in Slovenia—the Second Stage," in *Politics, Power, and the Struggle for Democracy in South-East Europe*, ed. Karen Dawisha and Bruce Parrott, 189–217

(Cambridge, UK: Cambridge University Press, 1997); Patrick Hyder Patterson, "On the Edge of Reason: The Boundaries of Balkanism in Slovenian, Austrian, and Italian Discourse," *Slavic Review* 62, no. 1 (Spring 2003): 110–41.

35. Eric Gordy, *The Culture of Power in Serbia* (University Park: The Pennsylvania State University Press, 1999).

36. V. P. Gagnon, *The Myth of Ethnic War: Serbia and Croatia in the 1990s* (Ithaca, NY: Cornell University Press, 2004), 92.

37. Gagnon, *The Myth of Ethnic War*; Gordy, *The Culture of Power*.

38. Vladimir Matic, *Serbia at the Crossroads Again* (Washington, DC: U.S. Institute of Peace, 2004).

39. Many observers regard Koštunica's DSS as merely more savvy, not less nationalistic than SRS. See International Crisis Group, *Serbia's New Government: Turning from Europe* (Belgrade, Serbia/Brussels, Belgium: International Crisis Group, May 2007).

40. Ivan Siber, "The Impact of Nationalism, Values, and Ideological Orientations on Multi-Party Elections in Croatia," in *The Tragedy of Yugoslavia: The Failure of Democratic Transformation*, ed. Jim Seroka and Vukasin Pavlovic, 141–71 (Armonk, NY: M.E. Sharpe, 1992); Mirjana Kasapovic, "Demokratska Konsolidacija i Izborna Politika u Hrvatskoj 1990–2000" in *Hrvatska Politika 1990–2000*, ed. Mirjana Kasapovic, 15–40 (Zagreb, Croatia: Fakultet Politickih Znanosti, 2001); and Gagnon, *The Myth of Ethnic War*.

41. *The 1990 Elections in the Republics of Yugoslavia*, (Washington, DC: International Republican Institute for International Affairs, 1991); Suad Arnautovic, *Izbori u Bosni i Hercegovini 1990* (Sarajevo, Bosnia: Promocult, 1996).

42. European Commission for Democracy through Law, "Opinion on the Constitutional Situation in Bosnia and Herzegovina and the Powers of the High Representative" (March 2005). Available at www.venice.coe.int/SITE/DYNAMICS/N_RECENT_EF.ASP?L = E&TITLE1 = 62ND%20PLENARY%20SESSION&TITLE2 = 62E%20SESSION%20PLÉNIÈRE.

43. Sumantra Bose, *Bosnia after Dayton: Nationalist Partition and International Intervention* (Oxford: Oxford University Press, 2002), 117.

44. Donald L. Horowitz, *Ethnic Groups in Conflict*, 2nd ed. (Berkeley: University of California Press, 2000); and Paul Mitchell, "Party Competition in an Ethnic Dual Party System," *Ethnic and Racial Studies* 18 (October 1995).

45. Elizabeth Cousens, "Missed Opportunities to Overcompensation: Implementing the Dayton Agreement on Bosnia," in *Ending Civil Wars: The Implementation of Peace Agreements*, ed. Stephen Stedman, Donald Rothchild, and Elizabeth M. Cousens, 531–66 (Boulder, CO: Lynne Rienner Publishers, 2002).

46. See website for the Office of the High Representative: www.ohr.int/pic/default .asp?content_id = 5182#11.

47. Duncan Perry, "The Republic of Macedonia: Finding Its Way," in *Politics, Power, and the Struggle for Democracy in South-East Europe*, ed. Karen Dawisha and Bruce Parrott, 235 (Cambridge, UK: Cambridge University Press, 1997).

48. Robert D. Putnam, ed., *Democracies in Flux: The Evolution of Social Capital in Contemporary Society* (New York: Oxford University Press, 2002).

49. Leonard Cohen, "Prelates and Politicians in Bosnia: The Role of Religion in Nationalist Mobilisation," *Nationalities Papers* 25 (September 1997): 481–99.

50. Anthony Oberschall, "The Manipulation of Ethnicity: From Ethnic Cooperation to Violence and War in Yugoslavia," *Ethnic and Racial Studies* 23, no. 6 (2000): 994–95; Patrizia Poggi, Mirsada Mazur, Dino Djipa, Snezana Kojic-Hasinagic, and Xavier Bougarel, *Bosnia and Herzegovina: Local Level Institutions and Social Capital Study*, vol. 1 (Washington, DC: World Bank, 2002).

51. Other groups—the HOS in Croatia; Muslim gangs that operated in Sarajevo in 1992; the Kosovo Liberation Army in Kosovo; and the Albanian National Liberation Army and Macedonian Lions in Macedonia—have elements that are similar.

52. Cynthia Cockburn, *The Space between Us: Negotiating Gender and National Identities in Conflict* (London: Zed Books, 1998).

53. Poggi et al., *Bosnia and Herzegovina*, 83; Bose, *Bosnia after Dayton*, 127.

54. On NGOs, see Paul Stubbs, *Displaced Promises: Forced Migration, Refuge and Return in Croatia and Bosnia-Herzegovina* (Uppsala, Sweden: Life and Peace Institute, 1999). On good neighborly relations, see Tone Bringa, *Being Muslim the Bosnian Way* (Princeton, NJ: Princeton University Press, 1995). On work, see Paula M. Pickering, "Generating Social Capital for Bridging Ethnic Divisions in the Balkans," *Ethnic and Racial Studies* 29, no. 1 (2006); David Chandler, *Faking Democracy after Dayton* (London: Pluto Press, 2000); Sevima Sali-Terzic, "Civil Society" in *Policies of International Support to South-Eastern European Countries: Lessons (Not) Learnt from Bosnia and Herzegovina*, ed. Zarko Papic, 138–59 (Sarajevo, Bosnia: Open Society Institute, 2001).

55. Ashutosh Varshney, *Ethnic Conflict and Civic Life: Hindus and Muslims in India* (New Haven, CT: Yale University Press, 2001).

56. Jennifer Stuart, ed., *The 2002 NGO Sustainability Index* (Washington, DC: US Agency for International Development, 2003).

57. UN Development Programme, *Early Warning System in Bosnia-Herzegovina*, IV (2004, 52), www.undp.ba/index.aspx?PID = 14 (accessed October 30, 2005).

58. Leonard J. Cohen, "Embattled Democracy: Post-Communist Croatia in Transition," in *Politics, Power, and the Struggle for Democracy in South-East Europe*, ed. Karen Dawisha and Bruce Parrott, 112 (Cambridge, UK: Cambridge University Press, 1997).

59. UN Development Programme, *Early Warning System in Bosnia-Herzegovina*, 70; UN Development Programme, *Early Warning System Report, FYR Macedonia*, (November 2004, 20), www.undp.org.mk/default.asp?where = publications (accessed October 30, 2005).

60. Kasapovic, ed., *Hrvatska politika*, 301, 336; Institute for Democracy and Electoral Analysis, "Survey Results: South Eastern Europe: New Means for Regional Analysis," (2002). Available at http://archive.idea.int/balkans/survey_detailed.cfm.

61. Gabriel Almond and Sidney Verba, *The Civic Culture* (Princeton, NJ: Princeton University Press, 1978).

62. UN Development Programme, *Early Warning System in Bosnia-Herzegovina*, 70; UN Development Programme, *Early Warning System Report, FYR Macedonia*, 30.

63. European Values Study Group and World Values Survey Association, *European and World Values Surveys Integrated Data File*, 1999–2002, Release 1 (Computer file). 2nd ICPSR version, 2004.

64. Institute for Democracy and Electoral Analysis, "Survey Results: South Eastern Europe: New Means for Regional Analysis," (2002). Available at http://archive.idea.int/balkans/survey_detailed.cfm. The total survey sample, which includes Romania and Bulgaria, is 10,000.

65. Institute for Democracy and Electoral Analysis, "Survey Results." The other options for elements that are extremely important to have in a society in order to call it a democratic society include "at least two strong political parties competing in elections; a government that guarantees economic equality of its citizens; the freedom to criticize the government; and equal representation of men and women in elected positions."

66. European Values Study Group and World Values Survey Association, *European and World Values Surveys*.

67. Institute for Democracy and Electoral Analysis, "Survey Results." Numerous other students corroborate these concerns, including Kasapovic, *Hrvatska politika*; The International Republican Institute (IRI); and the National Democratic Institute (NDI).

68. Robert M. Kunovich and Randy Hodson, "Conflict, Religious Identity, and Ethnic Intolerance in Croatia," *Social Forces* 78 (December 1999): 643–74.

69. European Values Study Group and World Values Survey Association, *European and World Values Surveys*. Surveys during the socialist period revealed greater levels of interethnic tolerance in Bosnia than in Macedonia. See Bjiljana Bacevic, Stefica Bahtijarevic, Vladimir Goati, Goran Miles, Milan Miljevic, Dimitar Mircev, Dragomir Pantic, Nikola Paplasen, Niko Tos, and Marjana

Vasovic, eds., *Jugoslavia na kriznoj prekretnici* (Belgrade, Serbia: Institut Drustvenih Nauka, 1991). Despite low levels of interethnic tolerance, groups in Macedonia are more resigned to coexisting in the same state than are groups in Bosnia.

70. Paula M. Pickering, "Swimming Upstream: Grassroots Perspectives in Bosnia on Progress in Interethnic Relations since Dayton" (paper presented at the annual meeting of the American Association for the Advancement of Slavic Studies, Boston, December 2004).

71. International Commission on the Balkans, *The Balkans in Europe's Future* (Sofia, Bulgaria: International Commission on the Balkans, 2005), Annex.

72. European Values Study Group and World Values Survey Association, *European and World Values Surveys*.

73. European Values Study Group and World Values Survey Association, *European and World Values Surveys*.

74. Matic, *Serbia at the Crossroads,* 17.

75. OSCE Democratization Department, *Public Opinion Research* (Sarajevo, Bosnia: OSCE Mission to Bosnia and Herzegovina, May 2004), www.oscebih.org/documents/741-eng.pdf.

76. Anis Dani, Sarah Forster, Mirsada Muzur, Dino Dijipa, Paula Lytle, and Patrizia Poggi, "A Social Assessment of Bosnia and Hercegovina," (Washington, DC: The World Bank, Europe and Central Asia Region, Environmentally and Socially Sustainable Development Unit, ECSSD, April 1999).

77. International Commission on the Balkans, *The Balkans in Europe's Future,* 20.

78. Freedom House, *Nations in Transit 2005,* available at www.freedomhouse.org/template.cfm?page=17&year=2006. The corruption score includes a measure of government implementation of anticorruption measures, laws, and public perceptions.

79. Gagnon, *The Myth of Ethnic War;* and Cohen, *Serpent and Bosom,* 90.

80. *Bosnia-Herzegovina: Selected Economic Issues,* IMF Country Report 5/198 (International Monetary Fund, June 2005).

81. Robert Hislope, "Organized Crime in a Disorganized State: How Corruption Contributed to Macedonia's Mini-War," *Problems of Post-Communism* 49, no. 3 (May/June 2002): 33–41.

82. Poggi et al., *Bosnia and Herzegovina,* Appendix; Gordy, *The Culture of Power,* chapter 5.

CHAPTER 14

Romania since 1989

LIVING BEYOND THE PAST

John Gledhill and Charles King

We are not accustomed to thinking of the Romanians as historical winners, but that is what they have been, at least in relative terms, for most of modern history. Although much of the territory of modern Romania was a vassal state of the Ottoman Empire, it was never fully incorporated into the empire's political or social structures. Independence came in 1878, while the Poles, Czechs, Bulgarians, Albanians, and others would have to wait several more decades for the same. Later, Romania emerged from World War I with more people and more territory than it had when it entered the war on the side of the Allied powers. This "Greater Romania," created by the postwar peace treaties, was very close to the maximal demands of the most ardent Romanian nationalists. Some of that territory was seized by the Soviet Union and Bulgaria after World War II, but most of the rest remained inside Romania's recognized borders, including the sizable Central European region of Transylvania.

Romania was occupied by Soviet forces after the war and spent the next four decades inside the communist bloc. However, unlike many other countries within the Soviet sphere, Romania was under formal military occupation for a relatively short time. The last Soviet troops left Romania in 1958—and they stayed out: there was no Romanian equivalent of the Soviet invasion of Hungary in 1956, the Warsaw Pact's crushing of the Prague Spring in 1968, or the Soviets' threatened invasion of Poland in 1981. As epitomes of national disaster, the Poles have the eighteenth-century Partitions, the Serbs have the Battle of Kosovo, and the Hungarians have the Treaty of Trianon. But in Romanian national mythology, there is no central historical tragedy around which the narrative revolves. The reason is simple: for most of modern history, Romanians have usually gotten what they wanted.

So, many Romanians ask, how did things go so wrong? Why did Romania experience the most violent of all the anticommunist revolutions in Central and Eastern Europe in 1989? Why did the Romanian economy falter throughout most of the 1990s, while neighboring economies began to show strong, market-based growth? Why did the country lag so far behind most of its northern neighbors in the race for membership in the European Union (EU) and North Atlantic Treaty Organization

317

(NATO)? And why has it been so hard to convince the world that Romania really is "European"—not "Balkan"—and that it can be a real contributor to the political, economic, and strategic goals of Euro-Atlantic institutions?

In the early 2000s, things certainly began to look up. Romania formally joined NATO in 2004, and in 2005 the country's application for membership in the European Union was accepted, with full accession slated for 2007. These steps were due largely to the fact that Romania's democracy was functioning smoothly; a change of government and president came in November 2004, when new elections saw the Social Democratic Party voted out of power in favor of a center-right alliance. But there were lingering concerns. Political and economic corruption was rife, and the government's commitment to minority rights at times seemed questionable. Strategic ambiguities surrounded the future place of a generally pro-American Romania within a European Union whose foreign policy was diverging considerably from that of the United States, especially in the aftermath of the Iraq War. EU and U.S. influences have undoubtedly helped to shape Romania's postcommunist trajectory, but the full integration of Romania into the sphere of developed, consolidated democracies will depend on how Romanians themselves come to terms with the burdens, as well as the benefits, of being historical winners.

Precommunist History

The Greater Romania (*România Mare*) that emerged in 1918 was composed of territories that had formerly been part of very different states or empires. The core of this enlarged Romanian state was the old kingdom, or Regat, which had been a vassal of the Ottoman Empire until the late 1870s. At the end of the World War I, the Regat acquired the province of Bessarabia from the Russian Empire, Transylvania from the Hungarian component of the Hapsburg Empire, and Bukovina from the Austrian component of the Hapsburg Empire, among other smaller regions. The new Romania, rewarded for its participation on the Allied side during the war, thus doubled its territory and population.

Although 1918 was hailed as the natural union of all Romanian territories, the challenges of integration were legion. Romania spent the 1920s and 1930s with revisionist powers on nearly all its borders—countries that sought, in one form or another, to retake the lands lost in the postwar peace treaties. Bolshevik agents were active in Bessarabia. Bulgarian guerrillas worked for the liberation of parts of the Black Sea coast and hinterlands. The Hungarian government looked longingly at the fertile region of Transylvania. The lands that became part of the Romanian state were also populated by large non-Romanian minorities, such as Jews, Hungarians, Russians, and Bulgarians. These groups found an uneasy existence inside a kingdom that was defined in wholly national terms.[1]

The interwar period produced a great flowering of art and literature, with the capital city, Bucharest, commonly referred to as *micul Paris*, or the little Paris. But by the 1930s Romania followed the path taken by many European states: toward rising anti-Semitism and the growth of fascism. Some of the same intellectuals who were at the center of cultural life were also seduced by the anti-Jewish rhetoric of the time.[2] An indigenous fascist movement, the Iron Guard, grew in popularity and managed to place its members within successive Romanian governments. Increasingly, the Romanian military establishment, headed by the popular general Ion Antonescu, adopted much of the ideology of the Guardists (although Antonescu later suppressed the Guard after an attempted coup).

War descended on Romania from the east, when the Soviet Union suddenly annexed the old Russian province of Bessarabia and other territories in the summer of 1940. Romanian liberals had been critical of the government's warm relationship with Hitler, which had been developing throughout the 1930s, but the Soviet attack on Romanian territory left them with little choice but to support Germany's invasion of the Soviet Union. Antonescu was declared supreme leader of an openly fascist state, and under his aegis Romania spent most of the war fighting on the German side and actively pursuing the ethnic cleansing and mass murder of Jews and other groups from the occupied Soviet territories.[3] However, in the waning days of the war, a palace coup unseated Antonescu. The young king of Romania, Mihai, who had ruled alongside Antonescu, deposed the authoritarian leader in 1944 and switched Romania's loyalties to the Allied side—only shortly before the Red Army marched into Bucharest. Mihai himself was forced to abdicate three years later, when a communist government was installed with the assistance of the Soviet Union.

Communist Experience

Romania was one of the last communist bastions to fall, but that was precisely because of its background as a relative winner.[4] The oppressive regime of Nicolae Ceauşescu, which collapsed suddenly in December 1989, wrapped itself in the mantle of Romanian nationalism. Ceauşescu came to power as general-secretary of the Romanian Communist Party (PCR) in March 1965 on the death of his predecessor, Gheorghe Gheorghiu-Dej. Romania had already begun to distance itself from the Soviet Union under Gheorghiu-Dej, whose support had been crucial to the establishment of communist power in Bucharest after World War II. Ceauşescu then continued and expanded that policy. Romania also began to assert its independence from Moscow in the economic sphere, refusing to participate in Soviet plans for greater integration of the East European satellite states. In the cultural arena, Ceauşescu continued Gheorghiu-Dej's policies of easing out the mandatory study of Russian and rehabilitating many of the great writers and intellectuals of Romania's "bourgeois" past. Most spectacularly, in 1968 Ceauşescu refused to participate in the Warsaw Pact invasion of Czechoslovakia. In arguably the most important speech of his political career, Ceauşescu denounced the move against the Prague Spring and prepared his countrymen for what he predicted would be a coming Soviet invasion of Romania.

Throughout the late 1960s and early 1970s, Ceauşescu's nationalist stance also endeared him to the West. Seen as a maverick within the Soviet camp, Ceauşescu became the darling of Western governments. He and his wife, Elena, were invited to tour Western capitals. In turn, major political figures from the capitalist world visited

Romania. (Richard Nixon's 1969 state visit was the first by an American president to any communist country). But Ceauşescu never threatened to dislodge Romania from the Soviet bloc. Rather, he found a carefully balanced position between East and West, supporting the Soviet Union on most foreign policy issues but always holding out a welcoming hand to the capitalist West.[5]

At least until the 1980s, this foreign policy goal brought Ceauşescu a good deal of popular support within Romania itself (insofar as one can determine the popularity of a political leader in a system without free elections). At various periods, he allowed something of a cultural thaw in Romanian cultural and artistic life. He promoted Romanian culture abroad. He rehabilitated figures from Romania's past and introduced a cult of the nation that was fully supported by nationalist writers, historians, and other intellectuals. As in Albania and, later, in Bulgaria, Romania's brand of communism was closer to what might be called "national Stalinism," a skillful blend of a centrally planned economy, the ideology of national uniqueness, and the cult of a supreme leader.[6] Rather than abjuring the idea of nationality as a fundamental social category—one of the basic tenets of Marxism—Romania's communists largely embraced it, seeing Ceauşescu's regime as the endpoint in the historical development of the Romanian people.[7]

As the 1970s and 1980s progressed, however, the ideology of the nation was rarely enough to sustain any goodwill that the young Ceauşescu might have enjoyed in his early years in power. He became more radical in his desire to defeat any rivals to his supreme authority. His sycophants crafted a more and more outrageous cult of personality, centered not only on Ceauşescu himself but also on Elena and their children, a development that led some analysts to label the system "socialism in one family."[8] Grand schemes for economic development ruined the countryside and displaced tens of thousands of farmers.[9] Around a fifth of central Bucharest was cleared in order to make way for Ceauşescu's socialist "systematization" of the city, a project that involved the construction of wide boulevards and the world's second largest building (the massive House of the People), at a time when food was being rationed across the country. The cult of the nation also led to serious complaints from ethnic minorities, particularly the large ethnic Hungarian community, which accounted for around 8 percent of the population in the last communist-era census.[10] Pronatalist policies designed to stem the falling birthrate led to increasing intrusion of the state into private life. Abortions and contraceptives were banned.[11] Faced with mounting economic problems, Ceauşescu adopted a radical policy line, turning his back on his erstwhile friends in the West and endeavoring to pay off all of Romania's considerable foreign debt. By the end of the decade, Ceauşescu had in fact accomplished that task, but at the price of destroying the economy and severely impoverishing the population.

Transition from Communism

It is no coincidence that the peoples who saw themselves as the biggest historical victims in Central Europe—Poles, Czechs, and Hungarians—were the first to throw off the Soviet yoke. The revolutions of 1989 in Warsaw, Prague, and Budapest were

Photo 14.1.   Bucharest's youth celebrate the flight of Nicolae Ceauşescu in December 1989.

(Source: Dan Dusleag)

not simply popular uprisings against a bankrupt political system. They were also genuinely national revolutions against what was perceived to be a foreign occupying power, the Soviet Union. In countries that had completed their "national" revolutions earlier—that is, communist states that had always been relatively clear of major Soviet influence—the end of communism was a reckoning less with an external oppressor than with a corrupt and bankrupt local elite. The latter process was predictably a far more traumatic experience for the societies concerned than the former; it was a national reckoning that led to the breakup of Yugoslavia, a near civil war in Albania, and repeated instances of social violence in Romania. This is, of course, one of the great ironies of the end of communism and its aftermath: it turned out to be a rather beneficial thing to have been occupied by the Soviets. Those countries that had been invaded and occupied after the Second World War found a unity of purpose in their desire to build truly independent and successful countries after 1989. Those countries that had been most free to govern their own affairs—from Yugoslavia under Tito to Romania under Ceauşescu—faced terrible difficulties in exiting from communism and crafting a stable postcommunist government.

Romanian communism ended in the most violent and, in many ways, most classic way possible: a street revolution, with rioters waving flags and calling for the army to join them and the tyrant fleeing from the capital city, only to be tracked down and executed by firing squad on December 25, 1989. But when the smoke cleared, Romanians found themselves rather disappointed. The revolution—a genuine popular revolt launched in the western city of Timisoara—unfolded simultaneously with what amounted to a coup d'état: an effort by senior party and state officials to manipulate popular discontent, oust Ceauşescu, and take over power for themselves.[12] A provisional government, headed by a group calling itself the National Salvation Front (hereafter, the Front), swiftly assumed control and placed a former Ceauşescu loyalist, Ion Iliescu, at its head.

The Front initially promised to be a transitional government, to offer wide representation of Romania's many social groups, and to pave the way for free elections. Soon, however, Iliescu and his associates transformed the Front into a political party that proposed its own candidates for the first parliamentary elections. Iliescu also declared his candidacy for the presidency. With huge resource advantages over the opposition, the Front won overwhelmingly in the May 1990 ballot. Iliescu received 85 percent of the vote and his party 66 percent, although there were some allegations of irregularities throughout the campaign.[13]

Romania thus began the 1990s with a mixed legacy. It had a history of relative independence from the Soviet Union, which meant it faced few of the problems encountered by its northern neighbors in terms of decoupling from the Soviet economic and military embrace. But this advantage was balanced by an enfeebled economy, a civil society battered by decades of Ceauşescu's isolationism, and the emergence of a "new" political class whose democratic credentials were doubtful. As a result, in each of several policy areas, Romanians found that undoing the past proved to be far more difficult than was expected in the heady days of the December 1989 revolution.

Political Institutions

According to the constitution of December 1991, revised in 2003, Romania is a representative democracy with a bicameral parliament consisting of a Senate and a Chamber of Deputies, each with a four-year term. The Chamber of Deputies, the lower house of parliament, consists of 332 seats, of which 314 are filled by election and 18 are allocated to minority formations that failed to meet the threshold standards. The Senate is a 137-member body. Romania uses an electoral system of proportional representation on party lists, and individual parties must meet a 5 percent threshold to gain entry into parliament. The new government that came to power after the 1990 elections was composed largely of former members of the party *nomenklatura*, albeit functionaries who had at some point fallen out of favor with Ceauşescu. Initially, they proved to be very much products of the old regime. As president, Iliescu was ambivalent about the nature of the new system that was being built. His early rhetoric referred to the need for "original democracy" in Romania—a system somehow different from that being constructed in the rest of postcommunist Europe. As he saw it, the new regime would be a "form of political pluralism . . . [based on] maintaining and consolidating the national consensus."[14] Early in 1990, the Front showed itself willing to make that consensus by force. When student protestors occupied downtown Bucharest between April and June 1990, demanding the removal of communist-era elites from the government, the president dispatched police and several thousand coal miners from Transylvania's Jiu Valley to act against the demonstrators. The headquarters of opposition parties were sacked, and pro-democracy advocates were beaten and arrested. Although there was clear evidence of the Front's involvement, the government denied any direct control over the miners' actions.[15] Scenes of street violence in Bucharest shocked observers, who had hoped that the end of the Ceauşescu dictatorship would lead to more civilized forms of political life. For the next several years, however, those hopes proved largely illusory. The miners returned again in 1991 to oust the prime minister, Petre Roman, a rival of Iliescu.

By the time of the 1992 elections (which were conducted under a new constitution), street politics had given way to a more formal consolidation of power by Iliescu and his core supporters, who had renamed themselves the Democratic National Salvation Front (hereafter, Iliescu's Front). In those elections, Iliescu again emerged as the presidential winner and his party garnered just over a third of the seats in parliament. Although carrying a reduced mandate, the new government and its prime minister, Nicolae Vacaroiu, followed the lead of its predecessor by introducing only minimal reforms. Indeed, Vacaroiu's government seemed primarily interested in ensuring that the basic structures of power remained in the hands of the ex-communist elite that had dominated Romania's postcommunist system. Ninety-six percent of the members of his cabinet, for example, were former Communist Party activists.[16] As the political scientist Vladimir Tismaneanu has argued, rather than progressing toward a consolidated democracy, Romanian politics between 1989 and 1996 was "very close to a populist regime, [a] corporatist, semi-fascist" system—one in which "corruption [was] the principal form of perpetuating the elite."[17]

Elections and Political Parties

Despite the illiberal face of Romania's new political order, relations among factions within and among the emerging political parties became hotly contested by the mid-1990s. Through formal and informal coalitions, two primary political blocs emerged.[18] On one side of the divide were those parties that rallied around the government and whose ideologies were of secondary importance to the charisma of the party leaders and their will to power. This faction was led by Iliescu's Front, but included smaller government coalition parties such the Socialist Workers' Party and two nationalist groups, the Greater Romania Party and the Party of Romanian National Unity.

Setting itself against this bloc were the parties of the self-proclaimed "democratic opposition." Although dominated by factions that declared themselves to be right of center (the National Peasant Party–Christian Democrats and the National Liberal Party), this bloc was unified more by a desire to see Iliescu's Front removed from power than it was by any real ideology. Indeed, in order to realize their common goal, a coalition calling itself the Democratic Convention of Romania (hereafter, the Convention) was formed in November 1991. The coalition grew in strength in the years that followed, as diverse political groupings coalesced under the slogan "We can only succeed together." By the end of 1995, the Convention had developed into a formidable opposition under the leadership of the university administrator Emil Constantinescu. Taking a lesson from Newt Gingrich, Constantinescu promulgated a "Contract with Romania"—a document that formed the basis of the Convention's 1996 electoral campaign and promised sweeping reforms across a broad spectrum of interest areas.[19] The contract highlighted the need for swift economic restructuring, including privatization, and called for the introduction of a serious anticorruption program. The public popularity of these policies led new parties to join the coalition bandwagon. By time of the 1996 elections, the Convention could claim more than ten parties among its ranks.

Confirmation of Romania's turning political tide came with the victory of the Convention in the parliamentary elections and Constantinescu's taking the presidency from Iliescu, who had held office since the revolution. The Convention garnered 30 percent of the vote in the lower house of parliament, while Iliescu's Front (now renamed the Party of Social Democracy in Romania) came in second with 22 percent. The Convention then entered into a coalition with other anti-Iliescu parties and formed a new government under Prime Minister Victor Ciorbea.

Despite the promise held out by "the Contract" and the steps toward democratic consolidation that came with the first genuine transfer of power, neither the Convention nor Constantinescu was able live up to expectations. Once they were faced with the realities of governing a systemically corrupt bureaucracy and a structurally weak economy, the fragmented coalition found effective and popular government an elusive goal. The coalition's initial moves toward reform were accompanied by high levels of public support but, as the social costs of economic restructuring hit, that support began to dwindle. Moreover, as it became increasingly clear that Constantinescu would not be able to deliver on the promises of his ambitious "Contract," divisions began to open up within the Convention itself. Those divisions ultimately caused the Democratic Party, the new vehicle of Petre Roman's political ambitions, to withdraw from the government and forced Ciorbea out of the prime ministerial post. Later, the withdrawal of the Liberals from the coalition saw the Convention reduced to a shell organization, which was sustained only by the presence of the National Peasant Party. Indeed, the implosion of the Democratic Convention had become so evident by 2000 that Constantinescu refused to run for a second term as president. In an impassioned declaration of his refusal to seek office again, the president warned that incumbent politicians, seeking only private gain, had imperiled the country and made real change nearly impossible.

With a crumbling government and an opposition that had retained control over significant political and economic resources (now Iliescu's renamed Social Democratic Party of Romania), Romania experienced a major realignment in the 2000 elections. The Social Democrats took 36 percent of the vote in the lower house, and Iliescu was returned to the presidency. But in many ways, this outcome was of secondary importance. Of more immediate concern, particularly from the point of view of the international community, was the remarkable rise of the strongly nationalist Greater Romania Party. Its substantial share of the vote in the lower house (20 percent, up from 4 percent four years earlier) was accompanied by the party's strong showing in the presidential race. The Greater Romania candidate, Corneliu Vadim Tudor, garnered almost a third of the vote in the first round of elections. During the communist period, Vadim (as he is generally known) had effectively been Ceauşescu's court poet, a writer known for his bombastic paeans to the Romanian nation and to the dictator's genius. He then went on to endorse the miners' violence of the 1990s and served as editor of his party's mouthpiece newspaper, *România mare* (Greater Romania), a publication known for its anti-Semitic and anti-Hungarian articles.

Some international observers reacted to the success of Vadim's party by immediately writing off Romanian democracy and the potential for the development of a stable democratic culture.[20] Indeed, a leading British newspaper argued that "just when Europe had begun to hope that the Balkans were entering a period of stability after the downfall of Yugoslavia's Slobodan Milošević, it could face a new hotbed of tension."[21] But these fears proved excessive. In fact, the execution and results of the 2000 elections were encouraging in a number of ways, and the strong showing of an extreme nationalist leader was hardly exceptional for a European state in the early 2000s. What emerged from the election, in effect, was a party system that closely resembled that of other European states: the consolidation of parties along a left-right spectrum, based on reasonably clear electoral platforms. Moreover, the success of the Greater Romania Party in 2000 was not a reflection of a deeply xenophobic citizenry; it was a product of Vadim's vehement anticorruption campaign and Romanians' disenchantment with the other major parties on offer. Vadim's capacity to catch the protest vote proved short-lived, however, and support for the Greater Romania Party dwindled after 2000. The party was able to take only 13 percent of the vote in the parliamentary elections of November 2004. One of the party's leading figures, Gheorghe Funar, lost his seat as mayor in the local elections of Transylvania's major regional center, the city of Cluj.

By contrast, center-right parties, particularly the Liberals and the Democrats, experienced a resurgence after 2000 by working together under the coalition banner of the "Truth and Justice Alliance." The 2004 elections confirmed both the broad appeal of a centrist coalition and the charisma of the Alliance's presidential candidate, Traian Băsescu, the popular former mayor of Bucharest. During the election campaign, Băsescu and the Alliance made it clear that they were aligning themselves with the turn toward democracy that had begun with Georgia's Rose Revolution in 2003 and continued with Ukraine's Orange Revolution in 2004. The Alliance even adopted the same orange banners that were seen waving on the streets of Kyiv earlier that year.

The result of this association was a major realignment in Romanian politics. Băsescu took the presidential post in the second round of voting, defeating the favored Social Democrat candidate, Adrian Năstase, who had served as prime minister during Iliescu's presidency and had been groomed as Iliescu's successor. Although the Social Democrats retained their position as the largest single party in parliament, Băsescu's win drew smaller parties to the Alliance, which allowed for the formation of a coalition government under a Liberal prime minister.

The creation of the Alliance government seemed to mark a clear generational shift in Romanian politics, as young ministers were appointed to important portfolios such as foreign affairs and justice. Polls suggested that these moves met with the approval of the Romanian electorate. Momentum also began to gather in favor of punishing those who had ties with the communist regime. Most significantly, the Social Democrats removed Iliescu as party leader, and replaced him with the younger Mircea Geoana. Soon after, Iliescu was formally indicted for his role in the miners' attacks in Bucharest in 1990; former prime minister Adrian Năstase was indicted on corruption charges. Judgment of the past was not restricted to affiliates of the Social Democratic Party, however. In 2006, new legislation opened parliamentarians' communist-era secret service files to public scrutiny. Several leading figures from the Liberal and Conservative parties were disgraced after their records showed collaboration with the Securitate, Ceauşescu's notorious secret police. The question of the communist past, in fact, became one of the central issues of Băsescu's presidency. After commissioning a blue-ribbon panel of historians and other intellectuals to investigate the nature of the communist period, Băsescu publicly denounced the communist system as "an illegitimate and criminal regime."[22] That stance—and the threat of possible lustration legislation—caused the parliament to seek to oust Băsescu in 2007, an attempt that failed after a national referendum yielded strong public support for the president.

Economic Transition

Under Ceauşescu, the Romanian economy ground to a creaking halt. Enormous industrial enterprises, constructed in the 1970s, generated more pollution than products. Oil refining, one of the mainstays of the economy, contracted. Agricultural production, burdened by outdated technology and a collectivized system that provided few incentives for individual farmers, declined.

Although the economy had become ossified by the late 1980s, Romania did have one relative advantage over a number of neighboring transition states. Throughout the 1980s, Ceauşescu was obsessed with the eradication of Romania's foreign debt. Imports were cut drastically, and radical austerity programs were introduced in order to allow for the export of Romanian foodstuffs. Although the social repercussions of this step were severe, Romania did begin its transition to a market economy with no foreign debt. Furthermore, the state had large quantities of foreign reserves and was the only country in the region that was already a member of the International Monetary Fund (IMF). But in spite of these seeming structural advantages, today Romania remains among the poorest states in Europe. Its fragile economy is based on a workforce that is concentrated in the mining of raw materials and the production of low-tech industrial goods, and an inefficiently managed agricultural sector. This economic underdevelopment can be partially attributed to the redundancy of certain sectors of the Romanian economy that the Front inherited in 1990. But for most of the following decade, the country's poor economic performance was a simple function of the triumph of political self-interest over collective economic rationality.

There were early moves from Petre Roman's government to liberalize, but Iliescu and the Front leadership were reluctant to make the hard decisions that would have jump-started the economy in the early 1990s. State-owned enterprises were allowed to continue functioning, and few moves were made to encourage large-scale privatization. This policy meant that over half the economy was still controlled by the state sector in 1995; the figure was below 40 percent in neighboring Hungary and Poland.[23] Iliescu consistently argued that he felt a responsibility to Romanian citizens not to apply the shock therapy reforms that had been advocated in other parts of Central and Eastern Europe. But there may also have been a deeper fear: that large-scale unemployment would turn the population against the government and erode the ambiguous legitimacy with which Iliescu and his associates had begun the postcommunist transition.

The election of the center-right Convention government in November 1996 was accompanied by an immediate increase in the level of structural reforms, which were introduced largely under pressure from international financial institutions. Some observers described this new reform program as Romania's own version of shock therapy; the Convention's program of rapid reforms saw the adoption of more than a hundred pieces of privatization and liberalization legislation during 1997 alone.[24] The mining sector, which represented about a quarter of all losses in the economy since 1990, came in for special attention.[25] In December 1998, the Convention government announced its plan to close down 140 mines in the Hunedoara region of Transylvania. However, in 1999 local miners repeated their violent mobilization of the early 1990s and once again moved on Bucharest, where they were able to coerce the government into backing away from its decision. The sector remains a large drain on the Romanian economy.

Since the late 1990s, the Romanian economy has grown in absolute terms, and the government has achieved a certain level of fiscal stability. GDP growth has remained above 4 percent since 2000, inflation has dropped to around 9 percent per year, and unemployment figures have hovered around the 7 to 8 percent mark. In its regular reports on the Romanian economy, the World Bank has attributed these positive indicators to the country's increased integration with the EU and world economy.[26] Exports are focused on textiles, clothing, footwear, and furniture. But structural economic concerns remain. The large focus on agriculture and heavy industry means that the country is unlikely to undergo rapid growth and development in the short term and will remain two steps behind its high-technology and service-oriented neighbors.

With its high level of education, low labor costs, and strategic geopolitical position on the Black Sea, Romania presents itself as an ideal candidate for intense foreign investment and development in the high-technology sector. However, high levels of corruption and the reluctance of successive governments to privatize large firms swiftly

Photo 14.2.   Poor technology and infrastructure is rendering Romania's coal-mining industry obsolete.
(Source: John Gledhill)

have meant that foreign direct investment has been low compared with neighboring states. As a result, Romania has not been able to take advantage of its potential comparative advantage in the technology sector. Forty percent of the population continues to work on highly inefficient farms, the produce of which accounts for only 14 percent of Romania's national income[27]—an inefficiency that can be traced to the way in which Romania's collective farms were privatized after 1990. Although the process was handled swiftly, political expedience saw tiny plots of land awarded to a large population base. This policy has ultimately meant that there are a huge number of inefficient "minifundia" dotted over the Romanian landscape, which can only produce subsistence and small-trade crops.

Further basic monetary and fiscal reforms are also needed. On the financial side, the state retains control of over 40 percent of the assets of the banking sector,[28] which has kept both foreign and domestic investment low. Moves toward the overall fiscal stabilization of the Romanian economy need to start with reforms in the energy sector. Governments (acting through state-owned enterprises) continue to allow for tacit subsidies in the energy sector, through nonpayment of debts and below-cost pricing of output. As the energy industry sits at the cornerstone of much of the Romanian economy, slow reforms in that sector have had resonant effects.

Corruption has remained an impediment to structural reform. The EU and Romanian citizens themselves agree that systemic corruption is the number one economic concern, ahead of poverty and unemployment.[29] World Bank surveys suggest that one out of every two Romanians sees corruption as a "part of everyday life."[30] This abuse of public office for private gain is perceived to be most widespread among customs officials, the judiciary, parliamentarians, the police, and health officials—but no sector is thought to be free of its effects. Some Romanian commentators have pointed to the country's history as the origin of corruption (Ottoman rule and the Orthodox Church have come in for particular blame),[31] but all transition economies across the region have fallen victim to corrupt practices. Differences in the current levels of corruption across the region seem to be a function of two factors: (1) variation in the level of engagement of the state in the economy under communist rule and (2) the kind of measures taken since 1989 to stem the abuse of public office. In the Romanian case, the state's hand delved deep into the economy under Ceauşescu. Then, throughout the 1990s, few of those in power had any interest in changing that basic arrangement, for they were in large part the very individuals who benefited from the shady system.

The transfer of power in 1996 saw certain anticorruption programs introduced. Yet the real impetus for reform has come from the EU, which has been harsh in its criticism. With the carrot of EU membership dangling in front of Romania, real efforts were made to curtail corruption before Romania joined in January 2007. In 2000 a "Law on Preventing, Detecting and Punishing Acts of Corruption" was introduced, which provided for the creation of a "National Section for Combating Corruption and Organized Crime" under the direction of the general prosecutor's office. A 2003 law brought Romania further into line with EU norms by increasing the freedom of information and clarifying the kinds of acts that actually constitute corruption.

Civil society was arguably slow off the mark in supporting the anticorruption fight, but an alliance known as the "Coalition for a Clean Parliament" has had some real success in bringing down corrupt politicians through public awareness campaigns that focus on obvious disparities between public representatives' relatively low salaries and their often vast wealth. This coalition played a large role in turning power over to the rightist Alliance during the elections of 2004. Civil rights activist Monica Macovei was then appointed justice minister under the new government, and she immediately made corruption her number one priority.

Despite problem areas, Romania's economy has been on the upswing since the early 2000s. EU membership should only encourage that positive trajectory. The prospect of increased trade with EU partners, a flow of technology and best practices from the West, and the immediate benefit of EU structural funds should all provide a further boost.

Civil Society

During the communist period, there was space for a certain number of voluntary associations to exist in Poland and Hungary, and a small dissident movement was able to develop in Czechoslovakia. By contrast, Ceauşescu's national Stalinism managed to crush civil society altogether. Indeed, the Romanian poet and political activist Ana Blandiana has described Romanians under Ceauşescu as a "vegetable people."[32] Citizens may have been coerced into demonstrating their support for the Ceauşescus and the party, but this forced hypermobilization was accompanied by an absolute lack of freedom to organize independently around common interests. Moreover, when certain Central and East European states began to liberalize in the 1980s, Ceauşescu merely tightened the grip of his secret police on Romanian dissidents. It is no surprise, then, that Romania's revolution was not characterized by a pacted transition between reformers and the old regime or the transfer of power to an organized opposition. Mobilized opposition groups simply did not exist in Romania.

Intellectuals were swift to organize after the revolution, once space was opened up for them to do so. Early movers gathered under the banner of the "Group for Social Dialogue" in January 1990 and began immediate publication of the journal *22*. This review served as a mouthpiece for anti-Front intellectuals throughout the early 1990s. Working alongside this group was a set of Transylvanian intellectuals who managed to coordinate a mass signing of the "Declaration of Timisoara" in March 1990—a document that called for strong lustration laws and a commitment to reform, multiethnic tolerance, and European integration. By April 1990, these groups had combined with nascent student organization to organize a seven-week-long sit-in demonstration in Bucharest's University Square. A tent city was set up and a "neo-communist free zone" was declared. These encouraging movements were, however, dealt a severe blow by the miners' attacks on opposition associations in June 1990.

Since then, the development of civil society has been rather slow. Formally, more than 17,000 nongovernmental organizations (NGOs) exist today; however, most of these registered groups are inactive, and even those that are engaged in real programming are largely dependent on external funding. Among those NGOs that are operative, there is a clear concentration of organizations in the more prosperous region of Transylvania, where 48 percent of NGOs are based; the poorer region of Moldova— the area of northeastern Romania bordering the Republic of Moldova—is home to only 16 percent.[33] The interests of active NGOs are diverse, bringing in a range of political and social issues. The highest priority issue for these organizations remains the provision of social support to neglected communities, such as street children. But there has also been an expansion in the level of NGO-driven political advocacy on issues such as domestic violence, anticorruption, the environment, and constitutional revisions. It is perhaps surprising that NGOs have not received significant support from the mass media in publicizing their campaigns, given the prominent role of the press in civic life since 1989 and the common alignment of NGOs with the free media against the ex-communist elite.

Although there is little official censorship in the broadcast media, a form of self-censorship is often at work, particularly when issues of national importance are at stake, such as Romania's candidacy for the EU. When these topics are addressed, criticisms of government programs may be muted. The EU continues to call for further liberalization of the mass media and has shown distress over reports of the harassment of journalists by regional authorities.[34] Reacting to these criticisms, the Năstase government decriminalized libel and gave the state media agency—ROMPRES—legal assurance of its editorial independence.

Foreign Policy

In the foreign policy field, Romania's initial moves seemed destined to repeat the strategic balancing of the Ceaușescu era. Romania hastily signed a treaty with Moscow in early 1991, but the treaty became moot with the Soviet Union's demise. That turn to the east worried many observers, who questioned the future of Romania's relationship with the Euro-Atlantic alliance. As the decade progressed, however, Romania became one of the staunchest supporters of the West, particularly the United States. Under Iliescu's successor, Constantinescu, Romania signed a "strategic partnership" with Washington. The document ultimately had more public relations value than substance, but it was a signal that the United States was looking fondly on Romania's ambitions for membership in NATO.

That goal was finally realized in 2004, when Romania joined the alliance in the second wave of NATO enlargement. Romania's potential contribution to NATO was clear. It is the second-largest country (after Poland) in Central and Eastern Europe, and its geographic location on the Black Sea gives it access to an increasingly significant Eurasian waterway. By 2005, negotiations had begun over the relocation of U.S. military bases from Germany to Romania and Bulgaria, placing them in closer proximity to the strategic hotspots of the Middle East and Central Asia. Romania was also an active participant in the war in Iraq, a point frequently made by Romanian politicians as a way of proving their good-faith commitment to the Euro-Atlantic alliance and to the United States in particular.

The potential problem with these developments was that Romania was also a keen contender for membership in the European Union. Romania became an official accession country in 2000 and began the process of negotiating the complex array of laws, treaties, and regulations known as the *acquis communautaire* that would allow for eventual full membership. Progress was slow, and Romania compared unfavorably with Bulgaria in the early phases of the accession process. But beyond problems of internal reform, the real issue for Romania was its ability to join a Europe that, in foreign policy terms, seemed to be distancing itself from the United States. Some EU member states, such as France, warned Bucharest that this unwavering support for unpopular U.S. foreign policy could put the country's EU prospects in jeopardy. Tensions peaked in 2005, when an EU investigation alleged that Romania had allowed the United States to establish secret prisons, where the United States could detain terror suspects indefinitely without charge. Romanian politicians ultimately negotiated their way through these troubles and again managed to balance two sets of interests—becoming a solid player in NATO, while also portraying the country as a potential asset to the EU. As the deliberation over the final date for Romania's accession to the EU approached, it became clear that Romania would be granted full membership in 2007.

These large-scale strategic debates about Romania's place in Europe had both positive and negative effects on its relations with neighbors. Relations with Hungary remained tense for the first half of the 1990s. The Hungarian government had frequently been critical of Bucharest—even during the communist period—for its treatment of ethnic Hungarians, concentrated in Transylvania. Ceaușescu had encouraged the settlement of ethnic Romanians in Transylvania, and the destruction of Hungarian villages and cultural sites was the concomitant of a policy that underscored the essential "Romanianness" of the region.

However, the race for membership in European institutions had a strong effect on Romanian-Hungarian relations. In fact, one of the great achievements of the 1990s was the rapprochement between Hungary and Romania, which was largely a product

Photo 14.3.   The street sign reads: "Romania: That'll do."
(Source: Ion Barbu)

of the EU and NATO enlargement processes. In 1996, Budapest and Bucharest signed a treaty on interstate relations, a treaty that had long been delayed because of persistent questions over historical borders and ethnic minorities. The easing of tensions came about largely because both countries understood that good relations with neighbors were a prerequisite for moving closer to Brussels. The treaty itself, however, did not solve all remaining problems. Hungary's efforts to carve out a special relationship with ethnic Hungarians abroad—via a 2001 law that granted certain privileges to Hungarians abroad based solely on their ethnicity, a law commonly referred to as the Status Law—harmed relations with both Romania and Slovakia, the two states with the largest indigenous Hungarian minorities in the region.[35] However, whereas past disputes over ethnic minorities were mainly a bilateral issue between the states concerned, the question of Romanian-Hungarian relations in an enlarged EU is now wrapped up with broader issues of European standards on minority rights.

As Romania moves closer to Western Europe, it will inevitably move farther away from the Republic of Moldova, the country immediately to Romania's east, which has a majority Romanian-speaking population. The situation between the "two Romanian states" is quite unlike that between Hungary and Hungarian-speaking minorities abroad, however. First, there is considerable debate in Moldova over whether the country is even culturally "Romanian" at all; the general consensus is that ethnic Moldovans speak the Romanian language but, nevertheless, form their own separate nationality.[36] Second, only a minority of the population and politicians of Moldova seriously desires a meaningful special relationship with Romania. And third, the Romanian government has not sought a real *droit de regard* over Romanian-speaking populations abroad, whether in Moldova or Ukraine, although interstate treaties, such as those with Hungary and Ukraine, routinely mention the special interest of Romania in the cultural life of Romanian-speaking minorities.

The 1990s saw a progressive weakening of the pan-Romanian ideal, both in Moldova and Romania. In the former, the Popular Front (the pro-Romanian movement that was at the center of Moldovan political life in the late 1980s) had been reduced to its core constituency of committed pan-Romanianists, a rather small portion of the overall population. In early 2000, 66 percent of ethnic Moldovans still favored stronger economic links with Romania, but that support was ambiguous: 59 percent and 70 percent desired the same with Belarus and Ukraine, respectively.[37] With the ideal of pan-Romanian union on the wane, many nationalists, convinced that the cause was lost, simply emigrated. Some of Moldova's foremost poets and writers, who led the national movement of the late 1980s, now live in Bucharest, in fact. The Popular Front, renamed the Christian-Democratic Popular Party, staged weeks of demonstrations in the capital, Chisinau, in early 2002, denouncing the pro-Russian cultural policies of the Moldovan government and calling for new elections. The result, however, was a strengthening of the government's hand. In a national poll, 73 percent of respondents said they would vote for the ruling Communist Party in the next elections, up from 67 percent a few months earlier.[38] In the 2005 elections, the Communist Party ultimately took 46 percent of the vote. That figure was sufficient to allow for the formation of a Communist Party government and the parliamentary nomination of Communist Party leader Vladimir Voronin to another term as president.

Similarly, in Romania, the Moldovan question elicits no great public response. This situation, of course, can change, but if anything, as one Romanian essayist has commented, there is a "growing Moldova-phobia" in Romania.[39] Given Romania's own economic problems and the desire for a stronger relationship with Europe, devoting serious energy to building bridges to a country farther east, less developed, and less Eurocentric than their own has not attracted the attention of many Romanian politicians. In fact, Romania has proved more than willing to sacrifice relations with Moldova to demonstrate its good faith to Brussels. Throughout the 1990s, Moldovans enjoyed easy, passport-free travel to Romania, but in July 2001 Romania imposed a passport requirement as part of the effort to control its eastern border, an important transit route for illegal immigration into Europe. A similar deepening in the division between the two states can be expected, as Romania's government seeks to capitalize on its European credentials following EU accession.

Conclusion

Romania has been as much a country burdened by historical successes as by historical failures. That, in fact, was the essential irony of Romania's twentieth century: how things can go terribly wrong even when they seem to be going remarkably right. But what are the prospects for the twenty-first?

As Romania has grown closer to the European Union, its political and economic star has brightened. Economic growth rates are now impressive. Romanians travel freely in the European Union, and their ability to work within the EU space will likely be sealed now that the country has acceded to the EU along with Bulgaria in 2007. Foreign investment, although dwarfed by that coming to the states of north-central Europe, is now far more substantial than in the past. Romanian politics has also begun to look far more similar to that of "normal" democracies in Central or Western Europe. Parties have begun to carve out rather clear ideologies along a left-right spectrum—the Social Democrats on one end, the Liberals and Democrats in the middle, the Greater Romania Party on the other end. While the former communist elite was able to dominate the early electoral cycles, competition between distinct political factions is now real. Extreme nationalists are present, of course, but as voters in France, Austria, and Holland know, having an anti-immigrant and extremist party to choose from in the voting booth seems to be a defining element of a genuinely European political system, not an aberration.

Romania has in many ways long been an exceptional place: a country of Latin culture in a largely Slavic part of Europe; a relatively large country surrounded by much smaller ones; a country that has always carved out a great deal of autonomy for itself within the boundaries set by more powerful neighbors, whether Ottomans, Russians, Soviets, or, perhaps now, bureaucrats in Brussels. That exceptionalism, moreover, has been central to Romanian national identity and has produced a sense that the country's chief survival strategy should be to protect its own interests by playing both sides of any political table. However, with its fate now lying with the European Union, Romanian exceptionalism may be at an end. As a medium-size country with a relatively poor but developing economy, Romania may come to look like many other new EU member states. Yet being rather unexceptional within a united, peaceful, and prosperous Europe may not be such a bad thing.

Suggested Readings

Badescu, Gabriel, Paul Sum, and Eric Uslaner. "Civil Society Development and Democratic Values in Romania and Moldova." *East European Politics and Societies* 18 (May 2004): 316–41.
Boia, Lucian. *History and Myth in Romanian Consciousness.* New York: Central European University Press, 2001.

Deletant, Dennis. *Ceauşescu and the Securitate: Coercion and Dissent in Romania, 1965–1989*. London: Hurst, 1995.

Gledhill, John. "States of Contention: State-Led Political Violence in Post-Socialist Romania." *East European Politics and Societies* 19 (Winter 2005): 76–104.

Hitchins, Keith. *Rumania: 1866–1947*. New York: Oxford University Press, 1994.

King, Charles. *The Moldovans: Romania, Russia and the Politics of Culture*. Stanford, CA: Hoover Institution Press, 2000.

Kligman, Gail. *The Politics of Duplicity: Controlling Reproduction in Ceauşescu's Romania*. Berkeley: University of California Press, 1998.

Siani-Davies, Peter. *The Romanian Revolution of December 1989*. Ithaca, NY: Cornell University Press, 2005.

Tismaneanu, Vladimir. *Stalinism for All Seasons: A Political History of Romanian Communism*. Berkeley: University of California Press, 2003.

Verdery, Katherine. *The Vanishing Hectare: Property and Value in Postsocialist Transylvania*. Ithaca, NY: Cornell University Press, 2003.

Notes

1. See Irina Livezeanu, *Cultural Politics in Greater Romania* (Ithaca, NY: Cornell University Press, 1995); and Lucian Boia, *Romania: Borderland of Europe*, trans. James Christian Brown (London: Reaktion Books, 2001).

2. See the important diary by Mihail Sebastian, *Journal, 1935–1944*, trans. Patrick Camiller (Chicago: Ivan Dee, 2000).

3. See Radu Ioanid, *The Holocaust in Romania* (Chicago: Ivan Dee, 2000).

4. For overviews of Romania during the communist period, see Vladimir Tismaneanu, *Stalinism for All Seasons: A Political History of Romanian Communism* (Berkeley: University of California Press, 2003); Katherine Verdery, *What Was Socialism, and What Comes Next?* (Princeton, NJ: Princeton University Press, 1996); Dennis Deletant, *Romania under Communist Rule* (Iaşi, Romania: Center for Romanian Studies, 1999); and Dennis Deletant, *Ceauşescu and the Securitate: Coercion and Dissent in Romania, 1965–1989* (London: Hurst, 1995).

5. See Michael Shafir, *Romania: Politics, Economics and Society: Political Stagnation and Simulated Change* (Boulder, CO: Lynne Rienner, 1985).

6. On the distinction between "national Stalinism" and "national communism," see Tismaneanu, *Stalinism for All Seasons*, 33.

7. The foremost general history text from the communist period is perhaps Mircea Muşat and Ion Ardeleanu, *From Ancient Dacia to Modern Romania* (Bucharest, Romania: Editura Ştiinţifică şi Enciclopedică, 1985).

8. See Martyn Rady, "Nationalism and Nationality in Romania," in *Contemporary Nationalism in East Central Europe*, ed. Paul Latawski (New York: St. Martin's Press, 1995).

9. On communist rural policy and its echoes in the postcommunist period, see Katherine Verdery, *Transylvanian Villagers: Three Centuries of Political, Economic, and Ethnic Change* (Berkeley: University of California Press, 1983); and *The Vanishing Hectare: Property and Value in Postsocialist Transylvania* (Ithaca, NY: Cornell University Press, 2003).

10. The last communist-era census was conducted in 1977. The 1992 census showed that 7.1 percent of the population claimed Hungarian ethnicity.

11. Susan Gal and Gail Kligman, *Reproducing Gender* (Princeton, NJ: Princeton University Press, 2000). See also Gail Kligman, "Political Demography: The Banning of Abortion in Ceauşescu's Romania," in *Conceiving the New World Order: The Global Politics of Reproduction*, ed. Faye Ginsberg and Rayna Rapp, 234–55 (Berkeley: University of California Press, 1995).

12. For a treatment of the fallout of the revolution, see Peter Siani-Davies, "The Revolution after

the Revolution," in *Post-Communist Romania: Coming to Terms with the Transition*, ed. Duncan Light and David Phinnemore (London: Palgrave, 2001). The most detailed treatment of the revolution itself is Peter Siani-Davies, *The Romanian Revolution of December 1989* (Ithaca, NY: Cornell University Press, 2005).

13. On the first elections and the early postrevolutionary years, see Tismaneanu, *Stalinism for All Seasons*; Vladimir Tismaneanu, "The Quasi-Revolution and Its Discontents: Emerging Political Pluralism in Post-Ceauşescu Romania," *East European Politics and Societies* 7 (Spring 1993): 309–48; Vladimir Tismaneanu and Matei Calinescu, "The 1989 Revolution and Romania's Future," *Problems of Communism* 40 (January–April 1991): 42–59; and Daniel Nelson, ed., *Romania after Tyranny* (Boulder, CO: Westview Press, 1992).

14. Quoted in Georgeta Pourchot, "Mass Media and Democracy in Romania: Lessons from the Past, Prospects for the Future," in *Romania in Transition*, ed. Lavinia Stan (Aldershot, UK: Dartmouth Publishing Company, 1997), 70.

15. For a treatment of these events, known as the *mineriade*, see John Gledhill, "States of Contention: State-Led Political Violence in Post-Socialist Romania," *East European Politics and Societies* 19 (Winter 2005): 76–104; Vladimir Tismaneanu, "Homage to Golania," *New Republic* (July 30, 1990); and Mihnea Berindei et al., *Roumanie, le livre blanc: La réalité d'un pouvoir néo-communiste* (Paris: Editions la Découverte, 1990).

16. Sorina Soare, "La construction du système partisan roumain entre sorties et entrées imprévues," *Studia politica* 4 (2004): 92.

17. Vladimir Tismaneanu (in conversation with Mircea Mihăieş), *Balul mascat* (Iaşi, Romania: Polirom, 1996), 31, 140.

18. Sorina Soare, "Sistemul partizan romanesc: Catalizator sau obstacol al consolidarii democraticice?" *Studia politică* 2 (2002): 115–40.

19. For an outline of the Convention's program, see "Contractul cu România: Programul celor 200 de zile" in *"Nu putem reuşi decît împreună": O istorie analitică a Convenţiei Democratice, 1989–2000*, ed. Dan Pavel and Iulia Huiu, 556–57 (Iaşi, Romania: Polirom, 2003).

20. For a recent overview of Romania's postcommunist period, in which the role of ethnic politics is highlighted, see Tom Gallagher, *Theft of a Nation: Romania since Communism* (London: Hurst, 2004).

21. "Haider, but More So: Romania's Unlovely Presidential Aspirant," *Guardian*, November 29, 2000. Also following the first round of elections, an article entitled "Romania Faces the Ghosts of Its Past" appeared in the French daily *Le Monde* and opened with the statement "Disaster. This word alone describes the current state of Romania." *Le Monde*, December 9, 2000.

22. Traian Băsescu, "Un regim ilegitim şi criminal," *22*, December 19–25, 2006.

23. Statistics taken from the World Bank's *Public Enterprise Reform and Privatization Database*, www.worldbank.org/ecspf/PSD-Yearbook.

24. Organization for Economic Cooperation and Development, *OECD Economic Surveys 1997–1998: Romania* (Paris: OECD, 1998): 22.

25. Vlad Fonta, "Valea Jiului: Un caz atipic in economia românească," *Sfera politicii*, 67 (1998). Available at www.dntb.ro/sfera/67/mineriade-4.html.

26. World Bank Country Memorandum, *Romania: Restructuring for EU Integration—The Policy Agenda* (Washington, DC: World Bank, June 2004): 6.

27. World Bank Country Memorandum, *Romania*, 8.

28. World Bank Country Memorandum, *Romania*, 10.

29. Southeast European Legal Development Initiative (SELDI), "Corruption Index of the Balkans: 2002." Available at www.online.bg/vr/SELDI01_e.htm.

30. World Bank, *Diagnostic Surveys of Corruption in Romania* (Washington, DC: World Bank, 2000), vi.

31. For examples of these arguments, see Alina Mungiu-Pippidi, "Crime and Corruption after Communism: Breaking Free at Last, Tales of Corruption from the Post-Communist Balkans," *East*

European Constitutional Review 6, no. 4 (Fall 1997). Available at www.law.nyu.edu/eecr/vol6num4/feature/breakingfree.html.

32. Quoted in Martyn Rady, *Romania in Turmoil: A Contemporary History* (London: I. B. Taurus, 1992), 58.

33. Todd Anderson and Jennifer Stuart, eds., *The 2003 Sustainability Index for Central and Eastern Europe and Eurasia* (Washington, DC: USAID, 2004), 152.

34. See Commission of the European Communities, *2003 Regular Report on Romania's Progress towards Accession* (Brussels, Belgium: Commission of the European Communities, 2003), 26.

35. For a detailed analysis of the Status Law, see Brigid Fowler, "Fuzzing Citizenship, Nationalising Political Space: A Framework for Interpreting the Hungarian 'Status Law' as a New Form of Kin-State Policy in Central and Eastern Europe" (working paper 40/02, University of Sussex, January 2002).

36. On the history of the Moldovan question, see Charles King, *The Moldovans: Romania, Russia, and the Politics of Culture* (Stanford, CA: Hoover Institution Press, 2000).

37. Stephen White, *Public Opinion in Moldova* (Strathclyde, UK: CSPP Publications): 27–28.

38. Institutul de Politici Publice, "Barometrul opiniei publice din Moldova," March–April 2002.

39. Andreea Deciu, "Moldova de dincolo de Prut," *România literară*, May 30, 2001.

CHAPTER 15

Ukraine

MUDDLING ALONG

Taras Kuzio

In December 2004 Ukrainian voters opened a new chapter in Ukraine's history. After over a decade of stop-and-go reform efforts capped by the increasingly corrupt and undemocratic actions of President Leonid Kuchma, Ukrainian citizens took to the streets and plazas to protest fraudulent election results in the 2004 presidential elections. These demonstrations, which came to be known as the Orange Revolution, brought Viktor Yushchenko to the presidency and ushered in a new period of reform. They also reopened the possibility that Ukraine would join other European countries in European and Euro-Atlantic institutions. As the unraveling of the coalition that formed Yushchenko's government in late 2005 and the difficulties of forming a coalition after the 2006 and 2007 elections illustrated, the process of consolidating democracy and creating a prosperous market economy in Ukraine continues to face serious obstacles. However, the prospects that Ukraine will achieve these goals remain brighter now than at any time since Ukraine became independent after the dissolution of the Soviet Union in 1991.

Precommunist and Communist Ukraine

Ukraine entered the twentieth century divided between three states. The largest part—central, southern, and eastern Ukraine—had been part of the tsarist Russian Empire since the eighteenth century. Volhynia in western Ukraine was also part of the tsarist empire. Galicia and Transcarpathia were within the Austrian and Hungarian components of the Austro-Hungarian Empire. Northern Bukovina was part of Romania.

Between 1917 and 1920, Ukrainians made various attempts to create an independent state, but these attempts all failed. Ukraine declared independence from tsarist Russia on January 22, 1918, and united with western Ukraine a year later. The White Russian armies who supported the post-tsarist provisional government, the Bolsheviks, and Poles all fought against the independent Ukrainian state.

In 1920–1921, Ukrainian lands were therefore divided up again between four states. The largest portion of Ukrainian territory that had belonged to tsarist Russia became the Ukrainian Soviet Socialist Republic (Ukrainian SSR). Galicia and Volhynia were transferred to the newly independent Poland, northern Bukovina to Romania, and Transcarpathia to the newly constituted Czechoslovakia and, when Czechoslovakia was dismembered in 1938 and 1939, to Hungary, then an ally of Nazi Germany.

It was the successor state to the Ukrainian SSR, one of the founding republics of the USSR in 1921, that declared independence from the USSR on August 24, 1991. Ukraine's territory was enlarged on two occasions. The first of these occurred at the end of World War II when western Ukraine (Galicia, Volhynia) was annexed from Poland, Transcarpathia from Czechoslovakia, and northern Bukovina from Romania as part of the postwar territorial shifts and settlements. Crimea was transferred from the Russian Soviet Federative Socialist Republic (RSFSR) to the Ukrainian SSR in 1954. Ironically, therefore, it was the Soviet regime that united ethnic Ukrainian territories into one state.

Soviet nationality policies bequeathed two important legacies for post-Soviet Ukraine. First, under Soviet rule, the non-Russian republics were designated as homelands for non-Russians. As a result, republican Communist Party officials were allowed a great deal of autonomy in their own republics in the post-Stalin era. In return, they were expected to keep nationalism in check in strategically important republics such as Ukraine. Soviet nationality policies also focused on Russification, which led to the growth of large numbers of ethnic Ukrainians who spoke Russian, as well as Ukrainians who were bilingual in Russian and Ukrainian and a large number of ethnic Russians.

Paradoxically, Soviet nationality policies also reinforced loyalty to the republics the Soviets created. Non-Russians came increasingly to look upon their republics as their homelands and the borders of those republics as sacrosanct. Public opinion polls in the post-Soviet era reflected a high degree of support for maintaining these inherited borders. In post-Soviet Ukraine, separatism never became an issue except in the Crimea, the only region with an ethnic Russian majority, in the first half of the 1990s.

In the 1920s, Soviet policies of indigenization (*korenizatsia*) supported the Ukrainization of life in Ukraine. If these policies had been permitted to continue, they would have led to the kind of modernization undertaken in Western Europe and North America, where industrialization and urbanization were synonymous with nation building. Indigenization in the 1920s included the migration of Ukrainian-speaking peasants to growing urban centers that became home to industry. State institutions and educational facilities provided a Ukrainian language and cultural framework. In urban centers, increasing numbers of people came to speak Ukrainian.

Josef Stalin deemed the continuation of indigenization to be too dangerous because of the fear that it would eventually lead to political demands, such as independence, propelled by a growing differentiation of Ukrainians from Russians. Stalin reversed early Soviet nationality policies in three areas. First, the Ukrainian Autocephalous Orthodox Church was destroyed. Secondly, there were widespread purges, arrests, imprisonment, and execution of Ukrainian nationalists and national communists. Third, Russification replaced indigenization policies, and there was a return to Russian imperial-nationalist historiography. From the 1930s, eastern Ukrainian urban centers, although including large ethnic Ukrainian majorities, became increasingly dominated by Russian language and culture.

The most devastating example of the reversal of these policies was the 1933 artificial famine that claimed 5 to 7 million lives in Ukraine. The nationally conscious peasantry based in private farms was decimated. Although widely publicized by the Ukrainian diaspora on its fiftieth anniversary in 1983, the *holodymyr*, or famine, only became a subject of public discussion in the USSR in the late 1980s as the result of Mikhail Gorbachev's policy of glasnost. The Communist Party of Ukraine only condemned the famine in moderate tones in 1990 and a law was not adopted until 2006 that described the event as "genocide."

Ukraine inherited a fifth of its population in seven *oblasts*, or regions, that had historically existed outside tsarist Russia or the USSR. Four of these western Ukrainian *oblasts* (in Galicia and northern Bukovina) underwent nation building under Austrian rule prior to 1918.

After its incorporation into the former USSR, nation building in western Ukraine was further facilitated by the Soviet regime. Urban centers in western Ukraine had been populated largely by non-Ukrainians prior to the Soviet annexation of the region in 1939. But after 1945, western Ukrainians moved in large numbers into urban centers that were largely empty due to the genocide against the Jews and the ethnic cleansing of Poles after the forced movement of Poland's borders to the west. Lviv, western Ukraine's largest city, was repopulated by Ukrainians after 1945 as the region underwent Soviet-style industrialization.

Transcarpathia also underwent nation building after its incorporation into the USSR. As a consequence of Hungarian asssimilationist policies, the region had always been the least nationally conscious of any western Ukrainian region. By the late 1930s, two orientations competed for the allegiance of eastern Slavs: Ukrainian and Rusyn, the adherents of the latter claiming that theirs was a separate and fourth eastern Slavic nationality. After 1945, Soviet nationality policies automatically designated all of the eastern Slav inhabitants of Transcarpathia as Ukrainians. Although a Rusyn revival developed in the late 1980s, it remained marginal in scope, unlike the revivals in Slovakia and former Yugoslavia.[1]

Thus, the Soviet Union pursued contradictory policies in Ukraine. The modernization of Ukraine ensured that its urban centers came to be dominated by ethnic Ukrainians, as seen in the capital city of Kyiv. This development, and the links between industrialization, urbanization, and nation building, made the Ukrainian SSR and independent Ukraine very different from what Ukraine had been in the early twentieth century, when the smaller number of urban centers in Ukrainian lands were dominated by Russians, Jews, and Poles. The eastern and southern parts of Ukraine were exposed to Russification and bilingualism. In western Ukraine, national consciousness grew in Galicia and Volhynia; in Transcarpathia, Soviet power came down on the side of Ukrainian rather than Rusyn identity.

By the postwar era, urban centers and institutions in the Ukrainian SSR were demographically dominated by ethnic Ukrainians. But, because nation building and modernization were only permitted by first, the Austrians, and second, the Soviets, in western Ukraine, the bulk of the republic's largest urban and industrial centers in eastern and southern Ukraine became Russophone or bilingually Ukrainian-Russian.

Soviet policies toward Ukraine deliberately played eastern Ukrainians against their western Ukrainian "bourgeois nationalist" counterparts. What differentiated inhabitants of the two regions was their attitude toward Soviet power. Eastern Ukrainians did not see Soviet power as imported and alien since they had lived with it since 1921 after the USSR was established. Western Ukrainians, on the other hand, saw Soviet power in the same manner as citizens in the three Baltic republics did: as imported, foreign, and "Russian." This division between eastern and western Ukraine, which independent Ukraine inherited, continues to complicate national integration in contemporary Ukraine. Starkly evident in the differing degrees of support for Viktor Yushchenko and his opponent Viktor Yanukovych in the 2004 elections that led to the Orange Revolution, differences in the perspectives of citizens in the west and east also complicate policy making and influence election outcomes.

The End of Soviet Rule and Ukrainian Independence

The differences discussed above between the western and eastern parts of Ukraine also influenced the development of opposition and civil society. As in the three Baltic states, nationalist partisans fought against Soviet power in western Ukraine from 1942 until the early 1950s. After the Ukrainian Insurgent Army (UPA) was destroyed, many members continued to operate underground. Others infiltrated newly established Soviet institutions in western Ukraine. Nationalist sentiment that built on a strong national consciousness influenced the creation of nationalist dissident groups in western Ukraine, such as the National Front, from the 1960s to the 1980s.

Ukraine was home to a relatively large number of dissident movements, such as the Ukrainian Helsinki Group. Ukrainian prisoners of conscience were the largest ethnic group proportionate to their share of the population in the Soviet gulag, or system of forced-labor prison camps. As in other non-Russian republics, Ukrainian dissidents promoted *both* national and democratic rights. Some groups called for Ukraine's separation from the USSR; others demanded the transformation of the USSR into a loose confederation of sovereign republics.

National communism was also never totally crushed. Its main adherents were either imprisoned or murdered in the early 1930s when Stalin reversed indigenization. But, during periods of liberalization, as in the 1960s and in the Gorbachev era, national communism again raised its head within the Communist Party in the Ukrainian SSR.

In 1990–1991, as the Soviet Union slowly disintegrated, the Communist Party within the Ukrainian SSR divided into "national sovereign" communist and "imperial" communist wings. The latter became discredited after it gave support to the hardline coup in August 1991 that was defeated by Russian pro-democratic forces led by President Boris Yeltsin. National communists coalesced around parliamentary speaker Leonid Kravchuk in parliament, which had become more of a real institution after republican semifree elections were permitted in March 1990. For the first time, a non-Communist opposition obtained a quarter of the seats within the Soviet Ukrainian parliament (known as the Supreme Soviet).

Radical and moderate tendencies appeared within the opposition movement in the late 1980s during the more liberalized Gorbachev era. Former dissidents and prisoners of conscience from the 1960s to the early 1980s played a strategic role in the creation of the moderate Ukrainian Popular Movement (Rukh) in 1987–1988.[2] These former dissidents were joined by the cultural intelligentsia concerned about Russification and the deplorable state of Ukrainian language and culture. More radical nationalists grouped within the Ukrainian Inter-Party Assembly.

Moderates and radicals only began to demand Ukrainian independence in 1989–1990. Only the moderates in Rukh had a real strategic influence because they had participated in the 1990 elections the radicals had boycotted. Through a combination of pressure from the more moderate Rukh and national communists, the Ukrainian SSR declared independence in August 1991 after the hard-line coup collapsed in Moscow.

All shades of Ukrainian political life (Rukh, radical nationalists, and national communists) supported the drive to state independence after the Moscow coup failed. The discredited "imperial communists" could not put up any opposition because the Communist Party had been banned for supporting the hard-line Moscow coup. This movement toward independence was crowned by the December 1, 1991, referendum on independence that was supported overwhelmingly by 92 percent of Ukrainians. A week later Ukraine, Belarus, and Russia signed an agreement to transform the USSR into the Commonwealth of Independent States (CIS), and the USSR ceased to exist later that same month.[3]

Political Institutions

Ukraine adopted a semi-presidential constitution in June 1996. This institutional framework created at times an uneasy balance between the executive and parliament. In contrast to the political systems in most other CIS states, the Ukrainian parliament continued to have power and influence throughout the pre–Orange Revolution era. Governments were controlled by the executive, which had the right to dismiss them, a power that was used extensively.

In roundtable negotiations in the Orange Revolution a compromise package was agreed upon that was voted on by parliament on December 8, 2004. The package amended the election law to reduce election fraud, adopted constitutional reforms to go into effect in January 2006, and replaced the Central Election Commission chairman. The reformed constitution transforms Ukraine into a parliamentary-presidential republic, a political system more common in Central and Eastern Europe and the Baltic states. The government is now responsible not to the president but to a parliamentary coalition. The president still controls foreign and defense policy, the National Security and Defense Council, the Security Service, and the prosecutor's office. The president also has a new right to disband parliament if it fails to create a coalition or government within a thirty-day deadline.

In April 2004 the election law was changed, and all 450 seats were contested in a proportional system in the March 2006 and September 2007 elections. Ukraine's 2006 elections were also conducted under a fully proportional system for local councils.

Postcommunist states that have adopted parliamentary systems have progressed further in democratization, and they tend to be based in Central and Eastern Europe and the three Baltic states. In Russia and the CIS, the dominant political system is super-presidential, with parliaments emasculated by overly powerful executives and opposition groups marginalized. In moving to a parliamentary system, Ukraine has therefore moved away from the CIS and toward the European norm.

Constitutional reforms did not lead to political stability, as the reforms themselves had been quickly introduced, with many issues not fully thought through. The Venice Council, the legal advisory board of the Council of Europe, had criticized many of the reforms in 2005 as insufficiently clear in dividing responsibilities between different institutions. These institutional conflicts and inadequacies in the reforms were made worse by a growing personal conflict between President Yushchenko and Prime Minister Yanukovych. The increasingly difficult relations between the executive and government culminated in the spring 2007 constitutional crisis. On April 2, 2007, President Yushchenko dissolved parliament and called early elections, the date for which was finally settled on as September 30. The decree to dissolve parliament had little constitutional legality, as the president had no legal right to dismiss parliament except in specific instances. The Constitutional Court was unable to make a ruling due to infighting between supporters of the president and prime minister that severely weakened this key institution.

Parties and Elections

On the same day as the referendum on independence in December 1991, parliamentary speaker Kravchuk was the victor in Ukraine's first presidential election, winning in the first round with 61.59 percent. The former ideological secretary of the Communist Party in Ukraine became independent Ukraine's first president. National Democrat reformers grouped in Rukh entered the election with Vyacheslav Chornovil, who obtained only a quarter of the vote compared to first place Kravchuk's 62 percent. Together the five National Democrat and Liberal candidates won a combined 35 percent.

In addition to the executive, the Ukrainian parliament also continued to be dominated by former Communists until the March 1994 elections. Domination of the executive and parliament by former Communists had a negative impact on economic reform and increasingly upon democratization in Ukraine's first years of independence.

During the Kravchuk era (December 1991–July 1994), Ukraine's political landscape continued to be dominated by three groups with little political party development. The Communist Party of Ukraine (KPU) returned, after being banned from August 1991–October 1993, as a new political party led by Petro Symonenko. Registering as a new Communist Party meant it legally had no connection to the pre–

August 1991 party, and no claim to Communist Party assets that had been nationalized after the party was banned. The newly registered KPU attracted less than 5 percent of the members of the pre-1991 Communist Party in Ukraine, which, at its peak in 1985 when Gorbachev came to power, had 3.5 million members. The post-1993 membership of the KPU has never exceeded 150,000 members.

The KPU's high point of influence was in the 1990s when it was ostensibly the main opposition to the ruling authorities. In the 1994–1998 and 1998–2002 parliaments the KPU had the largest factions, with 135 and 123 deputies respectively. In the October–November 1999 presidential election, KPU leader Symonenko came in second in a field of thirteen candidates and then faced incumbent Kuchma in round two. Kuchma defeated Symonenko, and the KPU's fortunes declined in the new millennium.

The 2002 parliamentary elections, in which Viktor Yushchenko's Our Ukraine bloc came in first with 23.57 percent of the vote, signified a break with the dominance of the left in opposition politics. Our Ukraine fared poorly in the March 2006 and September 2007 elections after many voters defected to the Yuliya Tymoshenko bloc. Our Ukraine, which had expected to be a close second to the Party of Regions, came in third in the 2006 and 2007 elections with 13.95 and 14.15 percent, respectively, nearly 10 percent less than what it had achieved under Kuchma. Many Orange voters punished Our Ukraine for removing the Tymoshenko government and dividing the Orange camp and for their disillusionment with President Victor Kushchenko.

In contrast to the parliamentary elections in 1998, when it received 24.65 percent of the vote, in 2002, the KPU, with 19.98 percent of the vote, failed to come in first in the election of the 225 parliamentary seats elected proportionately. In the 2002–2006 parliament, the KPU faction was halved to only sixty-six deputies. The KPU declined rapidly following the end of the Kuchma era, as many voters transfer their allegiance to the Party of Regions. In the March 2006 and September 2007 elections, the KPU obtained only 3.66 and 5.39 percent, respectively. As a political party of pensioners, the KPU, with less than 5 percent support, will have serious difficulties in surviving in the medium term.

The Socialist Party (SPU), led by Oleksandr Moroz, has been the only serious left-wing competitor to the KPU. This party was created in late 1991 when the KPU was illegal. The SPU is best described as a left-wing Social Democratic Party that is more committed to democratization but largely opposed to economic reform. The SPU is the only Ukrainian party member of the Socialist International. Its positive stance on Ukrainian statehood is different from that of the KPU, which has always seen Ukraine as part of a revived USSR. The SPU is progressively eclipsing the KPU in membership (100,000, compared to the KPU's 150,000) and electoral support. In the 2004 and 2006 elections, the SPU surpassed the Communists for the first time. In 2004, Moroz came in third with 5.82 percent of the vote followed by Petro Symonenko with 4.97. The SPU reached fourth place in the 2006 elections with 5.69 percent and thirty-three seats followed by the KPU with 3.66 percent and twenty-one deputies.

The SPU's fortunes have come to an end. Their voters have not forgiven them for defecting from the Orange coalition in summer 2006 and joining the Party of Regions and KPU in the Anti-Crisis coalition. Early elections in September 2007 marginalized the SPU as a political force that has played an important center-left role in Ukrainian political life since the early 1990s. The SPU can only hope to return to Parliament if it replaces its discredited leader, Oleksandr Moroz.

On the right there are a plethora of national democratic parties that grew out of Rukh. As in the Soviet era, these parties and movements combined national and democratic demands, such as affirmative action for the Ukrainian language, making them popular primarily in Ukrainian-speaking regions of western and central Ukraine. This changed in the 2007 elections when the Yulia Tymoshenko bloc obtained 15–25 percent throughout eastern and southern Ukraine outside the Party of Regions strongholds of the Donbas and Crimea.

The inability of national democratic candidates to win presidential elections or obtain parliamentary majorities created a dilemma. As pro-statehood parties, they felt inclined to cooperate with former national communists who were increasingly dubbed the "party of power." In the 1990s, these two political groups were allied in their support for quasi reform and the defense of Ukrainian statehood against a Communist domestic threat and a Russian external threat. Dealing with Russia's refusal to come to terms with Ukrainian independence and pressuring it to agree to recognize the border thus took up the entire first term of the Kuchma presidency (July 1994– November 1999). The threat from the KPU was only defeated in the 1999 elections, after which it went into terminal decline with many of its voters defecting to the Party of Regions.

Centrist-liberal and social democratic parties emerged in Ukraine in the late Soviet and early post-Soviet eras. They tended to attract those who were anticommunist but did not wish to join national democratic parties. Centrist parties therefore had a potentially respectable niche that lay between the left and the center-right. Throughout most of Kuchma's first term in office, centrist parties remained marginal, only to be gradually taken over by the "party of power" (former national communists). They made their public appearance in the 1998 parliamentary and 1999 presidential elections where they entered parliament and backed Kuchma's reelection.

By the late 1990s, Ukraine's center niche had been completely taken over by oligarchs who needed to convert their economic gains into political power. Unlike Ukraine's left and right parties, which have clear-cut ideologies, Ukraine's centrist parties have always been empty ideologically, acting merely as *krishy* (roofs) for regional, business, and corrupt interests. One of the first centrist parties grew out of the Democratic Platform of the Communist Party in Ukraine, which established the Party of Democratic Revival of Ukraine (PDVU) that became the People's Democratic Party (NDP). Kuchma failed in his attempt to establish the NDP as his party of power (i.e., ruling party) after the 1998 elections. A Liberal Party was also quickly established in Donbas and a Party of Economic Revival of Crimea (PEVK) in the Crimea. The PDVU created the New Ukraine bloc, which supported Kuchma in the 1994 elections, as did the Union of Industrialists and Entrepreneurs. In the second half of the 1990s, the PDVU, Social Democratic United Party (SDPUo), and Green Party, like other initially genuine centrist parties, were also taken over by oligarchic business interests. Genuine liberal reformers left to join national democratic parties, such as Viktor Pynzenyk's Reform and Order Party, which has aligned with the Tymoshenko bloc with whom it went into the 2007 elections.

Centrist parties faced three difficulties in Ukraine in the 1990s when they attempted to grow into respectable liberal and social democratic parties. First, although Ukraine has a history of social democratic and liberal political thought in the tsarist and Austro-Hungarian empires, this tradition was destroyed by the Soviet regime. Even in interwar western Ukraine under Poland, centrist parties were marginalized by the radical right Organization of Ukrainian Nationalists. Therefore, unlike other postcommunist states, Ukraine could not simply revive pre-Soviet parties banned under the Soviet regime. Genuine centrist parties have also found it difficult to compete with the national democrats because it has always been easier to mobilize Ukrainians by appealing to *both* national and democratic issues. This was as true in the late Soviet era with Rukh as it was in the 2004 elections and the Orange Revolution. By their very nature, centrist parties require an established middle class that supports the rule of law, private business and property, civil society, and an independent media. These aspects of Ukrainian society are only in the process of being slowly created. Genuine centrist parties should have been allies of Our Ukraine in promoting reform. Instead, centrist parties, during Kuchma's second term (1999–2004), had been taken over by oligarchs who backed authoritarianism, rather than liberal democracy.

In 1998 centrist parties made their first appearance in parliament as four of the eight parties that managed to cross the 4 percent threshold in the proportional half of the elections. Besides the SDPUo these included the Green Party and the NDP headed by Prime Minister Valeriy Pustovoitenko. The SDPUo was the last of the parties that reached the 4 percent threshold in both the 1998 and 2002 elections with 4.01 and 6.27 percent respectively, but reconfigured as the *Ne Tak!* (Not Like This!) bloc it failed to enter the 2006 parliament when its support collapsed to only 1.01 percent, leading it not to stand in the 2007 elections. The Dnipropetrovsk oligarch clan took over the Labor Ukraine party, and the Donbas oligarchs created the Party of Regions. The Regions of Ukraine party was created in March 2001 with the unification of five parties, including the Regional Revival of Ukraine, which had fared badly in the 1998 elections, when it obtained only 0.9 percent of the vote. The main base of the Party of Regions lies in Donetsk.

In the March 2002 elections the Party of Regions joined four other pro-Kuchma centrist groups in the For a United Ukraine bloc (ZYU). The other four parties included the Party of Industrialists and Entrepreneurs, the Agrarians, the NDP, and Labor Ukraine. With 11.77 percent of the vote, ZYU came in third in the proportional half of the elections, but was able to control half of parliament by adding a large number of deputies elected in single mandate (majoritarian) districts. In the 2006 elections, the Party of Regions came in first with 32.14 percent and 186 seats; it was the only former pro-Kuchma centrist party successful in entering parliament in that election. The Party of Regions won 34.37 percent in the September 2007 elections but obtained fewer votes and eleven fewer seats than in the March 2006 elections. Together the Party of Regions and KPU had insufficient seats to create a coalition, and even with the possible addition of the Volodymyr Lytvyn bloc the three party coalition would still fall short of the minimum 226 seats for a coalition. As in other parliamentary democracies with proportional election laws, the Party of Regions coming first did not guarantee that it would create the government.

In western and central Ukraine, oligarchic parties are unpopular. In the Kuchma era the Party of Regions and Labor Ukraine were popular in their local bases of

Donetsk and Dnipropetrovsk, unlike the SDPUo, which was never popular in Kyiv, a national democratic stronghold. The Kyiv clan's SDPUo barely scraped by the 4 percent threshold in the city of Kyiv in the 2002 election when it obtained 4.85 percent, a drop by half from the 8.48 percent it had obtained in the 1998 election. In local elections to the Kyiv city council held at the same time as parliamentary elections in 2002, the SDPUo fared even worse. Although it came in last in the proportional half of the 2002 elections, the SDPUo nevertheless succeeded in placing its members in many high places, due to the fact that SDPUo leader Medvedchuk headed the presidential administration in Kuchma's last two years in office (2002–2004). The Labor Ukraine party, NDP, and SDPUo have become marginalized in the post–Orange Revolution era.

In the late Soviet era and throughout much of the 1990s, eastern Ukraine remained politically passive, and its local leaders were not part of the national elites. This situation changed after Kuchma's election in 1994 when large numbers of officials from Dnipropetrovsk came to Kyiv. The Donbas leadership only entered the national central elite during Kuchma's second term in office, particularly when Yanukovych was appointed prime minister in November 2002 and then went on to become the authorities' presidential candidate in the 2004 election. Yanukovych was governor of Donetsk between 1997 and 2002.

All of Ukraine's centrist parties have three factors in common. First, many of them are Russian speaking. Second, all of them were pro-Kuchma and preferred the authoritarian political system increasingly evident in Ukraine during Kuchma's second term. This orientation reflected the strong influence of Soviet political culture among them and their preference for a hybrid system combining elements of Soviet and Western political-economic systems. In the realm of foreign policy, these orientations were translated into a vague and constantly shifting, multivector foreign policy. Domestic policies did not back up the stated foreign policy goals of "returning to Europe." Third, centrists are ideologically amorphous. Short-term economic and political gain and power are more important than ideological principles to centrist parties. Centrist parties are top-down virtual parties with memberships that are usually forced into joining at state institutions or through bribery. Their lack of real members is evident in their inability to mobilize supporters for demonstrations or rallies (as seen in their inability to organize a counterrevolution to the Orange Revolution). Those who attend centrist party rallies do so either because of intimidation or because they have been paid to attend, as evidenced during the paid anti-Yushchenko rallies in April 2007 in Kyiv following the dismissal of parliament.

Eventually, some former oligarchs turned against Kuchma. Both former prime minister Pavlo Lazarenko and Prime Minister Tymoshenko joined the anti-Kuchma opposition in 1998–1999. Fatherland aligned with other anti-Kuchma opposition forces such as the SPU and the national democrats and became the main party in the Tymoshenko bloc. The ouster of Yushchenko's government in April 2001 placed him in opposition to Kuchma, forcing him to join the SPU and Tymoshenko. Yushchenko then created the center-right reformist Our Ukraine bloc, which came first in the proportional half of the 2002 parliamentary elections, but obtained 10 percent less in the 2006 and 2007 elections when it came in third. Our Ukraine–Peoples Self-Defense, as its 2007 election bloc was called, improved its ratings in the 2007 elections after it underwent internal reforms, the purging of corrupt businessmen, such as Poroshenko, and the election of a popular leader, Yuriy Lutsenko.

Civil Society: The Orange Revolution

The events that came to be called the Orange Revolution occurred when government authorities attempted to blatantly rig the presidential elections in 2004. Orange was chosen by the Yushchenko team as an optimistic and neutral color to attract a broad constituency of voters, rather than using the national blue and yellow flag. Ukraine under Kuchma was a competitive semiauthoritarian regime. Such regimes are inherently unstable and very vulnerable during periodic elections where they can be challenged by united oppositions. Five of what have come to be called electoral revolutions that used mass mobilization to oust authoritarian leaders, those in Slovakia (1998), Croatia (1999), Serbia (2000), Georgia (2003), and Ukraine (2004), took place in semiauthoritarian regimes, which, unlike fully authoritarian regimes, provide space for and allow civil society and independent media to operate.

The victory of Our Ukraine in the 2002 election ensured that Yushchenko would become the main alternative to the authorities' candidate, Yanukovych, in the 2004 election. The 2004 election, therefore, became a choice in the eyes of many voters between consolidating democracy (Yushchenko) or consolidating authoritarianism (Yanukovych).[4]

National democrat reformers finally gained the presidency in 2004 as a result of the Orange Revolution, but this victory was a long time coming. National democrats failed to win Ukraine's first presidential election in 1991 and did not put forward major candidates in either the 1994 or 1999 presidential elections. The main competition in the 1994 race was between two wings of former national communists: former prime minister Kuchma and incumbent Kravchuk. Kravchuk led in the first round by 37.7 percent to Kuchma's 31.3 percent, but Kuchma edged him out in the second round by 52.1 percent to 45.1 percent. As former national communists, Kravchuk and Kuchma went on to become centrist allies in the late 1990s. The main competition in the 1999 election, then, was between the centrist Kuchma and communist Symonenko.

In the 1999 presidential election, the two candidates put forward by Rukh, which had split into two parties, together obtained only 3.4 percent of the vote, down from a quarter of the vote in the December 1991 elections for the national democratic challenger, Vyacheslav Chornovil. Some national democratic votes went to former Security Service chairman Yevhen Marchuk who obtained 8.1 percent. Marchuk's populist anticorruption and anti-Kuchma rhetoric was very reminiscent of the rhetoric of Yuliya Tymoshenko, who created the Fatherland Party, then the Tymoshenko bloc, and ran in the 2002 elections as the leader of the National Salvation Front. Marchuk sold out his voters when he agreed to become secretary of the National Security and Defense Council (NRBO), just prior to the second round of the 1999 election. His allies transferred their allegiance to Tymoshenko.

In the 1999 election Oleksandr Moroz, head of the SPU, obtained 11.3 percent, a result similar to his 13 percent in the 1994 election. Although Moroz came in ahead of the KPU leader Symonenko in the 2004 election, his vote dropped by half to 5.5 percent. After over a decade of Moroz's leadership, anger among Socialist voters at the SPU's defection from the Orange camp led it to defeat in the 2007 election. The lower combined vote for the two left-wing candidates (10 percent) reflected the fact that the 2004 election was largely a contest between Yushchenko and Yanukovych.

After his reelection in 1999 Kuchma set out to remove the leftist leadership of parliament. In early 2000, national democrats and centrists combined forces in parliament to create a majority of 253 that undertook, with executive backing, what came to be known as a "velvet revolution." These eleven nonleft factions were united less in their support for reforms or Kuchma than in their hostility to the left. The four left factions, in contrast, only commanded the loyalty of 171 deputies. The creation of a parliamentary majority was aimed at supporting Yushchenko's government. On January 13, 2000, 253 deputies from the national-democrat–centrist alliance created a "pro-reform" majority with the aim of speeding up reforms and harmonizing relations between parliament and the executive.

Kuchma also sought to increase his presidential powers in four questions in a referendum held in April 2000. The referendum was badly flawed, and its results were not internationally recognized: 84.78 percent of those who participated voted in favor of the right of the president to dissolve parliament if it failed to pass a budget within a month or create a majority within three months, 89.06 percent supported the withdrawal of immunity from parliamentary deputies, and 89.97 percent supported the reduction in the number of deputies from 450 to 300. The fourth and most controversial amendment on introducing a second parliamentary chamber was backed by 81.81 percent. Whatever the results, the referendum had no real international credibility: no international organizations sent observers.

Kuchma's plans to increase presidential powers were not implemented for two reasons. First, what became known as the "Kuchmagate Crisis" began on November 28, 2000. Excerpts of tapes made illicitly in Kuchma's office by presidential guard Mykola Melnychenko were released before parliament. Kuchma was heard on the tape ordering Interior Minister Yuriy Kravchenko to "deal with" opposition journalist Heorhiy Gongadze, who had been kidnapped on September 16, 2000. His decapitated body was found two months later. Second, mounting criticism of Prime Minister Yushchenko's policies from oligarchs close to Kuchma also blocked change. The oligarchs began losing large sources of corruptly earned income from the cancellation of privileges for their joint ventures and barter arrangements in the energy sector. Deputy Prime Minister Tymoshenko reorganized the energy sector and targeted distribution companies owned by leading oligarch groups. Anticorruption measures brought in over $2 billion into the government budget to pay off wage and pension arrears.

However unpopular he was among the oligarchs, Prime Minister Yushchenko's popularity soared among the public, reaching 50 to 60 percent. His government was credited by the public with bringing Ukraine's first economic growth in a decade and with repaying wage and pension arrears. In spite of this popular support, Yushchenko's government was removed by a parliamentary vote of no confidence in April 2001 with the support of centrist oligarchs and the KPU. From this moment on, centrists and national democrats stood in opposition to one another, culminating in the 2004 election contest between Yushchenko and Yanukovych.

The Kuchmagate Crisis mobilized the largest opposition movement since the late Soviet era in Ukraine. This movement against Kuchma was led by the Ukraine without Kuchma movement (based in Kyiv and dominated by radical center-left anti-Kuchma groups, such as the SPU and the Tymoshenko bloc) and the nongovernmental organization (NGO) For Truth (based in Lviv and dominated by moderate anti-Kuchma, national democratic groups). The Ukraine without Kuchma movement evolved into the Forum for National Salvation, which Tymoshenko took over as her personal election bloc in the 2002 elections. Throughout 2001–2003, these anti-Kuchma protests were followed by "Arise Ukraine!" rallies that brought together the opposition against Kuchma and his centrist allies. These protests were an important training ground for youth and election observer NGOs and political parties for the 2002 and 2004 elections and the Orange Revolution.

Ukraine's October 2004 presidential election was more than just the election of Ukraine's third president. Evidence had mounted, particularly during the Kuchmagate Crisis that President Kuchma had been involved in a wide range of illegal activities. Kuchma and his oligarchic allies, then, were doubly afraid of an anti-Kuchma victory. Not only would they lose their power, but they might also be prosecuted for their corruption and illegal acts. This, in turn, ruled out consideration of anything but a victory by the authorities' candidate, Prime Minister Yanukovych. As Kuchma correctly predicted, the 2004 election became Ukraine's dirtiest and most bitterly contested.

Ukraine was unique among the CIS states in that it had a large pro-Western, reformist opposition movement with experience in government. Yushchenko's Our Ukraine bloc came in first in the proportional half of the 2002 parliamentary elections, receiving more than double the support of the pro-Kuchma For a United Ukraine bloc. Yushchenko had remained the country's most popular politician since he led Ukraine's most successful government in 2000–2001.

The 2004 election was expected not only to decide who would become the country's next president, but also which trajectory the country would take. A victory by Yanukovych would have consolidated an oligarchic-autocratic political-economic system in Ukraine. This stark choice, coupled with the personal threat felt by the ruling elites, meant the elections would be bitterly fought to the very end by both sides.

A large proportion of the twenty-three candidates that stood in the election were virtual ("technical") candidates whose only purpose was to work on behalf of the authorities and against the opposition by taking allocated seats in electoral commissions. State-administrative resources were massively deployed in support of Yanukovych. The state-controlled mass media, particularly television, gave widespread positive coverage to Yanukovych but only covered Yushchenko in negative terms. Yanukovych had public and shadow election campaign teams. The official team was headed by the chairman of the National Bank, Serhiy Tyhypko. In the shadow campaign, Russian interests and the presidential administration were deeply involved in trying to bring Yanukovych a victory. In the process, the number of "dirty tricks" in the four-month campaign was legendary. The most dramatic of these was the poisoning of Yushchenko with dioxin in September 2004, which removed him from the campaign trail for a month.

Yushchenko won the first round of the election followed by Yanukovych on October 31, 2004. But the results were only released after ten days, the maximum permitted by Ukrainian law. Yanukovych's shadow campaign team and the presidential administration hacked into the Central Election Commission (CVK) server, which allowed them to manipulate results as they were being sent to the CVK. Despite the government's manipulation, and the poisoning of Yushchenko, he won round one.

The stakes were too high for the authorities to permit a Yushchenko victory in the runoff election on November 21, 2004. The Yanukovych forces ratcheted up their efforts to deliver him the election by using more blatant fraud, whatever the actual vote. The Committee of Voters of Ukraine, a well-known NGO, calculated that 2.8 million votes were fraudulently added to Yanukovych's tally in round two. Fraud was especially blatant in Donetsk and Luhansk, Yanukovych's home base, where turnout rates allegedly increased by 20 percent between rounds one and two. Ballot stuffing, massive abuse of absentee ballots, and voting at home were also used.

In making the decision to opt for blatant fraud in round two, the authorities miscalculated. First, they assumed that Ukrainians would remain passive. After all, during opposition protests in Kuchmagate and "Arise Ukraine!" in 2000–2003 the opposition had mobilized rallies of only 20,000 to 50,000 supporters, which had increased to 80,000–100,000 in the 2004 elections. But during the Orange Revolution, millions of citizens came onto the streets of Kyiv over seventeen days in bitter winter weather.

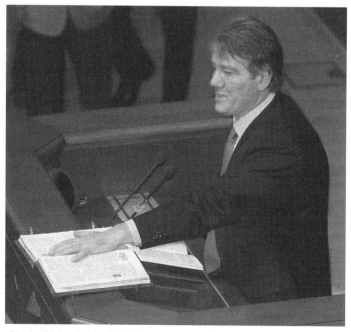

Photo 15.1.   Viktor Yushchenko after being poisoned by dioxin.

(Source: This photo was taken through joint efforts of the UNIAN news agency (www.unian.net) and the International Renaissance Foundation (George Soros Foundation in Ukraine, www.irf.kiev.ua).)

Surveys have found that one in five of Ukrainians participated in the Orange Revolution, with the highest number from western Ukraine (where a third took part) and the lowest from eastern Ukraine (where less than 5 percent did so). Second, the authorities underestimated the international reaction to their election fraud. They counted on the United States turning a blind eye because Ukraine had the fourth-largest military contingent in Iraq. They were again wrong. Three days after round two, U.S. Secretary of State Colin Powell refused to recognize the fraudulent official results released that same day, a step encouraged by Ukrainians themselves who were creating the Orange Revolution on the streets of Kyiv. Canada and the EU quickly backed the U.S. position.

The large numbers of Ukrainians who joined the Orange Revolution were responding to the stark choice facing Ukraine if Yanukovych became president through massive fraud. In round two of the election, Yushchenko received support from a very wide spectrum that ranged from the Socialists to the business community, led by Anatoliy Kinakh, and the liberal Our Ukraine to the center-left-liberal Tymoshenko bloc. Kyiv's popular Mayor Oleksandr Omelchenko provided crucial logistical support to the Orange Revolution.

Young people, such as students, were especially attracted to the Orange Revolution. A rally on the eve of the first round of the elections attracted 25,000 students in support of Yushchenko. Ukraine's normally apolitical youth were mobilized to take part in election-monitoring organizations (Znayu [I Know]), radical youth groups (Pora [It's Time] modeled on Serbia's Otpor and Georgia's Kmara), and pro-Yushchenko youth groups (Chysta Ukrayina [Clean Up Ukraine]).

The Ukrainian parliament and the Supreme Court overturned the fraudulent election results that declared Yanukovych the victor in round two. A repeat election was called for December 26. Roundtable negotiations brokered by Poland, Lithuania, and the EU led to a compromise; the election law was revised so that many of the fraudulent acts committed in round two could not be repeated. Yushchenko also agreed to support constitutional reform to go into effect after the March 2006 parliamentary election.

After winning by 8 percent in the rerun of round two, Yushchenko was inaugurated in January 2005 as Ukraine's third president. Ukraine's transformation into a parliamentary-presidential system in 2006 has brought it closer to the European norm and differentiated it from the super-presidential political systems of Russia and the CIS, where parliaments are emasculated. Pro-democracy reformers have won four elections since 2002 and Ukraine has held three free elections since 2004.

Orange Power

Yushchenko was propelled to power by the Orange Revolution that followed election fraud in round two of Ukraine's 2004 presidential elections. His election victory came about as a consequence of a very broad political alliance that included center-left (SPU, Tymoshenko bloc) and free market liberals, and center-right national democrats (Party of Industrialists and Entrepreneurs, Our Ukraine). There were few divisions within this election alliance over political and institutional policies. They agreed on democratizing political life, increasing respect for the rule of law, reforming the judiciary and court system, and battling corruption. The policy areas that strained the

Photo 15.2.   Viktor Yanukovych, the regime candidate in Ukraine's 2004 elections, and some of his supporters.

(Source: This photo was taken through joint efforts of the UNIAN news agency (www.unian.net) and the International Renaissance Foundation (George Soros Foundation in Ukraine, www.irf.kiev.ua).)

coalition were the trying of members of the former regime on charges of corruption and election fraud, the degree of reprivatization to be undertaken, economic reform (particularly land privatization), and foreign policy priorities (with the most divisive issue being NATO membership).

Tymoshenko had supported investigating a large number of privatizations while Yushchenko and the Yekhanurov government opposed reprivatizations in all but the most egregious of cases, such as Kryvorizhstal, the only reprivatization in Orange Ukraine.[5] Divisions over these issues divided the coalition fundamentally between limited state interventionists (center-left SPU and Tymoshenko bloc) and liberal free marketers (Party of Industrialists and Entrepreneurs, Our Ukraine). In Yushchenko's first 100 days in office, divisions over economic policies brought about an oil crisis, and concerns continued over economic policies that focused on social issues. In September 2005, Yushchenko dismissed the Tymoshenko government and replaced her as prime minister with Yury Yekhanurov, a technocrat and ally of Yushchenko's from the 1990s. The Yekhanurov government lasted until after the March 2006 elections, when it was replaced by one led again by Yanukovych.

The 2006 and 2007 Parliamentary Elections

Out of forty-five and twenty parties and blocs that stood in the March 2006 and September 2007 elections, respectively, only five crossed the 3 percent threshold. The

2006 elections brought three Orange parties to parliament (Our Ukraine, Tymoshenko bloc, SPU), but the SPU defected to the Blue camp represented by the Party of Regions and KPU. The 2007 elections brought two Orange and two Blue political forces into parliament. The 2006 and 2007 results were surprisingly similar to those in the repeat second round of the 2004 elections, with Orange and Blue (Party of Regions) supporters divided approximately 55–45. The Party of Regions with 32.14 percent was the key winner and came in first with 186 deputies, a threefold increase in its deputies that it possessed in the 2002–2006 parliament. The Party of Regions came in again as the clear winner in the 2007 elections with 34.37 percent.

In the 2006 elections the Tymoshenko bloc also scored a remarkable success, tripling its support to 22.29 percent, and became the second largest faction with 129 deputies and in the 2007 elections dramatically increased its vote by 1.5 million votes to receive 30.71 percent. Our Ukraine fared poorly, coming in third in the 2006 and 2007 elections with 13.95 and 14.15 percent respectively, a 10 percent decline in support. Clearly it was easier to win votes in opposition than in power.

In the 2006 elections the left came in fourth and fifth with 5.69 percent (SPU) and 3.66 percent (KPU), and together had only fifty-four deputies, down from the customary 40 percent of parliamentary deputies that the combined left controlled in the 1990s. In the 2007 elections the only left-wing force to enter parliament was the KPU with 5.39 percent of the vote. The SPU's decline came about as a consequence of its voters' anger at the SPU's betrayal of the Orange camp in summer 2006 when SPU leader Oleksandr Moroz sought the speakership of parliament.

The Party of Regions clearly was successful in both its ability to promote itself as the champion of Russophone voters in eastern and southern Ukraine and in its ability to marginalize all other former pro-Kuchma centrists, none of whom entered the 2006 and 2007 parliaments. Whether the Party of Regions can evolve into a post-Kuchma, democratic party remains an open question. The Party of Regions is an eclectic mix of oligarchs, businessmen, senior Kuchma-era officials, and former communist voters and therefore more akin to an anti-Yushchenko popular front than to an ideologically based political party.

Between April and June 2006, two attempts were made to create coalitions. An Orange coalition of the Tymoshenko bloc, Our Ukraine, and the SPU foundered over the unwillingness of Our Ukraine and President Yushchenko to agree on Tymoshenko's return as prime minister or Moroz as parliamentary speaker. An alternative grand coalition, made up of Our Ukraine, the Party of Regions, and possibly the SPU, agreed on maintaining Our Ukraine leader Yekhanurov as prime minister. It failed after Yushchenko heeded U.S. pressure and opted for an Orange, rather than a grand, coalition.

Following the defection of the SPU, the Orange coalition collapsed before it could put forward its government. The Party of Regions offered Moroz the position of parliamentary speaker, and the SPU agreed to join the Anti-Crisis coalition composed of the Party of Regions, SPU, and KPU with 240 deputies. The coalition proposed Yanukovych as prime minister after his party agreed to sign the Universal Agreement on National Unity negotiated by Ukraine's first roundtable of political parties and the president and signed on August 3–4, 2006. Our Ukraine, which was invited into the Anti-Crisis coalition, remained bitterly divided over the expediency of joining a coalition that included the KPU and with a government led by Yanukovych. The national democratic wing of Our Ukraine supported joining the official opposition led by the Tymoshenko bloc, while the centrist business wing opted to join the coalition. Between October 2006 and February 2007 Our Ukraine went into opposition to the Anti-Crisis coalition and revived its relationship with the Tymoshenko bloc. Our Ukraine also underwent a radical internal overhaul with the election of a new leader, Vyacheslav Kyrylenko; the expulsion of corrupt and discredited businessmen; and an alliance with Lutsenko's newly formed People's Self-Defense force. Hence, Our Ukraine fought the 2007 elections as the Our Ukraine–Self-Defense bloc, with a more national democratic profile (rather than a liberal business profile as in the 2006 elections) and more energetic leadership (Orange Revolution activist Lutsenko rather than technocrat Yekhanurov, as in 2006).

The Economic Transition

Between 1989 and 1999 Ukraine's economy collapsed by more than half, a fall far greater than what occurred in North America and Western Europe in the 1930s during the Great Depression. The shadow (unofficial) economy averaged 50 percent of economic activity throughout most of the post-Soviet period, reducing income of the state budget, facilitating corruption, and encouraging ties between business and organized crime.[6]

Frequent changes of government were a major problem that plagued Ukraine's

Photo 15.3. Yanukovych and Yushchenko after Yushchenko won the rerun of the second round of the 2004 Ukrainian election, after the fraud in the second round triggered the Orange Revolution. Yanukovych's party, in the parliamentary elections two years later, won enough votes to dominate the parliament and make him prime minister, but he lost the position in 2007.

(Source: This photo was taken through joint efforts of the UNIAN news agency (www.unian.net) and the International Renaissance Foundation (George Soros Foundation in Ukraine, www.irf.kiev.ua).)

economic policies. During the Kravchuk and Kuchma eras (1991–2004), Ukraine had ten governments. Of these, the one led by Yushchenko from December 1999–April 2001 was the only one genuinely committed to economic reform and not corrupt. Yushchenko had been chairman of the National Bank when Ukraine introduced its independent currency, the *hryvnia*, in 1996.

Economic reform under Kravchuk and Kuchma was always weak. Economic reform was never a priority for Kravchuk. Instead, he adopted nationalist protectionist policies directed against Russia. These policies proved to be disastrous and, in 1993, the country experienced massive hyperinflation and further economic collapse. Miners' strikes and social unrest were, in fact, a result of this failure and triggered an early presidential election in 1994, which Kravchuk lost to Kuchma. When Kuchma was elected in 1994, he introduced economic reform policies to stabilize the domestic economy. The IMF and World Bank began to provide assistance for the first time to Ukraine in return for a pledge to pursue reforms and relinquish nuclear weapons.

On the whole, Kuchma's economic policies were similar to his policies in politics and foreign policy, which lacked any clear direction. Privatization was undertaken in fits and starts from 1994, but it primarily benefited a small group of oligarchs who had good relations with the president. A small and medium business class did develop, but not to the extent that it did in Central and Eastern Europe where this sector became the driving force of the postcommunist transitions. The only regions where the small and medium business sector was developing was in western and central Ukraine with funds often transferred from Ukrainians working in the EU. Until 2004, Ukraine's vast corruption, overregulation, and unfriendly business climate discouraged large volumes of foreign investment from entering the country.

The first two years of the Yushchenko administration had a high turnover of three governments. The first, headed by Tymoshenko, only lasted eight months until President Yushchenko dismissed it during the September 2005 political crisis (see "Orange Power" above). The Tymoshenko government was plagued by infighting with another wing of the Orange camp led by Petro Poroshenko, a millionaire financier of the Orange Revolution who had been appointed as National Security and Defense Council secretary. Poroshenko's position aimed to balance the radicalism of the Tymoshenko government but in the end merely led to public infighting within the Orange camp. The main areas of dispute were over the extent of reprivatization, with Tymoshenko supporting sweeping attacks on the oligarchs, and over market versus state-interventionist economic policies. Tymoshenko was replaced by Yushchenko loyalist Yekhanurov, who led a caretaker government until the March 2006 elections. A month after Yekhanurov became prime minister, he ended all speculation on reprivatization by calling a meeting of Ukraine's oligarchs to mend relations between the government and Ukraine's largest businessmen. The new relationship could be seen when Prime Minister Yekhanurov described the oligarchs in a positive manner as Ukraine's national "bourgeoisie." Yushchenko continued to maintain close relations with Ukraine's oligarchs, many of whom saw him as an ally against the Party of Regions and the Tymoshenko bloc. Vitaly Haydiuk's Industrial Union of Donbas, Ihor Kolomoysky's Privat group, and Viktor Pinchuk's Interpipe were close to Yushchenko. A second meeting of Yushchenko with big business took place in July 2007 in an attempt at soliciting support for the upcoming early elections.

Prime Minister Yekhanurov's policies failed to revive Ukraine's growth to 2004 levels when it had reached a reported 12 percent. Growth had plummeted to only 3 percent in 2005 from 12 percent the year before. In 2006, GDP growth rose to 5 percent. Ukraine's economy only began to grow in 2000 during the Yushchenko government with a 5.9 percent GDP increase, followed by 9.1 percent the next year, 4.8 percent in 2002, and 8.5 percent in 2003. The 12 percent GDP growth in 2004 was therefore exceptional, rather than the norm. The January 2006 no-confidence parliamentary vote in the Yekhanurov government was ignored by President Yushchenko, who kept it in place as a caretaker government until after the March elections. The March 2006 election results would have led to the return of Tymoshenko as prime minister, as her eponymous bloc had come first among the three Orange political forces (Our Ukraine, Tymoshenko bloc, Socialist Party). President Yushchenko and Our Ukraine, although having agreed to the right of whichever Orange party came first to propose its candidate for prime minister, backtracked at the thought of Tymoshenko returning to government. From April to June, coalition negotiations were held within the Orange camp to create a revived Orange parliamentary coalition and government led by Tymoshenko. An Orange coalition was created in late June, but before Tymoshenko's candidacy as prime minister could be put forward, the coalition imploded.

The defection of the Socialist Party ended plans to replace Yekhanurov by Tymoshenko as prime minister. The Socialist Party joined with the Communists and the Party of Regions to create an Anti-Crisis coalition that proposed the return of Yanukovych as prime minister. Yanukovych's first stint as prime minister was from November 2002 to December 2004. He was voted prime minister by parliament again on August 4, 2006, following the signing of the Universal Agreement on National Unity the night before. He therefore became the first prime minister to benefit from constitutional reforms. Prior to 2005, governments lasted on average twelve months because they were regularly dismissed by the president, but under the reformed constitution the president can no longer dismiss them. Tymoshenko returned as prime minister to head an Orange coalition following the 2007 elections.

Ukraine's energy dependency on Russia is two pronged, as Russia is also dependent on Ukrainian pipelines for the export of 80 percent of its gas. The January 2006 gas agreement, following a gas crisis that affected gas supplies to Europe, was contested by the Tymoshenko bloc and the then opposition Party of Regions in a parliamentary vote of no confidence in the Yekhanurov government, but backed by President Yushchenko and Our Ukraine. The agreement stated that a nontransparent middleman, RosUkrEnergo, be given the right to transit Central Asian gas through Russia and Ukraine to Europe. The agreement has been upheld by the Party of Regions after they returned to government, doing an about-face on their January 2006 vote. Russia's strategic aim has always been, and remains, to obtain control over Ukraine's gas pipelines. An alternative pipeline being built from Russia under the Baltic Sea to Germany will only reduce Russian gas exports from 80 to 60 percent through Ukraine.

Social Change

Economic reforms, in particular privatization, coupled with a widespread tolerance of corruption, facilitated the rise of an oligarch class that survived due to close personal, economic, and corrupt ties to the executive during Kuchma's tenure as president.[7] Instead of experiencing real social change, Ukraine became known as the "blackmail state."[8] Corruption was tolerated and even encouraged by the executive branch, even as it was diligently recorded by the law enforcement bodies. If the corrupt elites remained politically loyal to the national leaders, their files were not acted on by the prosecutor's office. Political loyalty, therefore, was exchanged for large incomes ("rents") through corruption and preferential means.

This agreement largely held throughout Kuchma's rule. On two occasions, it broke down when dissident oligarchs challenged Kuchma. In 1997–1998, former prime minister Pavlo Lazarenko established an anti-Kuchma opposition political party Hromada, which elected deputies to the 1998 parliament. Lazarenko hoped to use this victory as a springboard to challenge Kuchma in the 1999 presidential election. Kuchma went on the attack and initiated criminal charges against Lazarenko, who fled abroad. In 1999 he applied for political asylum in the United States, where a criminal case was launched against him for money laundering. In August 2006, he was sentenced to nine years in prison and fined $10 million for laundering millions of dollars through U.S. banks. Ironically, Lazarenko remains one of only three senior Ukrainian officials who have ever been charged and sentenced (the other two being in Germany, convicted of the fraud of German funds sent for Ukrainian World War II slave laborers). No senior officials have been charged inside Ukraine.

Tymoshenko was a second dissident oligarch. Tymoshenko, who had cooperated in business with Lazarenko, left Hromada after Lazarenko fled abroad and created the Fatherland Party. Hostility to her from Kuchma and his allies intensified when she joined the Yushchenko government. Deputy Prime Minister Tymoshenko was first arrested in February 2001, released, rearrested, and again released on charges arising from her activities as CEO of United Energy Systems in the mid-1990s. An important ally of Yushchenko in the Orange Revolution, she served as prime minister until Yushchenko dismissed the government in September 2005. Following her dismissal, her relations with Our Ukraine and President Yushchenko declined further. Although an informal agreement was in place to permit the leading Orange party with the greatest votes in the 2006 elections to obtain the prime minister's position in an Orange government, Our Ukraine refused to abide by the agreement, dragging out negotiations until their late June 2006 deadline. Our Ukraine and the Tymoshenko bloc reforged an alliance in February 2007 and fought the 2007 elections in an Orange alliance, creating an Orange coalition and government following the elections.

The Tymoshenko bloc was the only political force in parliament that refused to sign the 2006 Universal Agreement on National Unity. The Tymoshenko bloc lobbied for President Yushchenko to disband parliament rather than agree to Yanukovych's nomination as prime minister. His return deepened the split between Yushchenko and Tymoshenko, which was only overcome when Our Ukraine went into opposition in fall 2006–winter 2007.

Women's rights have not greatly expanded since Ukraine became an independent state. Under the Soviet regime, women were theoretically accorded equality with men. Women were allowed to undertake many areas of traditional male employment, but usually for low pay and at the bottom of the social spectrum. Meanwhile, they continued to remain subservient in the home and were regarded not as equals, but belonging in traditional roles as housewives and mothers. In the late 1980s and first half of the 1990s, women became active in national democratic groups, such as Rukh, and formed offshoot NGOs, many funded by Western governments and endowments. At a time of the prioritization of nation and state building, national democratic groups looked upon women engaged in politics in traditional nationalist terms as "guardians of the hearth" (*Berehynia*), protectors of the family and nation. Gender equality was not on their agenda.

In the 1990s women's groups continued to grow, but they remained divided and dependent upon Western funding. After initially advancing, women's rights were gradually confined again to issues related to maternity and family. Ukraine, during Kuchma's decade in office, returned to many aspects of Soviet political culture, including the subservient role of women in society and the home. By the late Soviet era fixed quotas ensured that one-half of seats in local councils and a third of the seats in the Supreme Soviet (parliament) were allocated to women in the Ukrainian SSR. In the three parliaments elected in 1990, 1994, and 1998, women's representation initially declined and then slightly increased from 2.9 to 4.6 to 8 percent, but it still lags far behind that of the Soviet era. Women's issues continue to remain marginal to the concerns of mainstream political parties in Ukraine.

Five of Ukraine's over 100 registered political parties are devoted to women's issues. The All Ukrainian Party Women's Initiative (VPZI) was the first of these to be registered in 1997 and is the only party of the five that is based outside Kyiv in Kharkiv. Three others are also small parties—the Women's Party of Ukraine (1997), the Women's People Party United (1998), and the Solidarity with Women Party (1999). In the 1998 Ukrainian parliamentary elections, only one party, the VPZI, campaigned on a gender platform. Its poor result, only 0.58 percent, placed it twenty-second of the thirty blocs and parties that competed. In the 2002 election, Women for the Future, one of two election parties that had a gender platform, obtained 2.11 percent, coming in eighth out of thirty-three parties and blocs. Women for the Future was never intended to become a real gender-based party, as it is led by individuals with ties to the former Soviet Ukrainian *nomenklatura* and the Kuchma regime. The ideology of Women for the Future is Soviet and not in tune with gender issues and the women's rights movement in the West. Women for the Future does not oppose the Soviet-era stereotype of women's role in politics being confined to areas such as maternal and child welfare issues.

Yuliya Tymoshenko has been the exception, rather than the rule, of a woman at the center of what are still male-dominated Ukrainian politics. She rose to prominence in the mid-1990s as CEO of United Energy Systems and entered politics in 1998 within the Hromada Party. A year later she created her own center-left Fatherland Party that remains one of Ukraine's most popular (among Ukrainian parties, Fatherland has the second-largest number of regional branches). Her first taste of government was under Yushchenko in 2000–2001, where she earned the wrath of the oligarchs by undermining corrupt energy schemes. Her arrest and brief detention in 2001–2003 failed to dampen her anti-Kuchma political activity. The Tymoshenko bloc entered the parliament elected in 2002, and she became an important ally of Yushchenko during the 2004 elections and Orange Revolution. The Tymoshenko bloc entered the 2006 parliament in second place with 22.29 percent of the vote and the second largest faction of 129 deputies, a result that was improved in the 2007 elections with 30.71 percent. If Tymoshenko contests the 2009 elections, she has a good chance of being Ukraine's first woman president.

Ethnic Relations

Ukraine inherited a disunited polity from the former USSR with a wide diversity of regions. This regionalism was compounded by the lack of strong statehood traditions, few consolidating national ideas acceptable to the majority of the population, and a severe socioeconomic crisis. It was also complicated by the lack of resolution of the division of powers until the adoption of a new constitution in 1996 and laws on self-government and state administration in 1997 and 1999 respectively. As the economy plummeted and the center proved to be weak and inept, regional demands grew and reached their peak in 1993–1994. Regional elites saw their salvation in greater regional devolution, both as a means to enrich themselves and to overcome poor economic policies promoted by the center. These developments were echoed by growing demands to revive economic and political ties to the CIS, grant greater regional economic autonomy, and allow regions to hold on to more of their budgetary receipts. These demands were strongest in the Crimea and eastern Ukraine where calls for separation and federalism were the most acute.

Regionalism in Ukraine is not ethnically driven. Separatism has remained muted, except in the Crimea in the first half of the 1990s. Ukraine does not possess one regional divide but many that overlap and remain mutually reinforcing. The central issue facing Ukraine is reconciling regionalism with national integration.[9] As is evident in numerous other countries, such as Canada, Belgium, Spain, and Italy, regionalism is never likely to disappear completely. The key question is therefore *not* if Ukraine will continue to exist but in what form and how it will be structured.[10] Regionalism in Ukraine is *not* along ethnic lines but reflects different regional political cultures that have arisen due to historic, climatic, and economic factors. The eastern and southern parts of Ukraine are overwhelmingly Russophone, while the western and central regions of the country are primarily Ukrainophone.

In the 1990s Ukraine had a broad elite consensus in favor of a decentralized unitary state that simultaneously rejected what are regarded as two "dangerous" extremes—federalism and a centralized unitary state. The compromise option of a decentralized unitary state recognizes the need to foster national integration based upon shared values and common institutions that would bridge regional disparities. It also rejects the archetypal French model of a highly centralized and homogenized nation-state by accepting that Ukraine is composed of different regions.

Support for federalism in Ukraine has never been high, as it is widely believed that it would hinder national integration. Few political parties in elections advocate federalism. Polling data also confirm the lack of public support for federalism. Only 9 percent of Ukrainians favored federalism; support ranges from as low as 4 percent in the west to 11 and 16 percent in the east and south respectively.[11] All of Ukraine's regions—including the east and south—were willing to delegate greater authority to the center. Western Ukrainians were more inclined to favor regional devolution than other regions.[12] Other surveys found majorities in Lviv and Donetsk against federalism. A clear majority in both cities believed that the unity of Ukraine was more important than regional issues and linked the fate of their region to Ukraine.

The federal question only began to become acute in Ukraine during the latter period of the Kravchuk era (1993–1994), at a time of acute socioeconomic crisis and hyperinflation. Federalism was also raised again in eastern Ukraine in late 2004 by Yanukovych's allies because of their anger at having lost the 2004 election and their feeling of betrayal by their former allies in the Kyiv elites. The Party of Regions promoted federalism in the 2006 elections but this policy (federalism) failed to win sufficient adherents in parliament, even within their own party.

Despite these regional differences, interethnic relations have been exemplary, and no ethnic conflicts between Russians and Ukrainians have been reported. A sizable number of Ukrainians are Russian speakers, and an even greater number are bilingual, using both Russian and Ukrainian interchangeably.

The Crimea is unique in Ukraine because it is the only region with an ethnic Russian majority. In 1944 its autonomous status within the Russian SFSR was abolished after the Crimean Tatars were forcibly removed from their homes and relocated to Central Asia. A decade later the region was transferred to the Ukrainian SSR. Only in 1990–1991 did Crimean elites seek to upgrade and return their status to an autonomous republic within Ukraine. This demand was granted after a Crimean referendum overwhelmingly approved the decision in January 1991. Relations between the Crimea and Ukraine were strained between 1992 and 1995. At issue was the desire on both sides to either minimize the delegation of powers to the Crimea (the view of Kyiv) or maximize these powers (the view of the Crimea). Two of Crimea's three political forces—centrists and the KPU—supported the maximum delegation of powers to the Crimea but opposed separatism. Only Russian nationalists advocated the separation of the Crimea from Ukraine and its return to Russia. A Russian nationalist, Yury Meshkov, won the newly created Crimean presidency in January 1994, and his allies took control of the Crimean Supreme Soviet, but this influence proved short-lived. In March 1995 Kuchma issued a presidential decree abolishing the Crimean presidency, an event that progressively marginalized Russian nationalists. The KPU and centrists in the Crimea were able to reach agreement with Kyiv on the parameters of a new Crimean constitution that was adopted in October–December 1998. The constitution recognized the Crimea as part of Ukraine. In 1997–1999 the Russian state also recognized Ukraine's borders.

Interethnic tension in the Crimea exists between eastern Slavs and Muslim Tatars who began returning in the late 1980s. By the end of the Kuchma era, Tatars numbered 15 percent of the Crimean population. The 2001 Ukrainian census showed the progressive decline of ethnic Russians in the Crimea to 58 percent, down from 65 percent in the 1989 Soviet census, due to out-migration of Russians and in-migration of Tatars.

Foreign and Security Policy

In the first half of the 1990s, Ukraine was largely ignored by the West because of its orientation toward Russia, which was the only CIS state at the time with a reformist president, Boris Yeltsin. Ukraine under Kravchuk placed greater emphasis on nation and state building and the security of the state, principally vis-à-vis Russia, than on economic and political reform. This influenced its slow nuclear disarmament until 1996.[13]

From the mid-1990s, relations between the West and Ukraine improved dramatically. When Kuchma was elected president in 1994, he initially seemed pro-reform and agreed to de-nuclearize Ukraine. In 1994, Ukraine signed the Nuclear Non-Proliferation Treaty, which paved the way for de-nuclearization in 1994–1996, which helped transform Ukraine into an important strategic ally of the West. In the second half of the 1990s, the United States sought to support Ukraine both bilaterally in a "strategic partnership" and multilaterally through NATO as a "keystone" of European security.[14] Ukraine's geopolitical importance to the United States in curbing Russia's imperial ambitions within the CIS and acting as a buffer between Russia and Central and Eastern Europe, and Ukraine's support for NATO enlargement, were strategically important in U.S. policy toward Central and Eastern Europe. Ukraine became the third-largest recipient of U.S. aid and was the most active CIS state within NATO's Partnership for Peace (PfP), which it joined in January 1994.

During Kuchma's second term in office, several factors led to poor relations between Ukraine and the West. First, the West became exasperated by the widening gap between rhetoric and reality in Ukraine's domestic and foreign policy. The executive claimed in its foreign policy rhetoric that it was in favor of deeper political and economic reforms and "returning to Europe." As Kuchma said on a visit to Austria, "God wants Ukraine to be in Europe." However, Ukraine's record on human rights and democratization increasingly was assessed negatively by Western governments and experts. Ukraine's international image was also severely damaged by increasing restrictions on the media. Kuchma's constantly shifting and often contradictory domestic and foreign policies contributed to the image of a country unable to decide on its foreign orientation. Contradictory signals, one day pro-Western, the next pro-Russian, also damaged Ukraine's international credibility. Although Ukraine's elites portrayed the country's "multivector" foreign policy as a well-thought-out and "pragmatic" response to geopolitical realities, this policy received little international respect. Instead, it became a tool for the elites to adjust the country to short-term changes in the international environment that affected them personally. In other words, strategic foreign policy objectives (such as EU or NATO membership) were merely rhetoric to mask a foreign policy that served as a tool for corrupt elites. In 2002 Ukraine officially declared its intention to seek NATO membership. But the government did little to pursue this declared objective. During the 2004 election year, a wide-ranging anti-American campaign was orchestrated against Yushchenko, whose wife is American, by the Yanukovych government, which was officially in favor of NATO membership and which had a large military contingent in Iraq.

From 2000 to 2004, the U.S.-Ukrainian strategic partnership that developed under Bill Clinton foundered, and Ukraine's relationship with the West fell to a low level. After the September 11, 2001, terrorist attacks on the United States, Ukraine could no longer play off Russia against the United States to obtain geopolitical advantages. The United States under George W. Bush shifted its strategic alliance to Russia and away from the close relationship Clinton had built up with Ukraine. Assistance was reduced, high-level summits were not organized, and Kuchma was isolated. U.S. foreign assistance to Ukraine declined by nearly half.

As Kuchma became progressively isolated, he reoriented Ukraine toward Russia and the CIS. He became the first non-Russian to head the CIS Council of Heads of State. Ukraine also agreed to join a CIS Single Economic Space (SND YEP) with Russia, Belarus, and Kazakhstan. The SND YEP was to be created in three stages: Free Trade Zone, Currency Union, and Customs Union. Russia, Belarus, and Kazakhstan sought to join all three stages; Ukraine claimed it would only go as far as stage one. The opposition condemned the SND YEP as a threat to Ukraine's declared objectives of Euro-Atlantic integration. Russia's refusal to recognize Ukraine's borders until 1997–1999 led Kuchma to orient Ukraine toward the West in his first term in office to obtain security assurances from NATO and the West. Once Ukraine's borders were secured, Kuchma was able to return to his 1994 election platform, popular in eastern Ukraine, of a Russian-Ukrainian strategic alliance. Ukraine's reorientation from west to east was further deepened by the Kuchmagate Crisis that isolated Kuchma from the West.

Russia openly intervened in Ukraine's 2002 and 2004 elections. In the 2002 election, Russian media and Russian officials attacked Yushchenko and labeled his Our Ukraine bloc "anti-Russian." Russian president Vladimir Putin visited Ukraine on the eve of rounds one and two of the 2004 election to demonstrate his support for Yanukovych. Russian election advisors (political technologists) worked on behalf of the Yanukovych campaign and were behind many of the dirty tricks used against Yushchenko. In 2005 the Party of Regions and Unified Russia, President Putin's party of power, signed an agreement on cooperation, but in the 2006 and 2007 elections, Russia adopted a more restrained position toward providing support to specific parties.

Until the Orange Revolution and Yushchenko's election, the EU did not consider Ukraine or any other CIS states as potential future members. The Partnership and Cooperation Agreement (PCA) signed by Ukraine and the EU in 1994 and ratified four years later ends in 2007. A three-year Action Plan with the EU signed in 2005 will be completed at the same time as the PCA in 2007–2008. These agreements will not be replaced by an Accession Agreement. The EU will offer Ukraine a Free Trade Zone following its entry into the World Trade Organization. In 2008, the European Neighborhood Policy (ENP) is likely to be enhanced to an Enhanced Partnership agreement with greater avenues for integration, but not membership. Ukraine's post–Orange Revolution democratic path is therefore faced with domestic difficulties compounded by the lack of external encouragement from the EU that remains unwilling to provide it with a membership option.

As in other postcommunist states, NATO membership is the first step toward EU membership for Ukraine. Since 2003, Ukraine and NATO have developed annual NATO-Ukraine Plans of Action. After Yushchenko's victory and successful visit to the United States in April 2005, Ukrainian membership in NATO was put on a faster track. NATO upgraded Ukraine to Intensified Dialogue on Membership Issues and was ready to invite Ukraine to create a Membership Action Plan (MAP) after the March 2006 parliamentary election. Ukraine missed the opportunity to be invited into a MAP in the NATO summit in Riga in November 2006 because of the failure of pro-reform Orange forces to create a coalition and government. Ukraine's fast-track membership drive to NATO was frozen following the 2006 and 2007 elections. Membership will be dependent upon the formation of an Orange coalition, cross-elite consensus, and improved popular support. Popular support for NATO membership has declined from a third in the 1990s to 20 percent with especially low levels of support in eastern Ukraine. In Georgia, which also seeks NATO membership, popular support stands at 70 percent.

Yushchenko's foreign policy has not differed from the strategic goals of EU and NATO membership already articulated from 1999 to 2002. In contrast to the situation under Kuchma, under Yushchenko the strategic goals of NATO and EU membership have been backed up by greater support for democratic and economic reforms, the rule of law, and efforts to reduce corruption.

Critical Challenges

The Orange Revolution and two subsequent elections have produced a democratic breakthrough that has transformed Ukraine from a "post-Soviet" and "Eurasian" state to one that is squarely in the East European world. Ukraine's democratic revolution and the election of Yushchenko in January 2005 brought democratic gains for Ukraine in a number of key areas, such as free media and the holding of free and fair elections, making Ukraine's transition different from that of Russia and the autocratic majority of CIS states. Constitutional reforms transforming Ukraine from a presidential to a parliamentary system, a system that has successfully consolidated democracies in Central Europe and the Baltic states, has also reinforced Ukraine's democratic path. Following the 2007 parliamentary and 2009 presidential elections, Ukraine's transition could be set to consolidate the democratic gains of the Orange Revolution.

The continued strength of the Party of Regions in the 2006 and 2007 elections gives cause for doubt about the rapid pace of reforms. The Party of Regions could transform itself from a pro-oligarch and formerly proauthoritarian party into a centrist, probusiness democratic party. But the jury is still out, as such transformations of political parties take place over medium, not short, terms. In the short term, constitutional reforms will lead to growing institutional and personal conflict between parliament, government, and the executive reminiscent of the 1991–1995 era before Ukraine adopted its June 1996 semi-presidential constitution. The institutional and personal conflicts of 2006–2007 that led to early elections and a constitutional crisis in 2007 are evidence that a transition to a parliamentary system, although in the medium term positive, will be accompanied by short-term political instabilities and crises.

Democratic reform in Ukraine will inevitably be evolutionary because of two factors. First, regionalism has traditionally forced Ukraine's elites into pacted compromises. Second, Ukraine has no offer of EU membership that would externally stimulate radical domestic reform. The upside of this is that regional diversity by its nature in Ukraine makes it difficult for any political force to monopolize power, thereby making an autocratic system an unlikely outcome. The downside is that consensus politics leads to muddled progress in reform.

Following the 2007 elections, Ukraine could reinforce the gains of the Orange Revolution by gradually consolidating its democracy. Elements of such an optimistic trajectory would include relatively stable, competitive multiparty politics between three to four large parties; the pursuit of economic reforms; continued strong economic growth; and elite consensus on the state priorities to be pursued. Following the 2007 elections, the Ukrainian parliament is likely to be in place for five years, during which Ukraine could see domestic reforms that continue to transform the country along East European lines. The 2009 presidential elections will also be important in either returning Yushchenko for a second term or in electing a new president.

Ukraine's foreign and security policy is unlikely to change from that pursued since the second half of the 1990s. Ukraine's dilemma is that EU membership is popular in Ukraine but is not on offer, whereas NATO membership is on offer but is unpopular among Ukrainians. NATO membership will only become a reality if elite consensus is reached on attaining this goal. The EU could move toward offering Ukraine membership or associate membership in the medium term after the EU resolves its internal problems and if democratic progress takes place in Ukraine. Ukraine will continue to strive to maintain good relations with Russia while limiting its involvement in the CIS to economic cooperation. The downside is that Russia under Putin has had increasingly poor relations with the West, has become increasingly imperialist in its foreign policy toward its neighbors, and remains nondemocratic at home, and none of this is likely to change soon. The upshot is that an increasingly autocratic Russia has helped in marginalizing support for integration with Russia and the CIS.

Suggested Reading

D'Anieri, Paul. *Understanding Ukrainian Politics: Power, Politics, and Institutional Design.* Armonk, NY: M.E. Sharpe, 2006.

D'Anieri, Paul, Robert Kravchuk, and Taras Kuzio. *Politics and Society in Ukraine.* Boulder, CO: Westview Press, 1999.

D'Anieri, Paul, and Taras Kuzio, guest editors. "A Decade of Leonid Kuchma in Ukraine." Special issue *Problems of Post-Communism* 52 (September–October 2005).

Kuzio, Taras, guest editor. "A Decade of Ukrainian Independence." Special issue *Journal of Ukrainian Studies* 25 (Summer–Winter 2001).

———, guest editor. "Elections, Revolutions, and Democratisation in Ukraine." Special issue *The Journal of Communist Studies and Transition Politics* 23 (Spring 2007).

———. "The Orange Revolution: The Opposition's Road to Success." *Journal of Democracy* 16, no. 2 (April 2005).

———. *Ukraine: Perestroika to Independence.* 2nd ed. London and New York: Macmillan and St. Martin's Press, 2000.

Kuzio, Taras, and Paul D'Anieri, guest editors. "Regime Politics and Democratization in Ukraine." Special issue *Communist and Post-Communist Studies* (June 2005).

Magosci, Robert. *A History of Ukraine.* Toronto: University of Toronto, 1996.

Puglisi, Rosaria. "The Rise of the Ukrainian Oligarchs." *Democratization* 10, no. 3 (Autumn 2003): 99–123.

Subtelny, Orest. *Ukraine: A History.* Toronto: University of Toronto Press, 2002.

Way, Lucan A. "Authoritarian State-Building and the Sources of Political Liberalization in the Western Former Soviet Union, 1992–2004." *World Politics* 57 (January 2005): 231–61.

———. "The Sources and Dynamics of Competitive Authoritarianism in Ukraine." *Journal of Communist Studies and Transition Politics* 20 (March 2004): 143–61.

Wilson, Andrew. *Ukraine's Orange Revolution.* New Haven, CT: Yale University Press, 2005.

Wolczuk, Kataryna. *The Moulding of Ukraine: The Constitutional Politics of State Formation.* Budapest, Hungary: Central European University Press, 2001.

Yekelchyk, Serhy. *Ukraine: Birth of a Modern Nation.* Oxford: Oxford University Press, 2007.

Notes

1. Taras Kuzio, "Rusyns in Ukraine: Between Fact and Fiction," *Canadian Review of Studies in Nationalism* 32, nos. 1–2 (2005): 17–29.

2. Bohdan Nahaylo, *The Ukrainian Resurgence* (London: Hurst and Co, 1999); and Taras Kuzio, *Ukraine: Perestroika to Independence*, 2nd ed. (London and New York: Macmillan and St. Martin's Press, 2000).

3. Paul D'Anieri, Robert Kravchuk, and Taras Kuzio, *Politics and Society in Ukraine* (Boulder, Co: Westview Press, 1999).

4. Available online at www.taraskuzio.net/media/index.shtml.

5. Kryvorizhstal, Ukraine's largest metallurgical plant, was privatized in June 2004 for $800,000 to two Ukrainian oligarchs, one of whom was Kuchma's son-in-law, Viktor Pinchuk. It was reprivatized in October 2005 for six times this amount.

6. Robert Kravchuk, *Ukrainian Political Economy: The First Ten Years* (New York: Palgrave/St. Martin's Press, 2000).

7. Rosaria Puglisi, "The Rise of the Ukrainian Oligarchs," *Democratization* 10, no. 3 (August 2003): 99–123.

8. Keith Darden, "Blackmail as a Tool of State Domination: Ukraine under Kuchma," *East European Constitutional Review* 10, nos. 2–3 (Spring–Summer 2003): 67–71.

9. D'Anieri, Kravchuk, and Kuzio, *Politics and Society in Ukraine.*

10. Taras Kuzio, "Ukraine: Coming to Terms with the Soviet Legacy," *The Journal of Communist Studies and Transition Politics* 14, no. 4 (December 1998): 1–27.

11. Arthur H. Miller, Thomas F. Klobucar, and William M. Reisinger, "Establishing Representation: Mass and Elite Political Attitudes in Ukraine," in *Ukraine: The Search for National Identity*, ed. Sharon L. Wolchik and Volodymyr Zviglyanich, 213–36 (Lanham, MD: Rowman and Littlefield, 2000).

12. Vicki L. Hesli, "Public Support for the Devolution of Power in Ukraine: Regional Patterns," *Europe-Asia Studies* 47, no. 1 (January 1995): 91–121.

13. Jennifer Moroney, Taras Kuzio, and Mikhail Molchanov, *Ukrainian Foreign and Security Policy: Theoretical and Comparative Perspectives* (Westport, CT: Praeger, 2002).

14. Sherman W. Garnett, *Keystone in the Arch: Ukraine in the Emerging Security Environment of Central and Eastern Europe* (Washington, DC: Carnegie Endowment, 1997).

Part IV

CONCLUSION

CHAPTER 16

What Now?

Sharon L. Wolchik and Jane L. Curry

In 1989, the collapse of communism and the death of the Soviet bloc surprised almost everyone: the communist leaders and the opposition of Central and Eastern Europe, Western and Russian politicians, and observers and scholars of the area. The daily headlines of the *New York Times* heralded the changes as "the Year of Freedom." American foreign policy turned from fighting communism to helping the incipient democracies in the region make their transitions. The Soviet Union held on to the Baltic states and Ukraine for the next two years, but only barely. Then, the Soviet Union itself collapsed, as did Yugoslavia, and, two years later, Czechoslovakia.

The end of communism has been followed by efforts to create or re-create democracy, establish market economies, and once again be recognized as part of Europe. In contrast to the situation in the interwar period, when many of these states became independent for the first time or reestablished their independence, the international environment has been far more supportive of this process of transition. The road to achieving these goals, however, has not been smooth, and progress has been uneven, both among countries and within individual states. In part, these difficulties reflect the legacy of the communist period. They also reflect the complicated nature of the tasks leaders faced in simultaneously transforming their countries' politics, economies, and foreign policies.

The euphoria of the men and women on the streets from Berlin to Bucharest and in the rest of the world was palpable in 1989 and 1991. Most thought creating or re-creating democracy would be a matter of shifting to living without the shackles and hardships of communism and would guarantee them prosperity and the "good life." In actuality, the change was not as easy as many expected. Prosperity did not necessarily follow for most in these populations. Democracy proved hard to make work on the remnants of communism.

The difficulties involved in this process have been greatest in former Yugoslavia, where the end of communism coincided with the breakup of the state and was accompanied by a series of wars that killed hundreds of thousands of people and made many more the victims of ethnic cleansing. But even in states in which developments have been peaceful, the process has not been easy or straightforward. As the chapters in this book illustrate, the improvisations and reversals that marked the democratization process have, in many cases, been surprising and even agonizing.

The political institutions of the countries included in this volume are, on the whole, now similar to those of more established, and particularly European, democracies. The rule of law and guarantees of civil and political liberties and human rights have been or are being instituted. Popular support for democracy as a general concept, if not for current political leaders or even institutions, is high, and there is little desire to turn back to communism, although some look back nostalgically to the "good old days" of communist cradle-to-grave social support. The shift to a market economy has also been completed in almost all of these states. Thus, private enterprises account for the largest share of gross national product, and previously neglected sectors of the economy, such as the service sector, are booming—as are, with few exceptions, these economies after the sharp decline in production and living standards in the early 1990s. Economic reform and progress have come at a cost, however, as unemployment and rising inequality have caused hardship for less well-positioned groups in society and led to political backlash in some countries.

Most of the countries examined in this volume, with the notable exceptions of Ukraine and several states that were formed after the dissolution of Yugoslavia, have also succeeded in joining Euro-Atlantic institutions, most importantly the North Atlantic Treaty Organization (NATO) and the European Union (EU). As members of these institutions, they have achieved their original goal of returning to the European stage. They have asserted their independence in the international realm, but they have also surrendered part of their sovereignty to an outside power, this time voluntarily, in contrast to their required subordination to the USSR.

These developments, which suggest that leaders have achieved the major points on the political agenda following the end of communism, raise new questions. Two of the most important of these concern how we should view these polities now, and what the consequences of success, both intended and unintended, are for political leaders and citizens as they face new challenges both at home and in the international realm. These questions are closely related to another issue this chapter will consider, which is what theoretical frameworks are most useful in guiding study and research about politics in these countries now.

Theoretical Frameworks: Postcommunist or Emerging Democracies?

In the early years after the end of communism, the theoretical approaches that most frequently informed our study of these countries were based on the transitions from authoritarian rule in southern Europe and Latin America. These were used despite the many ways in which these transitions differed from the transitions in the postcommunist world.[1]

As the transition continued, some scholars of politics in this region came to rely on concepts drawn from studies of politics in more established democracies. These included studies of political values and attitudes, legislatures and their processes, the roles of presidents and other political actors, and electoral behavior. Other scholars used approaches developed in the rest of Europe and the United States to study the development of political parties. Studies of the intersection of politics and the economy, in turn, employed concepts and approaches used by students of political economy in other regions of the world. Increasingly, we became aware of the need to include international actors, such as international and regional organizations as well as transnational actors and networks, in our analyses of political change in the postcommunist world. To do this, scholars have drawn on the literature on norms in international politics and the role of international organizations, as well as on the democracy promotion literature.

Many of the studies based on these frameworks, including those by authors in this volume, have yielded valuable insights into the political process in these countries. At the same time, it soon became clear that use of these approaches had its own problems and that, although the postcommunist European countries included in this volume had much in common with their western neighbors and countries that underwent democratization elsewhere, there were and are important differences that must be considered. Simply put, these new systems are products of their special histories. Communist rule was different from the authoritarian regimes in southern Europe and Latin America. The political systems in place in the postcommunist European states today also differ in certain ways from those of their more established European neighbors. Although there are many similarities in the institutions of both sets of countries, and the leaders of Central and East European countries face many of the same problems evident elsewhere, it would be a mistake to lump these systems together with the more established democracies in what we used to call "Western" Europe. Due in part to their particular history and in part to the demands and opportunities created by the transition, institutions that look similar in the two parts of Europe sometimes operate quite differently if one looks more closely.

As the chapters in this book illustrate, the transition from communism seemed to be smoothest in Poland, Hungary, the Czech Republic, Slovenia, and the Baltic states for much of the first decade and a half. But in recent years, politics has turned "sour" in Poland and Hungary, with the election of a right-wing nationalist government in Poland and riots and demonstrations in Hungary after the prime minister's admission that he and his party, as well as all other parties, had lied to the public in order to gain or keep office. The Czech electorate was so divided in the 2006 parliamentary elections that it took seven months for the ruling parties to come up with a governing coalition that survived a vote of no confidence. In all of these countries, to a greater or lesser extent, politics has been affected by the economic disaffection of the population. That dissatisfaction has been mirrored in the demise of the political power of the old opposition and by a shift, particularly evident in Poland, by many politicians and voters to radical, populist politics as well as the rise of new concerns about communist-era abuses and agents. It is ironic that this shift has occurred after these countries have joined the EU and at a time when these economies are growing faster than most in Europe.

In the other countries we have considered in this volume (Slovakia, Romania, Bulgaria, Ukraine, and the successors to former Yugoslavia), the shift of power in the late 1980s and early 1990s was not so clear. In many, communist leaders maintained power while claiming to be democrats or nationalists for at least the first set of elections. In others, the initial victory of the opposition was quickly followed by the election of "old forces," or a period of de-democratization. Political institutions in these states that were ostensibly democratic often did not function democratically, and democratically elected governments sometimes took actions that were decidedly not the norm in more established democracies. Efforts to account for this fact led scholars to describe many of these polities as illiberal or hybrid democracies.[2] Others termed these systems semiauthoritarian or competitive authoritarian systems.[3] Whatever term was used, the basic elements of this depiction were the same: governments, some of whose leaders were elected in relatively free and fair elections, acted to restrict the freedom of action of their opponents; attempted to control the media and deny the opposition access; enacted legislation that disadvantaged minorities; worked to discourage the development of civil society; and reinforced values at variance with those, such as compromise and tolerance, supportive of democracy.

As the period we examine in this book progressed, some of these states went through democratizing elections. Often termed electoral or color revolutions due to the tendency of their supporters and leaders to use certain colors as symbols, such as orange in the case of Ukraine, these events involved the mass mobilization of citizens by unified oppositions in cooperation with nongovernmental organizations and campaigns to encourage citizens to participate in elections and, if necessary, protest in the streets if incumbents tried to steal the elections or failed to yield their offices if defeated. These events, which took place in Bulgaria and Romania in the mid-1990s, Slovakia in 1998, Serbia and Croatia in 2000, and Ukraine in 2004, as well as in two countries not covered in this volume (Georgia in 2003 and Kyrgyzstan in 2005), have had different outcomes. But in all, the ouster of semiauthoritarian leaders has been followed by movement in a more democratic direction.[4]

If we adopt a minimal definition of democracy,[5] which refers to the existence of free and fair elections and the alternation in power of different political groups, all of the states considered in this volume, with the exception of those parts of former Yugoslavia still under international rule, are democracies. If we adopt a definition of democracy that requires not only democratic political institutions and the rule of law, but also a well-articulated, dense civil society, a well-developed political society that includes political parties and movements that structure political choice for citizens by articulating different policy perspectives and link citizens to the political process, and a functioning market economy to provide resources for individuals and groups independent of the state and to keep the government in check,[6] many of the states under consideration in this volume have a way to go.

The question that remains is how we can best understand politics in the region now, particularly in those countries that have become part of the EU and NATO. Is it still useful, for example, to see these states as postcommunist? Or, as some have suggested and others feared, have they become "normal, boring European countries"? Václav Havel, for example, has noted that we no longer talk about the United States as a postcolonial country. Why then, he has asked, should we continue to talk about the countries of Central and Eastern Europe as postcommunist? We would argue that the term still makes sense, at least in certain areas. It is clear that the countries we have focused on in this book share certain characteristics and problems with the more established democracies of "Western" Europe. These similarities can, in fact, be expected to increase as these countries become more integrated into the EU and as generations of young people who have not had any meaningful experience with communism come of age politically.

However, at present, the countries we have analyzed in this book also face additional issues arising from their communist pasts and from the fact that they are newly established or reestablished democracies. Communism was a form of authoritarianism in which the state not only controlled politics but also the economy; communist leaders were not content merely to hold the reins of power but also wanted to transform their citizens into "new Socialist men (and women)," at least initially. Mobilizing citizens was important in these systems in which leaders used propaganda, mass political demonstrations, and police control to insure that there were no public questions or alternatives to the march they claimed to be making to "socialism."

The experience of democratization and the transformation of the economy were often not what people either had hoped for or expected. The lessons they learned under communism and during the period immediately after its collapse have stayed with them. Citizens learned, for example, that the system did not work as it said it did; that they needed to be part of informal groups that helped each other get the goods and services they needed but could not get on the market; and that they could have little voice in politics. In their lives, much had happened behind the veil of the secret police and their informers or in a bureaucratic morass about which people had little information. Indeed, people often read the media not for what was said but for what was not. They assumed that democracy and prosperity would be instantly linked. These legacies were carried into the transition period.

The remaking of the political system and the restructuring of the economy took place in a situation in which the population expected the changes to bring about almost instant gains in their living standards. This improvement did not happen immediately, or, for some groups of the population, at all. As a result, democratic institutions and traditions had to be built when people were disillusioned about what they were getting from their new governments. Political leaders also had to deal with citizens who had learned that politics was about appearing to support the top leadership's policies and not expressing their opinions or acting in groups to articulate interests or put pressure on political leaders to take action. Although many, if not most, citizens had seen through the claims of communism, they had also come, in some cases unconsciously, to expect the state to provide a wide array of services, however basic.

The impact of the communist experience, as well as of the transition itself, thus still makes it difficult to use concepts and approaches borrowed from studies of political phenomena in more established democracies in some areas. And, when these are used, differences often appear. As the chapters in this volume indicate, even in states that were early democratizers, such as the Baltic states, Slovenia, Hungary, Poland, and the Czech Republic, the future is not entirely clear. To a greater or lesser degree, a gulf remains between the rulers and the ruled. Party systems are still fluid in most states, and citizens have low levels of party identification and loyalty. They also tend to have lower levels of political efficacy than their counterparts in more established democracies. Despite high growth rates, current levels of economic performance and the functioning of social welfare systems do not please many citizens. Many also question how best to deal with the past and puzzle about what to do about increasing inequality. Other European governments also face a number of these questions, but they are particularly acute in the postcommunist region.

Membership in European and Euro-Atlantic institutions can be expected to strengthen movement in a more democratic direction in many of these areas. Generational change may also accelerate this process, particularly as those young people who have made good use of the ample opportunities to travel and study abroad come into positions of political responsibility.

EU membership itself also poses new issues and demands for leaders and citizens in these countries. As part of the broader community, political leaders in the postcommunist EU members obviously will also face many of the same challenges as their counterparts in other advanced industrial societies. As the section to follow discusses more fully, the postcommunist EU members in particular also face challenges in the international realm.

Central and Eastern Europe in the World: New Roles and Concerns

As the chapters in this volume demonstrate, the end of communism has also been accompanied by far-reaching changes in the foreign relations of the countries of Central and Eastern Europe. These are most evident in those states that have become members of the EU. However, there have also been significant changes in the international relations of others that have yet to or are unlikely to become members in the near future. With membership, postcommunist European states, as earlier members, have voluntarily taken on obligations that impose certain limitations on their freedom of action. Although the states of Central and Eastern Europe that have joined the European Union hold fewer seats in the European Parliament than those held by the older members, the new members and aspirants have played a larger role in the politics of the European Union than their numbers would suggest. Internally, there was a fear in many of the original members that the local labor markets of the original states would be flooded with workers from the new member states, where unemployment is far higher and wages far lower. In the states that did not put up restrictions on foreign workers, Ireland, England, and the Scandinavian countries, this influx has occurred, making Polish workers, in particular, ubiquitous. In France, in fact, this fear of "Polish plumbers" was one of the reasons for the defeat of the European Union constitutional referendum in May 2005.

Within the European Union itself, the new states, individually and as a bloc, have had a strong voice. Some, like Poland, have taken very different stands from the traditional members of the European Union on issues ranging from economic policy toward Russia to cultural issues such as the need to define Europe as a "Christian" union. Given that most of the EU deputies elected in 2004 were from conservative and Euroskeptic parties, they have helped shift the balance of power toward the right. Since the timetable for entrance had been set, Romania and Bulgaria were allowed to join in 2007 even though there remained huge gaps between the formal standards for EU accession and actual practice in areas such as transparency, control of corruption, and judicial reform. These countries were accepted but remain subject to continued monitoring in these areas after accession.

Even as they have succeeded in "returning to Europe," Central and East European states have been a key element of American foreign policy as well. Their transformation itself was a major issue in American foreign policy and also served as a platform for U.S. aid to be used in "democracy promotion and nation building." In the years immediately after 1989, nongovernmental and quasi-governmental organizations in the United States as well as the rest of Europe joined the U.S. and European governments in providing funds and expertise related to many aspects of the transition. Activists from many of these countries, including but not limited to those that experienced early democratizing elections such as Slovakia and Serbia, played important roles in supporting democratization in other semiauthoritarian countries by sharing their experiences, strategies, and techniques, in many cases with U.S. funding. A number of countries in the region have committed their own resources to these efforts by targeting all or part of the development funds EU members are required to establish for this purpose.

EU members, as well as those countries that still aspire to join that organization, also face the sometimes difficult task of reconciling their desire for, as many put it, "more Europe and more United States," or good relations with both the rest of the members of the EU and the United States. A number of countries in the region participated in the U.S.-led "coalition of the willing" by sending troops or peacekeepers to Afghanistan; the governments of some also bucked both domestic public opinion and the attitudes of several other EU members, most notably France and Germany, by sending troops or otherwise supporting the U.S. war in Iraq. The leaders of several of the postcommunist members of the EU have expressed a desire to strive for strong transatlantic relations, but this task can be expected to remain a difficult one when EU and U.S. perspectives and objectives clash.

As the chapters in this volume illustrate, the overwhelming focus of the leaders of Central and East European countries has been on relations with countries to their west. However, Russia and the countries to the east have remained important in Central and East European politics, particularly for those states that border Russia and other former Soviet states. The reorientation of trade from east to west took place relatively rapidly in the nineties, due in part to the collapse of the Council for Mutual Economic Assistance (CMEA). But, for Russia's neighbors, the flow of people and cheap products back and forth across the border has continued, and it remains important in their politics and economics. Russia's significance has been magnified by the fact that most of these countries are very dependent on Russian energy. For the Baltic states and Ukraine, this dependence has been a mallet for Russia to use to show its displeasure with their political and economic links with other Western countries.

What Next?

As this brief overview of some of this volume's main conclusions and of the utility of various theoretical frameworks for the study of the region's politics including the very designation "postcommunist" illustrates, leaders and citizens of the formerly communist countries in Central and Eastern Europe have achieved both more and less than might have been expected in 1989 or 1991. Both postcommunist and European, the countries we have considered in this book face problems that are peculiar to postcommunist states and also those that are common in other European, or more broadly, democratic governments. Their success in achieving the main goals outlined at the beginning of the transition period testifies to the ingenuity, sacrifice, and vision of both leaders and citizens. It also indicates that these countries, although they still differ in important ways from their European counterparts that did not have a communist past, either have become or are on their way to becoming "normal" European countries. Their failures, on the other hand, and the ongoing challenges they face, suggest that their politics will be far from boring for some time to come.

Notes

1. For arguments that advocate this approach, see Philippe C. Schmitter and Terry Lynn Karl, "The Conceptual Travels of Transitologists and Consolidologists: How Far to the East Should They Attempt to Go?" *Slavic Review* 53, no. 1 (Spring 1994): 173–85. For arguments against this approach, see Valerie J. Bunce, "Should Transitologists Be Grounded?" *Slavic Review* 54, no. 1 (Spring 1995): 111–27. See also Juan Linz and Alfred Stepan, *Problems of Democratic Transition and Consolidation: Southern Europe, South America, and Post-Communist Europe* (Baltimore: Johns Hopkins University, 1996); and Adam Przeworski, *Democracy and the Market* (New York: Cambridge University Press, 1991).

2. See Fareed Zakaria, *The Future of Freedom: Illiberal Democracy at Home and Abroad* (New York: W. W. Norton and Company, 2004); Thomas Carothers, "The End of the Transition Paradigm," *Journal of Democracy* 13 (January 2002): 5–21; Larry Diamond, "Thinking about Hybrid Regimes," *Journal of Democracy* 13 (January 2002): 21–35; Andreas Schedler, "The Menu of Manipulation," *Journal of Democracy* 13 (January 2002): 36–50; and Steven Levitsky and Lucan A. Way, "The Rise of Competitive Authoritarianism," *Journal of Democracy* 13 (April 2002): 51–65.

3. See Levitsky and Way, "The Rise of Competitive Authoritarianism."

4. See Valerie J. Bunce and Sharon L. Wolchik, "Favorable Conditions and Electoral Revolutions," *Journal of Democracy* 17, no. 4 (October 2006): 5–18; Taras Kuzio, "Kuchma to Yushchenko: Ukraine's 2004 Elections and the Orange Revolution" *Problems of Post-Communism* 52, no. 2 (April 2005): 117–30; and Sharon Fisher, *Political Change in Post-Communist Slovakia and Croatia: From Nationalist to Europeanist* (New York: Palgrave Macmillan, 2006) for examples of the growing literature on these elections.

5. See Adam Przeworski et al., *Democracy and Development: Political Institutions and Well-Being in the World, 1950–1990* (Cambridge, UK: Cambridge University Press, 2000).

6. See Linz and Stepan, *Problems of Democratic Transition and Consolidation.*

Index

About the Contributors

Federigo Argentieri received a degree in political science from the University of Rome and a PhD in history from Eötvös Loránd University in Budapest. He currently teaches history and politics at John Cabot University and Temple University Rome Campus. He specializes in European affairs, East and West, and transatlantic relations and has published widely on Eastern Europe under communism, particularly on the 1956 Hungarian Revolution, and on security issues after the Cold War. Recent books include *L'Europa centro-orientale e la NATO dopo il 1999: Il futuro politico-strategico dell'Europa* (2001), and *Ungheria 1956: la rivoluzione calunniata*, 3rd ed. (2006).

Mark Baskin is a senior associate at the Center for International Development at the State University of New York (SUNY) and research professor at the University at Albany's Department of Political Science. He was a public policy scholar at the Woodrow Wilson International Center for Scholars in Washington, D.C., from 2003 to 2004 and served as director of research at the Pearson Peacekeeping Centre in Canada from 2001 to 2002. From 1993 to 2000 he worked as a civil affairs and political officer for the United Nations Peace Operations in Croatia, Bosnia-Herzegovina, and Kosovo, and he held Fulbright and IREX fellowships in Yugoslavia and Bulgaria in the 1970s and 1980s. His research has focused on ethnicity and nationalism in socialist Yugoslavia, the economic and political transitions in the Balkans, and the establishment of rule of law and governance in conflict zones. He has published and lectured in North America and Europe. Dr. Baskin received his PhD in political science from the University of Michigan.

Janusz Bugajski is the director of the Eastern Europe Project at the Center for Strategic and International Studies in Washington, D.C. He has served as a consultant for the U.S. Department of Defense, the U.S. Agency for International Development, the International Research and Exchanges Board, and several private organizations and foundations. He has lectured at the Smithsonian Institution, the Woodrow Wilson Center, the National Defense University, and numerous American universities. Mr. Bugajski also runs the South-Central Europe area studies program at the Foreign Service Institute (FSI) at the U.S. Department of State. He has testified before various congressional committees and in 1998 was the recipient of the Distinguished Public Service Award granted jointly by the U.S. Department of State, the U.S. Agency for International Development, the U.S. Information Agency, and the Arms Control and Disarmament Agency. His books include *Cold Peace: Russia's New Imperialism, Politi-*

cal Parties of Eastern Europe: A Guide to Politics in the Post-Communist Era; *Ethnic Politics in Eastern Europe: A Guide to Nationality Policies, Organizations, and Parties*; *Nations in Turmoil: Conflict and Cooperation in Eastern Europe*; *East European Fault Lines: Dissent, Opposition, and Social Activism*; and *Czechoslovakia: Charter 77's Decade of Dissent*. His most recent book is *Atlantic Bridges: America's New European Allies*, with Ilona Teleki. He received an M.Phil. in social anthropology from the London School of Economics and Political Science.

Valerie Bunce is the Aaron Binenkorb Chair of International Studies and the Chair of the Government Department at Cornell University. Her research has addressed four issues, all involving comparisons among the postcommunist states: patterns of regime change, the relationship between democratization and economic reform, the impact of American democracy promotion, and the role of nationalism on state dissolution and democratic politics. She is the author of over seventy articles and two books—most recently, *Subversive Institutions: The Design and the Destruction of Socialism and the State*. She is currently engaged in a collaborative study of electoral revolutions in Europe and Eurasia with Sharon L. Wolchik. She received her PhD in political science from the University of Michigan.

Zsuzsa Csergo is an assistant professor of political studies at Queen's University. Her research focuses on nationalism in contemporary European politics. Her articles have appeared in *Perspectives on Politics, East European Politics and Societies*, and *Foreign Policy*. She has received a number of prestigious awards and fellowships from the American Council of Learned Societies, the Social Science Research Council, the European University Institute, the Institute for the Study of World Politics, and the Woodrow Wilson International Center for Scholars. She is the author of *Talk of the Nation: Language and Conflict in Romania and Slovakia* (2007) and is currently working on a collaborative research project about changing forms of nationalism in the European Union. She received her PhD in political science from George Washington University.

Jane L. Curry is a professor of political science at Santa Clara University. She is the author of six books on Polish and East European politics, including *The Left Transformed, Poland's Permanent Revolution*, and *Polish Journalists: Professionalism and Politics*. She has also written extensively on issues of civil society and pluralism in transitions. In 2003–2004, she held the Fulbright–University of Warsaw Distinguished Chair in East European Politics. In 2006, she received a United States Institute of Peace grant to examine the dynamics of the revolutions in Serbia, Ukraine, and Georgia. She holds a PhD in political science from Columbia University.

Daina Stukuls Eglitis is assistant professor of sociology and international affairs at George Washington University, where her research has focused largely on the social dimensions of postcommunist transformations in Central and Eastern Europe. Her recent publications include the chapters "Latvia," in *Women in Europe* and "The Uses of Global Poverty: How the West Benefits from Economic Inequality," in *Seeing Ourselves: Classic, Contemporary, and Cross-Cultural Readings in Sociology*. She is also the author of the book *Imagining the Nation: History, Modernity and Revolution in Latvia*. She is currently researching transition-era changes in courtship, marriage, and fertility behavior in Latvia. She received her PhD in sociology from the University of Michigan.

Sharon Fisher is senior economist at Global Insight in Washington, D.C., where she conducts economic and political analysis, risk assessment, and forecasting on a number of Central European, Balkan, and CIS countries. In that role, she has consulted on a wide range of subjects, including the impact of European Union enlargement. Fisher has published extensively on the politics and economics of Central and Eastern Europe, including the book *Political Change in Post-Communist Slovakia and Croatia: From Nationalist to Europeanist*. In addition, she is coeditor of *The 1998 Parliamentary Elections and Democratic Rebirth in Slovakia*. She has presented her work at numerous conferences and seminars in Europe and the United States and has lectured at the Woodrow Wilson Center, the Foreign Service Institute (FSI), and the Paul H. Nitze School of Advanced International Studies (SAIS) at Johns Hopkins University. Previously, she worked as an analyst with the RFE/RL Research Institute in Munich and the Open Media Research Institute in Prague. Fisher holds a PhD in politics from the School of Slavonic and East European Studies (SSEES) at the University College London, a master's degree from the University of Pittsburgh's Graduate School for Public and International Affairs (GSPIA), and a bachelor's degree from the College of William and Mary.

John Gledhill is a PhD candidate in the department of government at Georgetown University. His dissertation research concerns politics and social mobilization in post-communist Romania.

Charles King is Ion Ratiu Associate Professor and chair of the Faculty of the School of Foreign Service at Georgetown University. He has published widely on political change and ethnicity in Eastern Europe and the former Soviet Union, and his articles have appeared in such publications as *World Politics, Foreign Affairs*, and *Slavic Review*. He is the author of *The Moldovans: Romania, Russia, and the Politics of Culture* and *The Black Sea: A History*. He holds a PhD in politics from Oxford University.

Taras Kuzio is adjunct professor at the Institute for European, Russian and Eurasian Studies, George Washington University. He has previously been a senior resarch fellow at the University of Birmingham, resident fellow at the Centre for Russian and East European Studies, University of Toronto, and a visiting professor at the George Washington University. He is the author of *Ukrainian Security Policy*; *Ukraine under Kuchma*; *Ukraine: State and Nation Building*; and *Ukraine: Perestroika to Independence*. He is joint author of *Politics and Society in Ukraine*. In addition, he is the editor of *Contemporary Ukraine: Dynamics of Post-Soviet Transformation* and coeditor of *State and Institution Building in Ukraine*; *Ukrainian Foreign and Security Policy: Theoretical and Comparative Perspectives*; and *Dilemmas of State-Led Nation Building in Ukraine*. He has served as guest editor of six special issues of academic journals on postcommunist politics. Dr. Kuzio received his PhD from the University of Birmingham.

Ronald Linden is professor of political science at the University of Pittsburgh. From 1984 to 1989 and 1991 to 1998 he served as director of the Center for Russian and East European Studies at the university. From 1989 to 1991 Dr. Linden served as director of research for Radio Free Europe in Munich, Germany, where his responsibilities included supervision of the publication of the weekly *Report on Eastern Europe*. Dr. Linden is the author most recently of "Balkan Quadrilateral: Turkish Accession and the Future of US-Southeast European Relations" (*Orbis*); "Twin Peaks: Romania and Bulgaria between the EU and the United States" (*Problems of Post-Communism*); "Now You See It, Now You Don't: Anti-EU Attitudes in Central and Southeast Europe" (*Journal of European Integration*); and editor of *Norms and Nannies: The Impact of International Organizations on the Central and East European States*. He received his PhD from Princeton University.

Paula Pickering is an assistant professor of government at the College of William and Mary. Her research interests focus on ethnic politics and democratization in southeastern Europe. Her most recent publication, "Generating Social Capital That Bridges Ethnic Divisions in the Balkans," appeared in the January 2006 *Ethnic and Racial Studies*. Her book on grassroots influence on peace building in the Balkans, *The Groundfloor of Peacebuilding*, is forthcoming from Cornell University Press. She has worked for the Organization for Security in Cooperation in Europe's Mission in Bosnia (1996) and for the U.S. State Department (1990–1994). She received her PhD in political science from the University of Michigan.

Marilyn Rueschemeyer is professor of sociology emerita at the Rhode Island School of Design and holds an appointment in the Department of Sociology and the Watson Institute for International Studies at Brown University. She is an associate of the Davis Center for Russian Studies at Harvard University. Her research has focused on social and political life in Eastern and Central Europe before and after the end of communism. Her books include *Professional Work and Marriage: An East-West Comparison*; *Soviet Émigré Artists: Life and Work in the USSR and the United States* (coauthored with Igor Golomshtok and Janet Kennedy); *The Quality of Life in the German Democratic Republic* (with Christiane Lemke); *Participation and Democracy East and West* (edited with Dietrich Rueschemeyer and Bjorn Wittrock); *Women in the Politics of Postcommunist Eastern Europe* (1994, 1998); *Left Parties and Social Policy in Postcommunist Europe* (edited with Linda Cook and Mitchell Orenstein); *Art and the State: The Visual Arts in Comparative Perspective* (coauthored with Victoria Alexander); and *Women in Power: Women Deputies in Post-Communist Parliaments* (edited with Sharon L. Wolchik, forthcoming). She has been a Fellow at the Stockholm Institute of Soviet and East European Economics, the Swedish Collegium for Advanced Study in the Social Sciences in Uppsala, and the Department of Sociology at the Hebrew University of Jerusalem. She has also been a guest of the Wissenschaftszentrum, Berlin, and the Academy of Sciences of the Czech Republic. In 1972, 1982, and 1997, she was a senior associate member of St. Antony's College, Oxford University. She holds a PhD from Brandeis University.

Jeffrey Simon is a senior research fellow at the National Defense University's Institute for National Strategic Studies. Previously he served as chief of the National Military

Strategy Branch at the Strategic Studies Institute at the U.S. Army War College. He has taught at Georgetown University and has held research positions at System Planning Corporation and the RAND Corporation. Dr. Simon's publications include numerous articles and thirteen books, the most recent being *NATO Enlargement: Opinions and Options*; *NATO Enlargement and Central Europe: A Study in Civil-Military Relations*; *Hungary and NATO: Problems in Civil-Military Relations*; *NATO and the Czech and Slovak Republics: A Comparative Study in Civil-Military Relations*; and *Poland and NATO: A Study in Civil-Military Relations*. Dr. Simon holds a PhD from the University of Washington and an MA from the University of Chicago and has been awarded the Knight Cross of the Order of Merit with Star by the Republic of Poland.

Sharon L. Wolchik is a professor of political science and international affairs at George Washington University. She also serves as adjunct chair of the Advanced Area Studies Seminar on East Central Europe at the U.S. Department of State's Foreign Service Institute. She is the author of *Czechoslovakia in Transition: Politics, Economics, and Society* and coeditor of *Women and Democracy: Latin America and Central and Eastern Europe*; *Domestic and Foreign Policy in Eastern Europe in the 1980s*; *Ukraine: In Search of a National Identity*; *The Social Legacies of Communism*; and *Women, State and Party in Eastern Europe*. She has conducted research on the role of women in the transition to postcommunism in Central and Eastern Europe, and the role of women leaders, as well as on ethnic issues, and other aspects of politics in postcommunist societies. She is currently conducting research on postcommunist electoral revolutions in Europe and Eurasia with Valerie Bunce. She received her PhD in political science from the University of Michigan.